# S... BAR, C... NGE GUIDE 2001

Published and distributed by
Hangover Media, Inc.
65 Reade St. 5th Fl.
New York, N.Y. 10007
T: 212.420.BARS (2277)
F: 212.964.8026
E: sheckys@hotmail.com
www.sheckys.com
Bar Phone: 212.777.BARS (2277)
ISBN 0-9662658-8-2

Published by
Hangover Media, Inc.
65 Reade St. 5th Fl.
New York, N.Y. 10007

T: 212.732.BARS (2277)
F: 212.964.8026
E: sheckys@hotmail.com
www.sheckys.com
Bar Phone: 212.777.BARS (2277)

President: Chris Hoffman

Chief Operating Officer: Kim Zwingraf
Director of Marketing: Jocelyn Maas
Director of Marketing: Colleen O'Keefe

Content Design: Greg Evans
Cover Logo: Thomas Fuchs

Writers & Editors: A Muzich, E McKinnon, B Dale, B Niemietz, B Sloan, C Simpkins, C Entine, C Keegan,C Hensley, R Romero C O'Keefe, C Scollans, D Schwartz, D Blanes, D Brodsky, D Tese, E Killoran, E Buscher, E Van Tuyl, E Petit, G Capone, G Knott, G Cramp, L Cramp, I Smith, J Centola, J Gohmann, J Rubin, J Maas, J Carlucci, Kaos, K Dinlec, K Maddox, K Fusco, K McCabe, K Gunduz, K Madsen, L Lucas, L Price, M Lucineo, M Goodman, M Kauntz, M Kahn, M Brown, M Cohen, N Beer, N Doughty, O Shohamy, P Frankel, R Bates, S Sacks, S O'Shea, A Gargano, T Barzso, V Bazelais, Z Mackin and other contributing writers.

Publishers note: No fees or services were rendered in exchange for inclusion in this book.

Please note that while every effort was made to ensure the accuracy of phone numbers, addresses, hours, policies, prices and details at the time of publication, any of the criteria is subject to change so please call ahead.


Forth edition.
ISBN 0-9662658-8-2

Printed in the United States of America

# TABLE OF CONTENTS

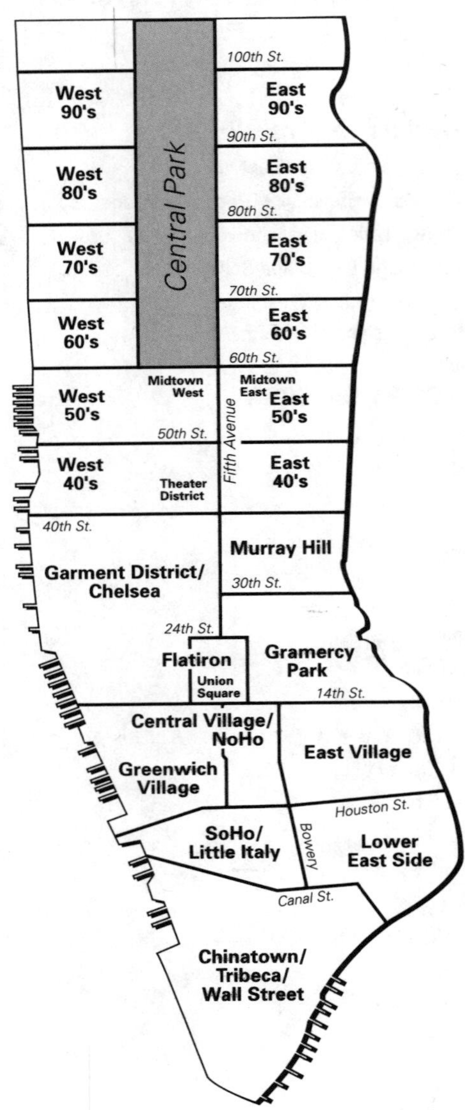
100th St.
West 90's
East 90's
90th St.
Central Park
West 80's
East 80's
80th St.
West 70's
East 70's
70th St.
West 60's
East 60's
60th St.
Midtown West
Midtown East
West 50's
East 50's
50th St.
Fifth Avenue
West 40's
Theater District
East 40's
40th St.
Murray Hill
Garment District/ Chelsea
30th St.
24th St.
Flatiron
Union Square
Gramercy Park
14th St.
Central Village/ NoHo
East Village
Greenwich Village
Houston St.
SoHo/ Little Italy
Bowery
Lower East Side
Canal St.
Chinatown/ Tribeca/ Wall Street

# ICON TABLE

 Lounge/Swanky/Upscale

 Neighborhood Bar

 Live Music

 Food

 Gay

 Lesbian

 Shecky's Pick

 Outdoor Space

 Dancing/Club

 Sports Bar

College/Frat Scene

 DiveBar/NoFrills
Inexpensive

# SHECKY'S TOP 10 LISTS

## After Work
Bank Cafe
Bryant Park Grill
El Rio Grande
Heartland Brewery
Houston's
Moran's
Tortilla Flats
Typhoon Brewery
Wall St. Kitchen
White Horse Tavern

## Cool Places
Art Bar
Bar d'O
Black & White
Eau
Guernica
Leopard Lounge
Passerby
Void
Waterloo
Zum Schneider

## Dancing/Club
bOb
Centro-Fly
Etoile
Float
Fun
Lotus
Ohm
Tunnel
Twilo
Webster Hall

## Date Spots
AZ
Bottino
Boughalem
Casimir
Chez es Saada
Double Happiness
Fressen
'ino
Lush
Torch

## Dive Bars
CBGB's & OMFUG
Coyote Ugly
Doc Holiday's
Hogs & Heifers
Holiday Lounge
Mars Bar
Red Rock West
7B
Siberia
Sophie's

## Gay Bars
Barracuda
Cubby Hole
Duplex, The
g
Hell
Henrietta Hudson
Meow Mix
Stonewall
Town House
Works, The

## Lounges
Angels' Share
Church Lounge
Eugene
H2K
Joe's Pub
Lotus
Lot 61
Luahn
Rhone
Sweet & Vicious

## New Spots
Bar Demi
Bar Veloce
Cachette
Chicama
Esperanto
Gustavino's
Lotus
No Malice Palace
Plant
Rue B

## Neighborhood
Corner Bistro
d.b.a.
Failte
L-Ray
Niagara
Peter's
Ruby's Tap House
Sin Sin
Solas
Tom & Jerry's

## Outdoor Spots
B Bar
Bottino
Blue Water Grill
Chelsea Commons
Coffee Shop
Luna Park
Miracle Grill
North West
PenTop Bar
Tavern on the Green

## Pick-Up Spots
Angelo & Maxie's
Belmont Lounge
Drinkland
Le Colonial
Lemon, The
Merchants
Moran's
NV
Union Bar
Whiskey Blue

## Sports Bar
Bar None
British Open
ESPN Zone
Mickey Mantle's
Nevada Smith's
Park Ave Country Club
Ship of Fools
Sporting Club
Third & Long
Time Out

A

## The Abbey

365 Driggs Ave. (N. 7th & 8th Sts.) Brooklyn
718-599-4400

THE BEST LITTLE Iggy Pop stop in the 'burg. Don't be put off by the uneventful interior, this place has libido up the wazoo. For years, people have tried to explain the Abbey as Williamsburg's "gay-friendly" bar. But we're really not sure it's that simple. In the old days, this was the gun club or the Elks of God-knows-what. Now, it is an inscrutable watering hole with a 4p.m.-8p.m. happy hour. The Abbey is part of the old-meets-new renaissance and is the youngest of the hipster bars. It has a young crowd and a killer jukebox. The shark bites here too, the pool playing gets pretty serious.

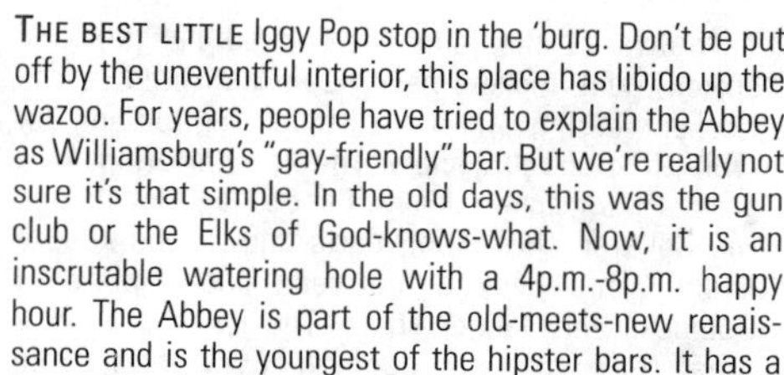

## The Abbey Tavern

354 3rd Ave. (@ 26th St.)
212-532-1978

FOR AROUND HALF a century, this brightly lit Irish pub and restaurant has been home to a steady and mature neighborhood crowd. The bar is decorated with enough hanging crockery and tea kettles that it could double as a Pottery Barn. Stained glass separates the bar from the restaurant that serves a usual assortment of American and Irish favorites. The no-frills happy hour from 5p.m.-7p.m. takes $1 off beers and drinks. After that, you'll pay $4 for pints, $3.50 for bottles, and $4.50 for drinks. Unless you're a local, you'll find the Tavern as bland as milk toast.

## Absolutely 4th

228 W. 4th St. (@ 7th Ave. So.)
212-989-9444

BRAND NEW AND completely overhauled from its dumpy predecessor Karma, Absolutely 4th's owners beautifully and tastefully transformed their "baby" into a chic lounge. The tile and copper bar, spectacular low hanging Murano glass lighting and large white candles on tables create an intimate atmosphere perfect for a date, a quiet chat or hanging out with friends. The husband and wife team plan to have live jazz beginning in September and a simple menu of tasty treats is available. The house drink is the apple martini, a crisp and delicious concoction, but watch out, it'll catch up to you by the end of the evening.

## Ace Bar

531 E. 5th St. (Aves. A & B)
212-979-8476

THE DAYS OF the longhaired, head bangers and spiked, punk rockers have been infiltrated by the Docker wearing collared shirts looking to hang out with the dregs of society. The Ace Bar brings in a great mix of punk rockers, East Village locals and Mr. Collared shirt. Pool, darts and pinball keep a lively group busy in between cheap pints of Guinness and Jaeger shots. The jukebox plays a great mix of head-banging MTV hits from Motorhead to the Ramones. This huge bar is a great place for the hard-core drinker to hang out with the friendly staff and stare down some dork playing air guitar.

## Acme Underground

9 Great Jones St. (@ Lafayette St.)
212-420-1934

A CHEESY TOURIST trap where Southern visitors can be overcharged for food they'd buy at the local diner for half the price, the upstairs bar at Acme is strangely designed so half the customers stare at the other half. However, there isn't much interaction between anyone since most people come to eat with friends. The downstairs is a bit more interesting offering live rock and roll for a $6 cover. However, there isn't much room to sit down – just a large space for you to dance, or more likely, impatiently wait for your friends to move on.

## Alchemy

12 Ave. A (E. Houston & 2nd St.)
212 477-9050

STILL TRANSITIONING into a sweet, more sophisticated Hip-Hop spot, Alchemy offers a layed back atmosphere to shake that ass, your gourdor or your Kangol to the DJ. While your time at the bar will be quick (efficient service), painless (a friendly wait staff) and buzz-inducing (a wallet-friendly price list), beware of the bathrooms, which smell like a stail piece of ________. But like Forest Gump would say, "Life is like a box of ass don't smell, you never know when you're gonna need it."

## Allegrias

46 Bedford St. (@ 7th Ave. So.)
212-741-1935

THIS RELATIVELY NEW Flamenco and tapas bar is a superb change of pace for a date or an evening with friends. The tiny stage in the back corner of the bar explodes with stomping heels, castanetas and the sultry twirling of traditional Spanish dance. Just listening to the skillful guitar playing is exciting and excuses the sparse décor. Friday and Saturday cover is $5. Happy hours are 4p.m.-7p.m. weekdays serving two for one beers, sangria and well drinks. Once a week at 7:30 p.m. a free salsa class takes place (call for day).

## The All State Café

250 W. 72nd St. (Broadway & West End Ave. )
212-874-1883

WHAT APPEARS TO be just another bar from the outside is actually one of the neighborhood's best spots for ample tables, authentic pub décor and a laid back atmosphere. This local institution is a great place to meet friends for a drink or wind down after work. Apart from the few daytime drinkers at the bar, All State functions as a restaurant while the sun's up. By nightfall, the crowd is more into getting lit, but the kitchen still serves food until 1:30 a.m.

## Alligator Alley

485 Amsterdam Ave. (83rd & 84th Sts.)
212-873-5810

IF YOU CAN get over the tacky neon green nameplate illuminating the watering hole section of Amsterdam Avenue, the no-nonsense atmosphere inside Alligator Alley might pleasantly surprise you. Comfortable red leather barstools, an inviting pool table and the most kick-ass jukebox north of 14th St. will keep you entertained for hours. The crowd is over 25, the bartenders are tattooed from head to toe and everyone here is serious about drinking. A decent selection of draft and bottled beer is sold at very reasonable prices, especially before 8p.m. when all pints and well drinks go for $3. Ladies drink Coors on tap for free all night on Sunday and Monday, and chances are they will drink for free any night of the week, what with the 6-to-1 male to female ratio. Regardless of age or gender, you'd be hard pressed to walk out of here sober. Beware the rowdy rabbles of post-grads late night and on weekends.

## Alphabet Lounge

104 Ave. C (@ 7th St.)
212-780-0202

WANT DANCING WITHOUT the steep cover? Low-key without the malaise? The feel of being tucked away without the loneliness? Head on down to this recently opened lounge in the heart of Louisaida and swing your hips to Latin, tribal and deep house grooves. The intimacy of Alphabet is its real strength, and these people can dance! You can't help but root for this cozy, friendly lounge with its young locals and in the know hipsters alike. Beer is $5, ( more than you would expect to pay on Ave. C) but considering the eye candy and the great dancing, it's all a bargain no matter what crack den of a neighborhood you happen to be in.

## Alva

36 E. 22nd St. (Park Ave. & Broadway)
212-228-4399

CATERING TO AN upscale Gramercy Park crowd, Alva defines what you want your neighborhood spot to posess; bartenders that give a new meaning to the three second pour, cool '70s tunes pumping through the stereo and food so good that it could give Bob Hope a hard on. With a deco setting and low romantic lighting, Alva is a great spot to hang with a buddy, or hang with a buddies girlfriend you always wanted to screw.

## America

9-13 E. 18th St. (5th Ave. & Broadway)
212-505-2110

GOOD LORD IN HEAVEN, will you please make this place die and put an ultra-swank dance club in its space? So eighties and so over, this huge loft restaurant is great for screaming children and stroller toting parents. The bar is tremendous as with everything else in this tourist filled space, but as we all know, size doesn't matter.

## American Spirits

1744 2nd Ave. (90th & 91st Sts.)
212-289-7510

AMERICA RULES, DUDE. Frat boys come to hang, pick up chicks and get trashed during the 5p.m.-8p.m. happy hour which features $1 Bud and Bud Light Drafts, $2 frozen drinks and $5 pitchers. On Friday and Saturday they have 5p.m.-11p.m. "power hours" serving all you can drink for $10 (but do you really want to see how much a frat boy can drink?). Monday is open mike night, Tuesday and Thursday is Karaoke, Wednesday features live music from whiney Eddie Vedder wannabes and Thursday is ladies night. Enjoy the Americana-crap on the walls or get toasted on lawn furniture at their sidewalk tables.

## American Trash

1471 2nd Ave. (76th & 77th Sts.)
212-988-9008

ACCORDING TO ITS owner, American Trash is one of the first authentic biker bars in Manhattan. You can't miss the glaring neon sign out front, and as you enter you'll be assaulted with the bar's décor; kitschy ornaments, decrepit surfboards and even a few bras plastered on the walls. Called a "Professional Drinking Establishment," American Trash offers 20 bottled beers and seven on tap, and a whole mess of bar diversions. The clientele is comprised of down and dirty bankers and bikers who are lookin' for beer goggle love in all the wrong places. J. J.'s Sunday Night Trash Band emerges from the dumpster every (you guessed it) Sunday night to jam from 10 a.m.-2 a.m. This institution will live on long past the cockroach.

## Amsterdam Billiards Club

344 Amsterdam Ave. (@ 77th St.)
212-496-8180

THIS POOL HALL is not known as "the best pool club in America" for nothing. Thirty-one regulation size tables are often all occupied by city dwellers of all walks of life playing the clean game in a not-so-seedy environment. On any given day or night, you can spot a local celeb who happens to live in the neighborhood or one of the renowned pool sharks whose portrait hangs above the bar. A digital sound system pumps out a vast variety of music while the staff busily serves drinks and good ol' greasy pool hall eats. Note to the smokers and the non: no cigars allowed, and there IS a non-smoking area.

## Androgyny

35 Crosby St. (@ Broome St.)
212-358-5094

MEN WHO LOVE men dressed as women fancy this frilly cross-dresser pick-up lounge. Only beer and wine are available, but there is enough entertainment available just by gazing around the room and checking out the wacky goings on. Cover charge is $5 for cross dressers and $10 for their admirers.

## Angel

174 Orchard St. (Houston & Stanton Sts.)
212-780-0313

THIS FORMER JAZZ club with its soft blue, dim lights and cloud-like rounded mirrors succeeds in giving the breed known as "hipsters" a taste of paradise. As a friendly staff serves up strong, tasty drinks in fishbowls and a DJ spins everything from sub-ambient techno to trip-hop, you can relax in the plush velvet couches, find your inner Buddha and contemplate how to splice DNA. While the place won't start bouncing until late night, we recommend that you arrive early to grab a seat in the loft. Don't forget to try the cocktails while you contemplate the theory of relativity.

## Angelo & Maxie's

233 Park Ave. So. (@ 19th St.)
212-220-9200
1285 6th Ave. (@ 52nd St.)
212-459-1222

THIS ART DECO steakhouse caters to a young professional male crowd with expense accounts. The concept of this place is harmless enough, but its execution gets muddled somewhere along the line. Granted the food is wonderful; juicy steaks, buttery potatoes; the stuff of steakhouses, but the presentation is pushy. At first the staff seem friendly, but they're really just trying to pump your check. They're not dumb, they know the majority of guys eating/drinking here have corporate cards burning holes in their pockets. Half the time these same guys are too drunk or too busy scamming on the very limited selection of women they wouldn't know if a few extra bottles of Silver Oak got added to their checks. (We're not saying that they do.)

## Angel's Share

8 Stuyvesant St. (9th St. & 3rd Ave.)
212-777-5415

HIDDEN AWAY IN the back of a Third Avenue sushi restaurant, there's a sign declaring quite politely that screaming, shouting and standing at the bar will not be tolerated... welcome to Angel's Share. The music is jazz, the drinks are the best in the city and the atmosphere is sultry. The decor includes a fairly bizarre mural of a greedy looking devil surrounded by a bunch of naked, lazy angels above the bar. Everything here is crisp, clean and civilized, right down to the bartenders' tuxedos. Angel's Share could be described as nothing less than an extremely civilized place to have a drink. (Try the Lichee daiquiri.) A very romantic date spot.

## Annie Moore's

50 E. 43rd St. (Vanderbilt & Madison Aves.)
212-986-7826

THIS POPULAR COMMUTER bar has six beers on tap, a dining area in the back and a sprawling bar. During the late afternoon and early evening the place is packed with customers stopping in for a quickie before they wearily plod to nearby Grand Central Station. In between the sporting events, they helpfully flash the Metro North train schedule on the TV's so your spouse doesn't give you the third degree if you are late coming home. Overall, this Irish pub is one of the better choices to hang out in this area. It is not a destination and stay-all-night bar, but a good place to come and drown the stresses of the day.

## Another Bar

543 2nd Ave. (@ 30th St.)
No Phone

IT WOULD NOT be surprising to find a banner hanging directly over the door reading "Welcome to the sleaze ball pit from hell." That sign isn't there but there is one above the bar reading "No Tabs and No Checks Cashed." After reading that you'd have to be completely sedated or partially lobotomized to not realize that this bar is a haven for dirty old men and neighborhood degenerates. Even if they were giving drinks away for free it wouldn't make sitting in this stale smoky dump worthwhile.

## Anotheroom

249 W. Broadway (Beach & N. Moore Sts.)
212-226-1418

A little more than just "another room," this is a pretty laid back art-rock hangout with better than average décor and a friendly staff. The prints on the walls are gallery-caliber and the bar seems to have put a good amount of time into its color and light scheme. A good place to take a small crowd, but not much of a place to meet one. The clientele is fairly young and comprised of people who are somewhere between college and career, as well as somewhere between art and commerce. This bar is strictly beer and wine, featuring 12 beers on tap, dozens in the bottle and a better than average wine selection.

## Antarctica

287 Hudson St. (Spring & Dominick Sts.)
212-352-1666

Who knew that a bar named Antartica could be so warm and fuzzy? This bar attracts a young collegiate crowd that hangs out at the long bar, church pews and tables. Antarctica has all the essential ingredients for your basic bar: pool table, cheap drinks, a diverse jukebox and it is open until 4a.m. Check out the nightly Name Game; if your name is written above the bar, then you drink for free from 5p.m. to 11p.m. Before making the long trek to Antarctica, call ahead to see if your name is up!

## Anyway Café

34 E. 2nd St. (Bowery & 2nd Ave.)
212 533-3412

THIS CAFÉ SITS about ten feet below sidewalk level, but feels like it's two thousand miles away from New York City. Upon entering the Anyway Café, you are immediately immersed in what's going on, simply because you cannot hide at a bar with only five stools in a café with only five tables. For those seeking privacy, there is an outdoor sub-level patio space with two tables. The beer and wine list is limited, but fairly priced, and the same can be said for the food. The crowd is a bohemian mix of New Yorkers with romanticized notions of Russian culture and homesick Russians searching for the American ideal. On most nights, a guitarist sits in the corner and fills in the few quiet moments.

## Apple Restaurant & Bar

17 Waverly Pl. (Mercer & Greene Sts.)
212-473-8888

THIS DARK, COZY, mellow hangout is just what the doctor ordered for all vegetarians who have cool friends who are carnivores. It's got two kitchens to satisfy both, with meat and seafood dishes made to order. With a 100 inch television screen in the curtained off front lounge area, you can just sink yourself in the comfy leather couches and think how awesome you will be when you "do your thing" in the Karaoke room on Thursday nights.

## Aquagrill

210 Spring St. (@ 6th Ave.)
212-274-0505

THE DÉCOR OF this lovely lounge is cramped, but its only purpose is to serve as a holding area for guests waiting for a table. The glowing staff will glide through the underwater atmosphere offering you wine and a delicious assortment of bi-valves. The menu is reasonable for SoHo, so if you plan on coming, make a reservation, especially if you want to sit on the patio. A fantastic date spot.

## Aquavit

13 W. 54th St. (5th & 6th Aves.)
212-307-7311

LOCATED NEAR THE MOMA in Midtown, Aquavit is a great place for a romantic date, a splurge lunch or some serious drinking, Nordic-style. The bar is named after "aquavit," a potent Swedish potato vodka that comes several flavors, ranging from cloudberry to caraway. If you can't decide which flavor to select from the 10 bottled and 14 homemade aquavits, order a flight and sip shot after shot out of elegant fluted glasses. A casual and affordable ambiance awaits you in the upstairs café, while the lovely downstairs dining room offers multi-course Scandinavian meals, at a price; the prix fixe goes for $58. Jump through firey hoops if you have to in order to obtain a seat near the towering waterfall,a feng-shui monolith. The crowd is mostly upscale and very reserved, so don't get too loosey-goosey after a half-dozen of those aquavits.

## Aria

539 W. 21st St. (10th & 11th Aves.)
212-229-1618

IN THE SPACE that used to be called Opera, way, way West of Chelsea, miles beyond the thriving gay scene, a good-looking downtown meat-market reigns. With newly installed velvet ropes and an impressive line of people trying to make the "rope-cut", this place is definitely a happening scene. The cover charge is $20 on weekend nights, $15 reduced and no cover during the week. The main room has women in black bikinis dancing on elevated cubes, slightly-cheesy techno music and a black gothic gate with glowing candles running through the center, separating the dance floor from the lounge area (with tables that are always taken or bearing a "reserved" sign). They just added a new large room (enter it by walking towards the bathrooms), called the 'Garden" with indoor trees, its own DJ on weekends and a more intimate party feel.

## Arizona 206

206 E. 60th St. (2nd & 3rd Aves.)
212 838-0440

OUTSIDE TABLES, A dimly lit cave-like interior and an overly flirtatious service staff make Arizona 206 a surprisingly cool bar and restaurant in an otherwise dead neighborhood. With fabulous margaritas and an interesting array of drinks, Arizona 206 is a nice place to stop for a quick drink after a Bloomies shopping excursion. Just one caveat, drinkers; beware of the unexpectedly high prices! You'll be paying SoHo prices for Upper East Side ambiance.

## Arlene Grocery

95 Stanton St. (Ludlow & Orchard Sts.)
212-358-1633

HOUSED IN A space that was once a Spanish bodega, this dark hole offers live music and cheap drinks. In a space more conducive to catching a case of the clap than watching an indie rock showcase, you will most likely see an a act on the verge of fame and an A&R dude looking for said act. In what many consider the CBGB's of the the new millenium, Arlene's is definitely your best bet for live, creative tunes during a period in Manhattan starved for this kind of entertainment. Bring your right guard, lysol and some ear plugs, and you could survive unscathed.

## Arlo

140 7th Ave. So. (10th & Charles Sts.)
212-242-1200

FLAKY SERVICE SETS Arlo apart from many other bars on 7th Ave. The predominantly tourist clientele sit at the lower level dining area bar or in the solarium wondering if this is all New York has to offer. The bartenders would rather opine about all of the wonderful things to do and see in the city rather than greet or, God forbid, serve new guests. It looks as though they began to redecorate then ran out of ideas because the frosted red deco track lighting strongly disagrees with the ornate wooden bar and booths.

## Art Bar

52 8th Ave. (Jane & Horatio Sts.)
212-727-0244

THIS INTERESTING LOUNGE/BAR has been a popular West Village after work hangout and weekend rendezvous spot for years. Don't be fooled by the dicey look of the entrance, if you walk past the long bar you'll find a huge lounge filled with gigantic oil paintings, mismatched antique couches, and a happening singles scene. Art Bar is a great spot for dates or casual outings with friends. If you are lucky enough to snag a couch in the back room you'd best sit tight, relax and enjoy the high ceilings, fireplace and candlelight because roving groups of bar hoppers are continually looking to slip into your spot.

## Arthur's Tavern

57 Grove St. (7th Ave.& Bleecker St.)
212-675-6879

THE UNIQUENESS OF Arthur's is baffling. Apparently the Ghost of Holidays Past haunts this festive bar or the changing of seasons is so unbearable that they leave the decorations hanging up. Live jazz music fills this small smoky bar nightly and is played to an aging set of New Yorkers and young tourists. There is a one-drink minimum per set at the tables. With many jazz bars to choose from, Arthur's suits those who are casual jazz listeners who enjoy engaging in light conversation. You won't be stifled here as you are in many other West Village venues.

## Asia de Cuba

237 Madison Ave. (37th & 38th Sts.)
212-726-7755

ADJACENT TO MORGANS HOTEL, the upstairs portion of this posh eatery is normally filled to the brim with under-worked, overpaid fashionistas and their companions. Its ultra chic décor including a lovely waterfall (be careful looking over the balcony after downing large tropical drinks with too many straws) makes for a romantic setting. You'd better hit the ATM before climbing the stairs for a cocktail here because a couple of bucks just won't cut it. Despite the fact that Asia de Cuba has already enjoyed its heyday in the limelight, the tasty, strong drinks are a perfect fit with the aromatic, delightful cuisine for a splurge among friends.

## Astor Bar (City Eatery)

316 Bowery (@ Bleecker St.)
212-253-8644

A TASTE OF Morocco in the East Village, the Astor bar is a lively lounge decorated with leather chairs and Middle-Eastern tiles. The downstairs includes a French/American bistro which reels in the early-thirties professionals sipping pink lemonade and wine. Prices for the good booze start at $6, but the beer is a little less. With its low lighting and comfy booths, the Astor is a great place to take a date for a drink or dinner. However, those that want to chill out may find the noise a little distracting.

# Asylum

149 Bleeker St. (Thompson St. & Laguardia Pl.)
212-254-8492

AN EXCITING NEW bastardization of a club and bar, the just-born Asylum has quickly become one of the best pick up joints in the Village area. Ladies night is legendary, giving unlimited free drinks to every woman who walks through the door all night long. Their doormen can be somewhat obnoxious, and the weekend $5 cover for a crappy DJ is fairly annoying, but you just can't deny a place that attracts beautiful women looking for a good time. Oh, and when you're really plastered the gargoyles of the seven deadly sins mounted above the bar are amazing.

# Au Bar

41 E. 58th St. (Madison & Park Aves.)
212-308-9455

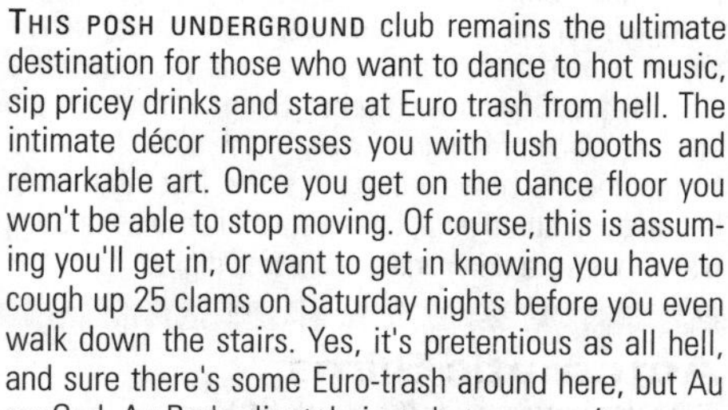

THIS POSH UNDERGROUND club remains the ultimate destination for those who want to dance to hot music, sip pricey drinks and stare at Euro trash from hell. The intimate décor impresses you with lush booths and remarkable art. Once you get on the dance floor you won't be able to stop moving. Of course, this is assuming you'll get in, or want to get in knowing you have to cough up 25 clams on Saturday nights before you even walk down the stairs. Yes, it's pretentious as all hell, and sure there's some Euro-trash around here, but Au my God, Au Bar's clientele is so hot you won't care.

# Aubette

119 E. 27th St. (Park & Lexington Aves.)
212-686-5500

THIS GORGEOUS LOUNGE decorated in red hues and modern accents is such a swanky scene, but for some reason it always escapes your mind. The crowd is laid back and way mellow on weeknights and weekend crowds tend to border on obnoxious, nevertheless, it's different from the pick-up joints lining Park Ave. For anyone sick of the nomadic herds of meatheads traveling to other bars in this area, Aubette is a classy alternative for drinks and conversation. The attentive staff is eager to educate patrons about their impressive list of wines by the glass. Cozy tables and a cigar lounge make this bar a Gramercy oasis.

## The Auction House

300 E. 89th St. (1st & 2nd Aves.)
212-427-4458

AN EXERCISE in compelling contrasts: name notwithstanding, the Auction House keeps drinks at a fixed price. Although on the Upper East Side, its ambiance is relaxed downtown: the techno music is at odds with the 19th century décor  resplendent with crimson drapes and velvet faux-antique sofas. The clientele, quite subdued and sophisticated for this neighborhood, sometimes enjoys the addition of lost frat boys lured in by the oil paintings depicting nudes. This bar is a required stop for anyone seeking something different Uptown.

## Aura

4 W. 22nd St. (5th & 6th Aves.)
212-463-0888

FORMERLY FRED'S BEAUTY BAR, the name has changed, but the look and feel is exactly the same. The space is long, narrow and loft like, and the crowd is a mix of frat/Downtown types. Snag a seat in the upstairs lounge for a great view of the cool glass light fixture and the crowd looking to score. Not the hippest bar on the Flatiron strip, but a safe and accommodating place to have a drink and score some digits.

## Automatic Slims

733 Washington St. (@ Bank St.)
212-645-8660

DURING THE WEEK, this place hosts good music, good food and good locals. However, the weekend sucks poodle dick. Frat boys, cheezy girls and bridge and tunnel folk take over this West Village stand by. If only they could place this bar in Hoboken during the weekend, the world would be a perfect place.

## Avenue A Sushi

103 Ave. A (6th & 7th Sts.)
212-982-8109

SQUEEZING ITSELF IN somewhere between hip, drum-and-bass playing, East Village bar and fine yet affordable sushi restaurant, stands Avenue A Sushi. If the tasty, raw fixin's don't get you here then the relaxed club-like atmosphere should. With its funked out, disco-balled interior and a DJ spinning all night, this could be the place for some friends to meet and greet or even a fine dating destination for the down towner. The weekends bring a wait so call ahead for a reservation.

## AZ

21 W. 17th St. (5th & 6th Aves.)
212-691-8888

THIS ASIAN INFUSED bar/restaurant is one of the coolest new spots to hit the Flatiron District this year. With its beautifully designed modern bar area and roof top dining room, AZ is a one of the best spots to dine and drink under the same roof. From the AZ martini to the spring rolls, the experience is A+. The crowd is young, hip and good-looking, but not too hip to be annoying. This is a great spot for a date, and a great spot to hang out with some Silicon Alley pals (you'll need their cash). We are glad to see this spectacular space once filled by "Flowers" has not gone to waste.

## Babalu

327 W. 44th St. (8th & 9th Aves.)
212-262-1111

OPENED AT PRESS time, Babalu is a new Latin restaurant and supper club created by music promoters Ralph Mercado and Jose Rosado. It looks promising but it's too soon to gauge what type of crowds will come.

## Baby Doll Lounge

34 White St. (@ Church St.)
212-226-4870

DESPITE WHAT CHRIS ROCK tells you, there is sex in the Champagne Room. Well, in this hole it's probably called the Malt Liquor Room. We always like to have one positive thing to say about any place, so here goes- you never have to fight for a dancer's attention, and the girls are sparkling conversationalists; especially if you have a fondness for monosyllabic answers. And, the dancing is, thanks to Rudy G., stopless.

## Baby Jupiter

170 Orchard St. (@ Stanton St.)
212-982-2229

In its three years of existence, Baby Jupiter has managed to build itself quite a reputation. The restaurant part is the Lower East Side's version of Union Square's Coffee Shop, a booth-filled diner style décor with a happening young scene that takes over every night after dinner. The kitchen is open until 2a.m. on weekend nights, which makes for a perfect late night meal. Adjacent to the restaurant is the Baby Jupiter performance space, where the best emerging bands in New York City play anything from jazz and funk to rock, pop, trip-hop and jungle. There is a 3-4 band line up seven days a week, with a $5 cover charge.

## Back Fence

155 Bleecker St. (@ Thompson St.)
212-475-9221

Bob Dylan played here. Okay, if that doesn't do it, how about chucking your peanut shells on the floor, listening to live rock 'n' roll every day, rubbing elbows with truckers, reminiscing with the folks who were doing more than beer in the hippie days, chatting with the beautiful and snapping your fingers to live poetry? This is a rap-with-the-bartender, homegrown bar with lots of wood and 15 beers on tap. Come in after work with some friends, order in some wings, and settle in with the rhythm that has kept this bar going for more than 35 years.

## The Back Page

1472 3rd Ave. (83rd & 84th Sts.)
212-570-5800

It bills itself as "New York's Hometown Sports Bar" which is a bit presumptuous considering it just opened in March 2000. But to its credit, The Back Page takes sports seriously. A wide-open space with tall ceilings, it features thirteen TV screens showing every major event. And when there's a big game they even turn the music off. Drinks and beers average from $3.50 - $5, and the 5 - 7p.m. weekday happy hour is two for one. A downstairs bar is available for private parties and the kitchen serves grub till midnight, with free goodies during happy hour.

## Baggot Inn

82 W. 3rd St. (Thompson & Sullivan Sts.)
212-477-0622

YOU KNOW THAT friend of yours that is in that shitty band and makes you go see him every single time he plays. Well, if you'e lucky you won't have to pay the $5 cover to get in to this slightly dumpy Irish bar underneath the Boston Comedy Club. This roomy, dark and smoky pub is a good place to listen to live music and grab a pint as you wait for the show. Young locals and a smattering of tourists frequent Baggot Inn making it a lively place to meet for drinks.

## Bahi

274 3rd Ave. (21st & 22nd Sts.)
212-254-5466

INTRODUCED AND WELCOMED with open arms over 3 years ago Bahi is now a Gramercy Park hot spot. The lounge hosts a DJ Tuesday nights spinning deep-funk, late-'70s and '80s tunes. Every other night you'll hear deep-groove oriented tunes.This dark, candle-lit, labyrinthine lounge attracts a boisterous happy hour crowd and gets packed on weekends. Bahi is a wonderful place for a blind date or any date because of its cozy anterooms and comfy antique couches. A second bar recently opened to service the throngs of thirsty customers.The Golden-tee and beanbag room attracts a young mix of ladder climbers to the back.

## Baktun

418 W. 14th St. (9th Ave. & Washington St.)
212-206-1590

THIS MULTIMEDIA TECHIE lounge with a tripped out vibe attracts a young, hip, multicultural crowd that cares more about shakin' some boootae than hanging around the block at the terminally disgusting (and popular) Hogs and Heifers. Baktun, The Cooler's little sister, is a long narrow space filled with sleek modern couches, an elongated steel bar and a large projection screen that displays funky films and colorful hypnotic psychhdelic shapes. DJ's spin everything from hip-hop to acid jazz and people can't help pumping and grinding "like a dog in heat, a bitch without warning"....(you finish the line). A refreshing change from the other places in the lounge/hood. This spot is definitely worth a visit.

## Balthazar

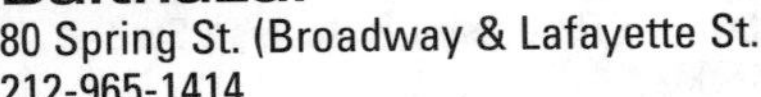

80 Spring St. (Broadway & Lafayette St.)
212-965-1414

THIS SHINING STAR in SoHo received an overload of media coverage as the locale where Jerry Seinfeld first encountered his wife, but no amount of buzz can undermine the elegance and charm of this beautiful French bistro. Limos full of the young and gorgeous flock here to be in the scene. The bar service is impeccable, but you'll pay a pretty penny for cocktails. If you're looking to impress friends by reciting your list of hangouts, a mention of Balthazar will do the trick.

## Bandito

153 2nd Ave. (9th & 10th Sts.)
212-777-4505

THERE'S NO logical reason for Bandito to still be around after eleven years. Granted, if you like to sit all day at a cheesy Mexican bar listening to Mariah Carey with a handful of drunks and a rotting bull's skull to keep you company, Bandito isn't half bad. It has a sidewalk seating area when the weather's warm that can be quite comfortable, as well some great margaritas which are only $3 'til 7p.m., making it a good place to stop and have a drink on your way somewhere else. Just don't get sucked in.

## The Bank Cafe

431 3rd Ave. (29th & 30th Sts.)
212-725-5999

AFTER 16 YEARS you'd figure The Bank Cafe could have developed more of a personality. A young crowd of frat boys and locals come in after work to watch sports and kick back a few. A full American pub menu can be enjoyed in their spacious back room until 10p.m. Beers range from $3.50-$5, and mixed drinks from $5-$6. The two pool tables in the back and the clean surroundings are what attract huge happy hour crowds.

## The Bar

68 2nd Ave. (@ 4th St.)
212-254-5766

THE EAST VILLAGE has this old-fashioned, Western, saloon type of bar to call its own. It seems to be a pick-up place for hustlers and their John Waynes. This bar is dark with the exception of the big medieval style lamp that hangs over the pool table and a few candles. The darkness seems to give this tawdry pick-up place its scandal. Specialty drinks this saloon can be proud of are its Long Island iced teas and red devils. Stepping inside feels like you have walked onto the set of Bonanza, but the prices remind you that you're still in New York's trendy East Village!

## Baraza

133 Ave. C (8th & 9th Sts.)
212-539-0811

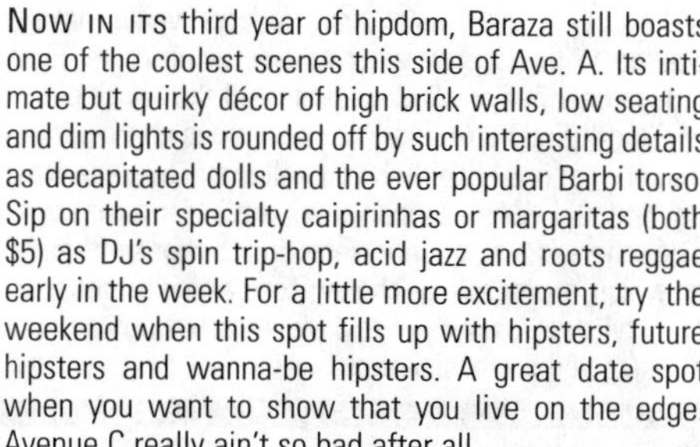

Now in its third year of hipdom, Baraza still boasts one of the coolest scenes this side of Ave. A. Its intimate but quirky décor of high brick walls, low seating and dim lights is rounded off by such interesting details as decapitated dolls and the ever popular Barbi torso. Sip on their specialty caipirinhas or margaritas (both $5) as DJ's spin trip-hop, acid jazz and roots reggae early in the week. For a little more excitement, try the weekend when this spot fills up with hipsters, future hipsters and wanna-be hipsters. A great date spot when you want to show that you live on the edge. Avenue C really ain't so bad after all.

## Barclay's Bar & Grille

111 E. 48th St. (Park & Lexington Aves.)
212-755-5900

Looking for an evening to drop some cash, smoke a stogie and sip martinis? Well, then, Barclay's is you answer. Great food, (try the jumbo shrimp) great service and a great bourbon menu make your heart a little fuller as your wallet feels a little lighter. The French doors that separate the dining area from the lounge add the perfect touch to an elegant evening in this Victorian atmosphere. Good spot for an upscale business drink with some clients.

## Bar Code

1540 Broadway (45th & 46th Sts.)
212-869-9397

How can you pass up an opportunity to play skeeball drunk? This 24-hour "barcade," is a boardwalk lovers dream. An escalator carries you up through video projections, glowing shapes and thumping house music to the second floor bar, a maze of tables and video consoles. The crowd is a mix of regulars, tourists and kids, and the bartender asserts that pickups are frequent. They advertise a host of specialty martinis ($8) and shots ($5), such as the blowjob, hard-on, brain tumor, etc., as well as hourly drink specials and competitions. Apparently, they set the bar on fire every Friday and Saturday night.

## Bar Demi

125 E. 17th St. (Irving Pl. & 3rd Ave.)
212-260-0900

IF FRASIER CRANE visits New York he would make a beeline to this teensy weensy, chic living room. Even though only five small glass tables fill the entire place, you'll still find more hilariously pompous characters in the room at one time than you will in the average Noel Coward play. Wine connoisseurs are in for a real treat since there is a staggering selection to choose from, all of which are specially chosen for particular seasons. The stylish classiness of this place makes any amount of perceived pretension worthwhile.

## Bar d'O

29 Bedford St. (@ Downing St.)
212-627-1580

DOROTHY, YOU'RE not in Kansas any more. Here you are more likely to hear a drag queen break out into "somewhere over the rainbow" than you are to see a football game on the tube. A cool lounge that features floor shows, DJ's and local transvestites, Bar d'O has become a local institution. Don't get us wrong, this is not a gay club, but it is very "gay friendly." The crowd is usually very laid back, good looking and is comprised of everyone from bankers to bike messengers. This is one of the best West Village nooks to visit if you want hang and spend the whole night in one spot.

## Bar East

1733 1st Ave. (89th & 90th Sts.)
212-876-0203

THIS RAW BAR space once occupied by Australia is just that, a raw bar space. A decent juke-box, cheap beer and a local post-college crowd fills this spot to shoot some pool and scam on some chicks (although the pickins are thin). Not worth traveling for, but an okay spot to meet. The downstairs is available for parties.

## Bar 89

89 Mercer St. (Spring & Broome Sts.)
212-274-0989

TRUE, THE CONCEPT BATHROOMS are what initially attracts newbies to Bar 89, but you'll come back for other reasons beyond being able to magically transform your unisex door from transparent to opaque with a click of the lock. In this lofty room, an attractive crowd consumes half-pound burgers and other dressed-up bar food staples in between sips of hearty (if overpriced) martinis like the sweet summer solstice.

## Bar 81

81 E. 7th St. (@ 1st Ave.)
212-598-4394

SOMETIMES WHEN YOU go to a dive bar you feel like you've landed on the concrete bottom of a bone-dry pool. This 30-year-old Ukrainian hangout used to have the Russian National Chorus sing there once a year. Nowadays it has a pool table and a jukebox. As one long time patron put it, "This is the type of bar that would appeal to a Mid-Western Finnish Lutheran." Another said, "Common sense tells me not to come here, but common sense is quite uncommon these days." Not everyone you'll talk to in here will make sense, but they will always make you feel welcome. The Ukrainian word Verchovyna adorns the front window. It means top of the mountain, but it should be bottom of the barrel. Bar 81 makes no excuses and neither do its patrons and that's why we like it.

## Bar 54

1701 Broadway (53rd & 54th Sts.)
212-247-0720

THIS PLACE DOES not suck quite as much as it probably should. It's located next to the Ed Sullivan Theater and other David Letterman landmarks, and attracts many thirsty tourists and "cool," young suburbanites looking for a good night of drinking. Mix in a few frat boys and a couple of tipsy old Irishmen and you have a pretty good picture of the crowd that packs this Theater District bar. The crowd may disappoint, but the beer selection doesn't; boasting 18 beers on tap, and a large selection of bottles. This is a great place to drink if your idea of a thrill is mocking the drinkers around you.

## Barfly

244 3rd Ave. (@ 20th St.)
212-473-9660

THIS TINY SPORT bar boasts many TV's and one giant boob tube. All sports all the time would be a good slogan for Barfly since each TV runs a different event simultaneously. Run of the mill bar food is served at the wooden booths or the bar. Bottled beer is only $3.75, not bad if you're staying for the whole game. The bartenders always seem too busy to be friendly but it's easy to strike up a conversation among the sports fanatics. On big game nights come early if having a seat is important to you.

## Barmacy

538 E. 14th St. (Aves. A & B)
212-228-2240

MEDICINE BOTTLES AND drugstore knickknacks line the walls of this former neighborhood pharmacy. The tables all feature old school jukeboxes and are filled with the cool East Village set and punks drinking concoctions like the Pepto-Bismol. DJ's keep things moving with a mix of rock, soul and exotica every night and a 2 for 1 happy hour runs between 5:30p.m. and 8:30p.m. Monday - Friday.

## Bar 9

807 9th Ave. (53rd & 54th Sts.)
212-227-6463

FOLLOWING THE SIMPLE formula of extreme dimness plus flea market couches, 9 has something-for-everyone. The bi-level space has a standing-room only bar with $4 tap beer up front, a living room in the center for the wine crowd and dining nooks in the back where you can sit by candlelight and choose from an eclectic menu. With live music and DJ's almost every night, Bar 9 has more character than most of its neighbors and remains a great stand by spot for those early drinks with the all-ages crowd from the office.

## Bar None

98 3rd Ave. (12th & 13th Sts.)
212-777-6663

THERE IS A saloon feel to the décor of Bar None, the kind that brings up memories of your 3rd grade trip to the old Western ghost town, but the old West didn't have bartenders as hot as the ones here! Alas, there are other things to do beside ogle the barmaids. You can play darts or shoot pool in the large back room. You and your friends can steal a booth, grab some cheap drinks-$4 well and domestic, and check out the mixed crowd of young suits and college kids. But whom are you kidding? You're going to ogle the barmaids. Happy hour runs from 5 to 8p.m. with $2 well drinks and pints.

## Bar on A

170 Ave. A (10th & 11th Sts.)
212-353-8231

THIS TINY MELLOW bar is quite the respite from the otherwise loud and trendified bars lining Ave A. Lots of cozy artist pallets are used as tables while real snakeskin lamps line the walls. This retro-style bar serves up inexpensive drinks and great American fare, such as tuna steak, calamari and vegetable dumplings. Open for 6 years, the crowd is mellow and the atmosphere is warm and comfortable. A daily happy hour serves up $3 margaritas and a $2 discount on all drinks until 9p.m. Definitely a mellow bar.

## Barracuda

225 W. 22nd St. (7th & 8th Aves.)
212-645-8613

HOSTING ONE OF the best nightly drag shows and packing in some of the cutest gay men on the island, Barracuda is quickly becoming a Chelsea landmark. From muscle boys, preppy tunnel and bridge travelers, to young Wall Street business types, this twentysomething crowd offers someone for even those boys with the most discriminating tastes. Play pool or relax in the comfortable retro lounge featuring modern chairs by Herman Miller. Club music pumps and the service is astonishingly quick for such a crowded bar.

## Barramundi

147 Ludlow St. (Stanton & Rivington Sts.)
212-529-6900

THIS AUSTRALIAN-OWNED bar has become somewhat of a staple during the Lower East Side's yuppification project. Dark and smoky, Barramundi has received a lot of press in the past couple of years, which has brought in an influx of uptowners and even some bridge and tunnelers. Barramudi is hip without trying too hard. When it's not packed you can snag one of the plush booths and enjoy an array of music from Fat Boy Slim to Latin Big Band. Check out their cozy back lounge complete with old couches and a fake fireplace. The weekends get very crowded since boys in dockers somehow got the impression that this is a pick-up spot. It's not.

## Barrow Street Ale House

15 Barrow St. (W. 4th St. & 7th Ave. So.)
212-691-6127

THIS BAR IS a very cool place to hang out with the NYU clan in this pleasantly non-crowded bar. As the jukebox plays a variety of feel-good music, you will feel like you are not in the midst of NYC, but in some West Virginia town hanging out with your boys. The atmosphere draws in chill, unpretentious people who come and drink beer, eat fresh hot pizza and play pool or keno. Throughout the bi-level bar, the patrons and bartenders are friendly and make this a great place to hang out. The hefty selection of beers helps too.

## Barrymore's

267 W. 45th St. (Broadway & 8th Ave.)
212-391-8400

MANAGED BY the Mayor of 45th St., this Theater District staple is an unassuming restaurant/bar that is ideal for either a pre-theater drink or dinner, or post-theater stargazing. Populated primarily by lucky tourists or in-the-know locals before show times, they begin blasting show tunes around 7:30 to get you in the mood and alert you to finish your drinks. After the theatres let out, casts and audiences file back in to hash over a the night's performances and enjoy cheap drinks and a late supper. The place is decorated with playbills, memorabilia and headshots from current and retired shows, as if they were proud parents to the whole Broadway generation

## Bar 6

502 6th Ave. (@ 13th St.)
212 691-1363

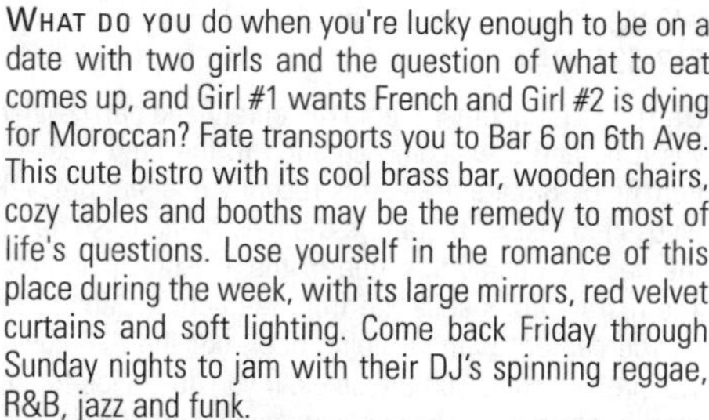

WHAT DO YOU do when you're lucky enough to be on a date with two girls and the question of what to eat comes up, and Girl #1 wants French and Girl #2 is dying for Moroccan? Fate transports you to Bar 6 on 6th Ave. This cute bistro with its cool brass bar, wooden chairs, cozy tables and booths may be the remedy to most of life's questions. Lose yourself in the romance of this place during the week, with its large mirrors, red velvet curtains and soft lighting. Come back Friday through Sunday nights to jam with their DJ's spinning reggae, R&B, jazz and funk.

## Bar Veloce

175 2nd Ave. (11th &12th Sts.)
212-260-3200

IT'S NOT A wine bar, insists the owner; explaining why we couldn't find our favorite box of wine in their selection. Attracting mostly thirtysomethings, this is a good place for couples and groups who enjoy Italian wines, or think they might enjoy them, but know nothing about them. Though it has the potential to one day become more ostentatious, for now Bar Veloce does wine without the whininess. A welcome newcomer to the East Village.

## B Bar

40 E. 4th St. (@ Bowery)
212-475-2220

THE BAR THAT everyone loves to hate but continues to visit. The common complaint is that it's filled with needy celebrities and one-dimensional beautiful people. Considering the fact that the outdoor space has been called "silicone alley," we can understand the

statement. B Bar, formerly a Gulf gas station, is a huge space, half indoors and the other half a walled-in patio space which makes you feel like you're on vacation even if you're only a block from your house. This place is never short on egos, the drinks aren't cheap, and it can come off as a bit tacky. But there's a reason for its appeal, besides the babes and the door goons: it has the best damn outdoor space in the city.

## B.B. King's Blues Club and Grill

243 W. 42nd St. (7th & 8th Aves.)
212-997-4144

OH NO!! Not another theme restaurant and bar!!! Why yes it is, and a welcome addition to the now Disney-fied Times Square area. This recently opened, bi-level blues club and restaurant is the new home to some of the best live blues this side of the Mason-Dixon line. The restaurant is separate from the actual club space so you can eat without going deaf, but the $20 cover will probably give you the blues. If you do decide to go, there's always a chance you could catch B.B. and Lucille wailing away on stage for your enjoyment.

## Bear Bar

1770 2nd Ave. (92nd & 93rd Sts.)
212-987-7580

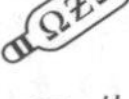

YOU MIGHT RUN into your college TA here so look around before you take off your bra so you won't feel weird taking it off in front of him. If you cannot stand the fact that college is over, come back to the good times of beer funneling and bear juice shots. This bi-level bar-restaurant boasts great wings and a great play land of sports games like foosball, pool, darts, video games, basketball and sporting events on TV. If you have Attention Deficit, you have come to the right place.

## Beauty Bar

231 E. 14th St. (2nd & 3rd Aves.)
212-539-1389

THIS BEAUTY-THEMED BAR owes its authenticity to the fact that it was at one point an actual salon. In fact, you may be confused, as the original sign for "Thomas Beauty Salon" still hangs over the entrance and the owner, Florence, still gives manicures Thursdays and Fridays for $10 (includes a beer!). This trendy, neighborhood bar is covered with beauty-paraphernalia including a row of electric dryers for seats, which although authentic, don't make for a comfortable evening. You can relax in the slightly more cozy back section and listen to a rotation of '50s cocktail music and rock-a-billy. They have daily drink specials such as Blue Rinse Monday's ($5 blue drinks) and Truck Stop Tuesday's ($2 Rheingold). Much like their other theme bar, Barmacy, it can get offensively crowded on the weekends.

## The Beekman

15 Beekman St. (Nassau & William Sts.)
212-732-7333

THIS WALL Street hang is a nice change from the usual Irish pubs found in this neck of the woods. The predominantly male clientele can enjoy continental fare while listening to a surprisingly up to date jukebox. The bar features a large room for parties and a happy hour from 5p.m.-7p.m.

## Beekman Bar & Books

889 1st Ave. (@ 50th St.)
212-980-9314

BEEKMAN IS SOPHISTICATED, classy, upscale and expensive; all the criteria for a divorcee to meet her future husband or lover. The jazz music in the background, dim lighting, book lined walls, premium liquors, wines, caviar and cigars politely whisper swank in unison. If you are in the mood to put on a jacket and revel in conservative stuffiness pick a night when a client is in town rather than bring your friends.

## Beer Bar @ Café Centro

200 Park Ave. (@ 45th St.)
212-818-1222

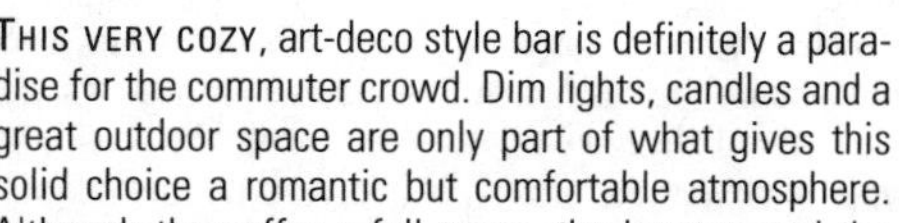

THIS VERY COZY, art-deco style bar is definitely a paradise for the commuter crowd. Dim lights, candles and a great outdoor space are only part of what gives this solid choice a romantic but comfortable atmosphere. Although they offer a full menu, the burgers and the

$10 stir-fry are true choices among the Metro North set. Thirsty? Try one of the reasonably priced martinis or one the many Belgian fruit beers to quench that trip before heading back to suburbia.

## Belgo Nieuw York

415 Lafayette St. (4th St. & Astor Pl.)
212-253-2828

GRAB A SPOT at one of the communal tables and experience mussels from Brussels at this unique NoHo hotspot. Belgo verges on being a theme bar/restaurant, with its monkishly robed wait staff serving steaming black pots of moules frites. Since February, Belgo's warehouse-looking front bar doubled in space, helping patrons focus on what the bar is all about: the over 100-count beer list.

## Bellevue Bar

538 9th Ave. (39th & 40th Sts.)
212-760-0660

A BIT OF the Lower East Side has landed in Hell's Kitchen tossing aside all yuppies on the way up. Formerly Hell's Kitchen Bar, the owner looked around at the oddly mixed clientele of his bar and the first word (or mental institution) to come to mind was Bellevue. With no cover charge, a great eclectic mix of live music, pinball and Pac Man, friendly bartenders and a great sushi bar, the Bellevue Bar is definitely a Shecky's pick. The place is very dog friendly (as in the animal not your girlfriend). Sunday is industry night which brings in your struggling actors, musicians and artists to mingle and schmooze. Red lanterns over the bar illuminates the art work on the walls and a statue of Elvis sets the scene for a very cool hangout in Hell's Kitchen.

## Belmont Lounge

117 E. 15th St. (Park Ave. & Irving Pl.)
212-533-0009

THIS FORMER UNION Square supermodel hangout is a good place to come with a bunch of friends and monopolize the back room. The waitress service is a bit slow and delivered with attitude. Eventually you'll get your drink, but the alcohol will have probably evaporated by then. If you can't snag a spot in the back room you'll have to mingle with folks in the front who are convinced they're interesting because they have a corporate job and/or a really bad ass tattoo. The soft pop music is oddly inappropriate for a lounge, but who cares; you're still waiting for that damn drink.

## Bemelmans Bar

35 E. 76th St. (Madison & Park Aves.)
212-744-1600

BEMELMANS BAR IS quaint, charming and makes you feel like you have been transported to the cafes of Europe as you sip (very expensive) wine and listen to the piano bar. Rich with history, Bemelmans Bar was named after Ludwig Bemelman, the author and artist of the widely popular Madeline stories. Original Ludwig Bemelman murals grace the walls of the bar and add to the European flavor. The crowd exudes class and the people are younger Euro-tourists and older locals discussing their portfolios.

## Bergins

89 South St., South Street Seaport,
(Pier 17, 3rd floor)

OPEN FROM NOON to midnight, Bergins has reasonably priced drinks (ranging from $4.50 to $6) including Fosters, Sam Adams, Heineken, Pete's Wicked Ale, Stella Artois, Harp and Bass on tap. The only food they serve are buffalo wings for $5. The decor offers nothing more than a modern-looking wooden bar illuminated with old fashioned light fixtures. A new addition to the seaport area, Bergins may be around for a while.

## Big Bar

75 E. 7th St. (1st & 2nd Aves.)
212-777-6969

COME ESCAPE the hype of the East Village in this 10 year-old local joint that's 10% less filling than your average bar. The obvious irony of the Big Bar is that everything is just a bit small, like someone left your usual bar in the dryer too long. Big Bar is a relaxing environment for the slightly older crowd of locals wishing to enjoy an evening without frat boys or beer pitchers. A rotation of Stevie Wonder and 50's cocktail music is kept at low volume to encourage the self-proclaimed "civilized clientele" to feel at home.

## Big Sur

1406 3rd Ave. (@ 80th St.)
212-472-5009

Big Sur is perfect for a date or anyone you need to impress. The dark and imposing lounge targets an older professional crowd. Drink prices are high but that's the price of warding off the youngsters. The restaurant features American bistro cuisine served to a mix of disco and house music. There's also a sidewalk cafe that's perfect for a summer dinner. At night, the tables move out to allow more room for crowds of Euro-trash and suits buying $8 martinis and $6 imports.

## Bill's Gay Nineties

57 E. 54th St. (Madison & Park Aves.)
212-355-0243

Originally a speakeasy, this comfortable, live music standby draws an eclectic mix of couples and post college students looking for some cover free, live entertainment. Whether you head upstairs for dinner or stay in the downstairs lounge, the turn of the century decor mixed with the moderately priced cocktails will keep you humming a Gershwin tune all the way home. This 1926 original is worth a visit if you happen across this touristy part of town. BONUS: A very safe spot to bring mom and dad.

## Billy's Stopless

729 6th Ave. (@ 24th St.)
212-242-8804

From the bathing-suit clad girls to the ridiculous added "S", what was once a thriving, semi-famous girlie bar part-local dive, part kitsch scene has suffered from Giuliani's moral crusade. But Billy's regulars have stuck it out. There are plans to renovate to satisfy the city's new 60-40 rule (40% nude, 60% empty). There's a grand re-opening planned for fall 2000 and we hope to again enjoy the only slightly over-priced drinks and entertainment sans cover. The friendly bar staff tells us the free Chinese buffet next to the stage is edible though no one's here for the sesame chicken.

## Birdland

315 W. 44th St. (8th & 9th Aves.)
212-581-3080

THIS SELF-PROCLAIMED "Jazz Corner of the World" is the perfect place for an eloquent evening of great jazz. Whether by music from Duke Ellington or Charlie Parker, you will be romanced out of your under pants when you hear the well-rehearsed band go at it. Twenty dollars will buy you at a seat at the candlelit and carpeted Birdland, where you can enjoy a delectable meal and get a great view of the orchestra. With no beer on tap, they have accumulated an extensive bottled beer and wine selection in the four years they've been making music here.

## Bishops Lounge & Grille

1650 3rd Ave. (91st & 92nd Sts.)
212-289-9982

BISHOPS IS EITHER a nondescript bar with a restaurant, or a boring restaurant with a bar. The owners probably aren't sure either. To further confuse the mix, they feature live cover bands Fridays and Saturdays. The good news is that you can muzzle up to the bar during their 4p.m.-8p.m. happy hour and enjoy $2.75 domestic beers and well drinks. You'll find a mix of Upper East Side yuppies and Irish locals hypnotized by the big screen TV and drinking $4 pints and mixed drinks. The Guinness isn't spectacular and don't expect anyone Irish to be making your shepherd's pie.

## Bistro Latino

1711 Broadway (@ 54th St.)
212-956-1000

LOOKIN TO LIVE la vida loca? Then mambo on down to Bistro Latino where you can sip sangria and munch on some Colombian sirloin empanadas in a truly authentic Latin atmosphere. The dining area offers a medium sized dance floor where you learn to shake like your favorite Menudo member for nada. If you're looking to hang with your frat amigos, samba on by. However it's not a bad choice for an off beat date.

## The Bitter End

147 Bleecker St. (LaGuardia Pl. & Thompson St.)
212-673-7030

SINCE ITS OPENING in 1961, the Bitter End has been all about the music, no question. Talents such as Billy Joel, Joni Mitchell and Neil Young have all played the stage here in their times, and the bar continues to get exceptional performers in a wide range of styles on a consistent basis. The atmosphere is relaxed but serious about the music and the drinks are reasonably priced. Of course, if the band is good nobody who belongs in The Bitter End really cares about cheap drinks anyway.

## Black & White

86 E. 10th St. (3rd & 4th Aves.)
212-253-0246

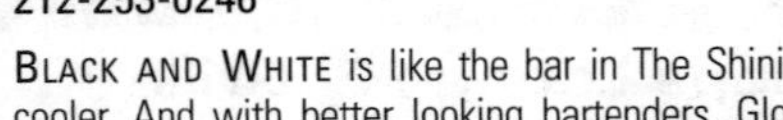

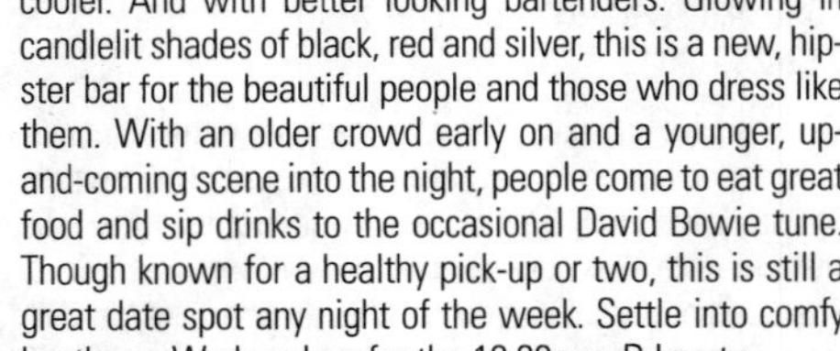

BLACK AND WHITE is like the bar in The Shining, only cooler. And with better looking bartenders. Glowing in candlelit shades of black, red and silver, this is a new, hipster bar for the beautiful people and those who dress like them. With an older crowd early on and a younger, up-and-coming scene into the night, people come to eat great food and sip drinks to the occasional David Bowie tune. Though known for a healthy pick-up or two, this is still a great date spot any night of the week. Settle into comfy booths on Wednesdays for the 10:30p.m. DJ party.

## Black Betty

366 Metropolitan Ave. (@ Havemeyer St.)
Brooklyn 718-599-0243

GET YOUR PASSPORT, it's time to go to Brooklyn. Over the past few years, Williamsburg has become the hip and semi-affordable artsy neighborhood that the Village once was. Black Betty's eclectic Moroccan/Caribbean mix attracts a stylish crowd who can afford to buy new clothes with the money they save on the potent and inexpensive drinks that set the mood at this sultry spot. Big, soft sofas, strong incense and heavy beats (DJ's three nights a week, free bands on the other nights), make this place all the sexier for those with enough style to compete.

## The Black Sheep

583 3rd Ave. (@ 39th St.)
212-599-3476

A MIXED CROWD of suits and locals cram into this Irish bar for a light, after-work nip that has the tendency to turn into a heavy pre-work hangover. Decorated in traditional T.G.I. Guinness, The Black Sheep serves up pints and drinks starting at $3. A huge "Game Room" sign beckons you to the rear of the bar, where you'll find a lonely poker arcade game next to the bathroom. On Sunday's they host an open blues/jazz jam from 7p.m. The session brings in around 20 artists that replace the usual jukebox of pop and rock hits.

## Black Star

92 2nd Ave. (5th & 6th Sts.)
212-254-4747

STILL PERSONALITY FREE and trying to figure out what it wants to be, Black Star has DJ's spinning every night of the week (no cover) and live grassroots musicians Tuesday nights. The small bar is friendly enough and draws fun crowds who play pool and pick up. We hear vanilla women come here to scam chocolate love.

## Blah Blah Lounge

501 11th St. (7th & 8th Aves.) Brooklyn
718-369-2524

WANT TO TAKE your honey to the Hamptons but haven't got the cash? Fear not, Blah Blah is here to save you from your woes. With its flowery wall paper, frilly lace curtains, a glowing fireplace and cozy furniture, Blah Blah has a sugar and spice and all things nice ambiance. The lounge/bar-cum-restaurant and coffee spot feels more like a cutesy little bed and breakfast in the country than it does a New York watering hole.

## The Blarney Cove

510 E. 14th St. (Aves. A & B)
212-473-9284

OH, THE GOOD ole days have come and definitely not gone here at the Blarney Cove. For 36 years the Blarney Cove has been pouring stiff, cheap drinks to the same loyal crowd who have not given up their barstools in all this time. Brightly lit with wood paneling and revolving beer signs, The Blarney Cove attracts ex-Vegas performers, Italians from the hood and a mix of locals. They have the cheapest drinks this side of Ave A and an eclectic jukebox spits out everything from Tony Bennett to Guns n' Roses.

## Blarney Rock

137 W. 33rd St. (6th & 7th Aves.)
212-947-0826

THE CLEANER OF two Irish sports-bars on this block and it's still pretty damn dirty. Sport memorabilia, beer signs and surly Irish bartenders who don't like too many questions, clutter this popular Madison Square Garden spot. Beer flows freely to the mainly blue-collar, after-work crowd. If watching games with loud, drunk people while eating shepherds pie is your idea of a good time, then this is the place for you!

## Blarney Star

43 Murray St. (Church & West Sts.)
212-732-2873

THIS AFTER WORK institution has been sporting its authentic Irish fare in TriBeCa for 30 plus years and is still going strong. Serving from 9:30a.m.-4a.m. (yes there are some die hard drinkers in there at 9:30a.m.), Blarney Star has kept the Financial District entertained with its live Irish music on Friday evenings and its reasonably priced drinks year round. Best as an after work spot, the crowd is a mix of professionals, blue collar workers and locals. If you're looking for a super-model try some of the trendier TriBeCa lounges, if you're looking to drink and relax in a real Irish bar, this is your spot.

## Blarney Stone

410 8th Ave. (30th & 31st Sts.)
212-997-9248

106 W. 32nd St. (6th & 7th Aves.)
212-502-5139
340 9th Ave. (29th & 30th Sts.)
212-502-4656

IF YOU'RE A toothless, dirty, smelly, ratty-haired old man, this chain of dumpy bars will be your heaven on earth. Any others need not enter, but if you do, go at you own risk.

## Blatino Bronx Factory

2999 3rd Ave. (@ 155th St.)
212-592-3632

OK, SO THE NAME caught your attention, huh? Well this place took us a little off guard, but it's in Manhattan and way uptown, and those who know it love it. This bar/club is only open on Thursdays and Fridays and has a very devoted crowd of black and Latino men who dance fiercely to the rotating DJ's who spin R&B, deep-house, salsa and hip-hop. The club itself is not so big, but has two metal cages with half-naked dancing boys. The cover charge varies at the door and there is a certain amount of attitude present that may unnerve a typical white, gay Chelsea boy, but generally everyone is welcome as long as you can hold your own on the dance floor.

## Bleecker Street Bar

58 Bleecker St. (@ Crosby St.)
212-334-0244

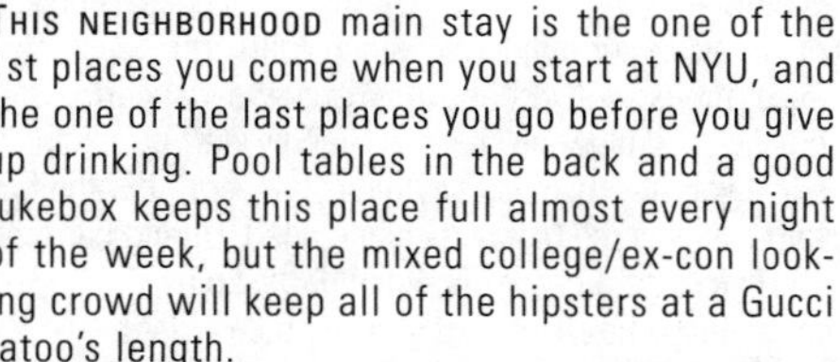

THIS NEIGHBORHOOD main stay is the one of the 1st places you come when you start at NYU, and the one of the last places you go before you give up drinking. Pool tables in the back and a good jukebox keeps this place full almost every night of the week, but the mixed college/ex-con looking crowd will keep all of the hipsters at a Gucci tatoo's length.

## Blind Tiger Ale House

518 Hudson St. (@ 10th St.)
212-675-3848

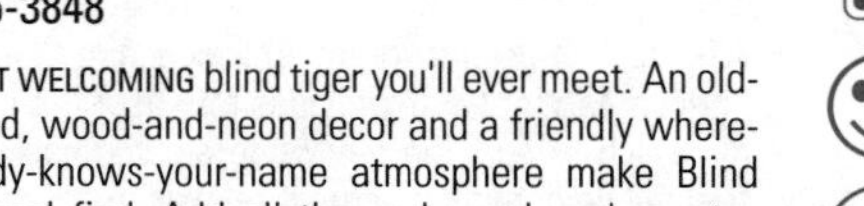

THE MOST WELCOMING blind tiger you'll ever meet. An old-fashioned, wood-and-neon decor and a friendly where-everybody-knows-your-name atmosphere make Blind Tiger a real find. Add all the perks and you've got a merry band of repeat customers, enjoying weekly newsletters, free cheese on Wednesday nights, free bagels on Sunday and a wee dose of fame. Drinking your way through the 51-beer Connoisseur Club gets you a permanent happy hour discount with your name emblazoned on a plaque on the back wall! Top it off with a choice selection of imported ales and liquor, and this is one of Manhattan's premier neighborhood bars.

## Bliss Bar and Lounge

256 E. 49th St. (2nd & 3rd Aves.)
212-644-8750

YOU COULDN'T TRIP in any direction without falling into one of the happy hour havens in this stretch of Second Ave. So why no drink specials? Visually more appealing than most, Bliss applies a clean, industrial look without coming across at all harsh. The uncomfortable barstools in the main room threaten to transform you into a hunchback, but they're pretty and chances are, you won't get one anyway. Mixed drinks here are pricey and diminutive, and you might find yourself waiting a while for another if you aren't a leggy blonde in a crop top. Out come the velvet ropes on weekends and in comes an attractive, less frantic clientele.

## Blondie's

212 W. 79th St. (Amsterdam Ave. & Broadway)
212-362-4360

ALTHOUGH TWO (not surprisingly, blonde) women own it, this neighborhood sports bar caters to a mostly male clientele. Seventeen conveniently placed television sets of all sizes surround you, along with frat house-style decorations like street signs and the Jaegermeister-emblazoned blow-up shark. A friendly staff is on hand to serve you "pretty much anything you want," but the buffalo wings come highly recommended. During halftime, you can catch a game of pool or darts, unless it happens to be happy hour (when it's way too crowded).

## Blu

161 W. 23rd St. (6th & 7th Aves.)
212-633 6113

A RECENT ADDITION on the gay scene in Chelsea, this bar-cum-Internet café provides four user-friendly kiosks on which to surf the net while sipping cocktails. The friendly neighborhood crowd relaxes in a lounge made comfortable with oversized furniture.

## Blu Lounge

197 N. 8th St. (@ Driggs Ave.) Brooklyn
718-782-8005

HERE ON THE sophisticated lagoon on Brooklyn's Barbary Coast lies Blu Lounge. Discrete pods at either end of a narrow hallway give this place a nautical feel, exemplifying the true lounge. Tastefully modern, discreet lighting, plush seating, two cockpit bars and dubbed world music make this location a perfect romantic hideout The martinis are transcendent. If you're on a bender, stop in here for a wake-up call with the slightly dirty gin martini or the unique sake-tini. A DJ plays French house music on weekends and happy hour is a bargain: From 6p.m-9p.m. every night you'll get $2 drafts and $3 sakes.

## Blue and Gold

79 E. 7th St. (1st & 2nd Aves.)
212-473-8918

IF YOU HAVEN'T been to Blue and Gold, you're missing out on what could be the most fashionable dive in town. The clientele is young, good looking and refreshingly hip. Small crowds of friends and strangers alike commune in front of a bitchin' jukebox and a large crowd assembles around the pool table. (Warning: these guys don't think it's cute if you suck). The bar staff varies from surly to hospitable depending on the night ; just be patient and smile, even if they don't smile back. The drinks are alarmingly cheap and the bathrooms shockingly heinous. Your best bet is to get here early and plant yourself in one of the booths that surround the pool table.

## Blue Note

31 W. 3rd St. (6th Ave. & MacDougal St.)
212-475-8592

THIS IS PERHAPS the best-known jazz venue in the city due to the big names and famous faces it attracts. Playing to a full house of tourists and music aficionados every night of the week, this is the Hard Rock Café of the jazz world. A mirrored den of seats provide good viewing of the stage which is nice considering the cover charges usually start at $30 per person not including a $5 minimum per person. The Sunday afternoon jazz brunch is a refreshing change from the norm.

## Blue Water Grill

31 Union Square West (@ 16th St.)
212-675-9500

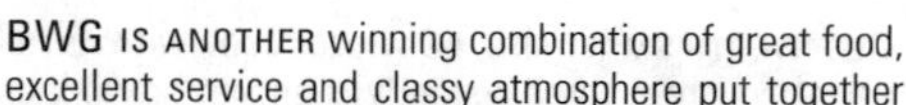

BWG IS ANOTHER winning combination of great food, excellent service and classy atmosphere put together

by Steve Hanson, restaurateur and owner of 8 amazingly successful spots in the city. BWG's grand atmosphere is pleasing to all senses with its marble, columns, flowers and chandeliers. The bar area on the main level is small and narrow and tends to burst at the seams with guests waiting for tables. In order to fully appreciate your time here you may want to head downstairs to the jazz room where a small bar with a few tables offers a calmer atmosphere and great music free of cover. BWG generally plays host to businessmen, pretty women, and B&T on the weekend.

## BMW

199 7th Ave. (21st & 22nd Sts.)
212-229-1807

SPORTING A FRIDGE full of bottles, three beers on tap and a couple coffee machines, BMW is the ultimate fusion of local bar and beatnik hideout. Enter, after coercing the door open, what looks like an artist's very cozy (and small) apartment, complete with stainless steel kitchen/bar, deep purple walls, taped up vinyl barstools and experimental artwork. A great bar for relaxing, meeting new people, and enjoying (OKAY, that depends) some experimental live music every night of the week/24 hours a day. Keep an eye out for friendly regulars like Mo, who haven't moved from their seats since the last millennium.

## Boat Basin Cafe

West 79th St. (@ the Hudson River)
212-496-5542

A PICNIC ATMOSPHERE pervades this spacious outdoor bar/cafe located underneath the Henry Hudson Parkway. From May to October a mixed crowd of local drinkers, dog-walkers and park-lovers crams into the Boat Basin for drinks and snacks. Weekends, folks come for a string quartet brunch until 3p.m. Weeknights, a younger crowd stops in for beautiful sunset viewing, with margaritas and electric lemonades in hand.

## bOb

235 Eldridge St. (Houston & Stanton Sts.)
212-777-0588

DESPITE ITS SMALL size, bOb oozes cool, with its red velvet couches, the constantly changing artwork on the walls (the lounge doubles as an art gallery) and DJ's spinning old school hip-hop and reggae. The low-key vibe and the $5 well drinks and drafts attract lots of Lower East Side cool kids. Happy hour runs from 7p.m. to 10p.m. when drinks are offered at half price. The door policy is casual and nice. If the small lounge gets too packed, single guys may have to wait outside till things calm down. The hip, low-key and cozy scene make this a nice place to bring a date for drinks.

## Boca Chica

13 1st Ave. (@ 1st St.)
212-473-0108

RESTAURANT FIRST, bar second, Boca Chica still bursts at the seams after 10 years. Alongside the single square room of tables is the slightly uncomfortable collection of would-be diners, elbowing their way to the bar for margaritas, Brazilian caipirinhas or pina coladas. Once seated, you'll get fresh seafood under the Christmas lights, loud conversation over the salsa tunes and another round of margaritas.

## Boiler Room

86 E. 4th St. (1st & 2nd Aves.)
212-254-7536

WALKING INTO THE Boiler Room, feels like you have entered someone's basement. Except this hot, gay East Village hangout has a cozier feel with its pool table and couches. This place has purplish walls and plain chairs in the back as if spectators were watching someone receive punishment or otherwise be slaughtered. The walls have stationary reflected lights with little white candles contradicting the rock-laden jukebox. If you're short on cash, go on Monday nights because they provide $1 well shots and $1 mugs of Bud/Bud Light.

## Bond Street

6 Bond St. (Broadway & Lafayette Sts.)
212-777-2500

PROFILE: EXPENSIVE DRINKS, Prada bags, cell phones, great sushi. Guilty party? Bond Street Lounge. Whether you decide to hang in the swanky, modern lounge for a $12 martini or scarf down some sea urchin in the beau-

tiful dining room, the experience is high end straight through. The main drawback is the over sized bouncer doing a DNA test at the door. Uber model genes need only apply.

## Bongo

299 10th Ave. (27th & 28th Sts.)
212-947-3654

BONGO OFFERS BIG (bongo drum) bang for your buck. This fresh oyster bar takes a retro look back at a swinging pad from the '50s. Green lounge chairs, vintage goods galore and a wall of colorful bottles allude to the kitschy rainbow array of mixed drinks in store for you. Bongo cocktails are big, look great and taste even better.

## Boots & Saddle

76 Christopher St. (7th Ave. & Bleecker St.)
212-929-9684

THIS WESTERN THEMED gay leather bar is one of those places where you can witness an overweight drag queen sipping Bud on the rocks while gawking at Marlboro Men dressed in cowboy gear. The awesome jukebox and friendly staff make this a great dive bar to take advantage of the two-for-one weekend beer blast.

## The Boston Comedy Club

82 W. 3rd St. (Thompson & Sullivan Sts.)
212-477-1000

SIFTING THROUGH THE mire of redundant airplane jokes can actually be fun at this clubhouse-style comedy club. Some of the comedians aren't quite there yet, but the dank frat-house atmosphere is the perfect place to get wasted on a weeknight and watch them hone their yuks. This is where the heavy-hitters try out their new stuff; it's not uncommon to see Chris Rock or Dave Chappelle drop by and warm up for a television appearance.

## Botanica

47 Houston St. (Mott & Mulberry Sts.)
212-343-7250

THOUGH SOMEWHAT SURREAL, sporting seventies psychedelic decor and some sort of earth goddess sculpture bursting through the wall, this is a comfortable semi-dive, offering cushy furniture and an atmosphere that'll make you think everyone is a regular. Make a selection from the no-frills alcohol selection and curl up with a book or a buddy. DJ's spin for free on weekends.

## Bottino

246 10th Ave. (24th & 25th Sts.)
212-206-6766

THIS HIP AND chic Chelsea Italian hot spot has quickly become a favorite among the gallery jet set. The area in the front offers a warm but modern setting to sip one of Bottino's many wines and specialty cocktails served by the very attentive and friendly bar staff. The food is great, the crowd is easy on the eyes and large outdoor garden serves as one of the best summer places to bring a date. Shecky's rates this one the best all around spots for dinner and drinks in NYC.

## Bottom Line

15 W. 4th St. (@ Mercer St.)
212-228-6300

PERHAPS NEW YORK'S only sophisticated venue to listen to bluegrass, country and folk music. There is always a line-up of aging hippies-cum-yuppies looking to recapture their youth. The stage is large enough to provide good views from any seat in the house and a limited menu of bar food is served. The Bottom Line is very organized so you can call up to one month ahead for ticket prices and performance dates.

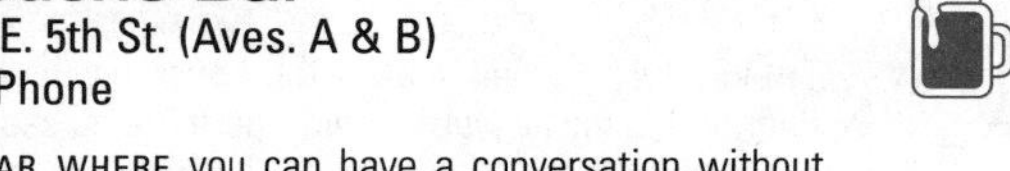

## Bouche Bar

540 E. 5th St. (Aves. A & B)
No Phone

A BAR WHERE you can have a conversation without yelling, now that is reason enough to go. The reasons do not stop there. Bouche Bar is a safe haven away from the super trendy scene where the bartenders are warm, friendly and remember your name. The clientele are an older and artistic neighborhood set that enjoys the comfortable, relaxed atmosphere. It is also a great place to have a drink and a cigarette while reading your favorite novel.

## Boughalem

14 Bedford St. (Downing & Houston Sts.)
212-414-4764

AN UNDISCOVERED GEM in the Village, Boughalem is a spectacular place to bring a date for a romantic meal. With its black stone bar, soft lit lanterns, soft piano music, and floral paintings, if this doesn't get your date in the mood, your best bet might be an inflatable sheep available in a Times Square porn shop. One of the best date spots in this area and definitely one of the more welcome additions to the scene this year.

## Bourbon Street

407 Amsterdam Ave. (79th & 80th Sts.)
212-721-1332

THIS MARDI GRAS theme bar packs it in late night with local 20-somethings (and younger, but who's telling?) ready to get down and let loose. Drown in a big easy fishbowl with friends or get smashed solo on a few tasty but lethal frozen hurricanes. Bourbon Street's selling points include a racially mixed crowd, Tuesday Karaoke nights (complete with occasional appearances by Dick Clark), free beads at the door and DJ and dancing nightly -- cabaret laws be damned! You're in N'Orleans now! On Wednesdays when the Buds and well drinks are free for the femmes, you might just find a few liquored up ladies dancing on the bar (or some-one's lap) before the evening comes to a reluc-tant close.

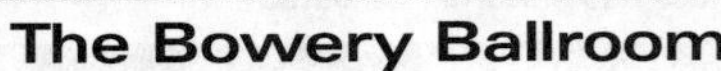

## The Bowery Ballroom

6 Delancey St. (@ Bowery)
212-533-2111

THERE ISN'T A bad seat in the house on the main floor of this music club. In fact, there are no seats at all. But there are tables on the balcony, where the sound and view are fine for those who don't wish to stand any longer. In the basement curves a spa-cious round bar serving 'em up to those sitting out the current gig upstairs. This is a great place to catch above-average bands on their way to rock star-dom.

## Bowlmor Lanes

110 University Pl. (12th & 13th Sts.)
212-255-8188

EVER THINK WHAT would happen if you cross-bred the movie "American Graffiti" and the television show "Battlestar Galatica" and threw in bowling to boot? This is it! What was once a staid ordinary old bowling alley in the Village has become a haven for parties and good times. This split-level bowling extravaganza is dark and cavernous on the upper level and well lit on the lower level. The bowling pins are fluorescent and glow in the dark, and the lanes have red runway-like landing lights streaking down them. There's a fun-loving young crowd here and everything's cheap--food, beer, thrills. You don't have to be a bowler to enjoy this place, because as the beer keeps flowing your bowling gets so much better!

## Boxcar Lounge

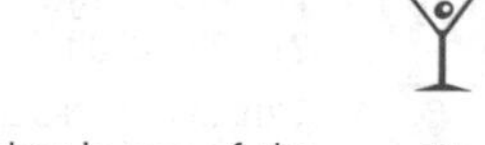

168 Ave. B (10th & 11th Sts.)
212-473-2830

THIS TINY WINE, beer and sake bar is one of the better choices for a drink in the East Village. In a space that looks like a boxcar (what a shock) drinks are served in a intimate setting to a mixed crowd ranging from locals to Upper East Siders. If you're really feeling wacky, try one of their signature drinks such as the sake screwdriver, or the Irish milkshake. If the boxcar/hobo feel is what you yearn for, you can always choose one of their 30 bottled brews. Although this has the appearance of a "velvet rope" spot, the vibe is cool, relaxed and free from "super scene-sters." The drinks are moderately priced, the atmosphere is kind and there's a garden to hang in. What more do you need in a bar?

## Brady's

1583 2nd Ave. (@ 82nd St.)
212-650-0567

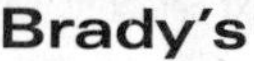

IF YOU LIKE playing darts, Brady's is the place to visit on a regular basis. Other than that, it's an average neighborhood joint with a pool table and all the obligatory beers on tap. The jukebox belts out an array of classic rock to jam to. Be careful when making your trek to the restroom, darts are flying everywhere. Brady's is another one of the typical uptown Irish bars that you can count on leaving contentedly drunk.

## Brandy's Piano Bar

235 84th St. (2nd & 3rd Aves.)
212-650-1944

BRANDY'S SEEMS TO HAVE snuck into the Upper East Side when no one was looking. This mostly gay bar and cabaret offers free live music nightly after 9:30 p.m., catering to an unusually diverse crowd for the area. While it's hardly a pick-up spot, the tall wood booths afford a little privacy. The beer bottles are around $4 and drinks are between $5 - $6. The talented performers belt out a mix of standards and jazz. You don't have to love show tunes to enjoy yourself at Brandy's but it helps.

## Braque

775 Washington St. (@ 12th St.)
212-255-0709

THIS CONVERTED GARAGE in the West Village serves as a home away from home for Manhattan's artist and model elite. Open seasonally from May to September, Braque serves expensive cocktails and finger food on tiny marble tables. This hidden treasure offers a tranquility that makes a trek to the west side worthwhile.

## Brasserie Bit

258 W. 44th St. (Broadway & 8th Ave.)
212-869-4440

A BIT OF brasserie meets Broadway where the pre-theater and the after-work crowd converge. Crack an egg at the bar or order from the steak-frites fare as you sip a fruit-infused champagne aperitif in this handsome, cream-colored space. Every hour is happy hour here and you never know when the next celebrity will walk through those French doors.

## Brassierie Centrale

1700 Broadway (@ 53rd St.)
212-757-2233

BRASSIERIE CENTRALE IS a beautiful restaurant featuring modern décor blended with a splash of '60s chic, and it never closes. Happy hour, from 4:30 to 7p.m., offers drinks at half price. Regular prices are standard: beers go for five bucks a pint and specialty frozen drinks come in at eight. Brassiere Centrale has been around 3 years and caters to business folk, laid-back drop-ins and out of town visitors.

## Brasserie 8 1/2

9 W. 57th St. (5th & 6th Aves.)
212-829-0812

THIS CHIC, BRAND spanking new edition to Midtown has the goods to be a finisher in the rat race of restaurant/bars. Upon entering a congenial host greets you, a refreshing change from clipboards and velvet rope. Then proceed down an orange spiral staircase to the lounge where the hub of activity awaits you. The back wall is adorned with an original stained glass window by Ferdinand Leger. Traditional hard-boiled eggs and other tasty bar treats work up the appetite of patrons enjoying the bar scene. For $9 you can get a little slice of heaven in a white chocolate martini. Drinks start at $6.50, so load up your wallet before you come.

## Bread Bar (@ Tabla)

11 Madison Ave. (@ 25th St.)
212-889-0667

RIGHT ON TARGET, Danny Meyer's newest NYC spot pleases on every level. The vibrant vegetable murals on the domed ceiling in the lounge area excite the eyes and the aromatic smells from the open kitchen will make your stomach grumble. There are a few tables outside looking onto Madison Square Park, but you must get here very early to get a seat because this place is no secret, especially to those who work in the CSFB building. The décor is modern, but respects the architectural history of the building. A unique list of $11 specialty drinks such as the tamarind martinis are a big hit with the thirtysomething crowd waiting for a seat in the upstairs dining room

## Brew's

156 E. 34th St. (Lexington & 3rd Aves.)
212-889-3369

IN THIS NIGHTLIFE dead-zone of Murray Hill, Brew's (named after the man who moved his ice cream parlor-turned-saloon to this site in 1948) is a cozy bar with a

very eclectic décor: The most noticeable prop being the moose head in the middle of the bar with yellow lights, a Yankees cap, and flag on top of it. Playing soft rock and oldies-but-goodies, Brews appeals to those visiting on business and a steak-eating set of regulars.

## Brewsky's

41 E. 7th St. (2nd & 3rd Aves.)
212-420-0671

With a selection of over 700 brands from around the world, Brewsky's is the quintessential beer lover's paradise. A no-frills, drinking man's bar and a place where the wildest decorations include a small train that circles overhead and a beer bottle collection that will put yours to shame. It's a home to both local beer connoisseurs and tourists who crave their own hometown brew. Many of the imports get kind of pricey, averaging $8 a bottle on the low end of the spectrum, the tap beers are much more affordable. Don't even think about ordering a cocktail here.

## The Bridge Bar

309 E. 60th St. (@ 2nd Ave.)
212-223-9104

Obviously near the bridge, this gay bar offers little more than a place for thirtysomething men to cruise each other or get drunk during happy hour. This neighborhood hang out is exactly that- yet comfortable, clean, sleek with attentive and friendly service. This bar is definitely one of the less well- traversed gay bars along the 2nd Ave. gay bar crawl, but one thing that makes this gay watering hole unique is its backyard garden.

## The British Open

320 E. 59th St. (1st & 2nd Aves.)
212-355-8467

British Open isn't just trying to be English, it really is English, and the Brits know it. Ask the bartender about the night Posh Spice watched her then-soccer star fiancé David Beckham get booted out of a World Cup match here, causing the team to lose and her to get booed by the other Brits there with her. The usual suspects here are middle-aged, trench coat sporting men and, of course, golf fanatics. You can also come alone and have a drink with the bartender. But remember to tip; he's still bitter about being snubbed by the Spice Girls.

## Broadway Lounge

**(@ The Marriott Marquis)**
**1534 Broadway (45th & 46th Sts.)**
**212-398-1900**

In the heart of Times Square this bar/restaurant offers titillating revolving views of the Manhattan skyline. Don't worry, the floor moves slowly enough so you won't get seasick or dizzy. Besides the view, this hotel bar is nothing extraordinary, they serve overpriced drinks to unsuspecting tourists that watch everyone riding up in the glass elevator. If you're a local, it's worth coming to listen to the pianist and complimentary jazz while you watch the world pass you by.

## Brooklyn Ale House

**103 Berry St. (@ N. 8th St.) Brooklyn**
**718-302-9811**

Brooklyn Ale House strikes one as slightly disingenuous considering it isn't as old as it looks and the young locals haven't been in Brooklyn as long as many of their "I was here before this neighborhood was popular" mentalities might imply, but tradition has to start somewhere. The floors are made of an unfinished wood and the furniture looks like it might have been built in the backyard (if they had one). The Ale House is known locally as Dog Bar since it's one of the few bars in the area that is dog friendly. But if you don't have a pup to play with, there is always pool.

## Brother Jimmy's

**1485 2nd Ave. (77th & 78th Sts.)**
**212-288-0999**
**1644 3rd Ave. (@ 92nd St.)**
**212-426-2020**
**428 Amsterdam Ave. (80th & 81st Sts.)**
**212-501-7515**

If you miss Spring Break, why not relive it at Brother Jimmy's? Tons of frat boys wearing baseball hats ogle ever-so-eager young girls. The bartenders are attractive and friendly, especially when the silicon enhanced ladies mount the bar, blow their whistles, shake their breasts and do shots. Awesome place to watch a sporting event, but you better get there early to avoid waiting in line and getting the bouncer's wrath. Eat some wings as you suck down drinks to the point of embarrassing intoxication. Brother Jimmy's is always a party waiting to happen.

## Brownies

169 Ave. A (10th & 11th Sts.)
212-420-8392

BROWNIES PLAYS HOST to most New Music parasites around the city. This tiny venue feeds many fresh music seekers with some of the newest indie-pop, electronica, math rock and touring Emo bands at a relatively cheap price ($5-$12 cover). Rock mongers are also leeches here, though most suck on this site for it's college music picks. Wednesdays are known Invisible Cities where you can hear DJ's of a local record store spin their electronica while submerging yourself in a sea of NYU kids. A few scattered tables and chairs, fairly cheap bottled beer and an eclectic copper-topped bar keep the locals around 'till the kids invade the space.

## Bryant Park Grill

25 W. 40th St. (5th & 6th Aves.)
212-840-6500

THIS POPULAR SPOT stretches for an entire block, combining an outdoor cafe and indoor dining room. The food and drinks are pricey, but that doesn't stop the sexy after-work throngs from making this their haunt. It might be a wise idea to stop by a deli and pick up a six-pack since no matter how loud you bellow or what denomination of greenback you're holding, it's impossible to get the attention of the inundated bartenders.

## BS New York

405 3rd Ave. (28th & 29th Sts.)
212-684-8376

QUITE POSSIBLY THE only gay bar in Murray Hill, BS gets a mixed clientele of locals and stray East Village guys. Non-stop music videos play to a rarely crowded bar scene.

The happy hour is decent worth two-for-one drinks, but other than that this places really has no special qualities.

## B3

33 Ave. B (@ 3rd St.)
212-614-9755

B3 OFFERS A relaxed bar and restaurant to start off your evening, and a downstairs lounge to help you finish it. The cozy, candle lit second floor serves as a dining room while the plush couch filled lower level hosts comedians, live music and DJ's. The beer and wine is afforble enough so that you won't get your panties in a twist and you can try the 2 for 1 happy hour every day from 6p.m. to 8p.m. Be advised: The lounge fills up early.

## Bubble Lounge

228 W. Broadway (White & Franklin Sts.)
212-431-3433

A HANDSOME LOUNGE dedicated to the bubbly and the beautiful. Stylish young 20-somethings can either sip sparkling house cocktails like the peachy $8 bubblicious or choose from the 400+ bottles of champagne available. With a good after work crowd, intimate cozy nooks, a downstairs lounge, and sumptuous treats like caviar and chocolate truffles, it's no wonder it's still so popular.

## Bull & Bear (@ The Waldorf Astoria)

301 Park Ave. (49th & 50th Sts.)
212-872-4900

BULL & BEAR IS no longer an old man's club. Old and young happy hour crowds co-exist here- even if they don't co-mingle. The young come to sample the fine single malt Scotches, and the old come to sample, well, the fine single malt Scotches. There is live jazz two nights a week and the free-pour drinks are generous. The bartenders go out of their way to remember the ames of regulars, but for 15% of a Bull & Bear tab most of us would memorize the Manhattan Yellow Pages.

## Bull McCabe's

29 St. Marks Pl. (1st & 2nd Aves.)
212-982-9895

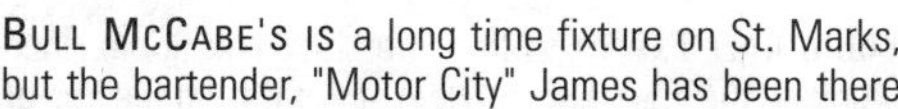

BULL MCCABE'S IS a long time fixture on St. Marks, but the bartender, "Motor City" James has been there longer. "I feel like I'm on the lease," rasps the front man for the band that bears his nickname. James has seen this bar go through three owners. The sidewalk sitting area, known to regulars as "St. Mark's TV," is one of the best places to "people watch" in the city. Standing behind the pine bar, wearing a white button down shirt, bow tie and dark rimmed glasses, you can almost picture "Motor" serving lager to the likes of Yeats, Joyce and Beckett. $2. Jaegermeister shots pour straight from the Jaeger-machine, it just doesn't get any better than that. Whether you're stopping by after work, taking a rest from your travels or waiting for Godot, "Motor" will make you feel right at home.

## Bull Moose Saloon

354 W. 44th St. (8th & 9th Aves.)
212-956-5625

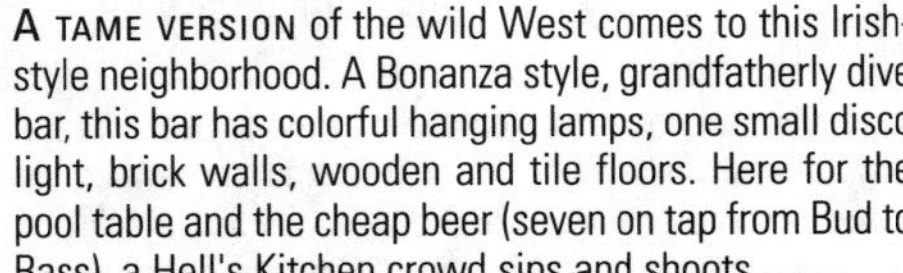

A TAME VERSION of the wild West comes to this Irish-style neighborhood. A Bonanza style, grandfatherly dive bar, this bar has colorful hanging lamps, one small disco light, brick walls, wooden and tile floors. Here for the pool table and the cheap beer (seven on tap from Bud to Bass), a Hell's Kitchen crowd sips and shoots.

## Bull's Head Tavern

295 3rd Ave. (22nd & 23rd Sts.)
212-685-2589

A LIVELY YUPPIE scene can be found at the Bull's Head, where loyal crowds congregate nightly. Live music packs them in Wednesday and Thursday nights. The daily happy hour serves up $3 drafts 'til 7p.m. and ESPN and Cartoon Network play to the delight of the successful and mostly male crowd. The indie-rock jukebox is packed with MTV-approved faves and the competition on the two back pool tables is slim, but steady. The Bull's Head is thankfully one of the few alternatives in a neighborhood plagued with Irish pubs, however the only serenity in this hopping space is the new back lounge--but even that won't last.

## Burp Castle

41 E. 7th St. (2nd & 3rd Aves.)
212-982-4576

YOU'D HALF EXPECT to find Friar Tuck and Robin Hood drunk on the counters, guzzling straight from the keg at this monasterial beer hall. Burp Castle features a heavy wooden bar dotted with candles, tables just big enough for your tankard, and little signs that urge "Please, whispering only". Definitely not your weeknight party spot, the Castle is meant for true-to-the-brew drinkers itching to pick from a list 500 beers long in a tranquil setting. Pay anywhere from a modest $2.50 to a high-rollin' $65.00 for delicious ale and discreet bartender service. A different spot and definite must.

## Cabana

89 South St., South St. Seaport (Pier 17, 3rd Fl.)
212-406-1155

THIS FUNKY SPANISH bar/restaurant features an art deco decor, snazzed up with tropical paintings on the wall, a marble floor and bar and gigantic green plants. There is live reggae here every Friday night; you'll see people dancing as they wait at the door, unable to contain themselves. No beer on tap, but the specialty drinks will knock your balls off. The south beach sangria and vacation martini are some of the more potent drinks, and at $6, they give more bang for your buck than a $5 vial of crack. The food is authentic caribbean fare and serves as a tastey sponge to soak up the lethal drinks.

## Cachette

14 Ave. B (Houston & 2nd Sts.)
212-260-7100

IT'S GREAT THAT the Lower East Side has developed into a hip, yet very gentrified area and Cachette represents just that change. Soft lighting and a romantic atmosphere is what you should expect when you come to this East Village newcomer. It's almost too soon to judge the crowd,, however it's certainly leaning toward the East Village hipsters and yuppies. But hey, the economy is so good, even the homeless guy on the corner is well dressed. This place should blossom in a few months.

## Café Carlyle (@ The Carlyle Hotel)

35 E. 76th St. (@ Madison Ave.)
212-570-7189

THERE'S NOTHING WRONG with the decor, it's purely beautiful retro '50s and '60s. Multicolored patterns accent the lounge chairs and large plants and statues set off the splendid marble floors. But good interior design doesn't save the spot. Bartenders are tiresomely vague about cocktail prices (don't worry, your credit card bill won't be), the wait staff is uptight and the clientele seems to consist of snooty Upper East Side aristocracy.

## Café des Artistes

1 W. 67th St. (Central Park W. & Columbus Ave.)
212-877-3500

AFTER WINDING THROUGH several small dining areas covered in naked nymph murals, you take your position with the regulars at the small quiet bar. "Regulars" in such a neighborhood includes the flawless 85-year-old beauty, holding court in the corner most every night for the last 25 years, and others who come as far as their CPW pads. The scene is infused with romance making so many New York men fall upon their knees and propose. There's no music, not even subtle ambiant tunes; the owner claims "it ruins the mood and the food." All the better then to hear the amazing New York stories from the man popping quail eggs to your right.

## Café Gitane

242 Mott St. (Houston & Prince Sts.)
212-334-9552

IF YOU'RE IN the mood to pretend you're with the literary ex-pat set of Hemingway in Paris kicking back with a glass of wine and smoking a pack of cigarettes, look no further. This French/Moroccan establishment embodies a trendy bohemian-like atmosphere that keeps coming back. This is one of the few places you can sit for hours and order a coffee, wine, or beer and not be bothered because someone else needs your table.

## Café Nicole Bar

226 W. 52nd St. (@ Broadway)
212-315-0100

EVEN IF YOU'RE not staying at the lovely Novotel Hotel, you can still enjoy a relaxed evening at Café Nicole Bar. Live piano and singing performances accompany your drinking experience in this blue and orange room in which the New York tropical shake and cosmos are key.

## Café Noir

32 Grand St. (@ Thompson St.)
212-431-7910

THERE ARE THE nights at Café Noir when a Mediterranean breeze blows, the minty mojitos are pressed with perfection, the baked brie and grape leaves glisten in candlelight and you too feel like one of the pretty people in your midst. This sexy French Moroccan bistro owned by the man behind Jules and Le Singe Vert is sexy because it doesn't try to be. You'll come again and again trying to reclaim that one perfect night.

## Café Pierre (@ The Pierre Hotel)

2 E. 61st St. (@ 5th Ave.)
212-940-8195

WALKING INTO THIS great old-world hotel bar you're immediately swept back to a more civilized time. In this world drinkers sit in plush chairs, wear suits, order $14 drinks and chat softly to the strains of live piano music. Café Pierre has none of the pretensions exuded by most swanky bars aiming for the attention of New York's youth. That explains why the patrons here range from 40 to 80. If a quiet, comfortable, evening appeals to you, consider plopping down on one of the Café's many couches, but if the guy next to you looks like he's napping, be warned, it may take a pair of paddles to wake him up!

## Café Remy

104 Greenwich St. (Rector & Carlisle Sts.)
212-267-4646

TRAVEL DOWNTOWN TO this bi-level venue and experience everything from Wall Street parties to hot salsa weekends. Downstairs the bar is dark, plush and comfortable with flickering candles setting off the red and black décor. Upstairs, there are always live Latin bands plus DJ's spinning salsa, merengue, Latin rock, Brazilian and house. Leave work early to take advantage of the free open bar from 5p.m.-6p.m. Saturday is "The" night at Café Remy; the dancing is great and the crowd is young, hip and full of energy. The cover charge varies so call for reduced admission.

## Caféteria

119 7th Ave. (@ 17th St.)
212-414-1717

NOW A VERY FASHIONABLE Chelsea staple, Cafeteria offers great drinks and decent food at moderate prices. Open 24 hours a day, this is "THE BEST LATE NIGHT EATERY PERIOD." The clientele is mixed and loyal, but the service is spotty. There is great outdoor seating in the summer and a cool LA-esque interior all the time. The food is one of the best bangs for you buck this side of the Mississippi. The macaroni and cheese is a sure remedy for a hangover. The small downstairs lounge is perfect for smoky intimate drinking, but if you're a straight guy in here at 3a.m. you might feel like Caféteria is a tuxedo and you're a brown sneaker.

## Café Wha?

115 MacDougal St. (Bleecker & 3rd Sts.)
212-254-3706

THIS VILLAGE INSTITUTION offers one of the best salsa nights in the city. With more energy than a truckload of Duracell batteries, Jazz, blues, comedy and funk are all reasons to visit this 30-year veteran of the music scene, all for $5.

## Caffe Torino

139 W. 10th St. (7th Ave. So. & Greenwich Ave)
212-675-5554

THE BAR AT Caffe Torino is like a miniature version of the restaurant. The restaurant is classic, decorated with brass lamps, polished wood, candles and a garden in the back. Your bartender, like the waiters, will be a strapping, flirty gay boy. The bar tunes will be whatever gay easy-listening music is currently topping the chart, Whitney Houston, Toni Braxton, etc. The restaurant serves excellent Italian food, wine, beer and cocktails. A well-rounded place to come and enjoy the outside and relax.

## Caliban

360 3rd Ave. (26th & 27th Sts.)
212-689-5155

IS IT A glitch in the Matrix or is it Caliban? A cool minimalist setting with beautiful exposed brick walls cov-

ered in rotating art exhibits, this bar/restaurant is marching to the beat of a different drummer. Since most of the other bars in the area are run-of the mill Irish pubs, Caliban offers a fabulous retreat for those looking for a change of pace. There is a secret garden patio in the rear that is a perfect oasis for post work-day cocktails or a quiet weekend dinner. This is a great date place due to the unobtrusive staff and low-key atmosphere.

## Calico Jacks Cantina

800 2nd Ave. (42nd & 43rd Sts.)
212-557-4300

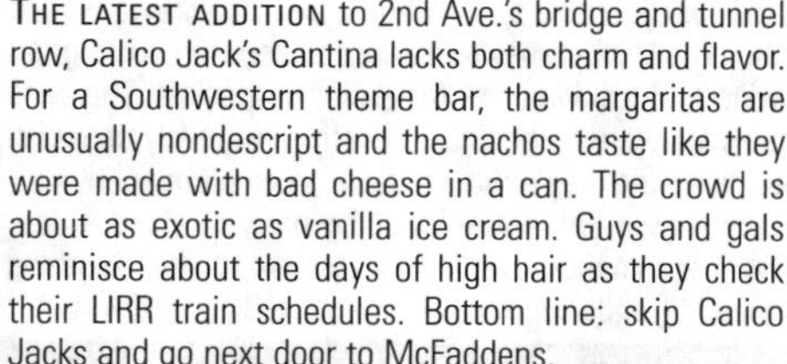

THE LATEST ADDITION to 2nd Ave.'s bridge and tunnel row, Calico Jack's Cantina lacks both charm and flavor. For a Southwestern theme bar, the margaritas are unusually nondescript and the nachos taste like they were made with bad cheese in a can. The crowd is about as exotic as vanilla ice cream. Guys and gals reminisce about the days of high hair as they check their LIRR train schedules. Bottom line: skip Calico Jacks and go next door to McFaddens.

## Caliente Cab. Co.

61 7th Ave. So. (@ Bleecker St.)
212-243-8517
21 Waverly Pl. (@ Greene St.)
212-529-1500

A RETURN TO spring break in Cancun, Jersey style. "Are spandex and Chess King still in fashion?" It is here that you can enjoy some of the most non-authentic Mexican food on Earth with some of the trashiest people on the East coast. If you're from Manhattan you would not be caught dead here. Cheap margaritas, cheap food, cheap people, enough said. Happy hour provides even cheaper drinks from 3 to 8p.m. The only good thing is the top-notch outdoor seating perfect for an afternoon drink-fest.

## Calle Ocho

446 Columbus Ave. (81st & 82nd Sts.)
212-873-5025

THE COLORFUL CALLE Ocho is a stylish and festive newcomer. A young, lively crowd sits at the long wooden bar under huge industrial fans and sips mojitos, caipirinhas and Spanish wine or beer. Those not wishing to holler over the blasting salsa music relax in two small lounge areas. Calle Ocho's bar presents a great prelude to their Nuevo Latino cuisine in the dining room.

## Candela

116 E. 16th St. (Irving & Park Ave. So.)
212-254-1600

HOVERING JUST THIS side of swank and just the other of medieval, Candela is a dark, atmospheric restaurant filled with sweet-smelling candles and a bat cave ambiance. Somehow managing to be both cavernous and cozy, it caters to a younger, dark-clad crowd who, if they know what they're doing, can order up some great wine and subdued, yet tasty dinner specials. The wise here are wary of the prices, which vary greatly from dish to dish. One may arrive to study in complete anonymity, burst in with an entire wedding party or show a date what a romantic evening in Lascaux is like. Anything goes at Candela.

## Candle Bar

309 Amsterdam Ave. (@ 74th St.)
212-874-9155

THIS LITTLE NEIGHBORHOOD gay bar on the Upper West Side has a very local feel. These guys like their very cruisey joint with daily drink specials, pool table, and theme nights. A comfortable but rather boring little spot that tries too hard, Candle Bar still pleases neighborhood guys by offering them a place to meet and get drunk.

## Canteen

142 Mercer St. (@ Prince St.)
212-431-7676

CANTEEN IS SEX and the City meets the Jetsons. With neon orange chairs and a metallic chrome bar, Canteen is sleek and sexy at its best. Throngs of successful, artistic thirtysomethings, donned in fuchsia sequined minis, black Gucci suits and snakeskin Manolo Blahnik sling-backs line the bar looking to exchange digits. If you listen closely enough, you can hear the patrons' cell phones ringing melodically to Barry White. With a great wine list, efficient service and a super cool ambiance, Canteen is a must.

## Captain Café
196 Orchard St. (Houston & Ludlow Sts.)
212-477-1033

ONE OF THE LATEST atrocities caused by the khaki invasion of the Lower East Side, the Captain Café is a rather plain-looking seafood restaurant/bar catering to the over-30 yuppie set. It's for those whose idea of fun is drinking from the pathetically small beer and wine list and listening to adult contemporary music. If that sounds appealing to you, then you'll fit right in. Although the food is quite affordable, the bar is not really worth a visit.

## Carnegie Club
156 W. 56th St. (6th & 7th Aves.)
212-957-9676

THIS BOOKISH BAR caters to midtown's elite and literate. The green wall-to-wall carpeting, gigantic windows, comfortable lounge areas, low lit lamps and candles and extensive wine list seem set to fuel good, quality conversations. You can even "Weekend with Sinatra" on Friday and Saturdays with Carcy Hoffman with The Stan Rubin Orchestra playing at 9:30 and 11 p.m. for a $20 cover and a two drink ($15) minimum.

## Carnegie Hill Brewing Co.
1600 3rd Ave. (@ 90th St.)
212-369-0808

A MICRO-BREWERY with good beer plus a bar/restaurant scene is a winning combinaton. The outdoor seating, windows and huge oak bar provide great people and TV watching. The bartenders and patrons are very friendly so if you just want to hang out, chat, watch the game and down some suds, then brave the nosebleed and mosey on over.

## Caroline's Comedy Club
1626 Broadway (49th & 50th Sts.)
212-956-0101

THERE'S SOMETHING FOR everyone at the most famous comedy club in America. In the '80's, Caroline's Comedy Hour was taped here, and for good reason. This is no small production. The club is located on

Broadway and has that big show feeling. Although more expensive than the other comedy venues, you definitely get what you pay for. The joint is fancy and you get much more yuk for your buck. Thursday through Sunday they usually have top-name headliners as well as two other comedians that you've either heard of or should have. The other nights of the week can be unpredictable, but this is by far the best comedy club in Manhattan to bring a date.

## Casa La Femme

150 Wooster St. (Houston & Prince Sts.)
212-505-0005

CASA LA FEMME is the kind of place that could only exist in New York, Soho to be specific. This Moroccan-inspired lounge/restaurant doesn't ignore a single detail whether it be the private, pillow-lined dinner and drink tents for two or the posh bar space up front. With an open front door bringing in fresh air and real sod rolled onto the floors, this is a great date-spot during the summer. The crowd is beautiful and the service accommodating. None of it's free, so bring your credit card. If you're doing dinner and drinks, bring the platinum one.

## Casa Mexicana

133 Ludlow St. (@ Rivington St.)
212-473-4100

CASA MEXICANA IS the latest Lower East Side establishment offering authentic Mexican food, Mexican beer and sangria. It also offers an attitude to those who don't look like a young, trendy professional. So if you go, dress the part. The restaurant has a dimly lit, romantic atmosphere that clashes a bit with the stereotypical sombreros and photos of hombres and mexicanos. Those not striving to impress a date may find the pricey beer and wine list off-putting. The lounge is decorated with paraphernalia lifted from an old West cat-house and is a decent spot to hang out, drink and enjoy the DJ's on Saturdays.

## Casimir

103-105 Ave. B (6th & 7th Sts.)
212-358-9683

OPEN SINCE DECEMBER 1998, this French bistro/bar has a habit of drawing one of the most attractive clienteles in the East Village. Stylists. models and up-and-coming dot-commers crowd the bar and occupy cozy tables in the grotto-esque lounge. Swaths of embroidered fabric and colored glass lamps blend with brick and mosaic tiles lending a taste of colonial Algiers to the otherwise modern Euro décor. Amidst the hum of foreign languages, enjoy a healthy assortment of aperitifs (the cloudy Pastis being among the most popular), a well thought out wine list and standard cocktails. Hooka not included.

## Catwalk

2 W. 35th St. (5th & 6th Aves.)
212-594-9343

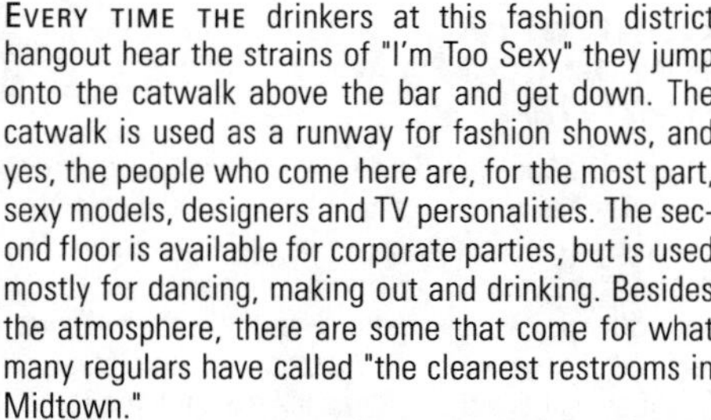

Every time the drinkers at this fashion district hangout hear the strains of "I'm Too Sexy" they jump onto the catwalk above the bar and get down. The catwalk is used as a runway for fashion shows, and yes, the people who come here are, for the most part, sexy models, designers and TV personalities. The second floor is available for corporate parties, but is used mostly for dancing, making out and drinking. Besides the atmosphere, there are some that come for what many regulars have called "the cleanest restrooms in Midtown."

## CBGB & OMFUG

315 Bowery (@ Bleecker St.)
212-382-4052

With all the renovating, buying and gentrifying this city has recently undergone, it's good to know that there is still one, butt-ugly pimple left. CBGB & OMFUG (or Country, Blue-Grass Blues and Other Music for Uplifting Gourmandizers) has always been and still is a staple for loud and obnoxious rock 'n' roll. With more of a stress on "Other Music" it's doubtful you'll ever find any Country & Blue Grass here. A year or two after CB's first opened in the early '70s, New York gave birth to an ugly, loud and rude child. They called it PUNK. It's offspring were bands such as "Blondie", "The Police", "Talking Heads", "The Ramones"... the list goes on and on. This was the only place that would allow these bands to play, and because it did, CBGB created a part of history. The cover charge ranges from $3 to $15 seven nights a week.

## CBGB's Gallery
313 Bowery (@ Bleecker St.)
212-982-4052

THE GALLERY IS CBGB's cleaner, more respectable older brother, featuring acoustic and rock acts that attract more hipsters and less punks than its world-famous neighbor. It's also cozier and more laid-back with plenty of couches and tables in the downstairs lounge. Its walls double as a gallery for up-and-coming artists with exhibits changing monthly. Drink prices and the beer list run about average for the Lower East Side (around $4.50) and there's usually a drink minimum. The cover runs between $5 and $7, so call ahead.

## CentroFly
45 W. 21st. (5th & 6th Aves.)
212-627-7770

ONE OF THE best new dance clubs to open on club row, CentroFly has a main dance floor with a mixed NYC crowd and a few conversation-pits off to the sides. The design is the coolest and freshest in the city with black and white psychedelic pattern on the floors and colorful futuristic furniture. The VIP room is a completely different animal and most attendees remain there for the entire evening. This exclusive lounge offers a different DJ, a long wooden bar, roughly 30 tables and a transparent swinging sofa. The VIP room is also a full service restaurant open for dinner.

## Chaeira
330 W. 38th St. (8th & 9th Aves.)
212-244-7101

A NEWCOMER CLUB with a dynamic vibe, Chaeria is a raw warehouse-like space with movies projected on the wall, retro-lounge chairs and a lamp-lit modern bar, diverse music, and an upscale/professional crowd. Too new to have a set schedule, Chaeria's does offer a no-cover Thursday with a finger food buffet.

## Chaos
225 E. Houston St. (@ Ave. A)
212-475-3200

TAKING OVER THE space once belonging to The Bank, a dark club catering to the tastes of goths, vampires and fetishists, Chaos has replaced it with a chic, slick and trendy dance club. A nice size dance floor plus a two level lounge area has a line snaking around the block for the opportunity to spend $10 for a mixed drink. The huge clipboard militia keeps the crowd attractive and as hip as you can get. Make a reservation or prepare to go elsewhere.

## The Charleston

174 Bedford Ave. (N. 7th & 8th Sts.) Brooklyn
718-782-8717

THE BEST THING about the Charleston? Any band can get a gig there. The worst thing about the Charleston? Any band can get a gig there. This family-owned bar in the middle of Williamsburg has been a starting ground for new bands since 1933 (the owner claims it was a speakeasy before that). The building is in a great spot and its heart is in the right place, but the mood depends on the band playing. A great place to visit if you're with a group that wants guaranteed seating, but bring your own atmosphere as this neighborhood joint has more space than character. You may also want to bring your own beer since there's no tap and the bottle selection is limited.

## Chase

225 W. 55th St. (Broadway & 8th Ave.)
212-333-3400

THIS HIP BAR/LOUNGE is trendy, multi-level space has DJ's spinning either house or lounge depending on the time of night and how crowded it is. Top shelf drinks start around $8. Like most upscale gay bars, their cosmopolitans make the trip worthwhile. The service is excellent and the servers are exceptional. They boast celebrity sightings, but they're referring to the actors performing at the theaters a few blocks away.

## The Cheetah

12 W. 21st St. (5th & 6th Aves.)
212-206-7770

DOING A NEW York clubbing experiment? Looking for a control club? Go to The Cheetah. It embodies everything standard of Manhattan clubs. Decorated with neon lights, disco balls, cushy booths (appropriately cheetah-skinned) and loads of mirrors. The upstairs room spins house and downstairs spins hip-hop. No big surprise but upon entering the club, the big bouncers pretend they are better than you by giving you the snotty once over. Once inside you and your friends will drink cosmos and guidos will ogle at you, typical. The only thing that sets this club apart from the other animals is the fab service. A snarling staff won't attack you here, but the overpriced drinks and weekend $20 cover will.

## Chelsea Bistro & Bar

358 W. 23rd St. (8th & 9th Aves.)
212-727-2026

LOOK UP THE word "charming" in one of those dictionaries with the little pictures and you just may see this place. The funny thing is that for all the glories that lie within, it has such an inconspicuous and unassuming front entrance. The decor is cozy and romantic, complete with an outdoor seating area and working fireplace. They make their own house orange wine that is delicious and serve excellent dessert drink concoctions.

## Chelsea Brewing Company

(@ The Chelsea Piers) Pier 59 (@ 23rd St.)
212-336-6440

A MICRO-BREWING company right on the Hudson River with huge copper and brass tanks filled with home-brewed beers (try the India Pale Ale and the Checker Cab Blonde Ale). Grab a brew and a seat on the outside deck or at the inside bar area which is quite large and impressive. If you're a large group this can be a good meeting spot, but once you're done with youre beer, you'll be stranded at The Chelsea Piers.

## Chelsea Commons

242 10th Ave. (@ 24th St.)
212-929-9424

WITH OLD-FASHIONED DRINKS, antiques, polished brass, varnished wood and a ruddy atmosphere, Chelsea Commons picks up where your favorite TV bar left off. The beer selection is tasty yet no-frills and the bar is large and adequate, catering to a mature, scotch-on-the-rocks kind of crowd. Chelsea's real allure, though, is in the lush garden area, a wonderful hideaway that, along with a few drinks, makes patrons forget how close they are to the West Side Highway.

## Cherry Tavern

441 E. 6th St. (Ave A & 1st Ave.)
212-777-1448

STRIKING OUT WITH the on-line dating and the personal ads? Didn't make the cut on Who Wants To Marry a Millionaire? Well then, get your ass to the Cherry Tavern where you can drink yourself into the arms of one of the attractive singles that flock to the Cherry Tavern nightly. Here's how you do it: Order a Cherry Tavern special for $4 and get a shot of tequila and a Tecate. Then play your favorite tune in the jukebox and stagger back to the pool table and partake in a flirtatious game of pool. This cozy, neighborhood watering hole gets packed on the weekend so sign off of Love at AOL and hit the Cherry Tavern for some real East Village love.

## Chez Es Saada

42 E. 1st St. (1st & 2nd Aves.)
212-777-5617

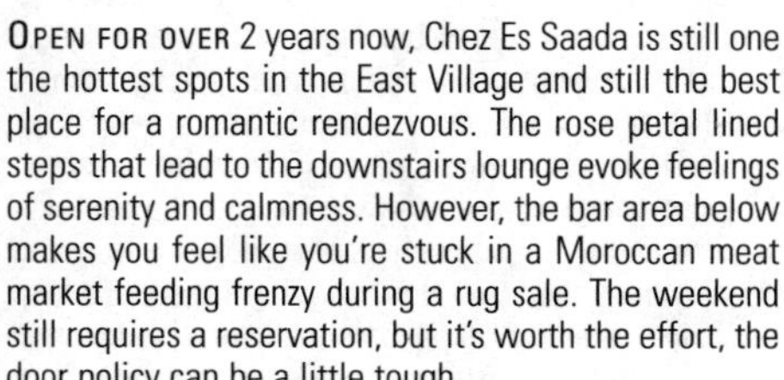

OPEN FOR OVER 2 years now, Chez Es Saada is still one the hottest spots in the East Village and still the best place for a romantic rendezvous. The rose petal lined steps that lead to the downstairs lounge evoke feelings of serenity and calmness. However, the bar area below makes you feel like you're stuck in a Moroccan meat market feeding frenzy during a rug sale. The weekend still requires a reservation, but it's worth the effort, the door policy can be a little tough.

## Chez Josephine

414 W. 42nd St. (9th & 10th Aves.)
212-594-1925

WITH BEAUTIFUL PORTRAITS, feathers and fiery red crush velvet curtains, this is Jean-Claude Baker's loving homage to his dancing diva mom. Despite this bungalow's Manhattan Plaza/Times Square surroundings, you will immediately feel the warmth and romance of Paris where Josephine spent most of her years. Food, booze.and the live piano performances will do their best to get you and your partner in the mood.

## Chi Chiz

135 Christopher St. (@ Hudson St.)
212-462-0027

THE TOTAL OPPOSITE of its name, Chi Chiz is a clean, polished, well kept bar without any chichi pretension at all. Heck, it's positively friendly. Serving a primarily African American gay crowd who have found the excellent, bargain bar food (the wings are particularly good), the two-for-one happy hour from 5p.m. to 8p.m., and the pool table in back to make Chi Chiz a great place to hang out. It's so good, in fact, that even if you aren't gay you might want to stop in for a beer or a bite to eat if you're in the neighborhood; especially if you're a PATH train rider, the Christopher St. train is right next door.

## Chibi's Sake Bar

242 Mott St. (@ Prince St.)
212-274-0025

THIS TWO-ROOM unassuming NoLita bar has the widest selection of sake this side of the Pacific. Named after the owner's French bulldog (who has a shrine to his name hanging on one wall), Chibi's decor is smart and slick with peach walls, a chandelier and velvet curtains. The appetizers are exotic with oysters, dumplings and caviar topping the list, but the best nibble food is the Japanese nuts that look like toys and come with every drink. No rowdy frat boys or pick-up chicks in this elegant neighborhood corner, so come to indulge in these pleasures with friends or a date.

## Chicago Blues

73 8th Ave. (@ 14th St.)
212-924-9755

THIS DARK AND COZY tavern, with its live music and blue lights will leave you feeling anything but blue. There is a no dancing policy but there is a broad line between what is and isn't dancing. Translation: Get loose my friend. The crowd seems to range in age between 25-45, but you would think they're teens at an

N'Sync concert by their behavior. The drinks are cheap, there's a 2-for-1 happy hour from 5p.m.-8p.m. daily. The area behind the stage, with its red sofas and candlelight is perfect for listening, a fun night out or an energy-release after work.

## Chicama

35 E. 18th St. (Broadway & 5th Ave.)
212-505-2233

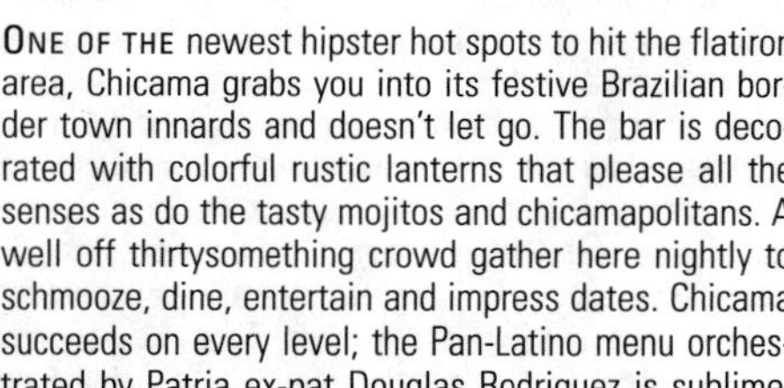

ONE OF THE newest hipster hot spots to hit the flatiron area, Chicama grabs you into its festive Brazilian border town innards and doesn't let go. The bar is decorated with colorful rustic lanterns that please all the senses as do the tasty mojitos and chicamapolitans. A well off thirtysomething crowd gather here nightly to schmooze, dine, entertain and impress dates. Chicama succeeds on every level; the Pan-Latino menu orchestrated by Patria ex-pat Douglas Rodriguez is sublime, the drinks don't disappoint, the music is hot and the crowd is spicy.

## China Club

268 W. 47th St. (Broadway & 8th Ave.)
212-398-3800

THIS IS ONE of the Manhattan nightclubs where you won't have to deck out in Prada in order to impress the doormen, they probably wouldn't know the difference between a Chinatown knock-off and the real thing. The whole idea of coming to this multi-leveled space that looks like a series of hotel conference rooms until you get drunk enough to appreciate the sparkling fiber optic lights and pulsating pop music, is to dance and check out the young energetic patrons. The cover charge on weekends is $20.

## Chow Bar

230 W. 4th St. (@ 10th St.)
212-633-2212

Chow Bar reopened in August of 2000 and has staked claim on this quiet corner. Unfortunately, it still hasn't produced a loyal following mainly due to its location, not its worthiness. Mellow and cool, the Chinese calligraphy on the walls and bamboo shoot accents give the dining room a sparse yet calming atmosphere. Pan-

Asian food is served at the bar or tables, amber lanterns cast a soothing glow over the bar and hip music plays at a perfect level. There are 9 beers on tap and bottled beer is a refreshing $4.

## Chumley's

86 Bedford St. (Barrow & Grove Sts.)
212-675-4449

AFTER YOU LOCATE the well-hidden front entrance, Chumley's reveals a friendly, 130-year-old ex-stable and ex-speakeasy, featuring 22 beers and micro-brews, reasonably priced pub fare and artery clogging, main courses. It's a trip into a Hemingway novel, where a slightly more mature clientele can down $5 pints and rub elbows with the occasional neighborhood film producer-type against a background accompaniment of Sinatra or swing from the jukebox. Three live-in dogs and a history of fire and restoration add a finishing touch to this tasty, atmospheric hideaway.

## Church Lounge

(@ The TriBeCa Grand Hotel)
2 6th Ave. (@ White St.)
212-519-6600

THE RECENTLY OPENED sister hotel to the SoHo Grand graces TriBeCa with its heavy door policy, club-like hotel lobby, pretty faces, beautiful wooden floors, sky-lit atrium that reaches for the clouds and $12 specialty cocktails. This lounge is a truly transporting experience that every jaded New Yorker must come see. It proves that not all modern construction must be uninspired. Unlike most fashionable haunts, the music gently drifts through the glowing space at an unobtrusive level. A screen wall of floating blue neon light complements the copper wall of glowing votive candles. Sheer red curtains line the entire space providing a voyeuristic show for the select group on the inside, which mainly consists of pretty girls on cell phones and Wall Streeters trying to bed them.

## Cibar

56 Irving Pl. (17th & 18th Sts.)
212-460-5656

TUCKED AWAY IN a garden-level space just outside of Union Square, this cozy little lounge makes clear that it's not seeking the collegiate clientele that frequents many of the bars in this area. With prices starting at $8 for beers and mixed drinks, this is a good place to flaunt reckless spending tendencies while trying to impress clients or dates. There is a nice, but small, outdoor space in the back where movers and shakers take in some air before closing deals over a third martini.

## Ciel Rouge

176 7th Ave. (20th & 21st Sts.)
212-929-5542

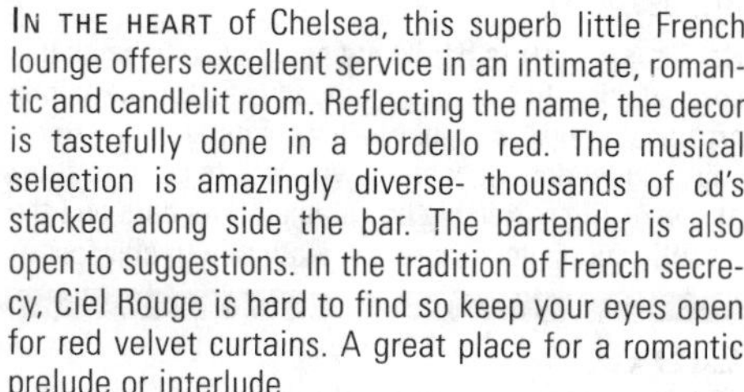

IN THE HEART of Chelsea, this superb little French lounge offers excellent service in an intimate, romantic and candlelit room. Reflecting the name, the decor is tastefully done in a bordello red. The musical selection is amazingly diverse- thousands of cd's stacked along side the bar. The bartender is also open to suggestions. In the tradition of French secrecy, Ciel Rouge is hard to find so keep your eyes open for red velvet curtains. A great place for a romantic prelude or interlude.

## Circa Tabac

32 Watts St. (W. Broadway & 6th Ave.)
212-941-1781

THE AUTHENTIC DESIGN of Circa Tabac make it one of the few tolerable theme bars in New York. The whole idea of giving smokers an oasis hideaway is truly original. Non-smokers can enjoy the period style of this place as well, since the air filtration system is state of the art creating a mysteriously smoke-free environment. The magical feeling of this lounge transports you to an era when things were sexy, clandestine and the three-martini lunch was standard. Come here with a date or with friends and bask in the time warp that is Circa Tabac.

## Cinema Classics

332 E. 11th St. (1st & 2nd Aves.)
212-971-1015

WITH A brand new beer and wine license and a 16mm movie projector in the back, this place has the potential to be a hot spot. Now you can enjoy the comforts of

home in a bar! The room in the front will always be a popular hangout for film students and freelance writers. The 55-seat theater has a variety of seats from couches to kitchen chairs. Movies play at 8:00p.m. and 10:00p.m. The marquee outside will tell you what's playing, but pick up a schedule anyway. You can have a beer while you peruse new releases, Hollywood classics and hard to find treasures on video.

## Citron 47

401 W. 47th St. (9th & 10th Sts.)
212-397-4747

HELL'S KITCHEN IS hardly the hell it used to be as this cozy addition to the neighborhood attests. In a comfy art deco lounge with big yellow umbrella-like lamps, you can feel right at home...if you tend to get this drunk at home. The extremely hospitable bartenders and the inventive drink list ensure a smooth ride to oblivion.

## Citrus

320 Amsterdam Ave. (@ 75th St.)
212-595-0500

FIRST THINGS FIRST: You want excellent tequila and margaritas? You got it, hombre. With over 80 kinds of tequila and over 13 different margarita varieties, Citrus is the place to go if you want to party like you're in Tijuana. But no bar south of the border will empty your wallet as quickly as Citrus. For some serious tequila tutoring, however, this joint is the place to hit; the bartenders know their agave and are generous with their knowledge. Line your stomach with some of their Southwestern eats before those shots.

## City Grill

269 Columbus Ave. (72nd & 73rd Sts.)
212-873-9400

THIS CLASSIC ESTABLISHMENT has stood on the same corner for over 100 years. Its name may have changed (from Kelly's during prohibition, to O'Neill's and most recently, Rupert's), but the solid mahogany bar, matching carved booths and genuine Tiffany windows continue to provide an intimate and comfortable atmosphere, whether for drinks with an old friend or dinner on that first date. And if that date bails on you, the bartender and his personal joke collection await.

## City Hall

131 Duane St. (@ Church St.)
212-227-7777

JUST TELL THE CABBIE to hang a louie on Duane St. and drop you off in the 1940's. You and your best twist can dress to the nines and stroll into this classy joint without getting the high-hat from any flunkies. City Hall oozes style and has character to spare. While there isn't much of a social scene at the bar - it is more of a compliment to the restaurant than anything else, - it does provide a great excuse to stop in and check this place out over a watermelon martini.

## CJ Knockouts

390 8th Ave. (29th & 30th Sts.)
212-563-5195

FOR $2, Knockout Ales in excess could fulfill the promise of its title. From noon until 3a.m., this newly renovated space caters to a sporty, beer-drinking, buffalo wing-eating crowd. And if the people-watching or the TV's don't provide much entertainment, there's always the aquarium.

## Clementine

1 5th Ave. (@ 8th St.)
212-253-0003

NYU FROSH SHOULD leave their fakes at home and make way for Wall Street, as this Village hot spot fills up early. Serving as the only cool place to go on the worst block in the Village (8th St.) Clementine does everything right: decor, drinks, music and crowd. Unwind at the one of the round booths, or flirt with one of the hotties lining the bar. Try the mojitos or one of the martinis from their extensive selection which should knock your wallet and your thong right off. A great menu and romantic lighting also makes this one of the more romantic spots to come if you already have your own hottie.

## Cleo's 9th Ave.Saloon

656 9th Ave. (@ 46th St.)
212-307-1503

THE CROWD as advertised is "serious-not sleazy", however the bartender must have been referring to the drinking ability of the gay men who hang here, not their personalities. Having said that, the bar has a cool happy hour where you peel off stickers that either say 25 cents, half price or full price and depending on what you get, that's what you pay drinks the whole night.

## Cloister Café

238 E. 9th St. (2nd & 3rd Aves.)
212 777-9128

If the Buddha were Mediterranean, he would be quite impressed. Falling somewhere between a nature hike and a prime vacation spot, the Cloister Cafe offers a soothing oasis from everything urban. The nervous yet knowledgeable servers will help you sip wine and eat duck amongst a garden of canopies, fountains and opera music. The stained glass monks will remind you of St. Francis studying away in his monastery. Simply a great spot for romance or just a quiet night out.

## Club Car

1696 2nd Ave. (87th & 88th Sts.)
212-348-4368

If you haven't had enough of trains between the subway, Metro North and random phallic dreams, check out this bar's rendition of an old-fashioned train car. Photos of old diesel trains hang on the walls and transport you back in time. Older, mellower crowds of locals come here to relax for happy hour, play darts and listen to the ecletic selection of tunes on the jukebox.

## Club Macanudo

26 E. 63rd St. (Park & Madison Aves.)
212-752-8200

This lavish cigar bar is surely the most expensive place in town. Cognacs and Louis XIII shots are $150 each and the bar's lengthy list of superb liquors are exceedingly pricey. Come on the right night and watch high-rolling conspicuous consumers such as Montel Williams (plus entourage) downing $200-$300 shots without blinking an eye. Cigar boxes dot the place and private humidors are available for rent. Macanudo also serves fine desserts such as the single malt scotch-filled warm chocolate truffles. Live jazz is featured through the fall and winter. Keep an eye out for Thursday night blackjack games and occasional cigar classes.

## Club New York

252 W. 43rd St. (Broadway & 8th Ave.)
212-997-9510

YES, THIS IS ground zero of Sean Puffy Combs' troubles last year. And Club New York has since called a cease-and-desist on its Sunday hip-hop nights. Still, the club claims that business has been unaffected and they remain the premiere Latin nightclub of NYC. They may be right. Wall-to-wall pretty people and it still registers a lion's share of the Latin celeb sightings. Friday and Saturday evenings are packed and the music gives you no choice but to start grooving. Though the space isn't particularly polished, you aren't going to notice with all the gorgeous people milling about. Getting past that velvet rope can be deadly after 1a.m. if you're not eye catching. But, don't let that Puffy thing scare you, security has been discreetly beefed up since.

## C-Note

157 Ave. C (9th & 10th Sts.)
212-677-8142

STILL A FAVORITE among local literati and jazz buffs alike, the C-Note will be seeing changes in its interpretation of bohemian revelry: more rock. But the bar with the vibe of a dive and the decor of an intimate lounge is not about to stop delivering the best in local and out-of-town jazz and blues talent, FREE. About the only noticeable difference at the C-Note these days is the more eclectic clientele, ranging in age from twentysomething to, well, some of the patrons were probably around in the heyday of Buena Vista Social Club. As always, a well priced bottle of beer or a powerful well drink ($3-6) welcomes you in off the street.

## The Cock

188 Ave. A (@ 12th St.)
212-946-1871

HOW OFTEN DO you see a mostly nude go-go dancer fornicating with a stuffed bunny rabbit on Easter? Known as the East Village's "Rock 'n' Roll Fag Sleaze Bar," the Cock is sure to shock unless you're one of it's usual patrons who enjoy dark humor, super skinny go-go boys and extravagantly vulgar trannies who advocate audience participation. In the darkly lit back lounge area, the boys don't only get down- they get down with each other! Not your usual cup of tea- but DJ's like JoJo America (The Bowery Bar) and Scott Ewalt spin non-trendy club tunes associated with Chelsea's gay set who frequent Roxy and Twilo. The Cock gets going after 11p.m. and on Tuesdays suck down $2 frozen margaritas.

## Cocktail Room

334 E. 73rd St. (1st & 2nd Aves.)
212-988-6100

THE COCKTAIL LOUNGE is a little bit of South Beach in the Upper-East Side. The bar is awash in orange, flowers and flamboyance. Pricey exotic drinks such as a $9 mint julep and a $28 champagne cocktail for two called the Romeo & Juliet will leave you feeling as exotic as the drink. The crowd is mostly female and very artsy. After three or four pink lemonades, you'll swear you saw Ricky Martin atop the bar singing Living La Vida Loca.

## Coco Pazzo Café

7 E. 59th St. (5th & Madison Aves.)
212-935-3535

ALTHOUGH THIS FASHIONABLE Italian restaurant (once the Playboy Club) has a small bar and a downstairs cigar lounge, the real draw here is the authentic Tuscan cuisine. The bar does offer amazing homemade potato chips; they're free, so wear something with big pockets or bring a backpack. If you can't make it here for dinner, at least try the ornate, beautifully-arranged desserts, those too are worth the trip.

## Cody's Bar

282 Hudson St. (Spring & Dominick Sts.)
212-924-5853

THIS LOCAL WEST side hangout is home to locals who love the unscene mellowness of this joint. A few tables and a smoky atmosphere provide all that is necessary for a long night of beer drinking and reminiscing with friends.

## Coffee Shop

29 Union Square West (@ 16th St.)
212-243-7969

BEST KNOWN for its outdoor seating and views of Union Square Park, this fifties diner-style venue is run by pretty people too busy practicing their monologues to realize you've been waiting a very long time for your drink. The Brazilian themed bar is reliable for decent drinks and food but the service ALWAYS BLOWS. Overall, though, Coffee Shop is a great place for after work jaunts and late night pit stops since it's open 23 hours a day.

## Collins

735 8th Ave. (46th & 47th Sts.)
212-541-4206

THIS INVITING YET chic Hell's Kitchen bar features live music, theme events from "Bourbon, Backgammon and Bridge" to Bingo, darts, a jukebox with everything from Mingus to Marley and a quality drink list. Whether sipping the specialty lilac collins or one of a dozen draft beers, the younger patrons chat and chill under ceiling fans and alongside the colorful artwork.

## The Comedy Cellar

117 MacDougal St. (3rd & Bleecker Sts.)
212-254-3480

DEFINITELY ONE OF the funniest shows in New York City. The club's lineup regularly features comedians that you'll recognize from Saturday Night Live and HBO specials. This underground hideaway has great middle-eastern food and one long show that runs from 9:30p.m. until 2a.m. every night of the week. Although the Chris Rock/Jerry Seinfeld/ Damon Wayans contingent tend to stop-by earlier in the evening, the best part of the show usually takes place after 11p.m. when innovative new stand-ups test the limits of hilarity.

## Commonwealth Brewery

35 W. 48th St. (5th & 6th Aves.)
212-977-2269

THE ONE THING that sets this brewery apart from the others is the odd mix of customers. Half of the patrons are business people from the Rockefeller Center area and the other half are tourists looking at the Rockefeller Center area. They come in and enjoy fresh draught beer while thumbing through guidebooks, while the after-work crowd chats loudly. So fill your wallet, grab your Fodor's and come on down!

## Commune

12 E. 22nd St. (Park Ave. & Broadway)
212-777-2600

Occupying a modern, rectangular, Asian-inspired space in the Flatiron District, this wannabe brand new New York nightspot gives the impression that its service and sophistication matches the sleekness of its decor. Nothing could be further from the truth. Upon entering, one is met with annoying hosts and a crowd of young singles perusing for love over domestic beer and cheap chardonnay. While the interior designer deserves accolades for the warmth of the black and red palette and the faux marble paneled bar, the furnishings of Commune, unfortunately, could never make up for the lukewarm-blooded personalities who inhabit this bar.

## Commuter Café

Path Station (@ The World Trade Center)
212-432-1633

Just get fired? Need a drink in one of Manhattan's more depressing holes before hopping back on the PATH train? You've found your spot. Ratty carpeting, a breath taking view of the PATH and a crowd filled with greyhound station rejects can only add to the ever pressing question, "How the hell am I going to pay my rent now?" The only bonus is that the friendly, chatty bartender might come up with a solution. Scotch, trains and transit check. Life is good.

## Continental

25 3rd St. (@ St Mark's Pl.)
212-529-6924

Continental is one of the few places left in this city to witness any up-and-coming or semi-established punk, hard core and good 'ol rock 'n' roll bands. It offers an intimate enough setting to actually get wet with the sweat (and sometimes blood) of your band of choice. Continental has a great live sound engineer (thank him on the way out for the buzz between your ears). Gaze around the walls and you're bound to see a snapshot of at least one of your rock idols playing in the very space that you're standing. During happy hour (4p.m.-8p.m.) drink prices are slashed in half.

## Cooler

416 W. 14th St. (9th Ave. & Washington St.)
212-229-0785

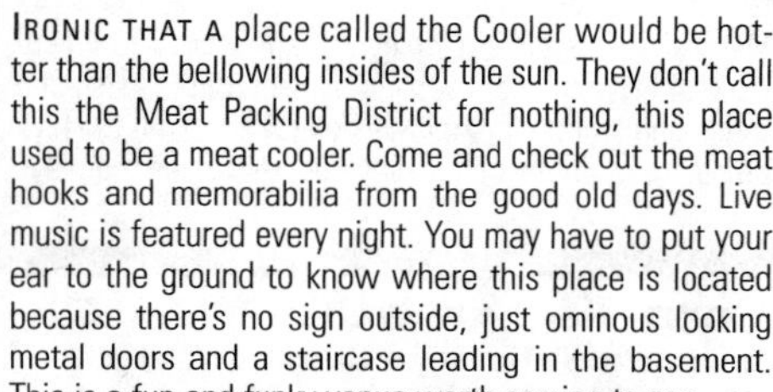

IRONIC THAT A place called the Cooler would be hotter than the bellowing insides of the sun. They don't call this the Meat Packing District for nothing, this place used to be a meat cooler. Come and check out the meat hooks and memorabilia from the good old days. Live music is featured every night. You may have to put your ear to the ground to know where this place is located because there's no sign outside, just ominous looking metal doors and a staircase leading in the basement. This is a fun and funky venue worth coming to see.

## Coopers Cigar Bar & Lounge

41 W. 58th St. (5th & 6th Aves.)
212-588-8888

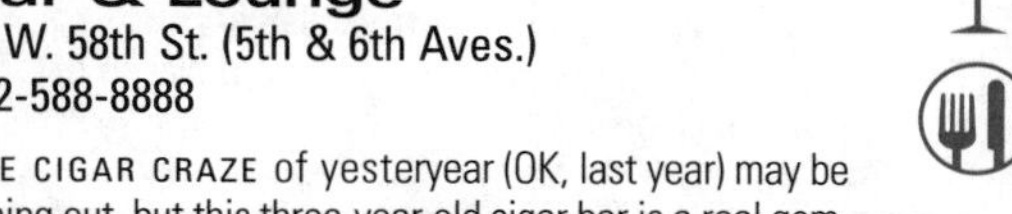

THE CIGAR CRAZE of yesteryear (OK, last year) may be ashing out, but this three-year-old cigar bar is a real gem. The beautiful trendy-contemporary space, including two private lounges in the back for the fabulous to chill in, caters to a diverse but demanding crowd of professionals, film folk and entertainers. There is definitely no shortage of alcohol: exotic martinis, a range of champagnes and imported beers are in decadent abundance.

## Copacabana

617 W. 57th St. (11th & 12th Aves.)
212-582-COPA

THIS LATIN CLUB is definitely a dance inferno with a central space big enough for a large wedding and a back "gringo" room with house music for younger folk who can't or won't salsa. The buffet-style menu features meatballs about three times the size of gallstones (and you can even help yourself to them for free on Tuesdays with the cost of $5 admission).

## The Copper Lounge

1629 2nd Ave. (84th & 85th Sts.)
212-485-2768

THIS IS A BAR with an identity crisis. As Sweet Melissa's, it had a solid local following. The newly gentrified version tries to appease everyone. The pub feel remains, as does the bar grub menu, 2p.m.-7p.m. happy hour and reasonable drink prices ($4 to $7). But now there are couches and live music on Tuesdays and Wednesdays which suggests the beginnings of a lounge. The woodwork and French doors seemed aimed at Euro-trash and bridge and tunnel-ers. And we don't know what the lava lamps imply. Someone please show this place the way!

## Cornelia Street Café

29 Cornelia St. (W. 4th & Bleecker Sts.)
212-989-9319

THE FRENCH DOORS opening onto the sidewalk welcome you into this charming, cozy café. This café/bar attracts artsy, pleasant patrons who listen to the live jazz, poetry readings and admire the art exhibits. A great place to relax with a glass of wine and grab a bite to eat. The locals and the staff are friendly and will have you coming back for the mellow, yet interesting atmosphere.

## The Corner Bistro

331 W. 4th St. (@ Jane St.)
212-242-9502

IF YOU CAN ever get a seat in this small, un-assuming little pub, you will enjoy what some call the best burger in New York (certainly the best bang for your buck). Filled with a mix of Downtown regulars (not the trendy kind) and visitors who have heard of the burger legend, Corner Bistro is a steady favorite and a reliable spot to have a beer that won't break the trust fund and food that works wonders with your waist line. Definitely worth a visit if you want to hang with some pals and catch up with some ketchup.

## Coup

509 E. 6th St. (Aves. A & B)
212-979-2815

A WELCOME CHANGE to the East Village, Coup offers a very romantic date spot, a casual lounge and garden seating all in one. The only major obstacle is convincing the locals that you can relax in an upscale post-modern minimalist showcase. The multi-level design, nominated for the James Beard Design award, is deceiving at first. The front Kubrick-like bar area

extends out into a roomy dining area. Coup entertains Atlantic Records executives for listening parties, juxtaposing a table of hungry Hell's Angels across the room. Theme nights occur regularly and DJ's spin Thursday thru Saturday. Look for the "Easy Tiger" night (a straight pick-up event) and Gay and Lesbian nights monthly.

## Cowboy Bar

1495 1st Ave. (@ 77th St.)
212-288-6636

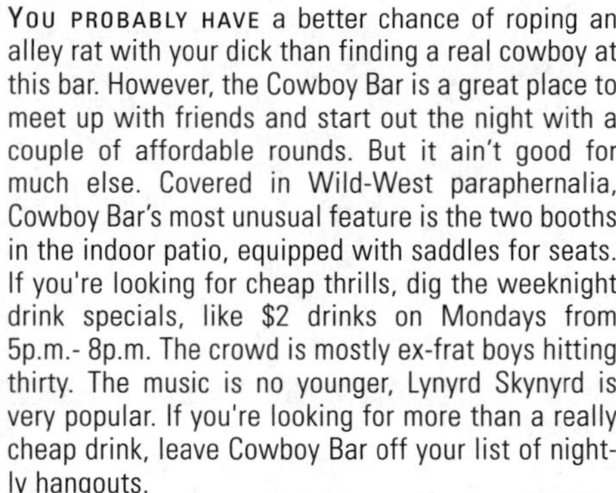

YOU PROBABLY HAVE a better chance of roping an alley rat with your dick than finding a real cowboy at this bar. However, the Cowboy Bar is a great place to meet up with friends and start out the night with a couple of affordable rounds. But it ain't good for much else. Covered in Wild-West paraphernalia, Cowboy Bar's most unusual feature is the two booths in the indoor patio, equipped with saddles for seats. If you're looking for cheap thrills, dig the weeknight drink specials, like $2 drinks on Mondays from 5p.m.- 8p.m. The crowd is mostly ex-frat boys hitting thirty. The music is no younger, Lynyrd Skynyrd is very popular. If you're looking for more than a really cheap drink, leave Cowboy Bar off your list of nightly hangouts.

## Cowgirl Hall of Fame

519 Hudson St. (@ 10th St.)
212-633-1133

RIDE-'EM COWGIRL! Bring the bachelor-ette or the birthday bashes and let the gut busting, side-saddling good times begin. Something of a less greasy, more girlie version of Dallas BBQ, the 10-year-old Hall's offerings include mind-numbing margaritas (try the bible belt with Jack Daniels for $6), oversized portions of Southern grub like spare ribs and chili and those hokey tunes you'll leave singing.

## Coyote Ugly

153 1st Ave. (9th & 10th Sts.)
212-477-4431

NO, THIS AIN'T NO disco this ain't no party. This is a REAL DIVE. Now that the bar has been imortalized by the movie (a classic, rivaled only by Ishtar), let's get the real deal. The drinks are cheap, the decor is part outhouse and part roadhouse, and the bartenders are rowdy and raucous. However, you will never find anything from the same gene pool as Tyra Banks drinking or working anywhere near this spot. It is a fun spot, but don't expect to sip a shot off a super-models boobs.

## Crazy Nanny's

21 7th Ave. So. (@ Leroy St.)
212-366-6312

THIS MIXED AND friendly bar/lounge literally has it all and it's delivered without any attitude at great prices. Open seven days a week with something going on just about every night and a daily half-price happy hour from 4-7p.m. Head over on Monday night to shoot pool in their tournament and compete for a cash prize. Wednesdays and Sundays host a free-for-all-no-cover super fun Karaoke night where you get your chance to be a star. Saturday is their famous mixer night where gay women biological or otherwise get down as they watch exotic dancers shake their groove thing.

## Cream

246 Columbus Ave. (71st & 72nd Sts.)
212-712-1666

THIS IS THE 3 karat diamond set in platinum engagement ring that every girl dreams of! The sweetness of Cream is just what the Upper West Side needs. It's hard to believe that the unassuming entrance hides such a great place. The underground space has five rooms of pleasure, with the two largest rooms divided by a glass wall so you're able to see in the next. With all the bodies rockin' to the hype beats of the DJ it's hard to decide which of the rooms to stay in. There are Victorian style velvet couches and tables available for either being picked-up or resting sore ankles and feet. The drinks are moderately priced and definitely strong. Be warned, the bouncer police will stop all who are not in compliance with the semi-strict dress code.

## C3

103 Waverly Pl. (@ MacDougal St.)
212-254-1200

C3 IS THE HOTEL BAR of the quaint and historical Washington Square Hotel. Walking downstairs to the lounge will leave you surprised and delighted at what you find. There exists at the heart of the NYU campus and tourist overrun Washington Square Park an underground hideaway that serves inexpensive cocktails and is rarely crowded. Sidle up next to your date or bring a book and relax in one of the cozy red banquettes. This unique treat closes at midnight so be sure to get in here early enough to enjoy the transporting art deco/speakeasy atmosphere.

## Cub Room

131 Sullivan St. (@ Prince St.)
212-677-4100

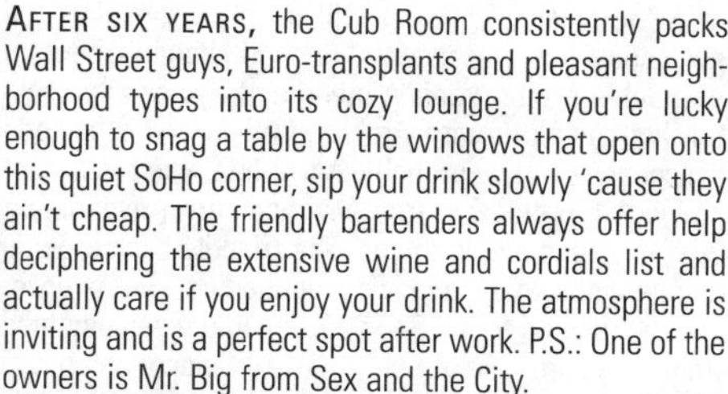

After six years, the Cub Room consistently packs Wall Street guys, Euro-transplants and pleasant neighborhood types into its cozy lounge. If you're lucky enough to snag a table by the windows that open onto this quiet SoHo corner, sip your drink slowly 'cause they ain't cheap. The friendly bartenders always offer help deciphering the extensive wine and cordials list and actually care if you enjoy your drink. The atmosphere is inviting and is a perfect spot after work. P.S.: One of the owners is Mr. Big from Sex and the City.

## The Cubby Hole

281 W. 12th St. (@ 4th St.)
212-243-9041

You walk in the place wondering who the hell designed this bar after ingesting psychedelic drugs. This place is just a little weird. The bar stools upholstered with Disney cartoon character's faces, continuous cartoons playing on TV monitors and fake flowers hanging amidst strands of Christmas lights don't make any sense. However, the mostly gay, more lesbian crowd seem normal enough. As you belly up to the bar and place your booty on either Bug's, Tweety's or Porky Pig's face, you can order moderately priced drinks and watch cartoons. The service and the crowd are friendly, it's just the decorations that make everyone seem out of sorts in this freaky play house that looks like it's meant for kids, not adults consuming alcohol.

## Culture Club

179 Varick St. (Charlton & King Sts.)
212-243-1999

Gag me with a spoon and throw on your Relax T-shirt for this aptly named megalopolis of '80s music and culture while dancing the night away to such classics as Video Killed the Radio Star and Come on Eileen. The cheesy Breakfast Club murals and theme drinks named after the Terminator and Ronald "I forget" Reagan would make anyone want to run out and buy Aquanet and blue eye shadow. Two floors of bitchin' music and dancing, are sure to quench your thirst for the '80s.

## The Cutting Room

19 W. 24th St. (Broadway & 6th Ave.)
212-691-4065

FORMERLY A FILM production space, this large comfortable Morrocan style spot will soon be the place on everyone's list. The recently opened kitchen offers an affordable Mediterranean menu and a specialty cocktail list complete with Arabic martinis and other odd concoctions you've probably never had. The restaurant provides a pretension free environment to experiment with new and exotic things. The friendly back room is unique, innovative and very happening. For a cover charge, ranging from $5 to $20, you might see anything from hip experimentation to a 19- piece orchestra. Members of the Conan O'Brien Show's band frequently play here and are becoming a house favorite.

## Daddy-O

44 Bedford St. (@ Leroy St.)
212-414-8884

IF YOU DON'T KEEP your eyes peeled it's likely you'll miss this one-year old, tiny corner bar. There is barely a sign and the dark interior doesn't give away the secret of this great hangout place owned by Steve Crane of Po. The few tables are filled with a mix of locals and yuppies that look like they accidentally stumbled in here while looking for something else. Regardless, everyone comfortably co-exists and conversations create a noisy din. After-hours the place gets cranking when the wait staff from area restaurants spill inside. A chalkboard menu hangs overhead listing a small yet creative list of snacks.

## Dakota Roadhouse

43 Park Pl. (Church & W. Broadway)
212-962-9800

QUIRKY AND CERTAINLY DIFFERENT; those are the two words that will come to mind when you see Dakota

Roadhouse. A combination live lobster tank and game (grab a crustacean with a mechanical arm for just two bucks!) will surely give any stressed working stiff a chance to unwind and forget any corporate-employment woes. And the mouse traps on the bar are always a gas. Games and a friendly staff make this Roadhose a nice change from all the lounges and Irish bars in this area.

## Dangerfields Comedy Club

1118 1st Ave. (61st & 62nd Sts.)
212-593-1650

WHEN YOU WALK INSIDE, you'll feel like you're in Reno, Nevada in 1962. Unfortunately, the comedians seem to be road hacks that travel great lengths into Manhattan to convince their wives that they're still in the business. Rodney Dangerfield opened this place during the comedy boom of the 1980's and he should have closed it during the comedy depression of the early '90s. The staff is rude, the drinks are weak and the comedians are downright horrible. You get the feeling that everyone from the waiters to the performers are working there because Rodney owed them a favor.

## Danny's Skylight Room

346-348 W. 46th St. (8th & 9th Aves.)
212-265-8133

WITH ITS PIANO BAR, stand-up comedy, mirrors, magnum-sized martini glass decorations and blue lights over the bar, Danny's Skylight Room has a live vibe. More exciting, perhaps, than its middle-aged crowd, but still an entertaining night out.

## d.b.a.

41 1st Ave. (2nd & 3rd Sts.)
212-475-5097

THIS BAR IS a gem in the East Village. Comfortable space, good music and an amazing variety of beer, wine and Scotch guarantee quality imbibing at d.b.a. On nicer days, the outside garden stays open until 10p.m. The clientele ranges from bikers to bankers, many coming for the huge draught beer selection. Beers change with the season; the list focuses more on wheats and whites in the warmer months and stouts and ports in the cold ones. d.b.a is a little crowded on the weekends, but what do you expect at a place this good?

## Dead Poet

450 Amsterdam Ave. (81st & 82nd Sts.)
212-595-5670

THIS LITTLE HOLE in the wall or, more accurately, little hole in the wall with a hallway attached, offers cheap drinks and $1.00 pool games. Although a large mirror behind the bar helps ease feelings of claustrophobia, there is no denying that this little neighborhood dive is indeed snug. Activity tends to congregate around the pool table in the back, while a few loyal local drinkers stick to the small bar at the front. Be warned, groups of more than five may be a fire hazard.

## Deanna's

107 Rivington St. (Ludlow & Essex Sts.)
212-420-2258

ATTEMPTING TO BRING a touch of class to the Lower East Side, Deanna's has all the trappings of a great date spot: candle light, soft jazz and a room brimming with antique couches. Beer and wine are served while owner Deanna Kirk sings Wed., Fri. and Sat. Music lovers are also attracted to the African drums, Brazilian sounds and jazz funk that play later in the evening.

## Decade

1117 1st Ave. (@ 61st St.)
212-835-5979

ONE DRINK? Hell no, patrons here are hitting their third or fourth. Watch those ever-adorable baby boomers getting their weekend groove-on to a DJ spinning James Brown and Mark Anthony. Younger folk shanghaied into paying the $20 cover are likely to bolt after downing a single $8 dollar drink. Decade offers a prix fixe dinner among wine bottle-lined walls in the VIP dining room. Different themes every night; on Monday go for a classic rock night sponsored by 104.3 FM, or Thursday night for Executive Decade when a DJ spins a chronological mish-mash of radio hits.

## Decibel

240 E. 9th St. (2nd & 3rd Aves.)
212-979-2733

ANY BAR THAT doesn't put its name on the entrance is probably too hip for its own good, and Decibel is definitely that. In fact, if it weren't for the obnoxious "we're cool -- are you?" atmosphere that infects Decibel it would be a very cool spot. The decor throughout Decibel is like an authentic Japanese bar, but with artistic flourishes to make it individual. The real triumph is the menu, which features an extensive list of high quality, reasonably priced sakes (cold and warm), as well as wide variety of low priced appetizers. An excellent place as long as you can get past the doorman.

## Delmonico's

56 Beaver St. (@ Williams St.)
212-509-1144

A BEAUTIFUL New York City landmark serving Wall Street hot shots, and more recently, the dot-commies who have invaded the area. The men's club bar area is beautifully appointed with gigantic flower arrangements and dark wood. Service is always top-notch which makes this the best venue in the area for entertaining and impressing clients.

## Delta Grill

700 9th Ave. (@ 48th St.)
212-956-0934

FOR AN ARTERY-CLOGGING good time, take a walk off Times Square and try the Delta Grill, a Cajun-themed bar/restaurant. While offering pretty tasty food, Delta is just a bit too far north for authenticity. Sip ultra-sweet hurricanes and Cajun martinis among precise simulations of ancient, southern awnings and decaying walls. Delta Grill offers a standard mix of seven beers on tap and a friendly place to sit for a while, eat some decent food and enjoy live music on the weekends. Though far from being an after work hangout, Delta Grill offers a fair, once-in-a-while drinking and dining experience.

## Demarchelier Downtown

100 W. Houston St.
(Thompson St. & LaGuardia Pl.)
212-254-7000

THE OWNERS OF Demarchelier transformed nightclub E&O into a trendy French bistro. The yellow hued Casablanca lighting that makes everyone look so damn

good and the red banquettes that surround the perimeter lends a beautiful interpretation of the classic Parisian bistro. Cute Euro waiters serve typical French favorites like steak-frites. Spicy olives are served gratis at the bar if you aren't hungry enough to warrant a table. Nice mixes of $9 house specials include the mojito, caipirinha and pineapple ginger martini. Outside seating is available in good weather and it's a perfect post for people watching on the SoHo/Village border.

## Dempsey's Pub

612 2nd Ave. (3rd & 4th Sts.)
212-388-0662

IN THE TRUE Irish spirit, doors open at 11:00a.m., so you can stop for an eye-opener before your meeting at noon or take the hair off the dog on Sunday morning. Sports are ever playing on the four TV's and the pool table is never two quarters away from your turn. Garrett and Maria are the resident lad and lass of the establishment and boast, in Irish brogue, "we serve da' best point of Guinness out soide the ol' sod." But with a happy hour that lasts from open till 7:00p.m., it's the regulars' opinion, "they serve the best $1.50 drafts and $2.00 cocktails this side of the Hudson."

## Denial

46 Grand St. (Thompson St. & W. Broadway)
212-925-9449

ALONG THE TRENDY, loud streets of SoHo lies a small comfortable retreat called Denial. This sake bar/lounge serves 15 high-end sakes and finger food. The DJ spins acid-jazzy tunes and the finger foods should keep you sockin' down the sake. The décor is simple, modern and comfortable with very peaceful music playing in the background. This isn't the place to come rage with your frat buddies, but it's not a bad spot to take your date and show that you have evolved from dragging your knuckles on the ground.

## Denizen

73 Thompson St. (Spring & Broome Sts.)
212-966-7299

WITH ALL THE panache and glamour expected of a SoHo venue, Denizen serves an extensive list of wines, and house special flavored cosmos (strawberry, raspberry and peach) minus the attitude expected South of Houston. Weather permitting, sit outside or simply enjoy a cocktail at the bar while chatting with ultra-friendly staff and locals. If not for the luxe of red velvet curtains, cushy forties style leather booths and dim lighting, you'd swear Norm and Cliff would make their well-received entrance at any moment, which is why locals have treasured this gem since its opening in 1997.

## Detour

349 E. 13th St. (1st & 2nd Aves.)
212-533-6212

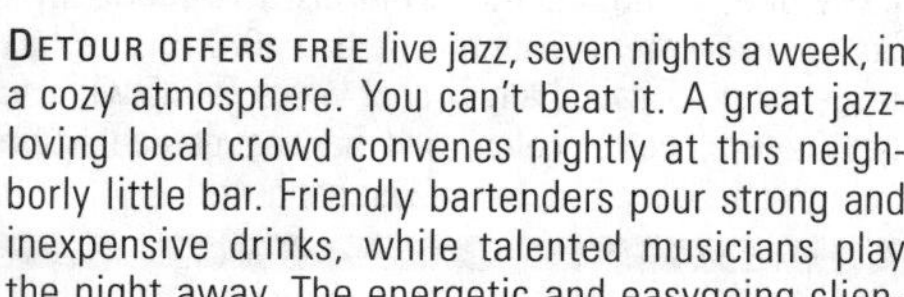

DETOUR OFFERS FREE live jazz, seven nights a week, in a cozy atmosphere. You can't beat it. A great jazz-loving local crowd convenes nightly at this neighborly little bar. Friendly bartenders pour strong and inexpensive drinks, while talented musicians play the night away. The energetic and easygoing clientele makes Detour a great place to meet new friends and have a good time.

## Dew Drop Inn

57 Greenwich Ave. (@ Perry St.)
212-924-8055

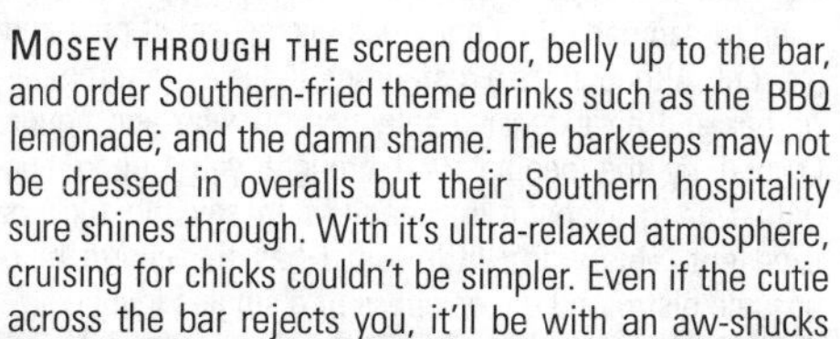

MOSEY THROUGH THE screen door, belly up to the bar, and order Southern-fried theme drinks such as the BBQ lemonade; and the damn shame. The barkeeps may not be dressed in overalls but their Southern hospitality sure shines through. With it's ultra-relaxed atmosphere, cruising for chicks couldn't be simpler. Even if the cutie across the bar rejects you, it'll be with an aw-shucks sorta smile. If only you had some hayseed to chew on.

## Dewey's Flatiron

210 5th Ave. (25th & 26th Sts.)
212-696-2337

PLACED IN THE Silicon Alley area, Dewey's looks like a run-of-the-mill watering hole for a lot of dot.com upstarts and other business types who don't mind spending $6 on a bottle of beer. But upon further examination, it's easy to see why they do. This spacious and friendly bi-level bar, topped by an elegantly arched brick ceiling, is a future landmark. Dewey's attracts a few sports fans, but their presence is by no means overbearing. Stop in to eat, shoot some pool or just hang out. They'll be happy to see you.

## Dick's Bar

192 2nd Ave. (@ 12th St.)
212-475-2071

SHOW NO FEAR of the plastic cock, because they are everywhere. This Eastside bar is also known for Musical Mondays showing old classics like Funny Girl starring Barbra Streisand (musicals and cocks . . interesting mix). If you don't fancy musicals, engage in a game of pool with the friendly locals. This 1980's style bar tends to cater to clientele in their 40's. This bar has a special drink called a dick shot which for $5 will you get Baileys, butterscotch, and banana poured down your throat. Delicious, to the last hangover!

## Diner

85 Broadway (@ Berry St.) Brooklyn
718-486-3077

THERE'S A DINER CRAZE sweeping Williamsburg and this one is not only the trendsetter, but it's the touchstone. This old diner from the '30s seems almost invisible from the outside but upon entry you'll see it has been re-vamped into a gorgeous microcosm of past and present. Although it's a restaurant, it has a great romantic bar and an extensive selection of wine and liquor. Owned by the people who brought you Odeon and Balthazar in Manhattan, needless to say the food is excellent. This warm little place has the charm of a upscale bistro and the sexiness of a singles lounge.

## Diva

341 W. Broadway (Broome & Grand Sts.)
212-924-9024

IN THE WORLD of diva's, this one is certainly no Jennifer Lopez. Opened a few years ago during the W. Broadway boom this red loft-like boite is hanging on by a string. A cool crowd used to hangout here, but recently European tourists from local hotels congregate at the long bar. Diva is enjoyable in the summer when the floor to ceiling windows open, letting the breezes blow in and the Euros spill out.

## Dive Bar

732 Amsterdam Ave. (@ 96th St.)
212-749-4358

YOU COULD MISTAKE this slightly seedier version of its sister bar Dive 75 for "Die Bar", with a crucial letter missing in its neon nameplate. In the dead stretch above 90th St., Dive Bar offers a healthy selection of draft and bottled beer (try the house brew for $2 a pint) as well as a most comprehensive list of blended and single malt Scotch and specialty bourbons. During the week, middle-aged working folk flock to the bar for happy hour specials and to watch the news on one of seven sets. On the weekends, local post-grads and Columbia students pack it in to play pool and tunes on the killer jukebox, unnerved by the giant bull's head leering at them on the wall.

## Dive 75

101 W. 75th St. (Columbus & Amsterdam Aves.)
212-362-7518

CONTRARY TO ITS name, the atmosphere is airy and refined, the staff friendly and knowledgeable and the patrons fresh from Wall Street. Lest you find the crowd perhaps a shade too subdued, Dive 75 is chock full of amusing distractions: ogle the African sicklets in the 155-gallon fish tank that pays homage to the space's former identity as a scuba shop, challenge a stranger to a game of Connect Four, make your way through a dense beer selection and pick a tune from the alarmingly diverse jukebox. Or, if you're feeling like a grown-up, order a specialty bourbon or one of 30 single-malt Scotches.

## Divine Bar

(downtown)
55 Liberty St. (@ Nassau St.)
212-791-WINE

THE FINANCIAL DISTRICT'S lack of cool after work spots has really worked in Divine Bar's favor. This two-story lounge is comfortable and close to Wall Street. Tapas and cocktails are served in this funky colorful spot. A large selection of wines and Scotches help many working stiffs iron out the kinks of their stressful day. Definitely one of the best spots to have a drink in this 'hood.

## Divine Bar

244 E. 51st St. (2nd & 3rd Aves.)
212-319-9463

A USER-FRIENDLY menu pairs tasty tapas with wine and cigars while a huge fireplace warms the romantic upstairs area in the colder months. Professional hops drinkers cavort at the bar below and live musicians jazz it up on Sundays. Even though the space is overrun with midtown professionals, it's a change of pace for a casual after-work drink.

## DJ Reynolds

351 W. 57th St. (8th & 9th Aves.)
212-245-2912

MIDTOWN RUSH HOUR crowds got you down? Duck into this quiet, simple woody space where, unlike "Cheers," no one knows your name and you can hide without any threat of anyone talking to you. Sidle up to the bar or languish in the lounge area and drown your sorrows in one of five beers on tap or the usual cocktails under the colorful hanging lamps. The bar's been around a while (11 years) and so has the somewhat older, just-chill kind of crowd.

## D Lounge

(@ The Delmonico Hotel)
502 Park Ave. (@ 59th St.)
212-355-2500

IF YOU DON'T LIKE the color blue you won't like this pricey hotel bar. If, on the other hand, blue is your favorite color, you may not want to drink anywhere else. The D Lounge feels like a deep shade of blue; with its mellow tone, low music and soft light. The crowd thins out late at night, making this relaxing bar even more appealing. Of course, spending an evening here requires a large financial investment, but it might just change your mindset forever.

## Doc Holliday's

141 Ave. A (@ 9th St.)
212-979-0312

READY FOR A GOOD TIME? You'd better be if you end up at this bar. Doc Holliday's is not for the faint at heart. With one glance you can tell that it's a dump. Be ready for a night of hard partying here; there are shots going 'round the bar and enough Pabst Blue Ribbon (here, they just yell PBR) to keep you guzzling until dawn. Amazing weekday specials: on Tuesday, drink all the Bud you want for $5, on Wednesday, ladies drink for free. Kitschy country posters coat the walls. Allman Brothers and Patsy Cline play on the jukebox. A TV, pool table and friendly bartenders (even to tottering lushes like you) are all here. What more could you ask for in a bar?

## Dock's Oyster Bar

633 3rd Ave. (@ 40th St.)
212-986-8080

IN A STYLISH, art deco setting with a wooden bar in the center, high ceilings, tiled walls and a black and grey lounge area, the older crowd of well-to-do folk line up for their succulent seafood suppers. For those here to drink at the equally packed bar area, bottled wines offer more bang for your buck than the by-the-glass options.

## Doc Watson's

1490 2nd Ave. (77th & 78th Sts.)
212-988-5300

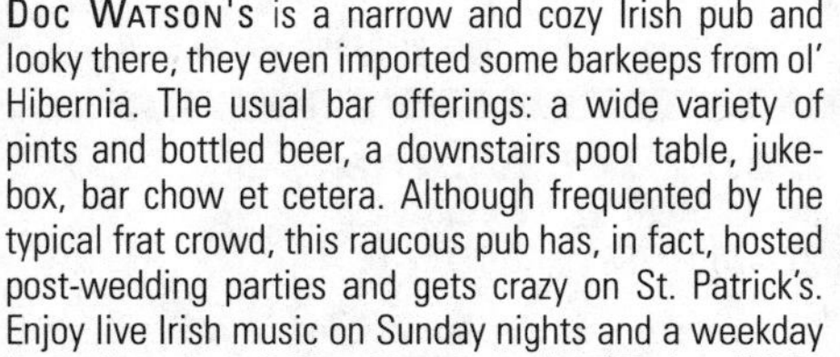

DOC WATSON'S is a narrow and cozy Irish pub and looky there, they even imported some barkeeps from ol' Hibernia. The usual bar offerings: a wide variety of pints and bottled beer, a downstairs pool table, jukebox, bar chow et cetera. Although frequented by the typical frat crowd, this raucous pub has, in fact, hosted post-wedding parties and gets crazy on St. Patrick's. Enjoy live Irish music on Sunday nights and a weekday happy hour from 3:30 to 7p.m., pouring $5 pints ($3.50 domestic bottles) and dollar discounts on mixed drinks.

## Do-Hwa

55 Carmine St. (7th Ave. So. & Bedford St.)
212-414-1224

IT SEEMS LIKE hip little Korean restaurants are popping up all over the place these days. Here is another one, brought to you by the same folks who own popular Dok Suni's in the East Village. Simply and sparsely decorated, this chic place is a nice addition to this area. The rumor mill says Quentin Tarantino is a silent partner, so while sipping your specialty martini keep your eyes peeled for celeb sightings. The food is moderately priced and satisfying, making this a good spot for a date.

## Don Hills

511 Greenwich St. (@ Spring St.)
212-219-2850

TRANS-GENDER MEETS fuel-injected rock 'n' roll at Don Hills. Drop your pants for Mistress Formika, bang your head to the Man Scouts of America and dance your ass off to the sweet sounds of rock 'n' roll. Don Hills boasts unique crazy theme parties every night, however, it's a good idea to call ahead for more info. Cover varies between $10 and $15, but do not be dissuaded, once you're inside you'll be immersed in NYC's best party environment. As the rock band Coyote Shivers states, "There will be sluts and drugs and fags and rock 'n' roll."

## Donald Sacks

220 Vesey St. (in 4 World Financial Center)
212-619-4600

DONALD SACKS IS a beautiful bar/restaurant with great specials. Monday-Friday, guzzle 1/2 price bottles of beer. Also available are fine martinis, margaritas and daiquiris. Entrees run from $10 to $18. After work, this place fills up with traders and their secretaries.

## Don't Tell Mama

343 W. 46th St. (@ 8th Ave.)
212-757-0788

A FAVORITE SPOT for tourists and natives alike, this piano bar offers great entertainment free of charge. Daily half-price happy hour is from 4p.m.to 7p.m. when drinks start at $4.50 and generally don't get more expensive than $6. Practice belting out your favorite Broadway tunes with the talented, good enough for Broadway wait-staff.

## Dorrian's Red Hand

1616 2nd Ave. (@ 84th St.)
212-772-6660

DORRIAN'S IS A BAR that people swear off but undoubtedly return to. If you stand close to the crowded bar you may be fortunate to catch an overweight frat boy making out with an extremely wasted stranger. This is a typical Upper East Side pick up bar that is as cheesy as getting a picture of yourself next to a celebrity cardboard cut out. During the day decent bar food is available and you can watch sporting events on one of the four televisions. If you're lucky you may spot a New York Yankee throwing back a pint since they have been known to hang here.

## Double Happiness

173 Mott St. (Broome & Grand Sts.)
212-941-1282

HIDDEN DOWN A STAIRCASE in the newly hip Chinatown, this trendy basement lounge gets packed with a sexy downtown crowd almost every night of the week. Varying DJ's spin every night of the week in this three-room dungeon space steeped in New York history (it used to be a member's only gay social club and later a mafioso hangout); this is its first reincarnation as a hipster hub. Some of its neighborhood appeal has been lost recently due to the doorman stationed outside on weekends.

## Down The Hatch

179 W. 4th St. (6th & 7th Aves.)
212-627-9747

GREAT TASTING CHEAP wings and watered down beer is what you can expect here. If you're in the mood for the college scene complete with dart boards and pool table then you've reached the apex. The underground haunt offers loud outdated music and re-runs of some of the funniest Saturday Night Live skits. If you just want to hang at no particular place with well priced happy hour, then viola! Otherwise keep the funnel moving!

## Downtime

251 W. 30th St. (7th & 8th Aves.)
212-695-2747

IT IS so very hard to pin this place offering a diverse crowd in a low key atmosphere. There is the B&T crowd, the hip-hip and R&B crowd. The live music showcase is good and musicians come not only to entertain but to have fun. The atmosphere is pleasant with a balcony accompanied by a small bar and candlelit tables. The only thing that you can pin down about this place is that you will have a good time and that the bar is reasonably priced. One thing to keep in mind: There is a velvet rope policy!

## Downtown

211 Pearl St. (John St. & Maiden Ln.)
212-344-3612

NEW TO THE AREA, Downtown is a refreshing departure from the Irish pub, good-ole-boy staples of the Wall Street area. Downtown actually achieves what all the 2nd Ave. Midtown bars are going for; a great place to bring that co-worker you've been eyeing for a quick drink after work. The jukebox has the ultimate collection of the best of three of the last four decades; the '90s are strategically ignored. A large back room boasts two pool tables that you can actually weasel on to. The bar offers a dizzying number of choices of draft beer and they pour a decent cocktail at prices that acknowledge that not everyone on Wall Street made a killing in that tech-stock frenzy.

## Drinkland

339 E. 10th St. (Aves. A & B)
212-228-2435

THIS SWANK, TRIPPY lounge exudes a Kubrick-esque motif and more style than many larger clubs. Eclectic, fashionable, young sophisticates cluster in one of three separate drinking areas. There is a long, slick bar in the main room that leads into a nook of glowing, spiral tables among velvet-draped walls. The piece-de-resistance is the notorious White Room, a wall-to-wall vinyl den right out of A Clockwork Orange. Drinks could be bigger, better and stronger but the atmosphere makes up for it. A cool meet-for-a-drink spot.

## Drip

489 Amsterdam Ave. (83rd & 84th Sts.)
212-875-1032

AHHHH. Romance in New York, what could be more exciting, more intriguing, more TERRIFYING? Well fear no more, for there exists in Manhattan a bar that eases the pressure of the pick-up scene. Besides cocktails, Drip offers coffee specialties, gooey desserts and a selection of sandwiches that make the joint seem very homey. But central to the success of this four year old bar is the popular dating service they offer. If you're on the prowl, just ask the bartender for a dating form and voila, you'll be in the loop. The whole mood of the place lends itself to a friendly flirtatious environment.

## Drover's Tap Room

9 Jones St. (Bleecker & W. 4th St.)
212-627-1233

THE SIMPLE AMBIANCE and hometown feel of DTR has people from all over town rushing here to sample the classic American dishes served the way mom makes them. The bar is very tiny, occupying only a small portion of the front room, but loyal New York beer drinkers can always be found here since the selection is limited to local brews only.

## Druids

736 10th Ave. (50th & 51st Sts.)
212-307-6410

IRONICALLY ENOUGH, we have Prohibition to thank for some of our best watering holes. (Makes one wonder what Guiliani's real legacy will be 80 years from now). Druids, housed in this handso 1920's building for the last six years, offers fine food, booze, live jazz, a great back garden and even a rotating art show appealing to connoisseurs of all sorts, especially the unpretentious kind.

## DT/UT

1626 2nd Ave. (84th & 85th Sts.)
212-327-1327

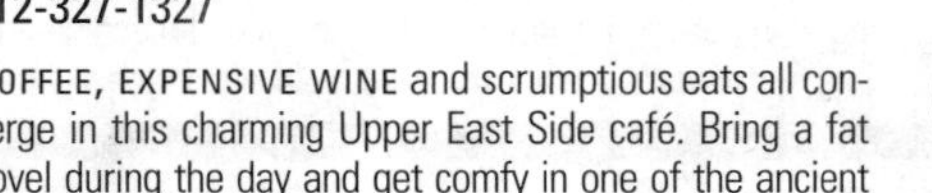

COFFEE, EXPENSIVE WINE and scrumptious eats all converge in this charming Upper East Side café. Bring a fat novel during the day and get comfy in one of the ancient couches. But be prepared to dog-ear your page at sundown, when they dim the lights and bring out the candles. Unique snacks are offered here; watch out for fondue, make-your-own smores and massive Rice Krispie Treats. If you're short on change, just get a simple tea and cookie.

You can't go wrong here on a lazy Saturday afternoon or weeknight when you're craving an hour of quiet chilling.

## Dublin House

225 W. 79th St. (Amsterdam Ave. & Broadway)
212-362-1274

REMEMBER THAT DEWARS ad campaign a few years back, the one that featured a surly-looking bartender and the question: 'Do you really want to ask this guy for a Screaming Orgasm?' Well, he's here, and the answer is an emphatic: No! No happy hour, no food, no dancing, no credit cards, no windows. Silver lining: No drinks over $3.50! This is the place to be in when you're broke and interested in some heavy, unadulterated drinking.

## Due South

399 Greenwich St. (@ Beach St.)
212-431-3318

THIS PLACE HAS the personality of a box of rocks. However, it has potential with a cute, airy space, high windows, red and white-checkered curtains and little bistro tables. There was no music, no hubbub, just a quiet neighborhood bar where you could go alone if you want to read a book or do some work. Beer is cheap, if you can get the bartender out of the Daily News Astrology page to serve it to you. Given the rising rents and stiff competition in the area, one has to wonder if they are laundering money or something.

## The Dugout

185 Christopher St. (Washington & West Sts.)
212-242-9113

THIS IS A CHRISTOPHER ST. landmark that attracts a mature, laid-back, daddy type. It is a great summer hang-out for those who like to check out the hotties roller-blading along the pier. With a pool table, pinball machine and free munchies at the bar, it's a great place to catch a game.

## Duke's

99 E. 19th St. (Park Ave. So. & Irving Pl.)
212-260-2922

THE NEON BEER lights in the entrance of Duke's, a self-proclaimed Southern dining room, may blind you. You will

also be bombarded with an assortment of decorations including old 45's, Christmas lights and other junkyard trinkets rejected by TGIF's. Suits and locals crowd the small bar nightly and listen to tunes by the Go-Go's and Ah-Ha. The 5-7p.m. happy hour is probably the best reason to come, $2 beers and $1 drafts are served. The after work crowd is fond of the dukirita, a special margarita for $7 and the spacious back dining where they convene with groups of friends and pig out on pulled pork sandwiches.

## Duplex

61 Christopher St. (@ 7th Ave. So.)
212-255-5438

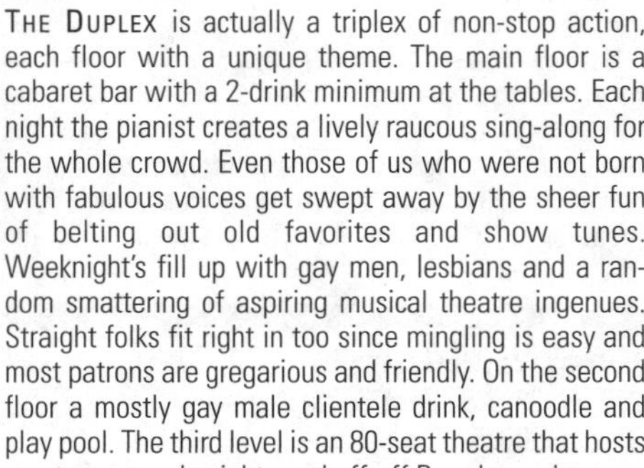

THE DUPLEX is actually a triplex of non-stop action, each floor with a unique theme. The main floor is a cabaret bar with a 2-drink minimum at the tables. Each night the pianist creates a lively raucous sing-along for the whole crowd. Even those of us who were not born with fabulous voices get swept away by the sheer fun of belting out old favorites and show tunes. Weeknight's fill up with gay men, lesbians and a random smattering of aspiring musical theatre ingenues. Straight folks fit right in too since mingling is easy and most patrons are gregarious and friendly. On the second floor a mostly gay male clientele drink, canoodle and play pool. The third level is an 80-seat theatre that hosts amateur comedy nights and off-off Broadway shows.

## Dusk

147 W. 24th St. (6th & 7th Aves.)
212-924-4490

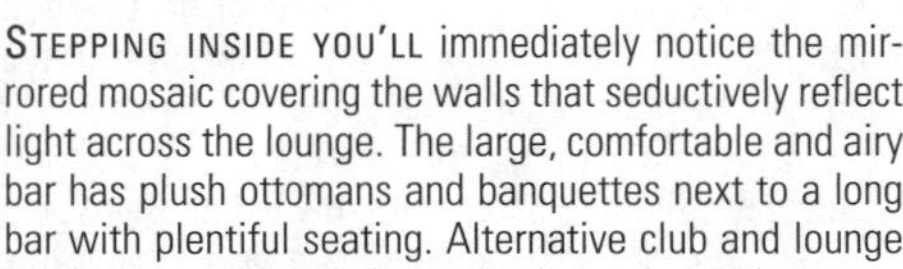

STEPPING INSIDE YOU'LL immediately notice the mirrored mosaic covering the walls that seductively reflect light across the lounge. The large, comfortable and airy bar has plush ottomans and banquettes next to a long bar with plentiful seating. Alternative club and lounge music creates a cool vibe and relaxes the soul.

## Dylan Restaurant & Bar

62 Laight St. (Greenwich & Hudson Sts.)
212-334-4783

IF IT'S TIME to impress your significant other and you're prepared to drop some dough in order to do so, Dylan is a sensory overload sensation built for reaching this goal. From the modern, swanky decor (elegant, but understated), to the food, which is a splendid mix of fine American, this pleasing bar/lounge area serves as a nice spot for an after work tryst or rendezvous spot for friends.

## The Ear Inn

326 Spring St. (Hudson & Greenwich Sts.)
212-226-9060

THE EAR has a long history, both as a historical landmark (built in 1817), and as a tavern. The walls are covered with old photos and souvenirs from the past. But what makes it worth the trip if the lack of pretension that one tends to associate with other SoHo watering holes. The slightly older crowd comes here for a meal, a cheap beer and a chance to sit on the seats out front. Live blues and folk on Mondays and Wednesdays and poetry readings on Saturday entertain the mellow crowd. Relaxing, jovial and relatively inexpensive, it's a great place when you want to get away from the "trend-setters".

## East of Eighth

254 W. 23rd St. (7th & 8th Aves.)
212-352-0075

IT WOULD BE EASY to walk by this unassuming spot on the 23rd St. strip, but you'd be missing out on a great Chelsea find. Whether you decide on cocktails in the lower-level, candlelit bar or dinner in the beautiful outdoor garden, this is a perfect place to bring your date. The restaurant serves up "eclectic American" fare at a good price and the wine list is one of the best in the area. On Monday nights, the upper-level restaurant hosts a spectacular drag show attracting a predominately gay clientele. It can get crowded on the weekends so show up early to claim one of the bar's few cozy tables.

## Eau (above Punch)

913 Broadway (@ 20th St.)
212-358-8647

YOU WOULD PROBABLY EXPECT a cool place to be hidden above an equally cool restaurant that occupies the main floor. And it does. Eau, (that's French for $H_2O$), has cool illusionary waterfalls under the bar and over the windows. The funky tin Zeppelin ceiling fans and unusual egg holder shaped stools make this lounge comfortable and an unexpected change of scenery from a typical lounge. Leather banquettes filled with local dot-commies sipping cocktails line the lofty space as DJ's spin hip hop every night of the week. There's nothing geekier than a Bill Gates look-a-like wearing a pocket protector acting like a homeboy.

## The Edge

95 E. 3rd St. (1st & 2nd Aves.)
212-477-2940

IF YOU'RE LOOKING for a crappy bar at a nice price, look no further than The Edge. Located three doors down from a genuinely rough biker bar, The Edge attracts people who aren't ugly enough to go there, but too ugly to be anywhere else. This 30ish crowd is a composite of ex-frat types, ex-art types and currently drunk types, all of whom share one commonality -- liquor. There's a nostalgia-inspiring jukebox, a pool table with ample playing space, and three dart boards at which you can fling darts carelessly without having to worry about accidentally hitting any super-models.

## Eight of Clubs

230 W. 75th St. (@ Broadway)
212-580-7389

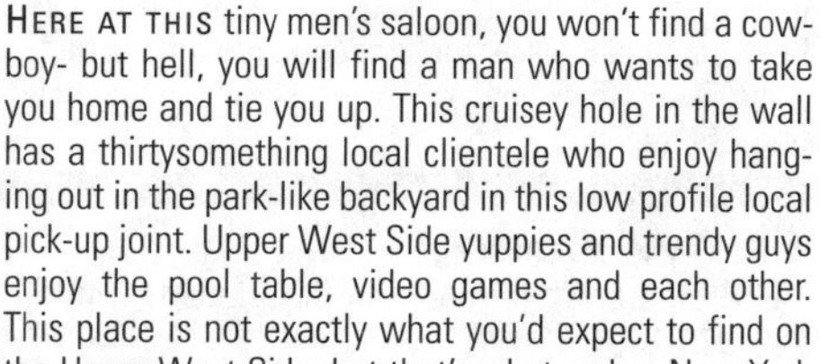

HERE AT THIS tiny men's saloon, you won't find a cowboy- but hell, you will find a man who wants to take you home and tie you up. This cruisey hole in the wall has a thirtysomething local clientele who enjoy hanging out in the park-like backyard in this low profile local pick-up joint. Upper West Side yuppies and trendy guys enjoy the pool table, video games and each other. This place is not exactly what you'd expect to find on the Upper West Side, but that's what makes New York so interesting.

## Eight Mile Creek

240 Mulberry St. (Prince & Spring Sts.)
212-431-4635

WELCOME TO THE coolest basement of a former bakery which houses a little bit of Australia in Little Italy. A half-hidden small neon cocktails sign welcomes you

underground to the comfy Down Under den. Once inside, underneath the restaurant of the same name, you'll find semi-darkness, '50s kitsch and the occasional breathtaking Aussie landscape. All summer long, this cozy lounge/bar provides the best bargain of the millennium with well drinks and Fosters at only $3 from 6-8p.m. every day except Mondays (closed). If you've got a craving for good down under cuisine, the restaurant above provides some of the tastiest food around.

## Eighty-Eights

228 W. 10th St. (Bleecker & Hudson Sts.)
Closed for renovations at press time!

## Elaine's

1703 2nd Ave. (88th & 89th Sts.)
212-534-8103

ANYONE WHO READS Page Six knows Elaine's is a hotbed of celebrity sparring and political intrigue. It's where hooker Sherry Rowlands regaled listeners with her Dick Morris toe-sucking adventures; where former Heads-of-State, Barbra Streisand and David Hasselhoff may show up together on any given night. Since the early '60s, it has been the uptown literati hangout. In fact, an exact replica of the saloon will be a regular set on Dick Wolf's new show "Deadline," in which real-life patrons will be recruited for cameos. The decor is nondescript, save a long, wall-length shelf covered in literary bric-a-brac, including Winston Groom's Best Screenplay Oscar for Forrest Gump. Drop in for the show, if you think you can handle such a stunning display of intellect.

## Elbow Room

144 Bleecker St. (Thompson St. & LaGuardia Pl.)
212-979-8434

PACKING IN standing room only crowds, this great space has an awesome sound system and dazzling lighting that gives a concert-like feel to every show. If you arrive early, take a seat on one of the couches so you won't have to slam elbows with the happy, sweaty yuppies comprising the bulk of the crowd on an average night. After 11p.m. Acid jazz and hip-hop stream out of the speakers and into the ears of Gen X'ers congregating in the new upstairs lounge.

## Eleventh Street Bar

510 E. 11th St. (Aves. A & B)
212-982-3929

APPARENTLY NAMED BY someone with a limited imagination, the décor in the dog-friendly 11th Street Bar is as interesting as its name. Deep ash trays and shallow pretzel boats are about it. The cd player oozes soft music chosen by the bartender, although live acoustic Irish music is strummed Sunday nights. If you're a virtuoso on the ivories, try the house piano, though if you suck you'll hear it from the pretzel gallery. The big back room accommodates yuppies and freaks alike. The prices are fair and they knock $1 off everything till 8p.m. In a changing neighborhood, this bar stands its ground.

## Eleven Madison Park

11 Madison Ave. (@ 24th St.)
212-889-0905

LOCATED IN the CSFB building, Danny Meyer's Eleven Madison Park is a work of art. The high ceilings and décor is breathtaking. As you slide on one of the leather barstools and sift through the wine list, suddenly life seems a little bit brighter. Everything about this place is first rate: service, food, décor and wine list. The crowd is a stylish after work crowd usually on an expense account. Overall, it's a great place with class and ambience, so it is worth the dent it'll put in your wallet.

## El Flamingo

547 W. 21st St. (10th & 11th Aves.)
212-243-2121

THIS IS the only place to see A Midsummer Night's Dream set to '70s disco, The Donkey Show. A great interactive performance and fun grooving afterwards, this show has drawn in a diverse crowd of tourists, locals and parties on the go. Worth every penny of the $35-$39 cover charge. Call ahead for times.

## Ellen O'Dees

130 E. 40th St. (Lexington & 3rd Aves.)
212-213-3998

YOU CAN'T MISS Ellen O'Dees, the 1960's bubble writing on the sign is a dead give away. This is a local bar through and through. If you just moved into the neighborhood, stay awhile and meet the regulars playing pool, video games and enjoying the cheap drinks. Otherwise you may want to move on to a more exciting bar in Midtown.

## El Quijote

226 W. 23rd St. (7th & 8th Aves.)
212-929-1855

IF YOU'RE in the mood for some old-world flavor, check out Chelsea's El Quijote, New York's oldest Spanish restaurant. The owner, Manny Ramirez, who claims to descend directly from the famous windmill-tilter, has the place decorated with medieval cavaliers and other memorabilia to recall the heyday of Spanish chivalry. Drink Manny's notorious sangria while digging into huge portions of very tasty Spanish dishes.

## El Rio Grande

160 E. 38th St. (@ 3rd Ave.)
212-867-0922

"WHAT THE FUCK is in those margaritas?" is what you'll ask the morning after downing the famous frosty South of the border favorites on the Mexican side of this Midtown happy hour legend. Don't miss taking the guided journey from one side of the restaurant to the other through the kitchen (much more exciting after you've finished your first drink). Expect long lines if you're heading over right after work, but you'll find it's well worth the wait. The food is good, but good luck getting a table.

## El Teddy's

219 W. Broadway (Franklin & White Sts.)
212-941-7070

THIS VERY POPULAR bi-level nuevo-Mexican bar/restaurant is always packed with after-work, young professionals soon drunk on big, tasty margaritas. Many of them come for the food but never get past the bar, which puts the predominantly single boys and girls elbow-to-elbow clamoring for the nacho trays. At first glance, the décor seems a bit over the top ( the walls and ceilings are adorned with smooth fragments of colored glass), but it fits the rowdiness. For a bit more serenity, the outdoor patio makes for a fun summer evening.

## Emerald

308 Spring St. (Hudson & Greenwich Sts.)
212-226-8512

CAN YOU SAY ANYTHING really terrible about a bar with pictures of the Quiet Man all over the walls? Open for 27 years and looking a bit blue collar and out of place in this neighborhood otherwise overrun with trendy spots; the Emerald is a good place for a $4 beer or mixed drink or to munch on some burgers and pasta. Don't lose any sleep at night thinking you're going to miss something if your friends decide to come here without you one night.

## Enid's

560 Manhattan Ave. (@ Driggs Ave.)
Brooklyn
718-349-3859

FINALLY, A NEW Brooklyn bar that feels like it's worthy of this borough's attitude. Just a year old, Enid's has established itself not only for the clever use of its cavernous corner space and uniquely angled bar, but also for dropping a necessary anchor off the Good Ship Hipster which its local competitors ride. True, the crowd is still on the young and sideburned side, however the owners, a couple of Kansas City ladies with a feel for the authentic, have created a relaxed watering hole that caters to the drinker in us all. With live country swing music, a juke box that plays 45's, Sunday movies and nary a cover in sight, Enid's didn't invade the neighborhood, it complemented the history.

## Ernie's

2150 Broadway (75th & 76th Sts.)
212-496-1588

THIS SPACIOUS EATERY, specializing in smallish portions of light Italian fare, attracts a somewhat trendy clientele. Everyone seems to be searching for the next hot spot in the neighborhood and falling short with this destination. Although the gargantuan room, lofty ceilings and minimalist décor at first seem calming, after 10 minutes at the bar it all begins to feel overwhelmingly shallow, empty and pretentious. The drinks are expensive, the staff is snooty and the atmosphere is almost antiseptic.

## Escuelita (La Nueva)

301 W. 39th St. (8th & 9th Aves.)
212-631-0588

THIS EXTREMELY FESTIVE gay nightclub features a warehouse style décor in the basement with lounging areas for relaxation. DJ's play hip-hop, R&B, salsa, merengue and house music to a predominately Latino and African American crowd. There are different parties Thursday through Saturday starting at 10p.m. until 4a.m. A drag queen named Harmonica Sunbeam performs with exotic dancers on Sundays to packed crowds. The festivities on Sundays start at 7p.m. Sometimes on Thursday nights centerfolds from Black Inches magazine (porn) will appear to sign autographs.

## Esperanto

145 Ave. C (@ 9th St.)
212-505-6559

AT THE END of its first year of operation in this up-and-coming part of Alphabet City, Esperanto knows how to deliver...Latino-style. Its open-air corner location, paneled in pale blue and yellow wood, suggests a surfer hut with soul. In addition to the unique and powerful cocktail selections like caipirinha, mojito cubano, batido de coco and kiwi roska ($5-6). Esperanto serves refined fare such as the Esperanto Steak, a classic Argentinean treatment complete with Chimichurri salsa and Feijoada, Brazil's national dish. A thorough, well-priced wine list (mostly Chilean) and a dozen or so bottled beers will keep you satisfied while you munch away at this new classic Loisaida restaurant/bar.

## ESPN Zone

1472 Broadway (@ 42nd St.)
212-921-ESPN

SURE, YOU CAN'T WIN if you don't play, but if you don't play you could just be drinking yourself stupid. Sporty types and those who just like to watch (with entire video walls it's hard not to) fill the latest theme spree in the "new" Times Square. This super-sized venue with its Super Bowl-like snacks and drinks, houses a Sky Box, a huge male playpen of arcade games and other such entertainment and the requisite TV screens for all things sports, all the time.

## Etoile

109 E. 56th St. (Park & Lexington Aves.)
212-750-5656

ONCE YOU FINALLY discover this new club unlabeled from the street, past the high-horse bouncer and tucked away behind zigzagging corridors and stairs - you'll be enveloped in Louis XIV décor. Posh seats in the lounge area, pink walls with high ceilings and attractive young people from every corner of the globe flipping fifties out of their gold money clips for drinks. The expansive back room jams great, worldly dance music and has plenty of seating for the exhaustingly late hours. This well-traveled, chic crowd does occasionally include the tipsy Long Island girl reminiscing about her semester abroad. Friendly and fun, Etoile is accommodating to all, and is a refreshing down- to- earth alternative to the predictably pretentious Au Bar scene.

## Eugene

27 W. 24th St. (5th & 6th Aves.)
212-462-0999

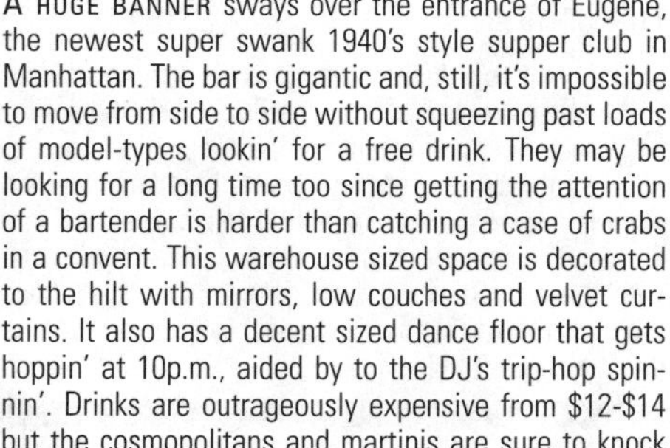

A HUGE BANNER sways over the entrance of Eugene, the newest super swank 1940's style supper club in Manhattan. The bar is gigantic and, still, it's impossible to move from side to side without squeezing past loads of model-types lookin' for a free drink. They may be looking for a long time too since getting the attention of a bartender is harder than catching a case of crabs in a convent. This warehouse sized space is decorated to the hilt with mirrors, low couches and velvet curtains. It also has a decent sized dance floor that gets hoppin' at 10p.m., aided by to the DJ's trip-hop spinnin'. Drinks are outrageously expensive from $12-$14 but the cosmopolitans and martinis are sure to knock your panties off. Your best bet is to get here early and stay late; this is a true destination spot.

## Eureka Joe's

168 5th Ave. (21st & 22nd Sts.)
212-741-7504

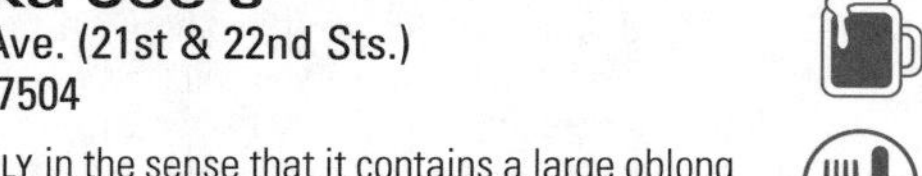

A BAR ONLY in the sense that it contains a large oblong piece of wood with bottles behind it, this place is kind of like a Starbucks with Heineken. Sandwiched between ritzy Fifth Ave. boutiques across from the Flatiron, Eureka is easily overlooked. The waitstaff may look at you as if you have ordered monkey juice when you don't order a mochachino, but then they will suddenly remember that they have a liquor license. An okay place for non-smokers to sip and read until about 11p.m. Just don't forget to order your Merlot decaf with skim.

## Evelyn Lounge

380 Columbus Ave. (@ 78th St.)
212-724-5145

ATTRACTIVE YOUNG PROFESSIONALS populate the four downstairs rooms and sip martinis from the vast list. The weekend DJ's spin a range of R&B, dance and standard pop, while the midweek live acts run toward jazz. This is one of the only tolerable spots on the Upper West Side. In an area with so many frat geeks, it's nice to see a spot where you can grab a drink, grab some digits and not feel like it's freshman oriontation.

## Excelsior

390 5th Ave. (6th &7th Sts.)
Brooklyn
718-832-1599

EXCELSIOR has pulled off a great coup in terms of New York bar culture. It manages simultaneously to be a little upscale, without reeking of the exclusivity prone to Manhattan's chichi establishments. Mostly a gay bar, but without the meat market vibe common to Chelsea, the decor combines Japanese art-nouveau influences with the decadence of the Oriental Express. Perhaps the highlight of this bar is its back garden, poked and pruned to perfection.

## Exit

605 W. 55th St. (11th & 12th Aves.)
212-582-8282

EXIT, formerly Carbon, is a mega tri-level club action-packed with disco dancing, hip-hop and techno clubbing. For the wallflowers you can observe the gyrating bodies from the second floor balcony. The VIP's, or people who think they are, congregate on the third level in any of the three lounges: the Living Room Loft, Blue Room or Jungle Room. You'll find every type in this club from drag queens to beauty queens. Expect an annoying door policy and cover, but that isn't a surprise.

## Faces and Names

161 W. 54th St. (6th & 7th Aves.)
212-586-9311

In such an anonymous city as this, sometimes it's nice to put a face to a name, a name to a face. Crazy Lou, Ann Marie, Bob Marley and others may not be sitting in the green or brown lounge chair next to you, but their named pictures gaze at you through the flickering candlelight. Have a few more of the six beers on tap, a cognac or cocktail and you might think one of those familiar strangers actually winked.

## Failte

531 2nd Ave. (29th & 30th Sts.)
212-725-9440

This quaint Irish tavern welcomes the young neighborhood crowd along with an influx of moviegoers from the Kips Bay megaplex. Failte serves as a welcome pit stop for an after work drink in the summer (ladies wear a sweater because the AC is cranked and headlights are sure to glare!) and as a cozy place to sit by the fire in the winter. The upstairs lounge is reminiscent of the Addams family living room. Wednesday nights from 10p.m.-1a.m. ladies can drink $2.50 well drinks, domestic beer and shots. Guys,wear warm under-roos, you know what they say about shrinkage.

## Fanelli's

94 Prince St. (@ Mercer St.)
212-226-9412

In a SoHo overrun with gallery-hopping Eurotrash and girls maxing out Mom's plastic, Fanelli's is a requisite reminder of a time long before our trendy times, the mid-1800's. It's a WYSIWYG establishment: red-checkered tables for hefty hamburgers and other pub grub, a wooden bar with seven beers on tap at about $4 for 12 ounces and a slightly more male, yet mixed, crowd on weeknights stubbornly swilling to the good ol' days.

## Fat Black Pussycat

130 W. 3rd St. (MacDougal St. & 6th Ave.)
212-533-4790

Choked to the gills with road signs, beer memorabilia, gumball machines, a pool table, dart boards, a big

screen satellite TV and a giant back room perfect for make-out sessions, Fat Black Pussycat is the basement party room every guy dreamed of in high school. Lured by the prospect of young, naughty girls who flow freely through the doors while NYU in session. The dirty old man quotient is high at FBP boasting more slicked back hair and leering gazes than your average strip club.

## Feinstein's (@ The Regency Hotel)

540 Park Ave. (@ 61st St.)
212-339-4095

THIS STUFFY Park Ave. cabaret nightclub is a joint venture between Michael Feinstein and the folks at Regency Hotel. The large elegant room is posh and intimate. Older couples and New York heavy hitters come here to hear the vocal stylings of Mr. Feinstein. The cover charge is steep ($50 min.), so be sure you're in the mood for some soulful crooning and Borscht Belt jokes.

## Fez

380 Lafayette St. (@ Great Jones St.)
212-533-2680

FEZ is the eight-year-old Moroccan lounge downstairs from the popular NoHo restaurant Time Café. This dark, somewhat swanky venue hosts live musical performances nightly. Tuck yourself away on a booth littered with cushions and pillows and gaze at the artfully tiled décor. Popular house creations include the fruity fez and flying carpet cocktails for $7 each.

## Fez North

2230 Broadway (@ 85th St.)
212-579-5100

THE SISTER BAR to Fez on Lafayette, this spot serves an uptown vibe, but no music like its downtown sibling. The large space draws a professional crowd that has quickly made this bar/restaurant a favorite in this good bar starved part of the city.

## Fiddlesticks

54-58 Greenwich Ave. (6th & 7th Aves.)
212-463-0516

THE FORMER HOME of Uncle Charlie's, the gyrating gay

theme park, has been transformed into Fiddlesticks, a huge Irish playground. Replete with accents from the homeland and cozy nooks for chatting, this bar has everything a homesick Dubliner could ask for. The 2 for 1 happy hours are Monday-Friday 5p.m.-7p.m. Current popular music plays in the background and bar fare is served at the quaint tables. Those who prefer a more traditional pub may not be impressed with the over the top décor but the staff and crowd are young and friendly making this a great after work meeting spot.

## 55 Bar

55 Christopher St. (@ 7th Ave. So.)
212-929-9883

IF YOU LOVE live jazz and blues, you will LOVE this West Village hangout! With live musical bands 7 nights a week, you have ample opportunity to drink it all up (you have to with the two drink minimum) and take it all in! This 35-year-old bar still has the décor of decades past, complete with entertainer's pictures and autographs. It is one of the last neighborhood saloons and can be a romantic atmosphere with the combo of jazz, blues, and of course, the margaritas they whip up.

## 5757 (@ The Four Seasons Hotel)

57 E. 57th St. (Park & Madison Aves.)
212-758-5757

LOCATED in the lobby of the Four Seasons Hotel, this chic and stunning bar/restaurant is large, elegant and just what you'd expect from the Four Seasons. Drink prices are some of the highest in the city, but the Mona Lisa isn't cheap either. With live jazz nightly, the deco-styled room with its 18-foot windows, 33-foot ceilings and bronze chandeliers, is a perfect setting for a romantic after dinner drink. Definitely worth the trip. Dress to impress!

## 53rd Street Cigar Bar

811 7th Ave. (@ 53rd St.)
212-581-1000

IF YOU'RE A BUSINESSMAN, 30-40 years old, preferably staying upstairs at the Sheraton Hotel, you'll fit right in with this high-class, martini-swilling, fun as a bag of plastic crowd. If you're hoping to add some romance to your trip, look elsewhere: the male/female ratio is only 10 to1 respectively. Although this elite establishment may be aesthetically pleasing it's not in the least bit interesting. End of story!

## Film Center Café

635 9th Ave. (44th & 45th Sts.)
212-262-2525

THIS FILM-FIXATED DINER/LOUNGE for the theater crowd has been around since the early years of the medium. Situated at vintage green tables and chairs or stools at the bar, low-maintenance patrons enjoy good American grub and one of eight beers on tap or experiment with house specialties like frozen fuzz and the cool operator.

## Finally Fred

765 Washington St. (12th & Bethune Sts.)
212-255-5101

FINALLY, the arduous search of finding a watering hole is over, so pick a stool, hunker down and get settled in at Fred's. You will feel right at home looking at a few '60s rock posters, a Mardi Gras shrine in the window and not much else. Finally Fred doesn't bother with the decorations because they concentrate on more important things like drinking, playing competitive, friendly pool and hiring bands to perform in the garage-like downstairs.

## Finnegan's Wake

1361 1st Ave. (@ 73rd St.)
212-737-3664

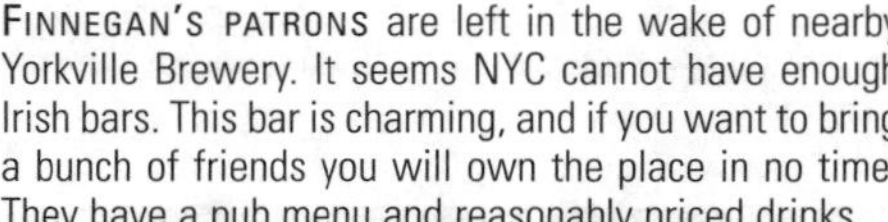

FINNEGAN'S PATRONS are left in the wake of nearby Yorkville Brewery. It seems NYC cannot have enough Irish bars. This bar is charming, and if you want to bring a bunch of friends you will own the place in no time. They have a pub menu and reasonably priced drinks.

## FireBird Café

365 W. 46th St. (8th & 9th Aves)
212-586-0244

THIS RUSSIAN BAR, which is adjacent to its restaurant, is one of the most lavish yet cozy hideaways in the

Theater District. One can get their own fire going with FireBird's own honey vodka while enjoying cabaret acts, harp and piano playing. The mature clientele may lead you to believe there is an underground KGB meeting going on, but be assured it is pure pleasure, not a conspiracy. FireBird is a great place for style, class, vodka dreams and caviar wishes.

## Firehouse

522 Columbus Ave. (85th & 86th Sts.)
212-787-FIRE

FOR ONCE, a theme bar/restaurant that isn't the slightest bit cheesy (or overrun with tourists). The Firehouse is decked with all things firehouse --- hard hats, ladder, hoses, extinguishers, and wheelbarrow --- gathered from Maine to Florida. The motif also applies to the menu, a robust and fairly priced collection of spicy numbers like boneless buffalo wings, burritos and the highest heap of nachos imaginable. To recapture the "inferno" flavor in the privacy of your own home, 125 hot sauces are available for purchase, along with cute Dalmatian tees. But, you'll certainly return to this casual neighborhood spot to hang with the eclectic, somewhat sporty crowd and hose yourself down with those happy hour two-for-one drinks.

## First

87 1st Ave. (5th & 6th Sts.)
212-674-3823

AT FIRST, this place seems overcrowded, but that somehow suits it. The dining area in the back is occupied by couples, while the small bar area in the front of the place is predominantly singles, hoping to meet the right person and graduate to the back. The drinks aren't cheap, but they are well made and served with care by a friendly and capable staff. The crowd is a combination of yuppies and aspiring yuppies who aren't always interesting but are approachable. The singles scene is helped by that sardine-can like seating.

## Fish Bar

237 E. 5th St. (2nd & 3rd Aves.)
212-475-4949

FISH BAR is pretty much the same as the Kastro Lounge it used to be a year ago, without the skeeviness of the bathroom. The fish theme is retained from the previous owner. A large aquatic mural with fish artifacts from Greece and patrons' own contributions adorn the wall. The bar has swimmingly tried to un-dive its act a bit. The neighborhood Kastro crowd has now resituated itself in their local living room with 20 martinis and 14 bottled beers on the wall. The owners are trying to think up some kind of fish-themed drink, but we're fine with those martinis, thanks.

## Fitzgerald's

336 3rd Ave. (25th & 26th Sts.)
212-532-3453

THIS TIGHTLY PACKED Irish pub has managed to fit a half dozen TV's around the bar. Low key and to the point, this local hangout draws a regular after-work crowd and some transients on the weekends. A normal beer or drink will run you about $4. Fitzgerald's is host to the New York Dart League who play Tuesday nights. The kitchen opens at 11a.m., and stays open late for your pub grub fix.

## Fitzpatrick's

1641 2nd Ave. (@ 85th St.)
212-988-7141

"WHERE THE PARADE ENDS, the party begins," says the manager to explain the popularity of Fitzpatrick's on St. Patty's Day. This family-owned bar's austere décor modestly belies its historical significance. Originally property of the Waldorf-Astoria, the beautifully kept bar itself is an antique of well over 100 years. The pub also enjoyed minor celebrity-status when it appeared in "Seinfeld" and a Woody Allen film. Whether unwinding after work, watching a game, trying to stump the bartender (impossible), or singing karaoke on Sunday, the always congenial mood makes quick friends of all who visit and inevitably return.

## Five Points

31 Great Jones St. (Bowery & Lafayette St.)
212-253-5700

HANGING TREACHEROUSLY over the precipice of pretentious yuppie-dom, Five Points provides such a warm-hearted atmosphere you almost tune out that person obsessively yammering on their cell phone. With its candelit ambiance, expensive American cuisine, and excellent wine list, Five Points is an ideal place to take a date for a low-key, romantic evening. It's also a crowded after-work spot, offering $1 oysters 5 p.m. to 7 p.m. Monday through Friday.

## Flamingo East

219 2nd Ave. (13th & 14th Sts.)
212-533-2860

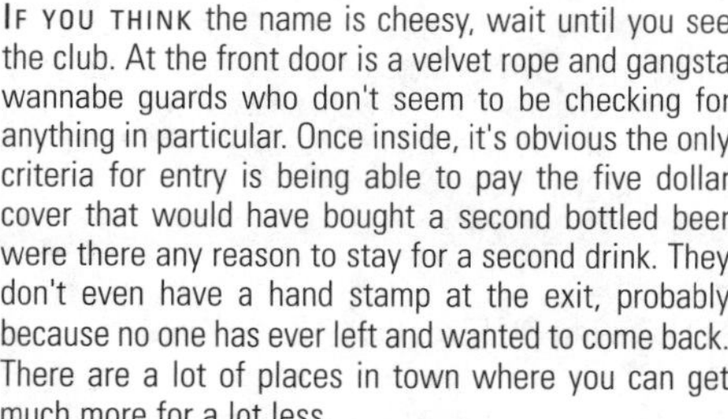

IF YOU THINK the name is cheesy, wait until you see the club. At the front door is a velvet rope and gangsta wannabe guards who don't seem to be checking for anything in particular. Once inside, it's obvious the only criteria for entry is being able to pay the five dollar cover that would have bought a second bottled beer were there any reason to stay for a second drink. They don't even have a hand stamp at the exit, probably because no one has ever left and wanted to come back. There are a lot of places in town where you can get much more for a lot less.

## Flannery's Bar

205 W. 14th St. (7th & 8th Aves.)
212-229-2122

LOOKING FOR a manly man bar? Cheap drinks, a rockin' juke-box and the occasional live band? Well, Flannery's is all that and a bag of missing teeth. Filled with construction workers, local drunks and some random stragglers, Flannery's is the type of place where Members Only jackets and Aqua Velva are all the rage. The place is filled with smoke and if you catch your breath for 2 seconds, you might start shakin' to the DJ's that spin on Saturday nights. But dancing, thanks to Rudy G, is not really allowed.

## Flight 151

151 8th Ave. (17th & 18th Sts.)
212-229-1868

AT FLIGHT 151, you can't beat the price or taste of the hamburgers and fries. Table service is great with friendly attentive waitresses. The jukebox is great and the crayons on the tables let the inner child in everyone shine. Happy hour is unbelievably cheap with $1 drafts and $1.75 well drinks. Overall an entertaining experience and one of the only straight bars in hood.

## Flight 1668

1668 3rd Ave. (93rd & 94th Sts.)
212-426-1416

DECKED OUT WITH airplane crap that no one cares about, the big draw here is the "Adult Romper Room" featuring a mix of creative drink specials and a mature sports-loving crowd. There are also video games and pool tables, and on nice days you can sit on their porch. The kitchen serves from 4p.m.- 4a.m. on weekdays and 11a.m.- 4a.m. on the weekends (with an all-you-can-eat brunch). There is also a 4 -7p.m. happy hour with half-price beers and $1.75 well drinks. If you ever visit during a rare moment with no specials, expect to shell out $3 - $6 for beers and drinks.

## Float

240 W. 52nd St. (Broadway & 8th Ave.)
212-581-0055

THERE'S NO DENYING that Float is the hottest club in Midtown, but that doesn't mean it's the hottest spot in the city. If your idea of fun calls for standing at a velvet rope holding pattern for seemingly hours, waiting to be stamped and accepted into the club, then this is your place. If you're lucky enough to be a celebrity, strike the previous sentence. Float caters to a young, well dressed, trust fund set. Girls in Gucci vie for attention from guys who spend too much time in front of the mirror. The interior is sexy, intimate and alive boasting a few VIP lounges and a sick dance floor where you'll see daddy's girls pump and grind to the progressive house music.

## Flor de Sol

l361 Greenwich St. (Hudson & Harrison Sts.)
212-334-6411

OF THE SEVERAL Spanish restaurants throughout Manhattan, only Flor de Sol has been creative enough to modernize itself into a sexy Gothic haunt. Decorated with black wrought iron chandeliers and tapestries hanging on the slaughtered-bull red walls, the large TriBeCa tapas spot lures groups of friends and those on dates into its flamenco infused depths. The sangria, tapas and sexy crowd please all five senses.

## Flute

205 W. 54th St. (Broadway & 7th Ave.)
212-265-5169

THIS IS A SUPER, sexy, chic place and a champagne lovers dream! Flute offers a serious champagne list that is served by the bottle or glass. The elegance and sophistication make for a wonderful romantic candlelit impress your date backdrop. The soft plush couches and tranquil effect will make you hate to leave! This is one of the most stylish places to have a drink in Midtown.

## 420 Bar

420 Amsterdam Ave. (@ 80th St.)
212-579-8450

ODDLY QUIET early in the evening, 420 is an ideal spot to start out if you forgot your Shecky's guide at work. Upstairs at 420 is sleek and chic with an older after-work crowd and after 11:30p.m. the younger set wanders downstairs to schmooze in the comfier sofa-and-dance-floor area and perhaps shoot a game of pool. Come to think of it, given the blithe, friendly crowds that populate the space after the witching hour, 420 is the ideal place to return after you've hit the more crowded, attitude-heavy frat bars common to this stretch of Amsterdam.

## 44 (@ The Royalton)

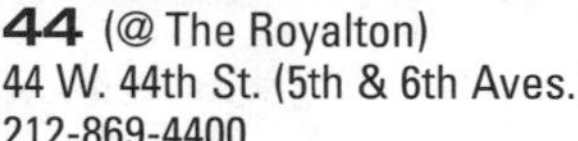

44 W. 44th St. (5th & 6th Aves.)
212-869-4400

ALL EYES are on you upon entering this swanky hotel bar- and they don't leave until you're settled into a seat and pose pretentiously enough to set your fellow drinkers at ease. Featuring oversized chairs, glass tables, white couches, flavored vodkas and astronomically priced drinks, 44 fuels your ego, warms your stomach and plunders your wallet. So, if you're dressed properly stop by, and enjoy being seen by some of NYC's hotties..

## Fressen

421 W. 13th St. (9th Ave. & Washington St.)
212-645-7775

FRESSEN is almost 2 years old now, and still going strong. It's probably the great food, romantic atmos-

phere and tasty, but expensive drinks that keep the trendy, attractive crowd coming back. Still a nice spot for a date, Fressen has the formula down to a T. However, if a cell phone rings, you'll probably see a full Chorus Line effect in the bar. Open lofty space, great lighting, good food and a great buzz. This spot should last long past the trendy lounge kick ends.

## Frying Pan

Pier 63, Chelsea Piers
(23rd St. & Westside Highway)
212-989-6363

CERTAINLY THE MOST UNIQUE venue in New York, even if it's only good for the few months of summer. The Frying Pan, docked off Pier 63, was a lightship off the Carolina coast from 1929 to 1964, until it sank. The boat's been raised, the barnacles scraped and for the last four years the creepy-cool vessel has served as the site for weekend tours, weddings, Sweet-16's, black tie events and regular open parties. Depending on the night and the promoter (call first to check), there may be a band and a bar on and/or off the boat. Bring your mates as the sunsets and raise your plastic cup to the land of Jersey across the river.

## Fubar

305 E. 50th St. (@ 2nd Ave.)
212-872-1325

IF YOU'RE A MALE over 30 looking to chat up your office temp after hours, this is definitely the place to do it. Once an appealing alternative for Turtle Bay professionals looking to escape the homogeny of the area's offerings, relative newcomer Fubar is now just another over-crowded, (though moderately priced) happy hour people mill. One ray of hope: if you arrive early with a large enough party, you can control the entire back room, where surprisingly decadent velvet curtains separate you from the melee, and low, lounge-worthy sofas await.

## Fujiyama Mama

467 Columbus Ave. (@ 83rd St.)
212-769-1144

ENJOY JAPANESE CUISINE in this black and futuristic space (like we thought 2000 would look in 1982) against a backdrop of '70s disco, '80s pop and '90s techno spun nightly. Mind you, this is not a bar with Japanese food, this is a Japanese restaurant with an in-house DJ. Fujiyama Mama is not for those on a tight budget, but the food is divine and the atmosphere is different. Though there is a bar and a couple of stools as you walk in, to truly groove here, you must eat a meal or at least sample off the sushi bar. Keep in mind: there is no smoking anywhere.

## Fun

130 Madison St. (under the Manhattan Bridge)
212-964-0303

THIS DOWNTOWN HOTSPOT surfaced on hipster radar last winter and has been making waves ever since. Strategically located far from the gentrifying hordes clambering through SoHo and the Village, Fun is tucked under the Manhattan Bridge behind a misleading awning that reads: 'white letters on a blue awning'. Once past the black-clad bouncers your senses are assaulted by a series of floor to ceiling projection screens that cast a frenetic glow on the crowd. Models and well-appointed dot-comers down beer at the bar or sip cocktails on the sofas covering the floor. Tuesday evening's larger-than-life Playstation games cover the walls. Admission is always free and drinks go from $5-10.

## g

223 W. 19th St. (7th & 8th Aves.)
212-929-1085

VOTED HOMO EXTRA'S 1999 Bar of Year, g deserves any kudos the press dollops on it. Even though there are long lines on the weekends, this ultra-swank gay bar in the heart of Chelsea has revolving DJ's, a living room area and a juice bar that will keep you coming back. You can expect long lines every day of the week-to enter the gay world of fashion and attitude. The service is quick and friendly and the bartenders serve up an excellent martini and delicious frozen cosmopolitans. Banquettes and huge ottomans offer comfortable lounging and a good place to check out some of Manhattan's hottest men. Everything about this bar is tight, upscale and chic.

## The Gaf

251 East 85th St. (2nd & 3rd Aves.)
212-472-8176
401 W. 48th St (9th & 10th Aves.)
212-262-2883

EVEN THOUGH THIS Irish pub may be one of the only bars in the city as small as your apartment, it has become a favorite watering-hole for many Upper East Siders. The rear wall of the bar is plastered with pictures of the regulars (who look plastered themselves), the bartenders are some of the friendliest in the city, the drinks are cheap and the jukebox is surprisingly good.

## Galapagos

70 N. 6th St. (Wythe & Kent Aves.) Brooklyn
718-782-5188

THIS LOUNGE BUILT inside the industrial corpse of a defunct mayonnaise factory marks the coolness trend permeating Brooklyn. High exposed white brick walls adorned with tons of candles, pipe networks in the ceilings and steel grating in the floors seem carefully placed and set the tone. Notice the black floor behind the guard- rail is actually breathing- it's a pool of water in the gutted shipping garage. This sexy lounge is a great place to have a relatively cheap drink and meet the young artistic crowd of Williamsburg. Daily events range from DJ's to a cabaret revue. Some fees do apply for the various features. The best time to come is during happy hour where the beer, and well drinks are cheap. A great space to come and see, but be sure to bring your registered Trendy-Cool Card, the customers may give off a whiff of pretension.

## Galaxy

15 Irving Pl. (@ 15th St.)
212-777-3631

FLY THE FRIENDLY skies at Galaxy. What was formerly a diner by the same name for 20 years, has for the last four years, been home to the starry nights of this unique bar/restaurant. All edges are curved, the ceiling is painted like the Milky Way and cosmic concoctions like the Big Bang Blackberry Lemonade ($7.50) keep the post-Irving Plaza crowd happy. The menu boasts "innovative ingredients for progressive palettes" like hemp tempura and tied Thai pizza. Far out.

## The Gamut Bistro Lounge

102 E. 25th St. (Lexington Ave. & Park Ave. So.)
212-598-4555

AFTER LITTLE MORE than a year, The Gamut has become a haven to locals and a treat to those that travel bridges and tunnels. The décor resembles its sister bar, Gaslight, with its heavy, burgundy velvet curtains and Victorian feel. And the staff is both competent and pretty, a true rarity. The only thing that's better than the staff's looks is the food. Chef Romchat Seneewong (known to regulars as Willy ) whips up an eclectic East meets West Asian-American menu mixed with old-fashioned bistro classics. Closed on Sundays.

## The Garage

99 7th Ave. So. (Barrow & Grove Sts.)
212-645-0600

THE GARAGE IS a large and airy restaurant with a circular bar in the center. Brick walls hang large bouquets of flowers and a wood burning fire on the second level create one of the tidiest, nicest looking garages you'll ever see. Every night there is a live jazz quartet entertaining the mixed crowd. There is never a cover charge, just a tip bowl passed amongst the crowd. There are 16 beers on tap and the menu offers a wide variety of seafood, steak and raw bar treats. Outside seating in the summer months provides a perfect people watching location.

## Gaslight Lounge

400 W. 14th (@ 9th Ave.)
212-807-8444

STRAP ON YOUR girdle and meander into the Victorian parlor at Gaslight. Instead of scones and tea, indulge in wine and beer on the wrought iron patio furniture while gazing at the view through the floor to ceiling French doors. The crowd is mixed (an interesting concept) and they have live music every night.

## The Gate

321 5th Ave. (@ 3rd St.) Brooklyn
718-768-4329

RIGHT NOW The Gate is popular for its extensive beer selection, but its catchall appearance hides the ominous truth. U2 is good but even they can be overplayed. Like Bono, The Gate is well on its way to becoming an old man, and soon no number of mirrored sunglasses will hid that fact. Brick work and candle lighting with a tasteful outside patio area give it appeal, but you can see the beginnings of a beer gut. It won't be long now before The Gate starts losing its shape, stops working out, has a little bit too much beer and goes to seed. Then the only people drinking here will look like Norm from Cheers no matter how plush the patio.

## GB Shaws

90 Fulton St. (Gold & William Sts.)
212-406-1380

POPULATED primarily by moderate sized groups of professionals from area businesses, GB Shaws could be one of the area's best Irish pubs to gather a gang from work. The most appealing aspect of this pub are the bartenders. They are a close knit group that leaves you feeling like you wandered into some surreal sitcom set.

## Gemini Lounge

221 2nd Ave. (13th & 14th Sts.)
212-254-5260

JUST LIKE A dual-personality Gemini, this lounge from the creators of Naked Lunch is not exactly as it seems. The velvet rope brigade towers over desperate patrons trying to prove their worthiness. This curbside pomp and circumstance is genuinely unnecessary considering the bar wore out its welcome eons ago. However, Gemini does seem to be making efforts to be a kinder, gentler place with a new Pan-Latino menu and a two-for-one happy hour Tuesday through Friday from 5 to 8p.m.

## Ginger

363 5th Ave. (5th & 6th Sts.) Brooklyn
No Phone

THE NEW KID of the block, this bar still has that squeaky clean, shrink-wrapped feel, as though all of its furniture was only recently let out of its plastic covering and the walls just got their last coat of paint. The bar is particularly popular amongst the gay and lesbian community in the neighborhood. On any given night you're liable to find couples and singles looking to be coupled, all generally in their early thirties, sipping on some beers and chatting. It all has a bit of that growing-up-and-feeling-good vibe, for people who regard themselves as to old to be part of the East Village scene, but too young to settle down and start talking mortgages.

## Ginger Man

11 E. 36th St. (5th & Madison Aves.)
212-532-3740

The Ginger Man doesn't cater to lovers of frozen cocktails, succulent wines or apertifs. Upon reaching the bar, patrons are assaulted by 66 taps, dispensing brews from around the world available in 13, 20 or 23 oz. glasses. But the selection doesn't end there. Another menu lists over 120 bottled beers including some that are rather obscure. Unfortunately, the crowded outer-bar may distract the focused drinker with wafting cigar smoke and roving bands of manly men. Fortunately there is a quieter room in the rear which allows one to relax and order a sandwich from the limited bar menu.

## Gin Mill

442 Amsterdam Ave. (81st & 82nd Sts.)
212-580-9080

In case $4 drinks seem too expensive, the Gin Mill offers any number of further bang-for-your-buck incentives. Weekday happy hours from 4 to 8p.m. knock 50 percent off your tab. Tuesdays are Ladies' Nights with $1 drafts and margaritas from 8 p.m. to close. And, a new tongue-in-cheek addition, White Trash Wednesdays, pairing a Pabst with a shot of Mad Dog for a mere $2. The outdoor seating is a draw in the warmer months, while the TV's play up to 11 (often collegiate) games at the same time to the sports-watching indoor crowd.

## The Girl from Ipanema

252 W. 14th St. (7th & 8th Aves.)
212-807-0150

Ahhhhhh. The name evokes visions of a hot, young Brazilian girl strolling on the beach in a tiny bikini sipping a fruity drink. Reality: This bar is filled with video

games, a pool table and bar girls dressed in Budweiser attire. Well, nothing is perfect. However the drinks are cheap, the location is central and the girls are cute. Maybe we were humming a Kid Rock version of the song.

## Globe

373 Park Ave. So. (26th & 27th Sts.)
212-545-8800

THIS MODERN AIRY eatery serves as a popular lunch and dinner spot for workers in this area, but doubles as a great pick-up spot during the after work drinking hours. Through the modern dining room that is filled with sleek high backed booths, you'll find a semi-circular bar with a few booths. Investment banker types gather here to down martinis with clients while trying to impress the overall good looking and well-groomed crowd of women.

## Gonzales y Gonzales

625 Broadway (Bleecker & Houston Sts.)
212-473-8787

A RESTAURANT WITH a bar the length of the entire place with stiff drinks to match, wonderful live Latin music and good looking people is truly all this place has to offer. From the outside you would think that this place belongs in Times Square with the large flashing neon sombrero that hangs less than daintily over the sidewalk. On the weekends this place has the nerve to act as if it's the hottest club on the New York City circuit with ID checks and a bouncer to boot. You can make this loud and large place fun if you take a group and participate in the salsa dancing in the back. Just do not go strictly for the wannabe chic Mexican food. Besides, the menu has not changed in over four years!

## Good Times

152 Metropolitan Ave. (@ Berry St.) Brooklyn
718-302-9161

NAME NOT WITH STANDING, there ain't no JJ Walker here. And it's anything but DY-NO-MITE! The walls are covered with old, stained, smoke-encrusted wallpaper garishly illuminated by several neon beer lights. There's a second room, but do no more than peek in; it's got that Blair Witch vibe. A full menu is available, however, unless you're sitting at the bar, you'll be standing, plate in hand. (Seats are generally few and far between.) Red devils and Long Island iced teas are the drinks of choice here. If that isn't cheesy enough for you, get a load of the Saturday night DJ. Ladies drink for 1/2 price every Thursday night, but Mama will be less than thrilled by anyone JJ could pick up at this joint.

## Good World Bar

3 Orchid St. (Canal & Division Sts.)
212-925-9975

HAVE YOU EVER strolled around Chinatown wondering where you can get a decent Swedish meatball? Probably not, but there are plenty of other reasons to visit this cozy spot. Bathed in low light and candles, a traditional Swedish menu is served at the bar and at the small tables around the front and back. Good World is a great place to meet friends and listen to a DJ spin a variety of music Wednesday through Saturday. The outdoor porch feels more like a prison gym with picnic tables, but it can be a sanctuary from what can become a crowded scene. The bar practically comes up to your chin and getting onto the bar stools can be a challenge, but it's worth your while to visit this cool spot before the word gets out.

## Googie's

237 Sullivan St. (@ 3rd St.)
212-673-0050

SINCE 1932, Googie's has provided the kind of neighborhood hang-out that drunks everywhere pray for: there's a pool table, decently priced bar food that's served until 3a.m. and friendly waiters and bartenders who will always lend an ear to your problems. There are also good songs on the jukebox, cheap beer, and most importantly, barrels of free peanuts you shell right onto the floor. While not exactly glamorous, it's dark, comfortable, and friendly; the kind of place that a college student might call home.

## Gotham Bar & Grill

12 E. 12th St. (5th Ave. & University Pl.)
212-620-4020

GOTHAM has cornered the market for the quintessential dining and drinking experience in the city. If you're

out to impress a date or a client look no further that this Greenwich Village institution. The bar scene will not have you hanging out all night, but the superb service and immense wine list provide the platform for an elegant pre-dinner drink. The high prices will leave those on an expense account undaunted, but for those of you pinching pennies, leave this experience for another time.

## Gotham Comedy Club

34 W. 22nd St. (5th & 6th Aves.)
212-367-9000

COMPARED TO SOME of the shit-hole comedy clubs that charge ridiculous covers and push drinks on you constantly, Gotham is a pleasant surprise. The interior isn't smoky or dingy and the bathrooms are clean and new. Depending on the night, you'll either see some unknown guys bombing so hard you'll want to throw a tomatoes at their heads or some talented up-and-comers trying out new material. Call ahead to find out what the evening has in store lest you get caught in a comedy conundrum.

## Grace

114 Franklin St. (W. Broadway & Church St.)
212-343-4200

THIS TRIBECA NEW COMER (opened in January 2000) is a sight for sore eyes in this Nobu part of town. A great space mixed with some excellent food has made this spot an instant hit among locals and frequent downtown visitors. The extremely large bar area and the friendly bartenders make this a great place to have a cosmopolitan or one their specialty martinis amongst a good looking but not too trendy crowd. The fact that the kitchen serves food until 4a.m. doesn't hurt the appeal. Definitely one the best places to hang in and a very welcome new comer.

## Gramercy Park Hotel

2 Lexington Ave. (@ 21st St.)
212-475-4320

WALKING INTO THIS hotel bar, you get the feeling there is something different in the air. Is it the seedy coziness? Are lovers meeting for a rendezvous? Was that a ghost of a literary old soul that just wisped by? Or it's all bullshit and it's just some locals and hotel guests sucking down bottled beer while munching on stale goldfish and pretzels in a 70-year-old bar. People come here for the nostalgic charm and classic Bette Midler and Marlene Dietrich songs the piano player belts out at 8 pm nightly. One can escape the bustle of every day life here, the pace is slower which is perfect to sit back, sip a Manhattan and enjoy the music.

## Gramercy Tavern

42 E. 20th St. (Park Ave. So. & Broadway)
212-477-0777

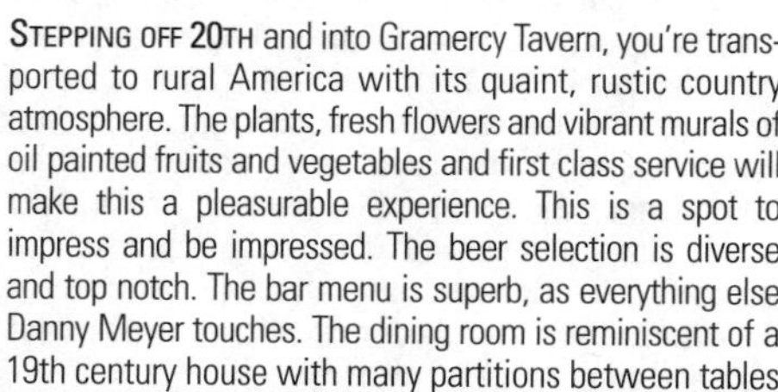
STEPPING OFF 20TH and into Gramercy Tavern, you're transported to rural America with its quaint, rustic country atmosphere. The plants, fresh flowers and vibrant murals of oil painted fruits and vegetables and first class service will make this a pleasurable experience. This is a spot to impress and be impressed. The beer selection is diverse and top notch. The bar menu is superb, as everything else Danny Meyer touches. The dining room is reminiscent of a 19th century house with many partitions between tables providing an intimate and elegant dining experience.

## Grand Bar (@ The Soho Grand Hotel)

310 W. Broadway (Canal & Broome Sts.)
212-965-3000

LOCATED ON THE second floor of the Soho Grand Hotel, the Grand Bar is a coo,l minimally decorated bar with huge mirrors and an awesome view of the streets. SoHo Grand attracts an upscale, young, hip and sometimes-famous clientele. There is no doorman standing behind a velvet rope making it difficult to get in, but it's always crowded, so expect to wait a while for your drink. Service from the well-groomed wait staff is generally pleasant, just hurried. Think of this hotel bar as a good spot to start out an evening.

## Grange Hall

50 Commerce St. (@ Barrow St.)
212-924-5246

IN THE RESTORED digs of the old Blue Mill Tavern, Grange Hall is Americana at its best. Vintage jazz, original wooden booths from 1941, antique lighting fixtures and a large mural commissioned in the WPA-style set the relaxed yet sophisticated tone. While you'd be in good company coming just for the 11 different martinis ($5 to $7.50), it would a be a shame to miss the comfort food that has kept this place on the map for eight years.

## Grassroots Tavern

20 St. Mark's Pl. (2nd & 3rd Aves.)
212-475-9443

GRASSROOTS IS A time capsule that serves liquor. It's not pretty, but the drinks are pretty cheap, the dartboard is usually available and the people, though often loud and drunk, are fairly harmless. Don't expect a smile from the bartender who is obliged to serve you but not under any obligation to be your friend. The wooden, rugged interior has an almost old western feel to it, befitting the general sense of lawlessness that marks this historic street. Difficult to tell whether this place is opposed to the times or indifferent to them, but it's still a great venue for slummin'.

## Great Hall Balcony

(@ The Metropolitan Museum of Art)
1000 5th Ave. (@ 81st St.)
212-535-7710

AMAZING VIEWS and well-dressed clientele make up for the limited hours. Sitting upon the rooftop garden of the Met, you suddenly understand why many New Yorkers are convinced that this, their home, is the center of the universe. Sipping wine and gazing out into Central Park it is easy to ponder the centuries of artwork beneath your feet. The overall effect causes you to reach a level of sublime happiness, a joie de vivre that can only come from the heady combination of culture and activity that personify New York. The view alone is worth it, but the trip through the artwork caps it. There could not possibly be a more romantic, beautiful spot to spend time.

## Great Jones Café

54 Great Jones St. (Lafayette St. & Bowery)
212-674-9304

WITH A VERY loyal local following, this tiny neighborhood bar/restaurant exudes more character than most places its size. Though friendly, the regulars don't have much use for newcomers. Management seems to share that sentiment, as evidenced by the fact they have never advertised in their 17 years. The excellent food and imaginative drinks are Creole/Cajun-influenced, but all New York when it comes to modest ingenuity. (Try the in-house pickled vodka or the spicy ginger ale and rum mixed "shaggy.") Also, be on your best behavior; this is a long-time neighborhood staple and you're a guest.

## Great Lakes

284 5th Ave. (@ 1st St.) Brooklyn
718-499-3710

DON'T MIND THE hip indie kids staring at you from under their furrowed brows. This is a great little neighborhood bar which borrows its fashion sense from Williamsburg and down home feel from Long Island. The decor flirts with an aquatic theme, and combined with the cavernous architecture and low lighting, gives the impression that you may have stumbled into a converted boat house. What people really come here for on any given night of the week is not the reasonably priced drinks, nor the friendly bar staff, it's the juke-box. The music selection is an out of this world indie rockers dream come true.

## Greatest Bar On Earth

1 World Trade Center, 107th Floor (@ Church St.)
212-524-7011

ALL HYPER-EXAGGERATIVE SUPERLATIVES aside, this airport lounge perched atop the city is a necessary visit just once. A giddy nausea pervades the massive elevators that shuttle roomfuls of whomevers from wherever to the top of the world. Once your ears are clear, you'll be sipping cosmos with the Euros. While overlooking Brooklyn and beyond sample the eclectic menu, be serenaded by a bad lounge singer or groove to the odd assortment of music being spun by a DJ that tries to please all tastes.

## Greenwich Café

75 Greenwich Ave. (@ 7th Ave. So.)
212-255-5450

WITH THE VILLAGE being the bastion of style and trends, there is a lot pressure on bars to keep up. However, some places just try too hard. Aside from its ostentatiously displayed modern art, antique lamps and lighting so dim you can hardly see your drinks, it's a nice place to go with a group of friends since they do have some very comfortable couches and are open 24 hours a day.

## Groove

125 MacDougal St. (@ 3rd St.)
212-254-9393

ALTHOUGH THE LIVE music tends to be pretty good at Groove, the owners don't seem to understand you don't need a Madison Square Garden sound system in an 800 sq. feet room. Beware, if you're one of the suckers coerced by the thugs doing promotions to come inside for a $5.50 beer, keep in mind you'll feel as if you have been trapped in a jet engine. Combine that with an obnoxious bar staff who don't know the meaning of "I don't want to pay for another shot" and you'll just wanna groove on by.

## Guastavino's

409 E. 59th St. (@ 1st Ave.)
212-980-2455

GUASTAVINO'S HAS CREATED the epitome of chic elegance with its cathedral ceilings, huge avant-garde light fixture and white marble floors. Queens cocktails and caipairinhas are considered the house specialties. This oversized palace caters to an affluent crowd here to eat on the brasserie-style first floor or in the more exclusive upstairs Club.

## Guernica

25 Ave. B (2nd & 3rd Sts.)
212-674-0984

THE SPACE THAT was once occupied by the legendary after hours club, Save the Robots, is now home to Guernica. This is one of the best bets in the East Village for a hipster on a date and a budget. The reasonably priced restaurant occupies the main floor with an eclectic menu and an affordable wine selection, while the lower level is a slick cool lounge where you'll find a crowd mostly in their mid-twenties grooving to a cool DJ and hanging with the hot bartenders. A great spot that satisfies any nightlife desire.

## Halcyon (@ The RIHGA Royal Hotel)
151 W. 54th St. (6th & 7th Aves.)
212-468-8888

AFFLUENT AMBIENCE ABOUNDS at Halcyon in the RIHGA Royal Hotel. The immaculately detailed space with its perfect curtains, plush carpeting, porcelain bar and pricey cocktails caters to the well-heeled set. But if you can't afford to dine at this highly praised restaurant, the lounge menu offers more affordable fare from $15 to $25.

## The Half King
505 W. 23rd St. (10th & 11th Aves.)
212-462-4300

JUST BECAUSE you can write a great book doesn't mean you can run a good bar. But in this case, it does. Sebastian Junger of The Perfect Storm fame is the latest celeb to try his hooks at the NYC nightlife scene. The bar is rustic, reasonably priced and as close to a pure bar as we've seen it the past few years. A quiet, cozy outdoor space that closes at midnight and a large tavern like dining room bucks the trend of celeb lounges that have invaded the city over the past years. A local, laid back crowd and a friendly bar staff only add to its appeal. A refreshing new comer to the scene.

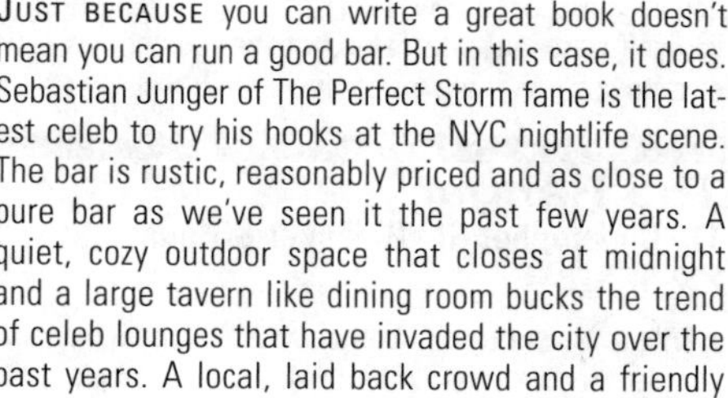

## Hallo Berlin
402 W. 51st St. (9th & 10th Aves.)
212-541-6248
626 10th Ave. (@ 44th St.)
212-977-1944

IF IT WERE any cheaper they'd be giving it away. This tiny Hell's Kitchen bier garten has an affordable menu of hearty German staples like Wiener Schnitzel and pommes frites, with good beer and wine to wash it down. There is no bar to speak of but feel free to down a few at the handful of tables inside or one of the sidewalk tables out front. Open eight years, they've expanded to several other larger spaces, including one on 44th St. and 10th Ave. that features a large full bar, pool tables, private rooms and expanded menu. But for our money, the off the-main street original location is the real find. Happy hour runs from 5p.m.-7p.m.

## Halo

49 Grove St. (@ Bleecker St.)
212-243-8885

FORMERLY KNOWN AS The Oaks, (an old Judy Garland haunt) this spot has been occupied for over forty years. This bar/lounge/restaurant serves decent food to a mixed twenty to fortysomething crowd who love drinking, people watching and listening to the DJ spin hip-hop, house, funk and lounge music. Drinks are expensive at $10 a pop, but the pour is heavy. As you walk down the stairs into Halo's cave-like interior you suddenly feel removed from the hustle and bustle of the city. The crowd is upscale, attractive and a tad snotty. Pull the Fendi and Gucci from your closet, put your cell phone away, flatter the doormen and maybe you'll be one of the chosen few. Don't be surprised if you find yourself partying with celebs of the moment as Halo cast its spell on the likes of Gwyneth, Ben and Leo.

## The Hangar

115 Christopher St. (Bleecker & Hudson Sts.)
212-627-2044

A WEST VILLAGE neighborhood staple with a gay pool league, this bar is packed from 4p.m. every night of the week with locals and tourists alike. This is a serious pick-up spot with lots of action around the pool tables and very interesting videos playing overhead. The space is designed to look like an airplane hanger with a central location where DJ's spin and go-go boys boogie to a wide variety of music. It's no wonder that this bar is the epicenter of gay pride.

## Hanratty's

1410 Madison Ave. (97th & 98th Sts.)
212-369-3420

SIMPLY PUT, if you enjoy cold service and managers that really don't want you around, Hanratty's is definitely for you. This spacious restaurant/bar doesn't seem to attract many clients and also has a very uncomfortable vibe of being exclusive and restricted. The manager himself stated, "I don't want people coming here." Behavior like this does cause one to wonder. Lunch and dinners range from $8-$11 on the average. Beers, wines and cocktails run about $5.

## Hard Rock Café

221 W. 57th St. (7th Ave. & Broadway)
212-459-9320

NEED YOU READ? Hard Rock, in case you've been encased in ice a la Austin Powers for decades, is that chain of music-themed restaurant/bars out to conquer every major city in the world. New York, Paris, L.A., it's all the same. Yet still the tourists come in droves to add to their T-shirts collections, pay too much for a hamburger, and decipher Jim Morrison's poetic scrawl. Surrounding the wooden space with green and white checked tablecloths and green light fixtures that loom like vultures, are those requisite rock "artifacts."

## Harley Davidson Café

1370 6th Ave. (@ 56th St.)
212-245-6000

THIS MIDTOWN THEME eatery attracts between three and thirty thousand tourists daily. Looking for that true New York City experience they flock here like a fat men going to a candy bar sale. There is no good reason to go to this bar, even if you're a tourist, but if you somehow wind up in here, make the best of it by ordering a flat tracker, it'll have you buzzed for hours.

## Harry Cipriani (@Sherry Netherland)

781 5th Ave. (59th & 60th Sts.)
212-753-5566

PLAYING HOST TO the snooty Euro crowd and older businessmen regulars, this place needs to get over itself. Overpriced drinks and a stale atmosphere may make some people feel important, but for the most part the décor and the service leave a whole lot to be desired. If your idea of a good time is hanging out and watching has-beens who think it's cool to spend 2 billion dollars on a gin and tonic.

## Harry's at Hanover Square

1 Hanover Sq. (Pearl & Stone Sts.)
212-425-3412

THIS BEAUTIFUL AND ancient medieval-style restaurant has been around for 30 years Antique pictures of pirates and century-old photos of New York lend this roomy and airy establishment a sense of history. Harry's is a wee pricey though; beers and wines start at $6, and their prime sirloin steak does $27 damage to the pocketbook. Lots of Financial District bigwigs and socialites frequent this spot.

## Headlines

1678 1st Ave. (87th & 88th Sts.)
212-426-6309

"UPPER EAST SIDE bar devoured by mediocrity" is the only headline this neighborhood sports joint will be producing. The big screen TV is pretty nice, the beers on tap are okay, the ambiance is non-existent, and the décor isn't anything you haven't seen before. If you're coming here, come with a bunch of friends, since it's quite possible that they'll be the only other people there. Self-entertaining activities to do while you're brainstorming of other places to go are playing pool in the back or throwing darts.

## Heartland Brewery

35 Union Square West (16th & 17th Sts.)
212-645-3400
1285 6th Ave. (@ 51st St.)
212-582-8244

AN OVERWHELMING SEA of people, house-brewed beers and seriously tasty, food at reasonable prices make Heartland Brewery one of the best casual watering holes in Gotham City. Down-to-earth staff are quick to pour a pint or mix a cocktail and chat about the game on the bar's two television sets. Sit outside, upstairs or on the main level, but don't forget your earplugs; Heartland is known for its boisterous atmosphere.

## Helena's

432 Lafayette St. (@ Astor Pl.)
212-677-5151

WEDNESDAY NIGHT FLAMENCO, Miro-esque murals, a year-round garden, a housecat named Gazpacho, colorful cocktails like the Helenita margarita with a twist of blood orange $6) and the best tapas in NYC, make Helena's a virtual trip to Spain without the jet lag. Now that Helena, a Barcelona native, has met her goal of recreating the "complete Spanish experience," she wants to start a chain.

## Hell

59 Gansevoort St. (Greenwich & Washington)
212-727-1666

STRAIGHT, GAY, BI, TRI? It doesn't matter. Everybody goes to Hell eventually. The red velvet curtains, red lighting and quasi-evil drinks make for a perfect setting to try and get down and dirty with the original sin. Serving up drinks like the Lucifer martini, Hell feels like a playground of drunken debauchery. This is a great location for this kind of place, considering some people feel that the meatpacking district smells like the pit of Hell.

## Henrietta Hudson

438 Hudson St. (Morton & Barrow Sts.)
212-924-3347

IF YOU'RE SEARCHING for an exciting atmosphere with reasonable drinking prices along side beautiful lesbians, search no more! This is a spot that is ever so mellow with just the right amount of lighting to set a tranquil mood. Women of every nationality can bug out on a friendly level while enjoying pool in the backroom. Off the hook parties with DJ's and dancing.are their signature draw.

## Hi-Life

1340 1st Ave. (@ 72nd St.)
212-249-3600

MORE OF A bring-your-mate than find-a-date, Hi-life is a cool, intimate '60s style martini lounge, surprisingly located on the Upper-East Side. The leather-upholstered booths make couples feel like they are steaming up the windows of an old Chevy parked at Make-Out Point. If your night didn't turn out like you expected, come to this old Manhattan standby for a killer martini and things will instantly get better.

## The Hog Pit

22 9th Ave. (@ 13th St.)
212-604-0092

WELCOME TO REAL Southern cooking and Southern fried spirit to go with it. Swill some beer and chow on their kick-ass ribs. Never mind the rough truckers who frequent the bar or the six stuffed hog's heads staring down at you in condemnation as you gnaw on one of their cousins. The Hog Pit is an agreeable down home sort of a place to hang out, play a game of pool and pretend for a second that you're not in New York anymore.

## Hogs & Heifers

859 Washington St. (@ 13th St.)
212-929-0655

ONE OF THE LAST havens where suits drink along side burly bikers and the bartenders are rowdier than the patrons. Clad in Texas style bikini tops and armed with bullhorns, these vixens are never short on wit or insults. Rub them the wrong-way, and you'll be out the door quicker than a shot of JD down the gullet of a red-neck on a Friday night. Hogs and Heifers is famous for its bra-laden walls, amateur stripteases on the bar and boasts celebrity visits from Julia Roberts and Drew Barrymore. But stay away from the pool table unless you're Paul Newman or Tom Cruise.

## Hogs & Heifers

1843 1st Ave. (95th & 96th Sts.)
212-722-8635

HOGS & HEIFERS in the trendy Meat-Packing district has become an unfortunate tourist trap, but this makes their uptown branch filled with locals a welcome site. The same elements that made Hogs & Heifers such a success are still present: bikini-topped bar maids shouting at you through a bull horn, bar top dancing, bras on display donated by daring inebriated patrons and, of course, the pool table. This version has the added pleasure of loud, live rock and blues. The layer of bras behind the bar is thin, but growing. Donate one tonite! Keep an eye on this place as Manhattanites begin to move further North into New Harlem.

## Holiday Lounge

75 St. Mark's Pl. (1st & 2nd Aves.)
212-777-9637

HOME OF THE cheapest drinks around, The Holiday Lounge has been around for as long as its drunken bartender has been hitting the bottle. Be prepared to wait a while for drinks; this family owned bar is well know for its perpetually drunken, elderly bartender who will stumble, sing and eventually forget what you ordered. This dive sports a jukebox, lots of tables and chairs and a decent mix of locals, NYU kids and old school St. Mark's drinkers. With $2.50 beers and $3 drinks, your brain will be on holiday after a night at the Holiday.

## Holland Bar

532 9th Ave. (39th & 40th Sts.)
212-502-4609

ESTABLISHED IN **1947**, this place is not for the faint of heart. It's a true dive catering to your starting at noon drunks to your toothless Port Authority lifers. This tiny bar is decorated with Christmas lights, posters of Marilyn Monroe and wallpapered with old pictures and ancient newspaper articles. A jukebox spits out an eclectic old school mix from The Doors to Tony Bennett and Billie Holiday. There is a mega-touch video game that can keep you entertained once the old toothless gentleman sitting next to you stops rambling on about the names of all his dead cats!

## Hooters

211 W. 56th St. (Broadway & 7th Ave.)
212-581-5656

IF YOU HAVE A BOOB and wing fetish, this is the place for you. Hooters is almost like a G rated strip club. The NYC branch of this national chain attracts ogling men and women who pretend they don't care about the heaving bosoms that bounce around dressed as waitresses. Bring in your softball team for a night of drinking and hardball. Every guy's wet dream can be found here: beer, girls, wings, and TV!

## Houston's

378 Park Ave. So. (26th & 27th Sts.)
212-689-1090
153 E. 53rd St. (@ 3rd Ave.)
212-888-3828

PERHAPS BECAUSE OF the location, the new Houston's in Gramercy isn't quite as irritating as it's Midtown cousin. However, the bar area is just as swamped with just as many yuppies on the prowl. The newest member of this upscale TGIF's is certainly swankier, but the corporate attitude still prevails. Good luck getting the bartender's attention right away, let alone getting a seat at the bar. If you do manage to make the cut, expect to drown in an intense sea of single professionals all laying down $10 for their 5oz. martinis. Stick to beer, it comes in a frozen mug. The dining room stays open till 11p.m. and serves consistently good food. Feel free to order munchies or even a full meal at the bar. You'll be able to pick out the girls who haven't scored by the number of empty cheese and artichoke plates lined up on the counter.

## Howard Johnson's

1551 Broadway (@ 46th St.)
212-354-1445

THE HOJO's you know and love/hate, even in midtown Manhattan. This frozen-in-time establishment employs the necessary brownish-orange color scheme, plain wood and bright lights. If ice cream sundaes don't suit you, the 16-ounce $6.25 cocktails include such dubious names as sunrise sunset, kiss of passion, Miami ice, and what a banana blast. There are 14 bottled beers to choose from as well as a surprisingly decent wine selection. As if anyone would come here for wine.

## H2K

219 9th Ave. (@ 23rd St.)
212-727-2616

PART LOUNGE, PART BAR, and wholly cool. This wonderful space in Chelsea is everything you want in a bar and a bag of chips. A large, surprisingly smoke-free space, killer drinks, great bar food and a friendly staff makes this one of our favorite bars in Manhattan. Keep an eye out for the rotating artwork for a nice change of scenery. The crowd ranges from actors to bankers and a good male/female ratio keeps everyone on their toes No attitude, no clipboard mafia and great drinks are still the formula for a great bar.

## Hudson Bar & Books

636 Hudson St. (@ Jane St.)
212-229-2642

WALKING INTO Hudson Bar & Books, you are transported into an English Manor, complete with butler and Rolls Royce. You can enjoy the Rolls Royce of cognac for a mere $125 by ordering a glass of Louis XIV. The West Village location is a bit more dress down and doesn't require a jacket. Enjoy a cigar from the well-stocked humidor and a glass of wine or port on one of comfortable couches. This English inspired bar attracts an older crowd of writers (somewhat successful ones), film industry types, locals and the work crowd sporting the corporate card.

## Hunter's American Bar & Grill

1387 3rd Ave. (78th & 79th Sts.)
212-734-6008

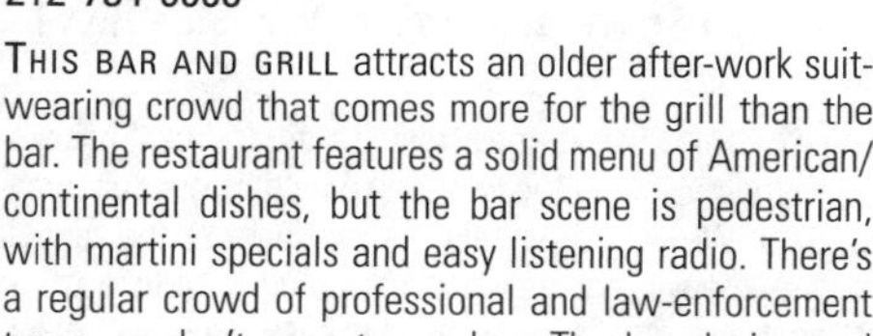

THIS BAR AND GRILL attracts an older after-work suit-wearing crowd that comes more for the grill than the bar. The restaurant features a solid menu of American/continental dishes, but the bar scene is pedestrian, with martini specials and easy listening radio. There's a regular crowd of professional and law-enforcement types, so don't expect a ruckus. The bar design and lighting leaves little to the imagination, but the comfortable dining room has better atmosphere. Expect to be surrounded by the bar staff drinking and playing cribbage on their night off.

## Hush

17 W. 19th St. (5th & 6th Aves.)
212-989-HUSH

THIS VERY HIP CLUB is decorated quite fiercely with disco globes hanging over the dance floor and conversation pits with seating and tables. A hot and hectic groove pulses through the ultra-trendy atmosphere where people dance and dine on decent food. Monday night is gay night, but other than that there is very straight crowd here scoping each other out.

## i

277 Church St. (Franklin & White Sts.)
212-625-0505

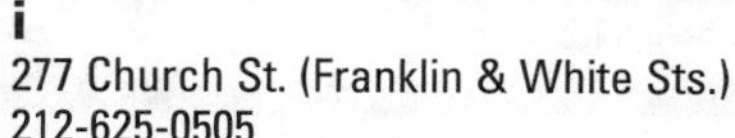

I, SHORT FOR ILENE, the owner, isn't short on anything else. The upstairs is quaint and stylish, and serves first class food. The downstairs has got to be the sexiest lounge in New York City. Marble floors, internally-lit tables and specialty drinks are just a few of the perks.

A laid-back, culturally diverse crowd gives off a warm vibe, either sitting on the homemade wooden stump stools or chilling against the plush high-backed benches. The downstairs holds 125 people easily and, with DJ's spinning every night, well, you can just imagine what might happen next. If you like exotic high-class drinks, try the molten lava. Better still, indulge in the chocolate martin. (Godiva Liquor and secret ingredients poured into an ice-cold, chocolate coated glass.) A TriBeCa staple for more than 3 years, I has pioneered south of Canal, and paved the way for what is becoming NYC's new hip strip.

## Ice Bar

528 Canal St. (Washington & West Side Hwy.)
212-226-2602

GREAT LOOKING AND refreshingly attitude-free, Shecky's predicted this out of the way club would be one to watch in 2000. We're still waiting. Its proximity to the tunnel means a heavy Jersey constituency though, to their credit, most river-crossers are here because they don't want to be in Jersey either. The white interior and cool blue lights make for a calm setting, but despite the name, the people at the Ice Bar are anything but cold. This place is still finding its niche, but if you need a new playground, there's a nice spot waiting on the lower west side.

## Ideya

349 W. Broadway (Broome & Grand Sts.)
212-625-1441

THIS TWO-YEAR-OLD SoHo restaurant and bar serves Latino food and drink to a good-looking-yet-unpretentious crowd. Caribbean appetizers and an all-around island feel make this a great place to sit and relax. The walls have colorful murals of beaches and carnivals, while the tables and bar are classically candle lit. The super friendly staff serves up potent tropical drinks, and most people come for the good bar vibe rather than the food (although it's superb).

## Idlewild

145 E. Houston St. (1st & 2nd Aves.)
212-447-5005

IDLEWILD LOOKS LIKE the inside of an airplane with the feel of a Stanley Kubrick film, intriguing and disarming.

Once you walk down the eerie jetway to the bar, you will notice the airliner seats along the wall. There are drink menus designed to look like seatback emergency landing instructions and bathrooms designed just like the ones on a plane. Man, you know how much fun they can be. The crowd is as diverse as the passengers in coach along with a few members of first class scattered about the cabin. Grooveilicious DJ's spin trippy music that flies through the air like the Concorde. This bar is a unique place to take friends from out of town or to check out for yourself. Bottom line, Idlewild is good for a layover or as a final destination.

## Iggy's

132 Ludlow St. (Rivington & Stanton Sts.)
212-529-2731

LADIES AND GENTLEMEN, children of all ages, cloned in the lackluster originality of Iggy's Kick Ass Bar on the Upper East Side is Iggy's Keltic Lounge!!! In the heart of the bargain district, on a street with many other neighborhood watering holes, this brand new bar doesn't try hard to stick out. It's an Irish pub with two satellite TV's and traditional music once a week. (You don't say!) This is a good place to catch up with a friend over drinks or enjoy a relaxing pint in a non-threatening environment. Whoever performed this experiment should stick to sheep.

## Iggy's Kick Ass Bar

1452 2nd Ave. (@ 76th St.)
212-327-3043

IF YOU WANT to play pool and stick to everything you touch, Iggy's is the place for you. Men in acid-washed jeans play air guitar to Def Leppard as their little ladies dance seductively a-top the bar. The pool table is cool, except for the mystery stain in the middle. Basically, Iggys is a typical dive bar with typical dive bar beer and typical dive bar ambiance. Avoid the bathrooms at all costs.

## Iguana

240 W. 54th St. (Broadway & 8th Ave.)
212-765-5454

FROMAGE, QUESO, KAESE, and formaggio- no matter how you say it you can find any kind here. You can have an after work drink or stay for the night in this all encompassing bar, club, and restaurant scene. The DJ comes out on Thursday, Friday and Saturday, so after you try every one of their 35 different tequilas maybe you can shake the white man's disease. If you want to get your groove on come in and chow on some Tex-Mex and suck down an Iguanarita.

## Il Bagatto

192 E. 2nd St. (Aves. A & B)
212-228-0977

STILL GOING STRONG, Il Bagatto is dishing out expensive, but delicious, Italian cuisine to neighborhood newcomers. The small, swanky basement bar serves up expensive drinks while you wait for your table. But this is really no place to hang out and imbibe. If you don't have a reservation, get one, for the food is superb. If you're just looking for a cocktail, leave your eating disorder elsewhere.

## Il Covo dell'Est

210 Ave. A (@ 13th St.)
212-253-0777

WINE RULES at this Italian Bar and Restaurant. They have, "a taste for every taste bud and a price range for any pocket, from $20 to $300 a bottle." The delicate décor and candlelit tables are accentuated by the soft, romantic, native Italian music filtering through the room. The live jazz on Thursdays and brunch on Saturdays and Sundays are drawing in more and more people. This place is brand new and word is spreading. If you want a good, clean, classy Italian restaurant, The Cove of the East (Village) is sure to please.

## Il Porto

11 Fulton St. (@ South St.)
212-791-2181

BUSY, BUSY, BUSY is this restaurant on Fulton Street serving pastas, pizzas and seafood. Sandwiches include lobster rolls, grilled chicken and cheeseburgers, all ranging from $10-$21. This restaurant is decorated green wood patio furniture and has a patio bar. Try their specilaty drink fantasia, you'll need it to get past the middle of the road.

## Isla

39 Downing St. (Bedford & Varick Sts.)
212-352-2822

THIS BAR/RESTAURANT doesn't have a sign but it sure doesn't need one. On a sleepy, West Village street, the red brick exterior has been replaced by ocean blue siding giving it the look of a misplaced indoor swimming pool. Inside, the smallish bar is lined with fashionistas lounging on sleek, white banquettes and orange, plastic scoop chairs. It's "Wallpaper: The Bar." But it's oddly cozy after downing a few generous cocktails. Be sure to go on the early side of the evening, as the place runs more on a restaurant schedule and closes shortly after 1a.m.

## I Trulli

122 E. 27th St. (Park & Lexington Aves.)
212-481-7372

LOCATED NEXT DOOR to a beautiful Apulian dining room is a little wine bar for serious oenophiles. The pastoral mural on the back wall provides the backdrop for a serene drinking experience. An extensive list of Italian wines by the glass and are also available as flights. Service is stuffy but helpful and attentive. A menu of cheeses, olives and meats are served at the bar. I Trulli is a good pit-stop for a strong espresso, a nightcap or some dessert before heading home from a night out.

## Il Violino Rosso

1803 2nd Ave. (@ 93rd St.)
212-426-8350

THIS CONTEMPORARY ITALIAN American restaurant has to house the best lounge bar this side of the park in a hood once populated with nothing more than Irish pubs. The words chic and cosmopolitan do not even begin to describe the décor of this laid-back and friendly venue. Because of a caring manager that caters to people from all walks of life, you can come in and enjoy the company of a very diverse clientele. A well-priced menu means you can frequently partake of Il Violino Rosso's delectable cuisine. The service is also, by the way, quite excellent.

## The Independent

179 W. Broadway (Leonard & Worth Sts.)
212-219-2010

WHAT THEY WERE going for in this TriBeCa gathering place was a modern take on the historic 1920's steak house. They nailed it with its striking, historically correct décor and sleek color scheme. A perfect place to split a bottle of wine from the selection of over 150, or sip an perfectly prepared cocktail. Upstairs, you can enjoy the open, airy dining room with a view of West Broadway. One might think of this spot as a starting point, but you might get caught up in the friendly vibe until closing time.

## Indigo Bar

487 Amsterdam Ave. (83rd & 84th Sts.)
212-362-0373

KHAKI ALERT, KHAKI ALERT! For a minute you will have an Upper East Side flash back but, relax, the place redeems itself with a DJ, good drinks and live jazz bands during the week. It gives the feeling of a neighborhood hang out where everyone knows each other and is willing to accept some outsiders. There is dancing and a lounge area in the back so take some friends and make new ones, Indigo will certainly not make you blue.

## International Bar

120 1/2 1st Ave. (St. Marks Pl. & 7th Sts.)
212-777-9244

INTERNATIONAL BARTENDERS are the people's people. They'll keep you entertained for hours just by shooting the breeze and the dirt cheap beer won't exactly have you heading to the door. Equipped with a kick-ass jukebox, rock away the day or night with the neighborhood crowd. But be quiet! The surrounding neighbors won't hold back in expressing their feelings about rowdy drunks. You just might get hit with a shoe.

## 'ino

21 Bedford St. (6th Ave. & Downing St.)
212-989-5769

NESTLED ON ONE of the prettiest blocks in the West Village 'ino is sure to please, be it for a night of drinking great wine, or a quick meal and half-bottle with

a friend. 'ino also offers delicious bruschetta and paninis for a quick app. The space is dark and cozy, looking as if it had been a wine cellar in a previous life. The wines are priced remarkably well (glasses range from $6-8.50), considering that $12 mojitos rule these parts.

## Iona

180 Grand St. (Bedford Ave. & Driggs St.)
718-384-5008 (Brooklyn)

IONA HAS MANAGED to merge the cozy, liquor driven Irish pub, with the hip, DJ oriented American bar/club. The inside of the bar is wooded and spacious but feels small and intimate. In back is a landscaped, candlelit patio. The combination of darkness and good liquor threatens to make this a lawyer bar, so watch your step. One other drawback is that Iona sits on the outside cusp of new Williamsburg, a stone's throw from rough ol' Williamsburg. On some nights, it may feel like you're spending an evening in Dublin, then exiting into Belfast.

## Iridium Jazz Club

48 W. 63rd St. (Broadway & Columbus Ave.)
212-582-2121

BELOW MERLOT LIES the popular, if pricey, Iridium Jazz Club. Borrowing the same loopy Dr. Seussian décor from upstairs, the club seats up to 160 for its nightly performances. The biggest and most expensive of shows is the legendary Les Paul on Mondays ($25 and a $15 drink minimum). Iridium is a unique jazz venue known for its serious wine fixation; the international list includes 600 bottles, 20 by the glass. The menu also offers food paired with various wine flights.

## Irish Pub

837 7th Ave. (@ 54th St.)
212-664-9364

THIS PLACE IS for serious drinking. Other pubs dick around with Irish surnames and Catholic names but they don't beat around the bush: the name says it all. It's full of Irish ex-pats, Irish tourists and earnest drinkers from all parts of the world. It stays open long after its theater district counterparts have closed, and open bright and early at 8a.m. Its décor consists of

Mets memorabilia and Irish-pride placards. The dim lighting does not create any mystique about what you're doing; there's no need to feel out of place getting smashed at 2a.m. on a Tuesday, or any night of the week for that matter, in this Irish Pub.

## Irish Treasury

325 5th Ave. (32nd & 33rd Sts.)
212-685-5049

If you're looking for the only crazy, non-drinking, record spinning, Irish bartender, you are set. Don't be confused by the lanterns, old Irish memorabilia and hard wood floors with the Will Smith's Get-Jiggy-With-It music. The vibrant crowds come for the beer and the hip-hop. It's all-good. If you can take the old with the new and the fact this bar is located in the midst of tourist central (in the shadow of the Empire State Building), you will have a fab time.

## Ivy Night Club

2130 Broadway (@ 75th St.)
212-579-1000

What? Say it isn't so; the Upper West Side has another star on top of the tree? Yes, it's true and this place is Ivy! Prepare for a sweat your hair out, limp home with broken heels good time. This spread offers five jammed packed rooms, a nice crowd, a DJ that is off the hook and the bar, fabulous! However, do not be fashionably late because you will be out of style and jealous when you can't get in due to the crowd. There is a $10 charge (sometimes this can be bypassed by coming before a certain time) but is all worth it, and all good!

## Izzy Bar

166 1st Ave. (10th & 11th Sts.)
212-228-0444

Any night of the week, one can expect to find kickin' live music at this hot spot on the edge of Alphabet City. Unfortunately, one can also expect to pay a cover, an action barely warranted by this modest lounge's somewhat bland decor and crowd. The velvet rope at the door is equally unnecessary, and one suspects that Izzy Bar is trying to be something it's not. All in all, a good bet during the week if you don't mind shelling out the

$3 to $5. If you don't dig the B&T crowd, stay away on the weekends.

## Ja

84 7th Ave. So. (Grove & Bleecker Sts.)
212-243-7888

Ja (pronounced "HA") opened two years ago by the brothers Ferrari. Disappointed with the typical lounge options in New York, they wanted to create something uniquely their own. Ja is hidden on 7th Ave. next to a jazz club, and we have a sneaking suspicion that the brothers wouldn't mind if the average passerby didn't notice their tucked away oasis. They strive to cater to patrons that want to be moved by the trance, tribal and progressive music that is spun by resident DJ Jon Ferrari. A $5 cover charge instituted on weekends which tries to keep the bridge and tunnel crowd to a minimum. The vibe is totally cool and anyone could make a night of hanging out in this mellow hideaway.

## Jack Rose

771 8th Ave. (@ 47th St.)
212-247-7518

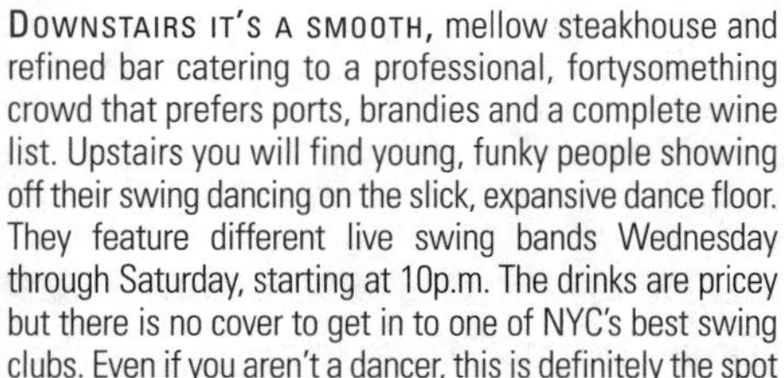

DOWNSTAIRS IT'S A SMOOTH, mellow steakhouse and refined bar catering to a professional, fortysomething crowd that prefers ports, brandies and a complete wine list. Upstairs you will find young, funky people showing off their swing dancing on the slick, expansive dance floor. They feature different live swing bands Wednesday through Saturday, starting at 10p.m. The drinks are pricey but there is no cover to get in to one of NYC's best swing clubs. Even if you aren't a dancer, this is definitely the spot to come watch or pretend you can dance.

## Jake's Dilemma

430 Amsterdam Ave. (80th & 81st Sts.)
212-580-0556

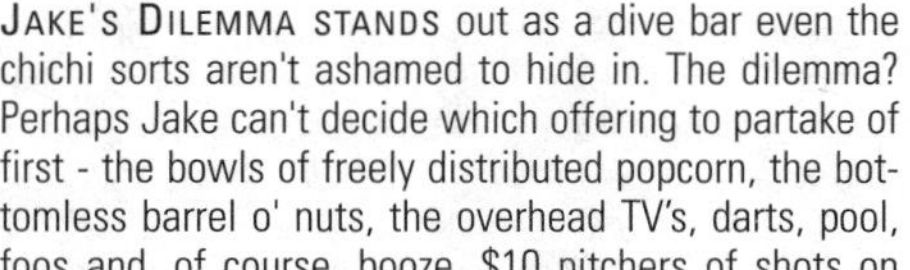

JAKE'S DILEMMA STANDS out as a dive bar even the chichi sorts aren't ashamed to hide in. The dilemma? Perhaps Jake can't decide which offering to partake of first - the bowls of freely distributed popcorn, the bottomless barrel o' nuts, the overhead TV's, darts, pool, foos and, of course, booze. $10 pitchers of shots on Thursday nights are a dangerous draw for the neighborhood fraternity crowd who can't seem to let their college days rest in peace.

## Jameson's

975 2nd Ave. (51st & 52nd Sts.)
212-980-4465

THIS UNPRETENTIOUS WATERING hole has a loyal local following, drawn in by the friendly atmosphere and reasonably priced food and drinks. An accommodating staff and $4 beers make it easy to understand why masses of neighborhood regulars flock here after work for dinner or a few drinks. While most of the other bars in the area have become yuppie havens in the past few years, Jameson's has stayed true to its Irish pub roots and maintained its status as a neighborhood favorite.

## Japas St. Marks

11 St. Marks Pl. (2nd & 3rd Aves.)
212-473-4264

IF THE KARAOKE community took over the world and there was no such thing as modern architecture, this would be the coolest place in history. But since that will never happen, this place blows. Its low, rounded adobe-like ceilings and howling patrons make you feel like you're in an underground torture tunnel. There's a $20 drink minimum, which isn't hard to achieve, since drinks average $7-$9, and even a bag of potato chips costs $3.75. I don't mind singing loud and off-key, but there is a time and place for it. It's called the shower.

## The Jazz Standard

116 E. 27th St. (Park Ave. S. & Lexington Aves.)
212-576-2232

THIS GORGEOUS MULTI-LEVEL restaurant/lounge/club is an excellent alternative to the tourist-trap jazz clubs such as Blue Note and Village Vanguard. Located on a quiet street in Gramercy, you can enjoy the house band in the main lounge area during an after-work drink. For a more intimate experience, the upstairs balcony has been renovated recently, but you lose sight of the band. The weekends get busy since The Jazz Standard is one of the most up and coming jazz venues in the city The downstairs club is dark and moody, like any good jazz spot. Cover charges are reasonable at $15-$25 (with a

$10 minimum) depending on the caliber of the talent. A great date spot all around, you should probably put on a jacket, and expect to pay a few extra bucks to impress whomever you're with.

## JB (Closed - now Diabla)

202 9th Ave. (22nd & 23rd Sts.)
646-638-1111

A NEW ADDITION to 9th Ave., and formerly known as Sydney B, this beautiful spacious bar/restaurant draws an upscale gay/straight crowd who enjoy excellent wines, extensive single malts, great bourbons and awesome cosmopolitans. Gay club promoter John Blair conjured all his talent to create a chic, comfortable and friendly bar. Famous drag diva Hedda Lettuce performs a live show with a keyboard accompanist every Monday. The bar serves one of Manhattan's best margaritas, and one is never enough.

## Jean Georges

(@ Trump International Hotel & Tower)
1 Central Park W. (60th & 61st Sts.)
212-299-3900

THE BAR OF the four-star Jean Georges restaurant has a summery, airy atmosphere. Mostly a pre-dinner meeting spot, the bar fills nightly with businessmen, celebrities and high rollers sipping one of the many $14 cocktails and working their palates into a frenzy for the wonderful meal waiting just a few feet away. If cocktails aren't your thing, the 700 bottle wine list should calm your nerves, unless you order the $12,000 bottle by accident.

## Jekyll and Hyde

91 7th Ave. So. (Bleecker & Christopher Sts.)
212-989-7701
1409 6th Ave. (57th & 58th Sts.)
212-541-9505

THIS 10-YEAR-OLD location of New York's popular theme park may be a real hoot for Mid-Western tourists on a tour staying at Howard Johnson's, but you'll be hard pressed to find any New York natives here. The haunted house is chock full of talking ghouls, goblins, human sized wax figures, anthropological prints and other freaky critters. Friendly staff garbed in safari wear look ready to serve you bar food on an outing down the Amazon. Every Friday and Saturday night there is a DJ and dancing in the upstairs Cannibal Café. There are 16 beers on tap available in yard glasses or pints. So, if you're a hungry tourist that missed going to the American Museum of Natural History, why not kill two birds with one stone?

## Jet Lounge

286 Spring St. (Hudson & Varick Sts.)
212-929-4780

Be prepared for a visual overload upon entering the super-trendy Jet Lounge. Every surface is covered with shards of mirrored glass mosaics providing thousands of reflective surfaces for the self-involved and a look said clients think is "edgy". On a good night you can find yourself surrounded by Upper East Side-socialite-wannabes getting crazy dancing on the bar. Or if the customers' moves aren't daring enough, cage dancers contort their sexy bods on Thursday and Friday nights. According to one bartender, the best way to describe the clientele is "everybody comes here looking for a little extra on the side." After you've exhausted the Jet Lounge, visit their sister bar, Jet East, in East Hampton.

## Jeremy's Ale House

254 Front St. (@ Dover St.)
212-964-3537

Jeremy's Ale House has got to one of the most eclectic dive bars in existence. It seems like decades of hearty-spirited business men and their lady-friends have spent many a Bacchanalia here, considering the many ties, bras, panties and loincloths (yep, loincloths) hanging from the vaulting, cathedral-esque ceiling. While this is clearly not a romantic spot, it does offer an excellent view of the Brooklyn Bridge. All beers are on tap and there are lots and lots of specials. Even though some people just come for the cheap pints and pitchers, there's plenty of seafood, salads and sandwiches to satisfy every food craving.

## J.G Melon

1291 3rd Ave. (@ 74th St.)
212-744-0585

Melon mania has invaded this homey local bar. Billy Joel's greatest hits emanate from the jukebox as the patrons sing with their beers in unison. J.G. Melon is the type of neighborhood bar where in any city besides NY, everyone would know your name. The crowd ranges from suit clad to gym clad. Don't miss the burgers; Kathie Lee Gifford thinks they are the best in NYC. (Is that saying much, though?)

## Jim Brady's

75 Maiden Ln. (William & Gold Sts.)
212-425-1300

THIS WALL STREET INSTITUTION, open for over 100 years, is where you might have found the likes of Joe Kennedy, Al Capone, Sinatra and other mid-century heavyweights hunkering over their old-fashions. The crusty mainstay is a great choice for an after-work, during-work, even pre-work drink. (you won't be the only one here tippling at ten a.m.) Drinks are all around $5 and the entrees are in $13 range. History, good drinks, good food and a comfortable atmosphere; that's about all you need, and exactly what you'll get from Jim Brady's.

## Jimmy's Corner

140 W. 44th St. (Broadway & 6th Ave.)
212-944-7819

ONE OF THE longest running venues in the theater district, Jimmy's Corner has been dispensing liquid cheer for 28 years. The walls, and even the counter-top, are lined with pictures of boxers past and present, and Jimmy's gets big crowds, as well as a cover charge, when they show a pay-per-view fight. Part of "Raging Bull" was filmed here, but tourists beware - this is not a place to bring the kids after a trek through the Disney Store. For all its history, Jimmy's Corner remains a neighborhood dive catering mostly to regulars with questionable hygiene reveling in cigarette smoke. Still, it's a friendly watering hole, welcoming all types.

## Jimmy Walkers Ale House

245 E. 55th St. (2nd & 3rd Aves.)
212-319-6650

LADIES, if you love men in uniform check out the firemen at Jimmy Walkers. This Midtown ale-house has all the necessary stuff for an all-out good time with beer, pool, darts, and lots of TV's for your sports viewing pleasure. Your basic beer-loving crowd can be found here.

## Joe's Bar

520 E. 6th St. (Aves. A & B)
212-473-9093

A LOCAL HANGOUT for the average Joe who likes cheap drinks, pool (good league pool out of Joe's) and a ton of rock and country western, which is loudly cranked out of a jukebox. Lots of Christmas lights, beer signs and pool trophies adorn the walls of this no frills East Village hangout. Despite its seediness, a cool vibe and friendly bartenders truly makes this locale a dive amongst dives.

## Joe's Pub

425 Lafayette St. (Astor Pl. & E. 4th St.)
212-539-8770

HOUSED WITHIN the landmark Joseph Papp Public Theater, is a new bar to add to the "Super Swank" list. The owner's of B Bar & Time Café have transformed the offices of the theater into an elegant martini fest. Lounge on comfy couches while devouring deviled eggs or lobster rolls or mingle with hipsters surrounding the illuminated bar. The mood is sexy and filled with beautiful New Yorkers and celebs chatting over light jazz music and flickering candles. The decor is warm and classy with a small, dimly lit stage. Certain evenings bring in an array of performers like salsa musicians, theater groups, piano players and spoken word series. Primarily an upscale, theater going crowd, Joe's Pub charges a hefty $20 cover Wednesday-Saturday nights.

## John St. Bar & Grill

17 John St. (Broadway & Nassau Sts.)
212-349-3278

THIS LOCAL WATERING HOLE is not much to write home about; however, it's a cheap, safe place to grab a quick one on the way there. Buds run about $ 2.50 a piece and pitcher specials are a mere $5.

## Johnny's Bar

90 Greenwich Ave. (12th & 13th Sts.)
212-741-5279

YEARS AGO, an older Greek man who lived on Greenwich would religiously sweep the sidewalk daily. Although he didn't speak a word of English, everyone called him "Johnny." And thus, Johnny's Bar on Greenwich Ave. came into being. This tiny gem is still going strong after many years serving up super cheap drinks to a very cool mix of loyal locals, East Villagers, construction workers and tourists. The jukebox plays an eclectic mix of tunes from the Grateful Dead, Joe Jackson, The New York Dolls, Sex Pistols and Patti Smith. Super friendly bartenders make you feel at home and create a warm and welcoming escape from the expensive, trendy bars popping up all over the West Village.

## Johnny's Fish Grill

220 Vesey St. (in 4 World Financial Center)
212-385-0333

LOCATED in the vast World Financial Center, and boasting an unusual décor highlighted by a large tropical aquarium and rock-slab walls covered with greenery, Johnny's is definitely a funky bar to show off to your visiting friends and family. $29.99 buys you a twin lobster special; and the other seafood specials are nothing to sniff at either. Drinks are fairly priced, unexpected for this location, and the sizeable crowd appears content to stand around the bar, downing cocktails and shooting the breeze for hours.

## Johnny Fox's

316 3rd Ave. (23rd & 24th Sts.)
212-673-5149

THIS SIMPLE SPACE with its light hardwood floors offers an alternative to Gramercy Park's over-populated Irish pub district. Small and cozy, locals and students from SVA and Baruch come here to kick back. A Monday through Friday happy hour from 4p.m.-7p.m. rotates weekly. Actors and patrons of Roundabout Theater have recently discovered the bar and made it their after-show hangout. The real draw here is a back garden with plenty of tables.

## The Joshua Tree

513 3rd Ave. (34th & 35th Sts.)
212-689-0058

EVERYTHING ABOUT The Joshua Tree is big and loud. From the beefy bouncer to the twin big screen TV's behind the bar, this Murray Hill hangout is a huge favorite not only for the single working crowd, but also for the slew of bridge and tunnelers that flock here every weekend. A solid bar staff serves up $5-$7 drinks drafts to this pub which reaches club-like proportions. Thursday through Saturday a DJ spins everything from rap to Top 40, (and they do take requests). If you can muscle your way though the front bar area, you'll find a more accomodating back section to stretch out. This bar offers full-contact drinking for those who are looking to score, or those who like to get lost in a crowd.

## Journey's Lounge

(@ The Essex House)
130 Central Park So. (6th & 7th Aves.)
212-484-5119

MIDWAY THROUGH the hall connecting the front and rear entrances of the famous Essex House Hotel lies the dark and handsome room known as Journey's Lounge. Businessmen cluster in intimate groups on dark red and green upholstered chairs surrounded by gold-framed oil paintings (and accompanied by live piano music on weekends). They're here for the "To Die For" Manhattans and other long-stemmed cocktails.

## Joy

263 W. 28th St. (7th & 8th Aves.)
212-244-3005

CONFUSION would have been a better moniker for this midtown club you've probably never heard of. The DJ can't seem to make up his mind, pumping anything from '80s house music to JAY-Z and the crowd is about the most random mix this side of the Mason Dixon. If you wish to step behind the velvet rope of the side room, good luck; even the staff members don't know how to get on the list. Beneath the Mondrian-esque foil and white wall opposite the main bar, are couches and square seats that nod to Calvin Klein. A comfortable respite to sip free vodka drinks served from 10pm to 11:30pm every Friday (in hopes of swallowing at least ten dollars worth of alcohol to make up for the cover charge).

## Judge Crater's

301 E. 91st St. (1st & 2nd Aves.)
212-831-1788

TINY, yet accommodating, Judge Crater's is a delightfully authentic hangout in the spurious Upper East Side.

The name comes from a Supreme Court justice who mysteriously disappeared in the '30s and was never found. What this has to do with this bar remains to be seen, but the young neighborhood crowd couldn't care less. The enjoyable bar staff will serve you from 5p.m.-4a.m. weekdays and 1p.m.-4a.m. weekends. It is an intimate space to bring a date or a small group of friends to hide from Manhattan for a while.

## Judge Roy Bean

38 W. 56th St. (5th & 6th Aves.)
212-262-8300

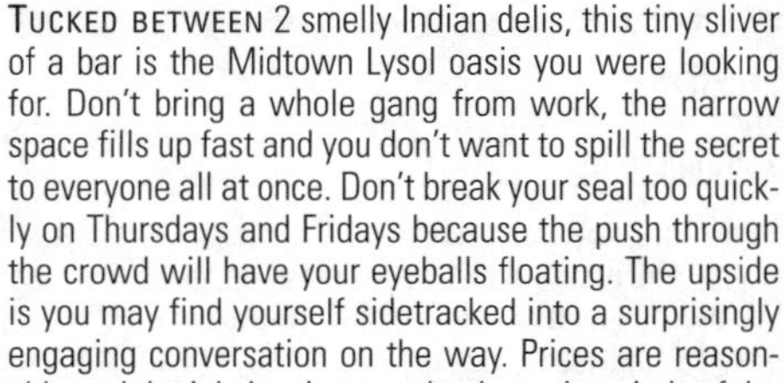

TUCKED BETWEEN 2 smelly Indian delis, this tiny sliver of a bar is the Midtown Lysol oasis you were looking for. Don't bring a whole gang from work, the narrow space fills up fast and you don't want to spill the secret to everyone all at once. Don't break your seal too quickly on Thursdays and Fridays because the push through the crowd will have your eyeballs floating. The upside is you may find yourself sidetracked into a surprisingly engaging conversation on the way. Prices are reasonable and the jukebox is geared to keep the minds of the 30ish crowd off the fact they are no longer in college.

## JUdson Grill

152 W. 52nd St. (6th & 7th Aves.)
212-582-5252

IF YOU WORK in Midtown then you already know this is the place to come after work. This big, airy bar/restaurant is packed with professionals, mostly single, who come to peruse the scene and check out the talent, inconspicuously of course! Even if you don't work in this area stop by for the action and the friendly service.

## Judy's

169 8th Ave. (18th & 19th Sts.)
212-929-5410

AS YOU WALK down 8th Ave., it's hard to miss Judy's; Chelsea's art deco inspired, gay piano cabaret. When you walk in, hopefully you will be lucky enough to hear Claire Cooper playing piano and singing. The atmosphere is very cordial and service is top notch. There are plenty of seats at the bar but crowds start filling in here around 10p.m. Judy's has two piano players nightly, one for happy hour and the second starting at 10p.m.

## Jule's Bistro

65 St. Marks Pl. (1st & 2nd Aves.)
212-477-5560

ONCE YOU GET PAST the giant instrument of death at the door, Jule's Bistro is a pretty French bistro with lacy curtains, an aged wood bar and a charmng outdoor seating area. The main attraction of Jule's Bistro is the live jazz, played during the week from 9p.m. to 12a.m. and from 11p.m. to 1:30a.m. on the weekend. The menu is a little pricey but the food is delightful, the beer and wine are reasonably priced, and for the most part the crowd is stylish and mellow.

## Julies

204 E. 58th St. (@ 2nd Ave.)
212-688-1294

EVEN THOUGH this lesbian pick-up joint is relatively small, the dance floor really heats up, especially on Wednesday nights (Latina night). This is a small, not so easy to find ladies bar where the boys are welcome, but you won't see many. This is a great place to go dancing and a good alternative to some of the bigger, trendier lesbian bars. Expect a crowd outside on Wednesdays and weekends.

## Julius

159 W. 10th St. (@ Waverly Pl.)
212-929-9672

JULIUS is a true West Village landmark and former celebrity haunt from the 1950's. The incredible photographs on the wall are worthy of a visit alone. A mature albeit loud neighborhood crowd enjoys awesome hamburgers and french fries that are especially excellent at 2a.m. Play quick pick lottery and think of your local VFW post and remember folks, buy bonds! A pool table is on the way and a two for one happy hour keeps things real.

## Juniper

185 Duane St. (Greenwich & Hudson Sts.)
212-965-1201

ALL YOU BALTHAZAR nay sayers, pay heed to this friendly and unpretentious bistro. A vivacious staff bustles back and forth in the cozy, wood-paneled space, delivering plates laden with tantalizing Gallic and American entrees. The bar itself runs through the center of the space and offers an astounding variety of foreign beers and over 30 excellent wines. An eclectic mix of neighborhood locals and Wall Street types convene here to sip cognac after catching a gig at the Knitting Factory. A good date spot, so long as you don't mind your significant other ogling the employees.

## Junno's

64 Downing St. (@ Varick St.)
212-627-7995

While you wait and wait for a table in Junno's cool little room, just tell the bartender to "sock it to me." That's saketumi, a fruit-infused sake cocktail on the large specialty list. Once seated, the tasty and aesthetically pleasing Japanese fare with Korean and French influences that will make you want to linger forever. The pack of beauties in the next booth won't have you heading to the door either.

## Justin's

31 W. 21st St. (5th & 6th Aves.)
212-352-0599

Named after Puff Daddy's son, Justin's is an ultra swank soul scene for the "seen and be seen." Beautiful and classy urbanites mill about the bar or dig into down home, southern-style meals. Specialty drinks like the p diddy and the faith will keep the vibe going all night. Tuesdays are industry nights, so be prepared for "the list" and prerequisite velvet rope.

## Kaña Tapas Bar & Restaurant

324 Spring St. (Washington & Greenwich Sts.)
212-343-8180

Open for two and a half years, Kaña brings a touch of Spain to Manhattan. On the outskirts of SoHo, this chic, yet cozy restaurant/bar graciously introduces downtown investment moguls to Prada-wearing SoHo-ites and bikers from the nearby Ear Inn. With a typical red velvet charm, Kaña serves a full tapas menu for reasonable prices. With lots of exposed brick and warm candlelight, Kaña plays host to live Flamenco every Tuesday evening. Open daily at 6p.m., they have six beers on tap, moderately priced drinks and an ever-flowing abundance of sangria. Kaña, which is Spanish for "a glass of beer", will quench your thirst for authentic Spanish food and drink.

## Karavas Tavern

162 W. 4th St. (@ 6th Ave.)
212-243-8007

IT SLICES, it dices, and does the laundry. Karavas tavern does it all or at least it tries. This West Village spot is sectioned off into a sidewalk café, neighborhood tavern, fast food joint and corner gyro stand. With wooden booths, a jukebox and the standard selection of drinks, the tavern offers comfort without the frills. There is no happy hour, but don't worry, the drink prices are always reasonable. The other parts of Karavas are rather unremarkable. Serving up gyros and greasy food with a seemingly overworked staff, Karavas tavern attracts twentysomethings who just want a nip and a quick bite.

## Kate Kearney's

251 E. 50th St. (2nd & 3rd Aves.)
212-935-2045

LOCATED JUST OUTSIDE the bustle of midtown, this dimly lit, friendly, Irish pub brings in an older and more subdued after-work crowd than other bars in the neighborhood. With a solid lunch and dinner menu, $3.50 beers, a pool table and a standard jukebox, this is a good spot to meet friends for after-work drinks or dinner. A live band plays traditional Irish music on Thursdays and Fridays.

## Kava

605 Hudson St. (@ 12th St.)
212-989-7504

THIS BAR AND LOUNGE, well known for its Australian and New Zealand wines, has a young, vibrant and mixed straight/gay crowd. The music varies from loungey to swank to ambient pop. Get cozy in the back lounge decorated with New Zealand inspired murals. With its low lighting and comfortable velvet banquettes, you'll feel right at home.

## Kavehaz

123 Mercer St. (Prince & Spring Sts.)
212-343-0612

A COMBINATION "gallery/café" (are there any bars left that don't exhibit art), and live jazz/world music space. Kavehaz is a good place for a romantic evening full of coffee drinks and desserts. There is rarely a crowd in the room, which makes it easy to stop by and relax in the art deco atmosphere and unwind with some tunes.

## K-Dee's

551 2nd Ave. (30th & 31st Sts.)
212-684-8769

THIS RUN-DOWN oddity situated across from the Kips Bay theatre serves booze and lends paperbacks. When it seems that most bars are leaning towards a comfortable airy "lounge" type atmosphere, K-Dee's is going for the summer-camp "lending library" feel. The large stack of books lining the shelf is accessible to patrons who want to peruse while drinking. As sad as it may sound, there is no rational reason this bar is in existence, other than keeping the senior citizen clientele off Prozac.

## Kennedy's

327 W. 57th St. (8th & 9th Sts.)
212-759-4242

IRISH EYES ARE SMILING at Kennedy's. For the past 30 years this comfortable bar/restaurant has gathered a loyal crowd that watches TV, hangs out and enjoys one of the best pints of Guinness in the city. Not surprising, this bar is named after the famous Kennedy family and plays host to an eclectic mix of monsignors, cops, neighborhood couples and young singles. The staff will delight you with their accents and no-fuss professionalism. The bartender in the back has been around for 25 years and is a real gem. His hospitality will make you feel at home, so much so you may never leave!

## Kenny's Castaways

157 Bleecker St. (Thompson & Sullivan Sts.)
212-979-9762

A WELL-KNOWN institution for jamming to live music, Kenny's Castaways has had its fair share of stars pass through its wooden arch, and it's got the gold records to prove it. Two of Kenny's longtime house bands, The Smithereens and Alan Davies Band, donated theirs and they're hanging proudly above the bar. It's a funky hangout and a true bar that just happens to have live music. Watch out for the $5 cover, which goes into effect when the better bands are playing, but as with everything Kenny's, even that is relaxed and reasonable.

## Kenn's Broome St. Bar

363 W. Broadway (@ Broome St.)
212-925-2086

"No cheese fries for you!" Even though they serve nachos with cheese, they adamantly refuse to compromise the integrity of their fries by adding any melted goo. Ken's has been on this SoHo corner for a century and will probably live through the next Ice Age. It is an institution that serves as a watering hole for young and old locals who prefer to hang out in jeans, not Gaultier. The menu has a variety of sandwiches, omelettes and pastas that won't get your panties in a jumble.

## Kettle of Fish

59 Christopher St. (@ 7th Ave. So.)
212-414-2278

Kettle of Fish has moved, for the third time, into these historical digs in the West Village. In an eclectic space where it's always Christmas (there are white string lights and a wreath), sports fans can stare at the TV while wordsters peruse the dictionaries and encyclopedias. The extremely cozy lounge area is accented by a red neon "BAR" light. Drinks are reasonably priced, and with their selection, you won't leave sober.

## Kevin St. James

741 8th Ave. (46th & 47th Sts.)
212-977-5984

A pleasant addition to an otherwise barren stretch of 8th Ave., Kevin St. James is a warm and friendly Irish pub and restaurant serving cold pints and a full Irish/American menu. Another good after work spot for all of the midtown professionals looking for a change of pace. Take off your tie, bask in the unpretentious atmosphere and strike up a conversation with the friendly patrons or staff.

## KGB

85 E. 4th St. (Bowery & 2nd Ave.)
212-505-3360

CLIMB THE STAIRS, pass the theater, round a corner, and enter a room with a few small tables, nothing more. The clandestine feel of this 1920's speakeasy-cum Russian Labor Club moves regulars to whisper sweet nothings to each other while sipping from a selection of over 30 vodkas. Free prose and poetry readings pack in the literary set on Sundays and Tuesdays.

## King

579 6th Ave. (16th & 17th Sts.)
212-366-5464

THIS GAY CLUB is a popular haunt all week long and late into the night. An eclectic mix of ethnicities gawk at each other and view silent porn on the TV monitors. There is no cover charge before 10p.m, and only $5 afterwards. There is a two-for-one happy hour every day but, unfortunately, the joint doesn't start hopping till much later. Sexy half naked go-go dancers "rock out with their cocks out." Three floors provide ample space for socializing, dancing and carousing. Every night has a different theme, but Wednesday is definitely the best with the "Amateur Strip" contest.

## King Cole Bar (@ St. Regis Hotel)

2 E. 55th St. (5th & Madison Aves.)
212-339-6721

OPENED IN **1949**, this hotel lounge only admitted men until the late 1950's when they realized what they were missing. The cherry oak bar is surrounded by comfortable seating and on the wall is a mural titled, "The Flatulence" depicting a farting king, which is now worth $4 million. High society convenes here to drink cognac, port and champagne. Good place for meeting a date before highbrow functions.

## Kings Carriage House

251 E. 82nd St. (2nd & 3rd Aves.)
212-734-5490

THE KINGS CARRIAGE HOUSE is unique because of its American Colonial décor. The exquisite venue features three excellent dining rooms: The Willow Room, The Mandalan Room and The Hunt Room. Because this romantic hideaway is near a church, no liquor is served; however, 40 wines and seven champagnes are poured. For dinner, partake in a $39, three-course meal. The menu changes nightly, so you never know what to expect. Stop by for high tea on the afternoons to sip Darjeeling and nibble finger sandwiches. If you're one who enjoys the feeling of old Williamsburg, VA, this is the spot for you.

## Kinsale Tavern

1672 3rd Ave. (93rd & 94th Sts.)
212-348-4370

THIS SIMPLE-LOOKING pub proudly serves 30 tap beers to the yuppies that swarm here, and a choice of 75 single malts for the former yuppies that come to dine with their children. Even with the lack of cheap beer choices the bar area can get mighty packed after work with local men on the prowl. Kinsale Tavern is a good place to watch a game and grab a bite, but little else if you live somewhere other than the Upper East Side.

## Knickerbocker Bar & Grill

33 University Pl. (@ 9th St.)
212-228-8490

WITH ITS MAROON WALLS, mahogany bar, old New York posters, jazz piano tunes playing softly in the background and dinosaurs at the bar talking about the good old days, Knickerbocker is steeped in New York history and a great place to come have a steak, smoke a cigar, and drink a lot of Scotch. The food is surf 'n turf and with the live jazz after 9:45p.m., it's a good place to go with a bunch of buddies you haven't seen for 20 years.

## Knitting Factory

74 Leonard St. (Broadway & Church Sts.)
212-219-3055

KNITTING FACTORY should be on any music loving New Yorker's list of thing s to do if it already isn't. This multilevel music megaplex in TriBeCa offers three shows on the main floor starting at 8p.m. for $10 (usually) and in the "old office" more live music, a one drink minimum and a lower cover charge (usually), and late night in the "tap room" is always free. This comfortable music venue always seems familiar and never disappoints. Call ahead for tickets and information.

## Kori

253 Church St. (Franklin & Leonard Sts.)
212-334-0908

IN A RATHER QUIet strip of TriBeCa there stands a unique gem. Kori's orange walls and minimalist setting induce a soothing effect on patrons. The glass-covered bar is unique and interesting with its rock garden and Nietzsche quotes. A variety of specialty drinks are served with Soju and fruity concoctions. Kori is an intriguing spot for a drink (or dinner) most anytime. This Korean bar/restaurant is a great place to impress that special someone.

## Korova Milk Bar

200 Ave. A (12th & 13th Sts.)
212-254-8838

THIS FORMER job placement office for the mentally disabled now houses the Clockwork Orange themed bar. Featuring naked mannequins, movies like Barbarella playing continuously on the 14 color TV's, lactose liquors like the white chocolate martini or the frozen embryo (the embryo being a Snickers bar), poetry every Tuesday, Gothic Fetish Wednesdays, the occasional vampire meeting (seriously), and many odd drink specials keep the freaks coming out at night.

## Kush

183 Orchard St. (Houston & Stanton Sts.)
212-677-7328

KUSH goes far to emulate a Moroccan speakeasy: Arabic music blasts into a very dark space where groups huddle around low tables or recline sultan-style on broad couches and sample one of the unusually named cocktails (Nana haleeb, anyone?), or a glass of Lebanese or Moroccan wine. An appetizing menu offers Middle-Eastern standards like hummus and stuffed grape leaves. On Tuesday nights, Kush pulls out all the stops offering henna hand painting, tarot card readings, belly dancing and a live Arabic band. In spite of the pre-determined fabrication of such specific ambiance, Kush is just elegant enough to avoid classification as a theme bar.

## La Cocina

217 W. 85th St. (Broadway & Amsterdam Ave.)
212-874-0770

THIS PLEASANT (if dull), orange-gold room walled with Frida Kahlo's and other Mexican works, considers itself a restaurant first and a bar second. But, the immediate nachos and salsa they present to patrons at the bar will alleviate any food envy. Magnificent margaritas are the draw, and at two for the price of one Mondays through Thursdays, a bargain to get buzzed on.

## Lafayette Grill & Bar

54-56 Franklin St. (@ Lafayette St.)
212-732-4449

THIS SHOULD BE called Lafayette Grill and Bar and Gallery and Ballroom and Theater and Belly Dance Review. It offers a little of everything. The art gallery is rumored to sell more than any gallery. A theater show takes place Wednesdays and Thursdays. Middle Eastern Night, with anywhere from 20 to 40 belly dancers, is on Fridays and tango dancing is featured Saturdays. All of this usually keep this place reservation-only, but you could get lucky and hit an off night.

## La Jumelle

55 Grand St. (W. Broadway & Wooster St.)
212-941-9651

ALMOST AN EXACT replica of its neighbor Lucky Strike, but with no affiliation, this French bistro is rarely crowded but is a great hang out place. La Jumelle serves its libations at a small bar in the main room or you can sit in the rear dining room. Typical French fare can be had at reasonable prices in this cozy, ochre tinted atmosphere.

## La Linea

15 1st Ave. (1st & 2nd Sts.)
212-777-1571

LA LINEA has been around for years and years; however, these days, it looks like it's falling behind the times.

Its "haute low rent" design featuring an antique hammered-tin ceiling, slaughterhouse-red walls festooned with red Christmas lights and zebra-striped banquette cushions, needs an update badly. When the East Village was scary, La Linea offered a gutsy stab at nighttime elegance. But these days, La Linea straddles the fence: too proud to be a dive, too broke to be chic. Like so many other neighborhood strongholds, La Linea may also soon disappear from this almost completely gentrified 'hood.

## Lakeside Lounge

162 Ave. B (10th & 11th Sts.)
212-529-8463

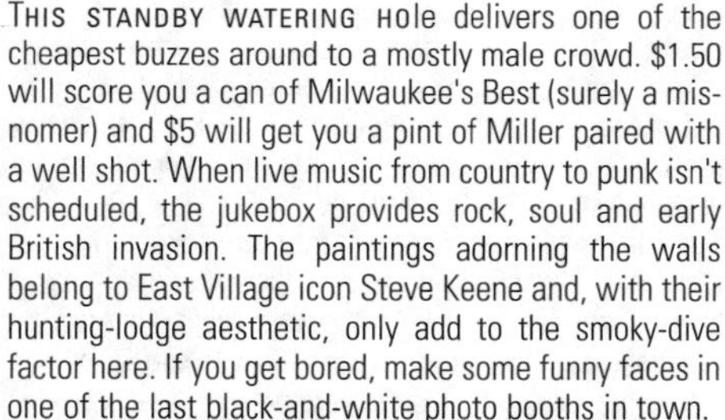

THIS STANDBY WATERING HOle delivers one of the cheapest buzzes around to a mostly male crowd. $1.50 will score you a can of Milwaukee's Best (surely a misnomer) and $5 will get you a pint of Miller paired with a well shot. When live music from country to punk isn't scheduled, the jukebox provides rock, soul and early British invasion. The paintings adorning the walls belong to East Village icon Steve Keene and, with their hunting-lodge aesthetic, only add to the smoky-dive factor here. If you get bored, make some funny faces in one of the last black-and-white photo booths in town.

## La Maison De Sade

206 W. 23rd St. (7th & 8th Aves.)
212-727-8642

LOOKING FOR a cozy downtown hideaway to entertain the visiting folks? This isn't it unless you want to see Mom cuffed to metal poles and spanked. In the meantime, you and a few pals can indulge in an evening of nasty voyeurism over calamari and cocktails in this sticky little hole in Chelsea. Pay $20 for a spanking, foot worship, dirty talk, or public humiliation. $8 specialty cocktails like the retisfist and the necrophiliac will numb your senses and make it easier to watch hot wax dripping from a sweaty stranger's nipple. So yeah, it's naughty, but with a Chuck E Cheese twist. There's a $5 cover Thursday thru Saturday.

## L'Angolo

108 W. Houston St. (@ Thompson St.)
212-260-8899

L'ANGOLO is a simple little space - a few tables, a few loungey crevices. If you love to linger outside in the warmer months but crave the ambience and intimacy you get when you're inside, L'Angolo offers a nice compromise. One assortment of comfy chairs settles into an open-windowed world of its own somewhere between bar and taxi. Those within can enjoy Italian soccer matches on the TV, cappuccinos and frozen drinks, sandwiches and salads, and the cool yet cozy vibe.

## La Nouvelle Justine

24 1st Ave. (1st & 2nd Sts.)
212-673-8908

WANT A SIDE OF S&M with your grilled chicken? Or the lash of whips with your mousse? In the back of Lucky Cheng's, discover a den of depravity: drag queens, BDSM...and French food. Frequented predominately by out-of-towners and gawkers during the week, the party really rocks on the weekend. Join roving dominatrices and jockstrapped leatherboys for "Glam 2001" on Saturday nights, where glittered-up rockers dig the Dead Boys, Iggy Pop and Ratt. Although both the cover charge and drink prices are steep, being burned by molten wax while Poison blasts on the stereo is way more entertaining than sitting at home. A great place for a date or for a family reunion. (If you're used to seeing dad in a leather thong and nipple chains and mom chained to the ground in front of the dog dish, that is.)

## Lansky Lounge

104 Norfolk St. (Delancy & Rivington Sts.)
212-677-9489

THE LANSKY LOUNGE is one of those bars that are so cool you wish you could keep it a secret spot just for yourself and your friends. No chance now, though. Accessed through an unmarked back alley at the rear of the institutional Rattner's Deli since its inception, the former speakeasy is about to go legit. Rattner's itself is switching from kosher to posh, which means the doors will open between the restaurant and Lansky's so the diners can explore without getting lost by the dumpster. Oh well. Now anyone can find this excellent, deco inspired lounge, with its stem glass laden bar and black and white photos of namesake Meyer Lansky and his morally challenged pals. Actually, word has been out for a while, as there are DJ's on weekends that draw a hip crowd.

## Last Exit

136 Atlantic Ave. (Clinton & Henry Sts.)
718-222-9198 (Brooklyn)

APPROPRIATELY TITLED, this oasis is WAY out of the way of any other nightlife. But it's worth the trip. Plush sofas and mood lighting set the stage for a slightly trendy, cool crowd. Sprawl out on a sofa or head out to the garden and sip one of the Exit's special martinis with names like the Gowanus. Every Saturday, DJ's spin techno, ambient and drum-n-bass; music good enough to dislodge you from your couch. Happy hour (4-7p.m.) is special here largely because the barkeep's a hottie. Ok, (blush)...Shecky's got a crush.

## Latin Quarter

2551 Broadway (@ 96th St.)
212-864-7600

DON'T LET the serious Salsa-steppers intimidate you in this formal Latin-American dance hall. From Thursday through Sunday, live bands play to an older crowd of couples for a $10 - $20 cover. But come by early on Thursdays (7 to 9 p.m.), and the folks there will teach you a few moves for free.

## Lava Lounge

28 W. 20th St. (@ 5th Ave.)
212-627-7867

THIS "VOLCANIC LAVA" THEMED lounge with its steroid induced muscle attitude at the door and $15 cover charge is sure to kindle a fire of burning hatred in your belly. Once inside the gigantic, beautifully decorated space, you'll be greeted with antique art, comfy couches and a less than attentive waitstaff. The place has serious potential but landed in a pit of mediocrity. Lava is best during the week when there is no cover and you can enjoy the ambiance minus the crowds. Usually booked with private parties and corporate events during the week, doors open to the public by 9:30p.m.

## Layla

211 W. Broadway (@ Franklin St.)
212-431-0700

MODELED AFTER the 15th Century headquarters for the Ottoman Empire, Topkapi Place, Layla offers an experience for all the senses to enjoy. The exquisite Middle Eastern cuisine, prepared by head chef Brian Wieler, is fit for a sultan. Fantastic drinks like the Moroccan margarita, fashioned with fresh squeezed pomegranate juice, are expertly mixed at the bar. Belly dancers shake their thing nightly.

## Le Bateau Ivre

230 E. 51st St. (2nd & 3rd Aves.)
212-583-0579

RELATIVELY NEW to the neighborhood, this gorgeous French restaurant sports a very chic and modern look. Wine and champagne bottles surround the restaurant and old-school oscillating fans provide a soothing, gentle breeze The selection of 250 wines and 30 champagnes will likely bedazzle even the most sophisticated wine lover, so make the decision easy on yourself and order their specialty drink, the vinopolinal. The appetizer menu offers marine delectables such as mussels, snails, oysters and clams, or settle in for the full experience.

## Le Colonial

149 E. 57th St. (@ Lexington Ave.)
212-752-0808

THIS BEAUTIFUL VIETNAMESE NIGHTSPOT serves some of the best food this side Mekong River. The hip upstairs lounge and great looking after work crowd makes this standard one of the best sure things for food and scene. This is one of the better pick-up spots in NYC. If you're out on the west coast, try their L.A. branch: one of the hippest scenes out there as well.

## Le Figaro Café

184 Bleecker St. (@ MacDougal St.)
212-677 1100

IT'S RIGHT TO ASSUME that the owners of Le Figaro Café had good intentions. However, the road to Hell is paved with them. What they have on their hands now is just that; an overcrowded café/bar on a grimy Greenwich Village street. They didn't even think to place a barrier around the sidewalk seating that gets so packed with annoying people that have no regard for pedestrians. There is nothing remarkable about the food or their drinks. However terrible this place might be, it still packs 'em in, so take word of advice and don't follow the herd.

## Lei Bar

112 Ave. A (@ 7th St.)
212-420-9517

YES, YOU'RE IN HAWAII; do not be confused by the sirens, horns and city bustle outside because this is the best Tiki bar in New York City. This tropical paradise once attracted an in-the-know crowd but has since been discovered by Upper East Siders looking to impress their sorority girlfriends. The bar and the drinks themselves are decorated in Hawaiian garb and twinkling lights line the walls. If you're lucky enough to snatch up a table, share one of their frozen cocktails for two, which are served in a monsterous glasses. Be advised: There are specific instructions for ordering conveniently posted on the wall to enhanse your drinking pleasure.

## Le Marais

15 John St. (Broadway & Nassau Sts.)
212-285-8585

THIS KOSHER RESTAURANT/BAR is one of the best choices for food if ham and foreskin ain't your cup of Manichewitz. The décor is tasteful and the staff is extremely attentive. The piano player and the brick walls add a romantic touch to what might otherwise have been a really stuffy night spot. Not much of a place for straight-up boozing, but a good choice if you need to entertain clients who keep kosher.

## Lemon

230 Park Ave. So. (18th & 19th Sts.)
212-614-1200

BYOC (Bring your own crowd) for a fun night at Lemon, because behind the menacing face of Lemon's cigar-smoking citrus logo, crowds of Armani-Exchange clad bridge and tunnelers practice pickup lines on anything without an Adam's apple. Reserve a table upstairs and try one of the house martini-style concoctions like the Memphis, Paris or Lexington. Try checking out Lemon in the summer months when the floor to ceiling windows open on to prime people real estate.

## Le Regence Bar & Grill

37 E. 64th St. (Madison & Park Aves.)
212-734-9100

IN THE BAR, discover a dim, yet quite comfortable, lounge area accented with old-school leather lounge chairs and green, wood-bordered walls set off by several nautical paintings. Sounds expensive, right? It is. Cocktails can run up to $16, while dinner starts at $20. But the well-dressed and polished businessfolk filling Le Regence don't seem to mind.

## Leshko's

11 Ave. A. (@ 7th St.)
212-777-2111

LESHKO'S is a "very nice bar". It used to be a divey Ukranian coffee shop until hip new owners transformed it into an Ave. A pit-stop. Now groups of Eastsiders nosh on pierogies and steak frites while tossing back cocktails at the tables or small bar.

## Le Singe Vert

160 7th Ave. (19th & 20th Sts.)
212-366-4100

THIS WONDERFUL LITTLE French bistro is cozy and very friendly. Old tin advertisement plaques, huge mirrors and photo books line the walls around striped maroon and green leather booths. The crowd is your average Chelsea cool, hip, trendy artist type or after-work professional out for a nice evening at a place with definite atmosphere. There's live jazz music on Mondays and Tuesdays. Shecky says this is a great first date spot.

## Let's Make a Daiquiri

89 South St., South St. Seaport (@ Pier 17)
212-406-1486

IF YOU HAPPEN to be hanging out in the mall when an uncontrollable craving for a frozen treat strikes, you can order from a variety of daiquiris from this crappy stand in the middle of the food court at the seaport. On summer days it could be a refreshing change, but other than that there is no reason to come here.

## Level X

107 N. 6th St. (Berry & Wythe Sts.)
718-302-3313 (Brooklyn)

First, the good news: this new Jestons-esque Williamsburg bar has excellent décor and lighting, and a strong DJ and sound system. But after that, Level X levels off. It's all show and no substance; the bathroom sink still has no faucet after having been open for months. The crowd is young, superficial, giddy and there to be seen. They can't be there for the booze, which is a lame selection of overpriced, second-rate bottled beer that keeps things simple for the pretty but unskilled bartenders. Level X should be applauded for trying something different but good intentions don't go far in club-land.

## Library (@ The Regency Hotel)

540 Park Ave. (@ 61st St.)
212-759-4100

With its large comfortable sofas, soft jazz music in the background, waiters at your beck and call and a menu to die for, Library serves as an example of why it's nice to be wealthy and live in the city. Decorated like a living room of a Manhattan millionaire, there is nothing about Library that is not exquisite. This is the kind of place, for instance, where the hamburger comes with Maytag bleu cheese and is served on brioche, not a bun. Cocktails start at $15, and don't be surprised to find yourself spending $45 for a glass of wine.

## The Library

7 Ave. A (Houston & 2nd Sts.)
212-375-1352

Remember all the time you spent in your high school library wishing you were getting drunk or laid? Well, don't let the name fool you. Ten years later and you're still getting loaded in The Library. Decorated in deep red with Christmas lights and shelves stocked with stolen library books, the atmosphere will make you glad you're not in high school anymore. Great bartenders pour strong and cheap drinks while the jukebox kicks ass with favorites from Television, The Stooges, The MC5 and Adam Ant. The Library supports local filmmakers by sporadically showing local independent films on the big screen in the back room.

Dim lighting, loud music and young East Villagers thankfully keep the tourists, yuppies and the studying types far, far away!

## Life Café

343 E. 10th St. (@ Ave. B)
212-477-8791

OPEN SINCE 1981, Life Café has luckily survived the gentrification of the East Village while still bringing in the native, artsy and tattooed crowd from the neighborhood. Either chill out with the friendly bartenders or take advantage of the outdoor garden and sidewalk seating for some healthy, cheap food. A great selection of music keeps the place hopping along with a most excellent happy hour: 5p.m.-9p.m. offers up a 2 for 1 discount on all types of drinks. The faithful crowds of Lower Eastsiders have kept this joint a true East Village relic.

## Lightship Frying Pan

Pier 63 @ Chelsea Piers (@ 23rd St.)
212-989-6363

IN A NUTSHELL, LFP is an old tugboat with a colorful history that's docked on the water and acts as a museum in the daytime and a helluva party spot at night. Built in 1929 and used by the Coast Guard as a lighthouse; it's considered a national treasure. The boat is available for rental as a private party space. This is an awesome and unique spot for a New York party outside of the normal clubs.

## The Limelight

47 6th Ave. (@ 20th St.)
212-807-7780

THIS CHURCH/MEGA club isn't where you go for confession. Sin is in the air, but be prepared, it'll cost you 20 smackers. Once inside, your senses will be dazzled by loud, pumping dance music and hypnotizing lights. Wait, that's only the main room. Stairs lead to many a hidden balcony and alcove. At the top is the famous Geiger Room bedecked with spooky alien imagery and loungy furniture to sink into with your overpriced drink in a plastic cup. From Wednesdays through Sundays from 10p.m. until 4a.m., you might end up rubbing shoulders with members of the Village People or catch a glimpse of gay sailors in mid-vogue.

## Lion's Den

214 Sullivan St. (3rd & Bleecker Sts.)
212-634-0427

THIS RELIABLE GREENWICH VILLAGE venue hosts a wide range of musical performers nightly. From reggae to soul to funk, Lion's Den fills its steamy insides with NYU students and stragglers from Bleecker Street. Cover charges start at $5 but do vary depending on the performer. Call 269-4TIX for show times and prices. For your listening pleasure the den is open 7 days a week and music generally begins at 9p.m. If you own anything made of hemp, throw it on and start making friends.

## Lips

2 Bank St. (Greenwich Ave. & Waverly Pl.)
212-675-7710

"HOLY TITS, ASS AND HAIR" is what you'll exclaim walking into this bejeweled, eclectic drag-queen heaven. This West Village restaurant is more known for its lip-syncing drag shows than for its food; it's a bachelorette party's planner dream come true. It's glittery, kitschy, sparkly and so "You Go Girl!". Silence grips the dining room when the high-pitched voice of a larger than life emcee decked out in a crazy wig and more make-up than Tammy Faye screams, One by one the beautiful "waitresses" saunter through the room singing to classics like "Voulez Vous Coucher Avec Moi" and hot blooded Tina Turner tunes. Lips is a perfect introduction to NY for that out of town cousin.

## Liquids

266 E. 10th St. (1st Ave. & Ave. A)
212-677-1717

A TIP: Get here early to avoid the doorman. Romantic and intelligent and very New York, Liquids caters to a hipster crowd that loves to look cool on a budget. Enjoy potent, expensive drinks served in fancy glasses that help to soothe the financial hurt, and groove out to top-rate DJ's on a supersonic sound system. A mix of "Come here often?" bar fare and "Do you read

Kafka?" lounge seating makes this an East Village hideaway for everyone.

## Liquor Store Bar

235 W. Broadway (@ White St.)
212-226-7121

THE LAID-BACK, dog-friendly Liquor Store still looks and feels like a neighborhood tavern. But, the neighborhood has changed, and TriBeCa's J. Crew-wearing residents don't do this place justice. However, the décor is pleasant and comfortable and, thankfully, there's no pool table, jukebox or dartboard. Kick back with a killer cosmo at an outdoor table and people watch to a soundtrack of Motown and familiar rock classics. There are four beers on tap and the liquor cabinet is always dependable. Relaxed and friendly, it's perfect for after work or late nite.

## Live Bait

14 E. 23rd St. (Broadway & Madison Aves.)
212-353-2492

THIS 14 YEAR-OLD Cajun-themed bar and restaurant was at one point a hip alternative in the Flatiron District. The folks who once arrived looking to score have since gotten married, and now just come for the food. Live Bait is still a decent place for some good after-work bar grub and drinks. Although armed with ESPN and a smattering of football paraphernalia, it's not a fully dedicated sports bar. Instead, Live Bait focuses on its Cajun food and music themes.

## The Living Room

84 Stanton St. (@ Allen St.)
212-533 7237

THIS MUSIC VENUE looks more like the rec room in your mustachioed uncle's basement than any living room you've probably seen. The cheaply made knotty-wood bar perfectly complements yellow-painted wood paneling, mismatched chairs and lingering New Year's decorations. The Living Room regularly books musical acts of the acoustic folk-singer/songwriter variety; you know, that pseudo Alanis/Fiona Apple longhaired, hairy armpit contingent. There is a one drink minimum, but unfortunately, the barkeep would have to employ a tire-iron to convince this teetotaling crowd to get loose and order a second Amstel. The Living Room is no doubt hot stuff for folk fans, but all this sobriety and heartfelt guitar strumming may make one feel more like they're at a Christian youth group than a legitimate nightspot.

## L'Ivre

1020 Lexington Ave. (@ 72nd St.)
212-717-3902

ENTER L'IVRE AND you will feel like you're on an acid trip. On the left, the bar is staid and looks like your grandfather's "smoking" room. On the right, there are disco lights blinking in unison to Abba blaring on the jukebox. The bartenders look like Siegfried and Roy as they serve you Glenfiddich. Bottom line: L'Ivre is having an identity crisis, a vast difference from its sister restaurant.

## Local 138

138 Ludlow St. (Rivington & Stanton Sts.)
212-477-0280

THIS BAR APPEARS modeled after a working-class pub somewhere in Dublin. Its no frills expanses of wood-paneled walls are interrupted only by the occasional wall sconce or Guinness beer mirror. Well-fed neighborhood hipsters in gas station attendant's shirts sit around simple square tables and talk about three things: rock, their cars and that bitchin' beer they're drinking. Although liquor is available, the bartender serves pints of several kinds of fine English brew, such as Newcastle and Strongbow Cider, to the locals. Local 138 is an ideal spot for an early start on a night out or a low-key tête-a-tête with an old friend.

## Loki Lounge

304 5th Ave. (2nd & 3rd Sts.) Brooklyn
718-965-9600

LOKI IS LOW KEY. The bar itself is gorgeous, with brick walls and wrought iron windows in the front giving way to plush red curtains and comfortable couches in the back. It all feels a bit like the stage set for the orgy scene in Eyes Wide Shut. In general, the bar is so relaxed it's practically asleep, as customers flick through magazines and occasionally shoot some pool.

Considering this spot is only a year old, it has gained a loyal following. On Friday and Saturday nights things liven up a little when a resident DJ spins house and soul classics.

## Lola

30 W. 22nd St. (5th & 6th Aves.)
212-675-6700

THIS HOTBED OF live R&B music provides a second home to the mostly African-American/Latino crowds that flock here on weekends. The bar and lounge areas are very large, but the popularity of this spot makes it almost impossible to move around comfortably and ordering a drink is not unlike trying to catch a cab in Midtown during a thunderstorm. Perhaps they should introduce a cover charge during the live music sessions Tuesday through Saturday to cut down on the fire hazard potential. The sex and sweat infused atmosphere make even rhythm-less souls kick up their heels and groove to the music.

## Looking Glass

108 3rd Ave. (13th & 14th Sts.)
212-777-3363

THIS TINY PLACE (so tiny anyone over 6 feet tall will have to duck down from the super-low ceiling) caters to the young East Village hipsters who want cheap beer and some Fishbone on the jukebox. Except for happy hour, 4p.m.-8p.m., and the occasional DJ or ball game, there aren't a lot of extras with this place. Really, the bar is just a dump that tries too hard to be hip.

## L'Orange Bleu

430 Broome St. (@ Prince St.)
212-226-4999

L'ORANGE BLEU: Who knew? A night at this festive restaurant/bar feels like a mini vacation to a happier, and more colorful, far-away land. Check out Monday's "Moroccan Night": $5 gains you admission to a world where live Arabian music soars, belly dancers shake and the sangria flows freely. The dining room is a feast for the senses; it's abundant with creative Mediterranean fare, vibrant décor and world music blaring from speakers in every corner. This place would be a hotspot if only it would extend its hours and spend some money on some well-deserved publicity.

## Lot 61

550 W. 21st St. (10th & 11th Aves.)
212-243-6555

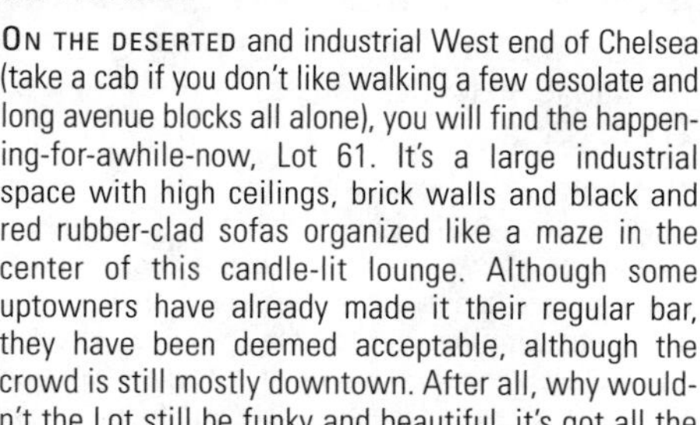

ON THE DESERTED and industrial West end of Chelsea (take a cab if you don't like walking a few desolate and long avenue blocks all alone), you will find the happening-for-awhile-now, Lot 61. It's a large industrial space with high ceilings, brick walls and black and red rubber-clad sofas organized like a maze in the center of this candle-lit lounge. Although some uptowners have already made it their regular bar, they have been deemed acceptable, although the crowd is still mostly downtown. After all, why wouldn't the Lot still be funky and beautiful, it's got all the New York requirements for a hot spot: an upscale dinner menu, room to dance, room to smoke, room to be anonymous and no sign outside.

## Lotus

409 W. 14th St. (10th & 11th Aves.)
212-243-4420

THE NEW THING this year seems to be the super posh, uber expensive, star laden supper clubs. Being a new flower on the block, Lotus smells like a rose in an area that usually smells like ass (the meat packing district). The sleek modern design as well as the cool acid jazz pounding through the sound system works as a perfect back drop to the wonderful food and the beautiful model types that are filling up the seats in this tri-level super-lounge. Sporting a well-stocked wine cellar and a premium cocktail selection matched only by the premium people enjoying them, you have the makings of the perfect hot spot. Now, try getting a reservation.

## Lotus Club

35 Clinton St. (@ Stanton St.)
212-253-1144

THE LOTUS CLUB truly has a split personality. By day, it's a mild-mannered deli offering soups, salads and smoothies. By night, it's a neighborhood hangout, with books on the walls, reggae on the speakers and

Guinness on tap, which goes for $2 during the 5 to 8 p.m. happy hours. And while the actual bar is tiny, the deli area offers plenty of room to put your feet up. There's also a friendly, fun staff and plenty of cheap beers. All in all, a nice hangout for locals in an area that has been less than friendly.

## Lounge at 203 Spring St.

203 Spring St. (@ Sullivan St.)
212-334-3855

THIS SOHO NEWCOMER, formerly known as Lili's, provides yet another 'tragically hip'; option to the easy to please local crowd. The lounge area is peppered with comfy antique furniture of all shapes and sizes, most of it covered with the same buttery, jewel-toned velvet that protects the door from bridge and tunnel intrusion. Drinks are pricey, but if you can hack it, the party's not half bad. A handful of DJ's and promoters are on hand to create an ever-changing variety of themed evenings, while a friendly staff is more than willing to help ease the pain that comes from being that damn cool.

## L-Ray

64 W. 10th (5th & 6th Aves.)
212-505-7777

AN AWESOME PLACE to go and get trashed with a super cool crowd who are hip and trendy, L Ray is decorated like a New Orleans oyster bar with the spirit to match. It also has absolutely stupefying margaritas, one of which will cause an out of body experience and make you do things you don't normally do (use your imagination). The only problem with L Ray is that it's not open nearly late enough - only until 12:30a.m. on weekdays, 2a.m. on the weekends if you beg.

## Luahn

59 5th Ave. (12th & 13th Sts.)
212-242-9710

THIS SPLIT-LEVEL chill restaurant/lounge, owned by hottie Stephen Baldwin, is totally mellow. The food is characterized as "Neo-classic American Seafood", so when you're out one night and your SOTH (Significant Other) says he/she wants "Neo-classic American Seafood"--please come on in. On weeknights, elegant couples and after work crowd hang out in the jazzy atmosphere. However, on weekends the place converts into Mr. Hyde. Check out the downstairs lounge with a DJ spinning and people hanging out on the over-the-top ultra-mod red velvet couch and you may not leave until closing time at 4a.m. Luahn's claim to fame: their specialty drink Rx was featured on Access Hollywood last May.

## Luca Lounge

220 Ave. B (13th & 14th Sts.)
212-674-9400

THIS RUSTIC ITALIAN restaurant/lounge brings good food and a genuine Italian glow to Ave. B. Worn antique tables and couches, dim candlelight and ambience provides the ideal date spot. An enclosed atrium in the back of the restaurant overlooks one of the most beautiful gardens in NYC. Drinks are reasonably priced and Sunday brunch is a must for bellinis and mimosas. It's a great family owned joint with lots of warmth, friendliness and a knack for keeping people coming back for more.

## Lucien

14 1st Ave. (@ 1st St.)
212-260-6481

ALTHOUGH CLAIMING TO be more restaurant than bar, the dining room itself looks a tad bipolar. While one half is straight-up elegant Manhattan bistro, the kitchen, an all stainless steel, clanging sauté pans and oven heat extravaganza, sits dead center in the room. But the contrasts will give you something interesting to watch while you poke at your escargots. Populated by artsy rich folk, Lucien has a good wine selection, expensive food and a lively, yet romantic, atmosphere.

## Lucky Cheng's

24 1st Ave. (1st & 2nd Sts.)
212-473-0516

LUCKY CHENG'S IS a great place to go for a nasty good time. Are they women? Nah! Well, maybe, I'm sure only their proctologists know for certain, but if you're open to anything you just might fall in love with your cross-dressing waitress. The walls are mirrored, the room is dark and there are animal prints everywhere from the tablecloths to the garter-belts. Have your drag queen geisha serve you an Imelda's chocolate shoe ($40). That's a pound of Belgian chocolate fashioned into a size 8 Prada stiletto full of chantilly créme, chocolate mousse and fresh berries. If this doesn't get you "pumped" to sing karaoke downstairs, just one of their famous scorpion bowls will.

## Lucky Strike

59 Grand St. (W. Broadway & Wooster St.)
212-941-0479

A TRAILBLAZER IN this neighborhood and still unchanged after 10 years, Lucky Strike remains one of the cooler brasseries below 14th St. The narrow space fills with a fashionable downtown crowd and (more recently) spillover tourists from the SoHo Grand. The soft yellow haze that fills this place makes you feel like you're inside of a wonderful French egg yolk that serves beer. It's better to come here on weeknights since the SoHo crowds get out of hand on weekends. Too bad you can't dance because the bar has great DJ's every night of the week.

## Lucy's

135 Ave. A (St. Mark's Pl. & 9th St.)
No Phone

A STAPLE ON the East Village scene, Lucy's is part of a dying breed of bars on Ave A. that refuses to be gentrified. Featured in the film, "Hurricane Streets", Lucy's has been around as long as Alphabet City has been pouring drinks. A loyal crowd loads up on cheap booze while listening to a great rock 'n' roll jukebox. Test your luck with a down and dirty game of pool with the best players in the 'hood. There's nothing to hide here at Lucy's, it's just an East Village dive with the will to survive.

## Ludlow Bar

165 Ludlow St. (Houston & Stanton St.s.)
212-353-0536

STEPPING INTO THIS place is like showing up at a last minute party in a friend of a friend's basement, albeit a very cool basement without a stairmaster or string art. You can find this handsome thrift store-meets-Old Navy crowd curled up on glittery plastic couches cradling their bottled domestics, or rubbing sweaty shoulders to a DJ's hip-hop or Latin jazz. There's also a pool table in back for the rhythm-impaired. Drinks are reasonable, pretense is low and the sexy red lighting encourages the possibility of a sleepover pal. Cover is $3 on Friday and Saturday after 11p.m.

## Luke's Bar & Grill

1394 3rd Ave. (79th & 80th Sts.)
212-249-7070

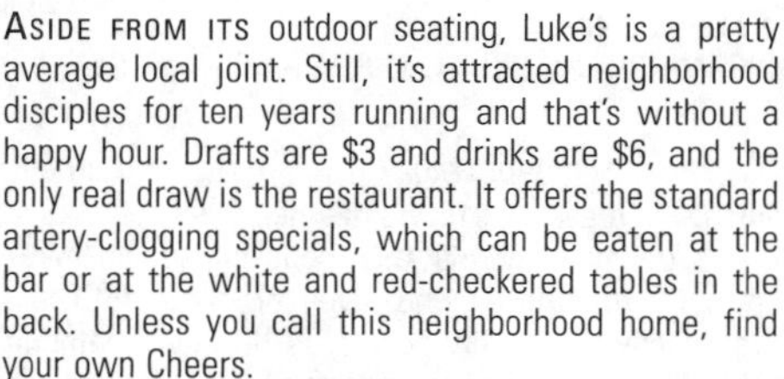

ASIDE FROM ITS outdoor seating, Luke's is a pretty average local joint. Still, it's attracted neighborhood disciples for ten years running and that's without a happy hour. Drafts are $3 and drinks are $6, and the only real draw is the restaurant. It offers the standard artery-clogging specials, which can be eaten at the bar or at the white and red-checkered tables in the back. Unless you call this neighborhood home, find your own Cheers.

## Luna Lounge

171 Ludlow St. (Houston & Stanton Sts.)
212-260-2323

LUNA IS A music venue first and foremost, but one can enjoy a $4.50 draft or $4 well drink in the front bar when the tunes get too loud. While the seasonal (i.e., not summer) Monday night comedy show "Eating It" is a draw, it's the thriving local band scene that has kept Luna around for five years without advertising or feeling the need to put its name on the door. Attracting talent like Elliot Smith and Nada Surf, this no-cover establishment decided to start its own label, Luna Sea. In between sets, pick out a tune on the famous alternate-rock jukebox. And if you think you can do better, drop off your demo tape with the bartender.

## Luna Park (@ Union Square Park)

1 Union Sq. E. (@ E. 17th St.)
212-475-8464

IF YOUR IDEA of happy hour conjures up images of being caught in a fisherman's net with a school of sharks while hanging on to an overpriced drink in a plastic cup, here you go. Only open in seasonable weather, Luna Park herds unthinking and uncreative groups of after work revelers into its pit. People actually line up in the park in order to drink stale beer from Dixie cups. Why not just tap a keg and have a house party? You might think, "Well, it's in the park and it's so nice to get some fresh air after sitting in a pea size cubicle all day!", but you'd be wrong. There is nothing romantic or bucolic about sweating through your work clothes while inhaling pungent, dog piss breezes.

## The Lure

409 W. 13th St. (9th Ave. & Washington St.)
212-741-3919

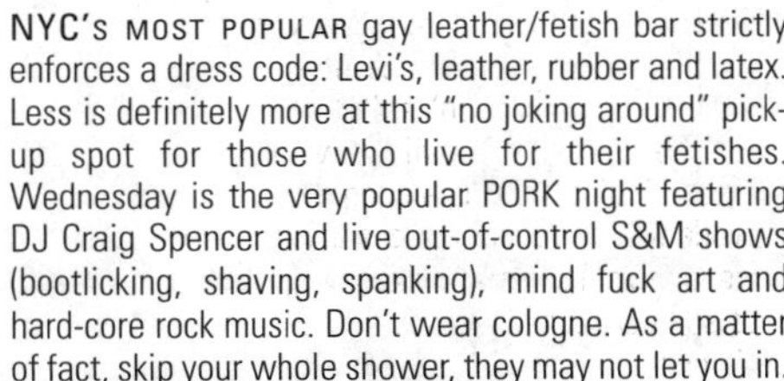

NYC's MOST POPULAR gay leather/fetish bar strictly enforces a dress code: Levi's, leather, rubber and latex. Less is definitely more at this "no joking around" pick-up spot for those who live for their fetishes. Wednesday is the very popular PORK night featuring DJ Craig Spencer and live out-of-control S&M shows (bootlicking, shaving, spanking), mind fuck art and hard-core rock music. Don't wear cologne. As a matter of fact, skip your whole shower, they may not let you in.

## Lush

110 Duane St. (Broadway & Church St.)
212-766-1275

PLEASE LET ME gush about Lush. This is a place to begin and end the evening. This spacious three-room club is designed for 25-35 year old singles, and the layout is conducive to making friends. But its best asset is its modesty. It could charge a cover, but doesn't. The drinks could be more expensive, but they're not. The crowd could have attitudes, but they don't. And while you can't be admitted every night, the bouncers are good about making that clear immediately so that you can get on with your evening.

## Luvbuzz

1438 3rd Ave. (81st & 82nd Sts.)
212-717-0100

LUVBUZZ is a swanky and friendly lounge for mature singles tired of schlepping downtown to feel at home.

It's famed for its "dating service" where, for $20, you can have a date arranged by the hip bartenders. Even if gambling on love isn't your thing, there are cocktails, which are pricey ($8-$9) but delicious. Try a buzzcone (a spiked snow cone) or their signature luvjuice (there's liquor in this?). The snack-serving kitchen is open until midnight weekdays and 1a.m. on the weekends. The front doors open to the street so you can sit outside and take pride in being hipper than your neighborhood.

## M&R Bar

264 Elizabeth St. (Houston & Prince Sts.)
212-226-0559

M&R BAR has been a NoLita staple for 5 years now. With three separate areas to chill out in including a crowded front bar, a dining room decorated with out of place nude paintings and a beautiful garden. M&R Bar's casual '50s atmosphere beckons crowds of very hip artsy locals. Not pretentious or annoying in any way, this intimate bar suits the drinking needs of the martini generation. DJ's spin sultry beats while friends and neighbors try to make love connections. An extensive beer, wine and cordials list is accented by specialty drinks that will make your head spin.

## MacDougal Ale House

122 MacDougal St. (Bleecker & 3rd Sts.)
212-254-8569

UNWIND FROM LIFE, pretend you're normal, get a couple pitchers and play a game of pool or darts. With a friendly bar staff, each of whom have their own specialty drink (I highly recommend Aly's pink drink), and a hard-rocking jukebox, it's an excellent little dive to tuck yourself away in for a couple hours and forget that you've got a job. As an added bonus, when NYU is in session it's an excellent spot to go and meet some good-looking co-eds. And if one has just dumped you, it's a great place to forget about her, too.

## Mad River Bar & Grille

1442 3rd Ave. (81st & 82nd Sts.)
212-988-1832

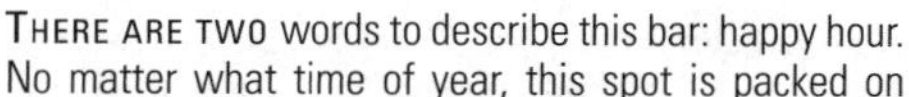

THERE ARE TWO words to describe this bar: happy hour. No matter what time of year, this spot is packed on

weeknights with young execs letting off steam after a day in the office. Super-friendly patrons and staff make for a fun time for all. If you head over early enough, you can catch a table and $1 off already reasonably priced drinks until 6p.m. Satellite TV makes Mad River overflow when big Yankees, Mets and Knicks games are on. And those cheap, greasy eats you'll soon be craving are served until 10:30p.m.

## Madame X

94 W. Houston St.
(LaGuardia Pl. & Thompson St.)
212-539-0808

MADAME X PLAYS such a great mix of hip-hop and R&B-loud enough to be heard around the block-that the absence of a dance floor doesn't stop patrons from getting down in the back room. Plan on wearing something lightweight since you'll be pushing your way through mobs of Villagers trying to nab drinks and head to the loo. If you're lucky, snag one of the sofas or overstuffed chairs in the back or on the upper level. Don't miss out on kinky drinks like "sex in the bathroom." There is a $5 cover charge Friday and Saturday nights.

## Madisons Nite Club

1584 York Ave. (83rd & 84th Sts.)
212-570-5454

MADISONS IS A second rate, cheese-ball, B&T night club that tries hard to be swanky. The door policy is 23 or older. Apparently, they're trying to keep a younger crowd out, which may or may not work. There is a large dance floor, a cigar lounge and they play loud pop hits for their frequent, private parties. The crowds here rent corny white limos and try to impress hoochie mamas. This place is good if you're in the area and want to dance because there are not too many other places on the Upper East Side like it. Madisons is only open for dancing on Friday and Saturday nights in the summer.

## Malachy's

103 W. 72nd St. (Broadway & Columbus Ave.)
212-874-4268

AS THE OWNER brags that Malachy's is the "working man's oasis," a nearby patron begins a story with "I remember when we were kids." Actors, college kids and old, blue collars alike seem to share the philosophy that the best things in life are (practically) free. Happy hour (more like happy day from 9:30a.m. to 7 p.m.) features domestic drafts at $2.50 a pint, $6 pitchers of Bud Lite, and burgers and fries for $3.50. "Why pay $6 for a Heineken when you can pay $3?" the owner asks. Why indeed.

## Manitoba's

99 Ave. B (6th & 7th Sts.)
212-982-2511

WELCOME TO AVE. B's punk rock museum. For those of you familiar with legendary punk rock songs such as "I Live for Cars & Girls" and Teengenerate", you will want to visit Dick Manitoba (frontman for the Dictadors) here. With walls adorned with punk icons, famous boxers and a dashing photo of Abe Bagota, Manitoba's beckons punk rock fans, local East Villagers and lots of European tourists looking to relive the '70s. Live music can be heard most nights while the coolest jukebox this side of the Catskills shoots out the Stooges, The Dead Boys, MC5 and Motorhead. If loud music ain't your thing, go downstairs to the comfortable make-out parlor to chill-out. Drinks are moderately priced with a good two for one happy hour from 4p.m.-8p.m.

## Marcel Lounge

323 3rd Ave. (@ 24th St.)
212-684-7610

RE-INVENTED FOR the third, and hopefully last time, Marcel Lounge is the "hotel bar" of the Marcel Hotel, which is around the corner and is accessible through the lobby. Marcel Lounge is pleasing to the eye with its comfortable sofas and chairs and soothing photography. The velvet red curtains give way so passersby may catch a glimpse of the scene, which is certain proof of the recent gentrification of this area. Marcel hasn't quite established a following, but they are giving it the old school try by offering a free comedy show and live music.

## Marie's Crisis

59 Grove St. (@ 7th Ave.)
212-243-9323

PREPARE TO BELT out "Hello Dolly" and "Gypsy" if you want to make friends. Drinks are cheap and there is no cover charge at this West Village institution. Seating is limited and tables are small so be ready to stand because it gets packed. On weekends, two pianos play and hordes of people sing along to favorite Broadway tunes. The music begins nightly at 9:30p.m. and 5p.m. on Sundays.

## Marion's

354 Bowery (4th & Great Jones Sts.)
212-475-7621

A TRULY BIZARRE little spot, Marion's is the perfect antidote to its pretentious neighbor, the Bowery Bar, offering friendly service and real quality. Granted, the fifties Hawaiian decor and dancing girls make it too kooky to spend a Saturday night here, but the menu is delicious and reasonably priced and the martinis are some of the best in Manhattan. A good place for an offbeat, memorable date, a large group of friends or anybody who has a thing for Frankie and Annette beach movies.

## Mark Bar

25 E. 77th St. (5th & Madison Aves.)
212-606-4544

THE MARK BAR is the epitome of a swank hotel bar - cramped, dimly lit, wonderfully decorated and reeking of cigar smoke. As sophisticated as the décor is, there is something surprisingly illicit about this place. As you sip an extra dry martini, you can't help but wonder if this is the type of place where Anna Nicole Smith might have met her sugar daddy. If you're looking to impress a client or your parents, come to Mark Bar and have a real drink.

## Markt

401 W. 14th St. (@ 9th Ave.)
212-727-3314

IT'S FITTING THAT A former fish-market has morphed into the seafood-centric restaurant, Markt. Now that all-things-Belgian are considered trendy, even the Meatpacking District can lay claim to its own moules-frites establishment. A longer-than-life bar lines this warm and woody brasserie where you can begin your trek through 34 Belgian brews before dining on water-zooi stew.

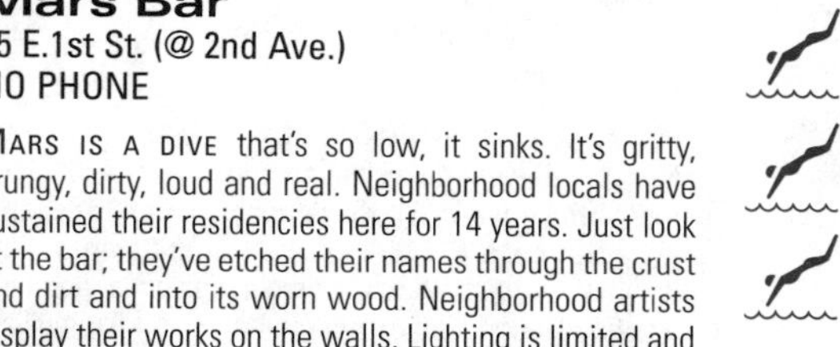

## Mars Bar

25 E.1st St. (@ 2nd Ave.)
NO PHONE

MARS IS A DIVE that's so low, it sinks. It's gritty, grungy, dirty, loud and real. Neighborhood locals have sustained their residencies here for 14 years. Just look at the bar; they've etched their names through the crust and dirt and into its worn wood. Neighborhood artists display their works on the walls. Lighting is limited and so are the blades of the two ceiling fans that actually spin. As far as music, the jukebox is so New York, it'll kick you in the hee-haww! It's chock full of local bands like "Heroin Sheiks", "Molotov Cocktail" and "Kung Pao". Friendly bartenders and really cheap beer ($2.75 for a bottle of Bass) will make you an excellent diver that doesn't mind heading straight for the bottom.

## Mars 2112

1633 Broadway (50th & 51st Sts.)
212-582-2112

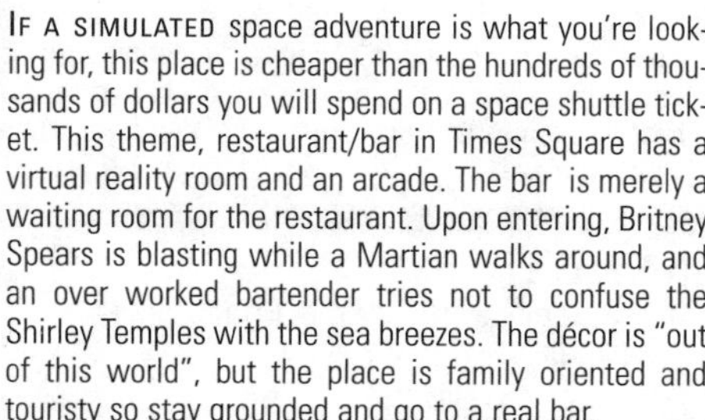

IF A SIMULATED space adventure is what you're looking for, this place is cheaper than the hundreds of thousands of dollars you will spend on a space shuttle ticket. This theme, restaurant/bar in Times Square has a virtual reality room and an arcade. The bar is merely a waiting room for the restaurant. Upon entering, Britney Spears is blasting while a Martian walks around, and an over worked bartender tries not to confuse the Shirley Temples with the sea breezes. The décor is "out of this world", but the place is family oriented and touristy so stay grounded and go to a real bar.

## Martell's

200 E. 83 St. (@ 3rd Ave.)
212-879-1717

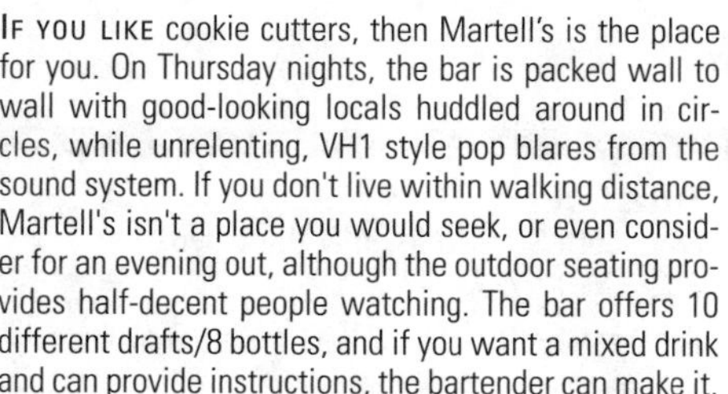

IF YOU LIKE cookie cutters, then Martell's is the place for you. On Thursday nights, the bar is packed wall to wall with good-looking locals huddled around in circles, while unrelenting, VH1 style pop blares from the sound system. If you don't live within walking distance, Martell's isn't a place you would seek, or even consider for an evening out, although the outdoor seating provides half-decent people watching. The bar offers 10 different drafts/8 bottles, and if you want a mixed drink and can provide instructions, the bartender can make it.

## Marty O'Brien's

1696 2nd Ave. (87th & 88th Sts.)
212-722-3889

FORMERLY CALLED THE CLUB CAR due to its small size, this cozy 85-year-old watering hole embraces Irish culture with both arms; if those arms aren't busy embracing a Guinness. Michael Collins' portrait sternly stares down at the bar, ready to admonish anyone who doesn't stick around long enough to hear live Irish music on Sunday evenings. The tight quarters lend itself to easy conversation amongst the eclectic crowd.

## Marylou's

21 W. 9th St. (5th & 6th Aves.)
212-533-0012

ONCE DINNER IS over, the bar at this odd joint takes on a life of its own. Marylou's is a quaint Continental restaurant in the early evening that morphs into watering hole for rock stars, movie stars and anybody else living the rock 'n' roll lifestyle. After 1a.m. you won't stand a chance of getting in the door unless you know somebody who knows somebody. Sometimes dinner leftovers are available for late night customers, but most of them aren't usually too hungry, if you know what we mean.

## Match

160 Mercer St. (Houston & Prince Sts.)
212-343-0020

CLOSED

## Match

33 E. 60th St. (Madison & Park Aves.)
212-906-9177

A PALER, DULLER version of its downtown sibling (which has since closed), Match is still cooler than its neighborhood. With a glass-covered garden room, an American/Asian menu featuring everything from Mahi Mahi to a rack of dim sum appetizers and house drinks like the fruity perfect match or sake spritzer, it may not be your perfect match, but it'll do just fine on nights when you're not too conscious of your wallet.

## Max Fish

178 Ludlow (Houston & Stanton Sts.)
212-529-3959

MAX FISH, THE frontrunner of the very established bar scene on Ludlow, is still fresh after 11 years. Even though the artsy locals are supplanted by the B&T and uptown crowds on weekends, during the week it's still the Max we know and love - the revolving art show on the walls, the videogames and alternative jukebox, cheap drinks ($3.50-$6.50) and colorful crowd.

## McAleer's Pub

425 Amsterdam Ave. (80th & 81st Sts.)
212-874-8037

MCALEER'S IS A refreshingly simple neighborhood Irish pub where you can bring friends and catch up on old times. An unassuming local crowd convenes here nightly to play darts and listen to classics pour out of the jukebox. You won't find singing drunks, hyper-glossed wooden bars or shamrocks hanging all over the place like you see at many new Irish places. Just local lads and lasses of all ages sipping on a $2 pint of McAleer's signature Red Ale.

## McCarthy's

345 2nd Ave. (@ 20th St.)
212-477-6201

THIS TYPICAL IRISH pub serves cheap drinks to the locals and other passersby that come here. McCarthy's is always filled with khaki-clad neighborhood guys and competitive dart throwers who seem to be more interested in their craft than in talking with young ladies. The food is average but the jukebox is filled with old favorites as well as new hits. If you leave late at night, don't worry, you are in good hands because the NYPD training facility is right around the corner. This is a good, comfortable place to hang out with friends and chat.

## McCormack's

365 3rd Ave. (26th & 27th Sts.)
212-683-7027

THIS IRISH PUB is a popular hang out for locals and those others who favor Guinness over water. A satellite TV brings you all the different European soccer leagues, no matter what time it happens to be in the U.S. It is not unusual to find hardcore Manchester United fans hanging out at 8a.m. to catch their latest victory. A typical American pub menu is offered in their back restaurant area, and free appetizers are served Monday through Friday. Pints and bottles will run you around $4.50, and drinks up to $5.50. This non-threatening Irish spot serves mostly men, so women that drink here are treated very well.

## McDooley's

133 W. 33rd St. (6th & 7th Aves.)
212-564-7424

MCDOOLEY'S BILLS ITSELF a bar and restaurant, but there is nothing on tap, and anyone who orders food in a place this dirty needs treatment for suicidal tendencies. You may need to wash your hands every few minutes, so be grateful that the management has placed cocktail napkins on the bathroom sinks to aid in drying. By the way, there are 12 TV's- if you don't count the large security monitor visible to everyone at the bar.

## McFadden's

800 2nd Ave. (@ 42nd St.)
212-986-1515

YES, MCFADDEN'S is yet another Irish pub located in the Midtown arena, but don't pass it by. The food is actually decent and there is enough space to move around, without getting hit by a Kate Spade bag or briefcase. Conveniently located on the corner of 42nd St. and 2nd Ave., this is the perfect bar to hang out with friends, clients or even your dad. There is a full restaurant adjacent to the bar, but the "McFadden's Barge," a load of tasty bar food, is the real crowd-pleaser. Laden with every type of a wing, chip and all other imaginable bar vittles, this $35 cornucopia of cholesterol offers enough food to feed that bunch of accountants placing bets on the Knicks game on TV. A fine beer selection, full bar, DJ spinning on weekends and a friendly, comfortable environment all make this bar stand out in the slew of nameless Irish pubs lining Second Ave.

## McGee's

240 W. 55th St. (Broadway & 8th Ave.)
212-957-3536

BARTENDERS WHOSE SPEED with their rack is matched only by their wit, call McGee's home. This Irish pub's tapsters swear otherwise, but it seems that you do indeed need a brogue as thick as a Guinness to pour at this first-rate midtown tavern. The almost authentic (the food is too good), dimly lit ambience sets the scene perfectly for drinking, catching the game, drinking, eating or drinking. Seating is ample for the lunch crowd and a second bar upstairs opens during the evenings for their typically large and fun company.

## McSorley's

15 E. 7th St. (2nd & 3rd Aves.)
212-473-9148

NOT LONG AFTER America was born, McSorley's Saloon opened its doors to the drinking public. This New York staple is a must-see for anyone in town, but be sure to get there early as the weekend brings a line down the block. The history and no-frills attitude make this Irish pub a drinking man's paradise, and thanks to a recent court order, women can now join their men in throwing back the best beer around. McSorley's 146-year-old recipe for "Light" or "Dark" is what they serve, so don't bother asking for anything else.

## McSwiggan's

393 2nd Ave. (@ 23rd St.)
212-725-8740

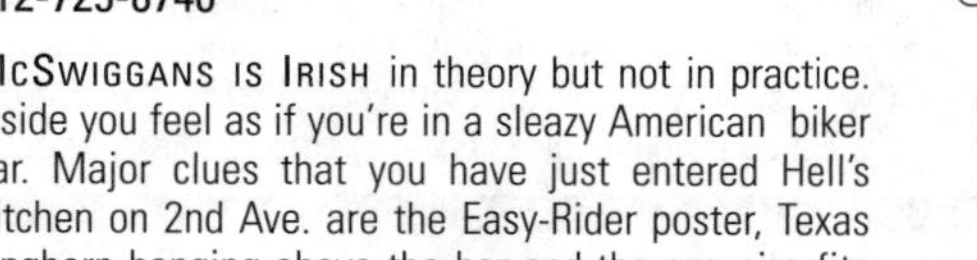

MCSWIGGANS IS IRISH in theory but not in practice. Inside you feel as if you're in a sleazy American biker bar. Major clues that you have just entered Hell's Kitchen on 2nd Ave. are the Easy-Rider poster, Texas longhorn hanging above the bar and the one size fits all "girly-tees" that are for sale. On the weekends you're sure to run into a mix of drunken neighborhood boys who stop here to play pool, darts or Golden Tee. From 9p.m.-12a.m. there is a $10 all you can drink draft beer special (16 on tap); not a bad deal considering the humans who frequent McSwiggans are not shy drinkers.

## Mekka

14 Ave. A (Houston & 2nd Sts.)
212-475-8500

MEKKA IS BY NAME ALONE; selling overpriced drinks and mediocre food, all in a decidedly un-vivacious setting. One would think people would skip Mekka and go to one of the other fun places on this block so crowded with hotspots. But they don't. Must be something in the water that appeals to the dullards who come here.

## Meow Mix

269 E. Houston St. (Suffolk & Clinton Sts.)
212-254-0688

APPARENTLY, RIGHT AFTER Chasing Amy arrived in theatres, the Meow Mix door was swarming with thirsty straight men looking for lesbians of their very own. Since then, the climate has returned to what it had been, a raucous but friendly girl bar. The renovated downstairs has produced a lesbian lizard lounge vibe but the pool table is still intact. Xena and WNBA games can now be viewed on spanking' new flat televisions. Thursday nights are packed at the Gloss party, which is highlighted by go-go girls. Perhaps this is why gay friendly celebs can sometimes be found here.

## Merc Bar

151 Mercer St. (Houston & Prince Sts.)
212-966-2727

"IT'S JUST A BAR," proclaim the matchbooks. True, true, and yet...as one of the first lounges in Soho, Merc Bar attributes its eight-year endurance to not trying to be hip. In a comfy-chic setting with a boat in the rafters and a woodsy lodge feel, the $10 cocktails (try the tropical vacation in your choice of colors) are strong and sweet.

## Mercer Bar

99 Prince St. (@ Mercer St.)
212-966-5454

MAKE SURE YOUR belly is full before heading over to the tiny bar located on the first floor of SoHo's Mercer

Hotel, because the sumptuous starters are barely visible even with the aid of a super-powered microscope. The drinks are strong, but the best part about the Mercer Bar is that you feel chic just walking through the door. The service is impeccable (The waitstaff in white watch closely and empty ashtrays almost before you've taken your last drag.) You'll swear you're a celeb while sitting at silver bistro tables looking out onto one of the prettiest corners in the city.

## Merchants

112 7th Ave. (16th & 17th Sts.)
212-366-7267
1125 1st Ave. (@ 62nd St.)
212-832-155
1521 Columbus Ave. (85th & 86th Sts.)
212-721-3689 -Closed

IF YOU'RE NOT feeling up for the whole chic scene but you want to hang out with your friends in a somewhat sophisticated New York spot, the chain of Merchants always delivers. Good food and booze in dimly lit digs attracts a nice young crowd to this not so "in" place to meet and impress.

## Mercury Bar

659 9th Ave. (45th & 46th Sts)
212-262-7755

FOR OBSESSED PEOPLE watchers, check out the French doors that lead to an outside patio for a streets' eye view of 9th Ave. Irish bar meets art deco lounge draws in a late 20's and 30's crowd. This Hell's Kitchen spot is a hybrid between pub and wannabe swanky. Be adventurous and make the best of it by trying all seven beers on tap. Or visit Monday-Friday and get giddy from 3-6 p.m. on frozen drinks.

## Mercury Lounge

217 E. Houston St. (Ludlow & Essex Sts.)
212-260-4700

WHAT WERE ONCE the servants' quarters for the Astor Mansion, then a tombstone showroom, is now considered the best venue for indie and folk rock bands on the verge of stardom. Jeff Buckley, Joan Jett, Luscious Jackson and Radiohead were discovered here. Everyone from music biz types on the prowl for the "next big thing" to NYU students rock out together in the large back room.

## Merlot (@ The Empire Hotel)

48 W. 63rd St. (Broadway & Columbus Ave.)
212-363-7568

THE DÉCOR HERE falls somewhere between quasi futuristic and, as the name indicates, eighties tackiness. In short, Luke Skywalker and Jack Tripper would feel equally comfortable hanging out here. The complete effect most closely resembles the bat cave on acid with slightly better lighting. Although there is not much activity at the tiny bar, Merlot houses a popular restaurant that bursts at the seams with Lincoln Center crowds and jazz fans heading to the Iridium Room (downstairs from the bar), one of the city's premier jazz/blues clubs.

## Mesopotamia

98 Ave. B (6th & 7th Sts.)
212-358-1166

ROUNDING OUT ONE of the most happening blocks on Ave. B, this Belgian-Turkish lounge/restaurant offers fresh fare at decent prices and some very good beer. Resisting the trendy interior and swank banquet-style dining that many in the area have fallen back on, Mesopotamia relies instead on honest revelry made interesting by a wide array of great imported beers. And boy, do they have a selection. Fin du Monde battles with the rubber stopper stuff that dreams are made of. These imports get pricey, but are worth every drop and go great with a plate of spicey steamed mussels. A perfect place to close your eyes and pretend you're dipping your toes in Nile while sipping a Raki.

## Metronome

915 Broadway (@ 21st St.)
212-505-7400

FROM THE OUTSIDE, Metronome looks like a very cool place with high ceilings and tall glass windows. And as you walk inside you will not be disappointed. This artistically impressive dinner club offers jazz nightly and caters to an after work crowd. A small bar adjacent to the elegant dining area offers an extensive wine and cocktail list to a thirtysomething crowd. On the weekends, however, it turns into a different place, especially during the summer when the rest of NY is in the Hamptons or the Vineyard. Then the bridge and tunnelers make their way in and it turns into a mass meat market that even the $20 cover cannot control.

## Mexican Radio

19 Cleveland Pl. (Spring & Kenmare Sts.)
212-343-0140

IN ITS NEW ten-times-bigger location on a busier corner with an expanded beer list, Mexican Radio continues to serve Mexican delicacies, amazing margaritas and sangrias, but this time with no wait. The two-floor restaurant has a long mahogany bar, cactus plants and red and green Aztec artwork. Although the new space is less intimate, the food and staff are as authentic and charming as they were on Mulberry Street. We would vote them best Mexican restaurant, but New York Press already did that, and we hate to be unoriginal.

## Mica Bar

252 E. 51st St. (2nd & 3rd Aves.)
212-888-2453

THE MAIN DRAW to this Midtown lounge is its rooftop deck where you can hangout and enjoy a quiet drink away from the maddening sidewalks below. The simple décor of bonsai trees and bamboo tables evoke peaceful tranquility. Its two levels give customers a choice of relaxing in a lounge or upstairs at tables with small velvet stools. The staff is friendly and cool, always trying to accommodate your wishes.

## Michael Jordan's

(@ Grand Central Station)
23 Vanderbilt Ave. (@ 44th St.)
212-271-2323

THE SPLENDIDLY REDONE Grand Central provides the perfect backdrop for the balcony bar of Michael Jordan's. This swanky little number overlooks the bustling terminal and is the closest thing to a SoHo lounge in Midtown. Drinks may drain your bank account, but they'll give you a nice buzz for the train ride home. This is a great place to knock back a few before heading back to the burbs.

## Mickey Mantle's

42 Central Park So. (5th & 6th Aves.)
212-668-7777

THEY SHOULD HAVE named this TGI Mickey Mantle's. It's the ultimate homage; a sports bar praising a great and unforgettable star. The bar is adorned with his memorabilia and has number "7" merchandise for sale, attracting throngs of tourists. The waiters are dressed like the Foot Locker salespeople, but at least they're friendly. Mantle's is considered one of the most popular sports bars in Manhattan.

## Milady's

160 Prince St. (@ Thompson St.)
212-226-9340

AN UNPRETENTIOUS BAR in SoHo, who'd a thunk it? This token local watering hole does its job and it does it well. Complete with drunken old man in the corner, the uncomplicated and stoic (40+ years) pub/sports bar/restaurant provides a refreshing alternative to the local "dress up" scene. Although Milady's tends to be more of a day bar, happy hour gets pretty lively and when late-night munchies kick in, come on in. Don't expect much of a pick-up scene; the male to female ratio is disproportionate.

## Milano's

51 Houston St. (Mott & Mulberry Sts.)
212-226-8632

MILANO'S is not as scary as it looks. It attracts neighborhood folks and has a distinct atmosphere of blue-collar beer drinking; all drinks are $3 - $4 bucks. Be prepared for plastic cups and to check your backside for ash stains (or is that dust?) when you leave. This place has been around for a whopping 110 years, and if cockroaches don't take over the planet, it will probably be here for another 110.

## Milk and Honey

**Lower East Side- No info/secret spot**

The first rule of Milk and Honey is never tell anyone about it. You can't get in unless you know someone in good standing with the owner. The other rules of this twenties-style speakeasy are posted in the bathrooms and strictly enforced. To the owner's chagrin, these policies have made this quiet bar all the rage to self-important Village idiots who can't fathom that someone somewhere doesn't love them. Once inside, there is no cover and the reasonably priced drinks are prepared with care and delivered on a (literal) silver platter. So if the opportunity to visit arises, go. Otherwise, get over it and yourself.

## Milo's

559 Lorimer St. (@ Metropolitan Ave.)
718-599-4444 (Brooklyn)

ALTHOUGH NEIGHBORHOOD PURISTS grumble that spots like Milo's symbolize the "burg's" imminent gentrification, its draws are irresistible. The tree-lined, sand pebbled outside garden provides a lush oasis next to the ubiquitous aluminum siding of neighboring dwellings. A powerhouse jukebox brims with gems from artists like Grace Jones and Al Green to Portishead. The Euro-accented staff is attentive and courteous, making this a hot new spot to hang out in the neighborhood.

## Miracle Grill

112 1st Ave. (6th & 7th Sts.)
212-254-2353
415 Bleecker St. (Bank & 11th St.)
212-924-1900

HEY, THIS WAS Bobby Flay's place, the goofy guy who has the show "Chilling & Grilling" on the TV Food Network. Grab a seat in the very large garden and order a cocktail. This place is more a restaurant than a bar, but that doesn't mean you can't get wasted on the property. Bring a date and start off with a few shots of the pineapple Absolut concoction that they keep fermenting on the bar. The Southwestern cuisine is so awesome that folks have been crowding in here for eleven years.

## Miri

179 Essex St. (@ Houston St.)
212-260-5690

A LITTLE BIGGER than a Manhattan studio apartment, dipped in red with a tiny bar and a wall lined with plush couches, this new Lower East Side sushi bar/lounge manages to give off a very relaxing vibe. This is more of a hangout for hungry young professionals than a party bar. You can munch on cheap sushi and try one of their 8 brands of sake. The wine list is small, but the beer list has some great imports. Happy hour is 6p.m.to 8p.m. Indulge in half-price beer and a 25% discount on food.

## Miss Elle's Homesick Bar & Grill

226 W. 79th St. (Amsterdam Ave. & Broadway)
212-595-4350

MAYBE IT'S NOT your home, but it's home to the blue haired octogenarians of the world. Welcome to grandma's Victorian lace and silk flower filled hideaway bar. You'll find old men and women who'd be better off with feeding tubes shoved in their arms downing gimlets while trying hard not to fall off their stools for fear of breaking a hip. Always an interesting spot to go if you're looking for cheap drinks and a jukebox filled with real oldies. Recommended, not for the homesick, but for the "nursing" homesick.

## Mitch's Place

134 Reade St. (Greenwich & Hudson Sts.)
212-226-8928

EVEN IF YOU'VE never been here before, you have. Mitch's is a typical Wall Street, yuppie sports bar complete with a pool table, a dart-board, big-screen TV and your standard vanilla, khaki-wearing clientele. On the plus side, there is an outdoor patio on a quiet tree-lined street and the service is friendly and prompt. It's also one of the few places in TriBeCa where you can still get a $4.50 premium draft. This is a good place if you're looking to stuff yourself on an $18 slab of ribs before that long trek home to Jersey.

## Mogos

1470 1st Ave. (76th & 77th Sts.)
744-8992

MOGOS, FORMERLY Beacon Hill Ale House, is a neighborhood bar by day, and a frat boy's wet dream by night. They come here in testosterone driven frenzies to pound beer and hit on neighborhood chicks. The pool table, darts and cheap beer attract a rowdy crowd of "looking to get laid" guys and girls. There is never a cover, but bouncers stand at the door on weekends to sift through the preppy riff raff.

## Molly's

287 3rd Ave. (22nd & 23rd Sts.)
212-889-3361

YOU HAVE TO be impressed by any place with a working fireplace and a floor covered in sawdust at the same time. But considering this is the neighborhood hangout for the local firehouse, you're probably in good hands. Molly's is a very cozy Irish pub that stands apart from its Gramercy Park neighbors with a touch of authenticity and intimacy missing from the Irish/sports bars that line 3rd Ave. New Yorker's consistently rank Molly's as the best Guinness bar in Manhattan. Come in the winter when you can curl up next to the fire and enjoy one of Molly's awesome burgers and a good brew.

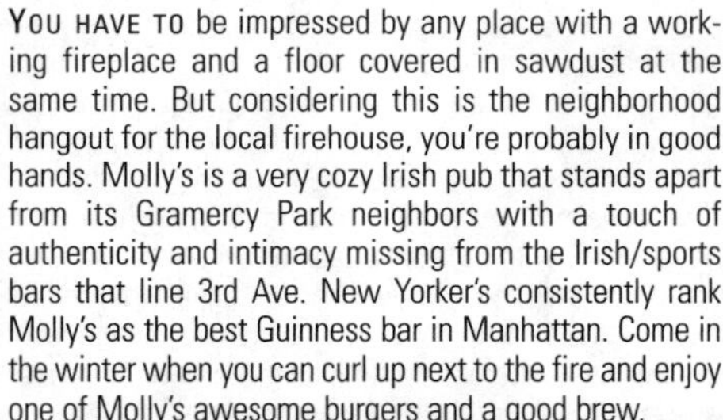

## Mona's

224 Ave. B (13th & 14th Sts.)
212-353-3780

THANK GOD FOR old school East Village dives! Around for 24 years, this "Cheers" of Ave. B offers a no-frills drinking experience for next to nothing. Mona's has some of the best bartenders in the East Village; they remember what you drink and it's ready in a flash as you walk in the door. And they do buy backs. Play some pool or listen to a great jukebox that spits out The Ramones, Patti Smith and Radiohead. Monday nights bring in a live Irish band with a very Irish following. Except for the occasional lost yuppie searching for the Musical Box located across the street, Mona's invites in a loyal East Village crowd and even the occasional stray dog.

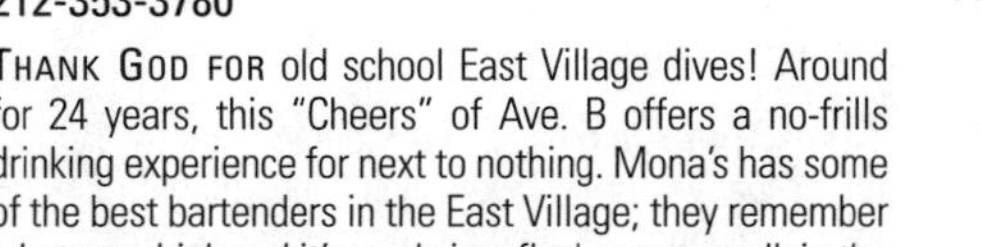

## Monkey Bar

60 E. 54th St. (Park & Madison Aves.)
212-838-2600

HISTORY, STYLE AND deep pockets are some of the reasons you might want to try Monkey Bar. Open since 1936, this beautifully romantic bar set in the equally stunning Hotel Elysee is one of the best midtown, after work spots available. A stylish art deco décor and an attentive staff keep this older crowd pick-up spot popular with the business folk. Offering live jazz after 9:30

p.m. nightly, Monkey Bar manages to give you that old Hollywood feeling without losing its NYC

## The Monster

80 Grove St. (@ Waverly Pl. & W. 4th St.)
212-924-3558

I GUESS THAT the name must refer to the yellow toothed, mean-spirited, nasty guy working the door. With the exception of that toad, The Monster is quite an agreeable place to be. Serving the West Village gay crowd for over 18 years, there's a high, happy energy buzzing through the place on a nightly basis, offering dancing downstairs for just a $3 cover and a happy hour from 4p.m.-9p.m. with reduced prices on all drinks. Unlike a lot of gay clubs where you feel as if the bathroom is doubling as a motel, most of The Monster's customers are primarily interested in minding their own business and enjoying a drink with a friend or lover.

## Montague Street Saloon

122 Montague St. (Henry & Hicks Sts.)
Brooklyn
718-522-6770

THANK GOD FOR a place like Montague Street Saloon. It'll assuage your city woes and send you on a holiday for a few hours. Settle down on the sidewalk patio and shift into low gear. Order yourself a piña colada and let it all slide away as you close your eyes and catch a cool breeze off the water. The bar hours (from 11:30a.m.-midnight, 2a.m. weekends), might convince you to extend your stay a little longer than planned. Arrange a trip to happy hour (4:30-7p.m.) for 1/2-price everything. Sojourn to brunch on any given Saturday and follow it up with Montague's live blues band. There's a friendly staff here, great frozen drinks and the place is a hell of a lot cheaper than Club Med.

## Moomba

133 7th Ave. So. (Charles & W.10th Sts.)
212-989-1414

MOOMBA PLAYS HOST to the ultra-chic, trendy, fashionista New York set. Every evening this restaurant-cum-celeb hangout is a veritable runway of blown-out blondes sporting Fendi bags scoping out men wearing

no socks and Gucci loafers. It's difficult to keep the attention of friends because their roving eyes suggest they are more interested in spotting the stick-figured model or checking to see if their cell phone is ringing. Moomba is undeniably modish right down to its red-hued lighting, well-groomed staff, and huge windows covered in sheer fabric offering voyeuristic sights of the street below. If you're marvelous enough to pass the sour-pussed gatekeeper to the third level you'll be surprised to find one of the most inviting lounges in New York.

## Moonlighting

511 Amsterdam Ave. (84th & 85th Sts.)
212-799-4643

THIS DANCE PLACE caters to a single, young professional crowd who like to sweat and be knocked around while they scope each other out. The downstairs bar usually hosts a private party leaving the upper two levels for gyrating horny twentysomethings. A fresh tropical nook complete with fake palm trees offers a cheap alternative to flying to Cancun. If you're still pining away about your spring break days and want to reminisce, get your butt over here and paaaarrrrrrttttyy.

## Moran's

250 Vesey St. (@ The World Financial Center)
212-945-2255

WHERE CAN I GO after work to get really drunk on some keg beer, pick up my old secretary and hang out with some naughty bankers? I know, let's try the old standard, Moran's. Although the crowd is mostly filled with beer swilling suits and the women who love them, Moran's does offer what is still the best outdoor drinking in Wall Street. Great water views, a convenient World Financial Center location and good people watching has kept this favorite packed for years. Maybe a required IQ test would thin out the crowd.

## Mo's Caribbean

1454 2nd Ave. (@ 76th St.)
212-650-0561

EVERYBODY LOVES A little variety so tear yourself away from an Irish bar and head into Mo's. Fruity frozen drinks and flirty, fun crowds fill Mo's Caribbean with a lot of fun energy. Like all good theme restaurants it has its share of goofy décor (neon palm trees anyone?) and each night has a different special. The most notable is Mondays when lobsters are $11 for the first and $7 for each additional. So the place is a bit cheesy, but the bartenders are friendly, as is the crowd, and everyone's out for a good time.

## Morell Wine Bar

1 Rockerfeller Plaza (@ 49th St.)
212-262-7700

THIS RELATIVELY NEW BAR and restaurant is a welcome addition to the Midtown scene. With over 120 wines by the glass, the wine list is not likely to disappoint anyone. The restaurant is pricey, at $17-$28 per entrée, but does offer creative and tasty entrees, such as an amazing ravioli made with Maryland crab meat and rock shrimp. Morell draws a lot of couples, who seem to just love that jazz drifting in from the speakers.

## Morgans Bar (@ The Morgan Hotel)

237 Madison Ave. (37th & 38th Sts.)
212-726-7600

THE PERFECT, SWANKY SPOT to impress your out-of-town friends, this small, candlelit downstairs space is located in the tres posh Midtown Morgans Hotel. Pretty patrons are only overshadowed by the prettier staff clad in barely-there black dresses. A much more laid back, friendly spot than most chichi hot hangouts, the music ranges from Pearl Jam to techno. Choose from a seat at the sleek marble bar or lounge on an overstuffed armchair at one of the clusters along the walls and revel in the high society around you.

## Moscow

137 E. 55th St. (Lexington & 3rd Aves.)
212-813-1313

AT $25 A HEAD, Moscow is a highly overpriced club that packs in a B&T crowd who file into the basement catacomb for dancing and drinking. This Midtown supperclub is decorated with giant statues that pay homage to famous Russian statesmen. Like all things Russian, Moscow is a little off, but interesting nonetheless.

## Motor City Bar

127 Ludlow St. (Rivington & Delancey Sts.)
212-358-1595

AHHHH....DETROIT. IT makes one think of cars, MC5, and this spacious dive on Ludlow. With enough automobile decor and furniture to rebuild a muscle car, Motor City will conjure up feelings of nostalgia even if you've never set foot in Detroit. Various DJ's, every night of the week, will take your requests without rolling their eyes and spin some of the best garage rock around. WARNING: Ask for Ricky Martin and you might be escorted outside to live your own Vida Loca.

## Motown Café

104 W. 57th St. (6th & 7th Aves.)
212-581-8030

WITH LIVE ENTERTAINMENT nightly, this theme bar/restaurant packs it in nightly with young tourists looking to get their groove on. If you love Motown, then get your ass over here and bask in the music and the specialty drinks such as "my guy," "abc" and "my girl" which will get you moving to the beat in no time. They are a bit steep at $13.75 but you can keep the glass. If you like Hard Rock Café, you'll be very happy here.

## Mr.Bigg's Bar & Grill

596 10th Ave. (@ 43rd St.)
212-246-2030

NO, THIS ISN'T Mr. Bigg's place from "Sex and the City." That would be The Cub Room. This Hell's Kitchen bar is a cross between a dive and a somewhat eclectic comfortable lounge. Mr. Bigg's is not big on décor but the French style windows open up to an awesome view of the neighborhood which makes up for the downfall. The locals give the buffalo wings rave reviews while taking advantage of happy hour and the reasonably priced drinks.

## Mudville 9

126 Chambers St. (W. Broadway & Church Sts.)
212-349-0059

DON'T CONFUSE THIS bar with the tagline for the movie Butterfield 8, "the most desirable 'bar' in town and the easiest to find." If anything, this dive bar is the polar opposite, it's the dive to end all dives. Its white trash décor makes the trailer park Britney Spears crawled out of look like the Malibu mansion Brad Pitt and Jennifer Aniston got married in. You're almost guaranteed to either see a brawl, or be involved in one while you down your cheap domestic draughts.

## Mug's Ale House

125 Bedford Ave. (N. 10th & 11th Sts.)
Brooklyn
718-384-8494

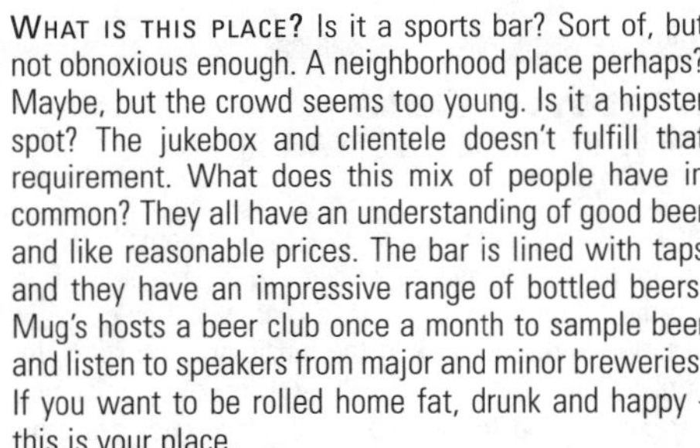

WHAT IS THIS PLACE? Is it a sports bar? Sort of, but not obnoxious enough. A neighborhood place perhaps? Maybe, but the crowd seems too young. Is it a hipster spot? The jukebox and clientele doesn't fulfill that requirement. What does this mix of people have in common? They all have an understanding of good beer and like reasonable prices. The bar is lined with taps and they have an impressive range of bottled beers. Mug's hosts a beer club once a month to sample beer and listen to speakers from major and minor breweries. If you want to be rolled home fat, drunk and happy - this is your place.

## Mug Shot Saloon

1446 1st Ave (75th & 76th Sts.)
212-772-6597

DID YOU KNOW that Suzanne Summers was once arrested? You would if you went to the Mug Shot Saloon. Celebrity mug shots adorn the walls of this otherwise no-frills Upper East Side bar. The owners were ingenious to come up with such a kitschy, different theme, because without the mug shots and the conversation that they invoke, the Mug Shot Saloon is dangerously close to being another annoying, frat-infested, yuppie dive bar.

## Muldoon's Irish Pub

692 3rd Ave. (43rd & 44th Sts.)
212-599-2750

THERE ARE ABOUT as many Irish pubs in New York as there are in Ireland and Northern Ireland combined. If the other bars are absolutely packed to the gills and you cannot get in, then come on in park your butt on a stool and order one of the eight beers on tap. The old-time bartenders are nice considering they have to serve a sketchy group of patrons all day long. If European soccer matches or hurling is your thing, then crash here and catch it on the telly.

## Mulligan's

267 Madison Ave. (39th & 40th Sts.)
212-268-0207

IF YOU ARE looking for an Irish bar in Midtown that has decent looking chicks, you have found the place. It must be all the advertising firms in the area that hire the fine lasses. The upbeat, friendly atmosphere makes this a good place to catch a game or hang and try to impress one of the girls. The after work crowd takes advantage of the happy hours.

## Mumbles

179 3rd Ave. (@ 17th St.)
212-477-6066

MUMBLES IS A STRANGE bird. Aging local alcoholics come here to hang out mid-afternoon sipping for hours on martinis and Manhattans. Never busy, Mumbles is an incredibly depressing and shabby place. If you're in a pit of despair, misery loves company at Mumbles.

## Murphy's Law

417 E. 70th (1st & York Aves.)
212-628-3724

TUCKED BETWEEN THE towering buildings of New York Hospital sits Murphy's Law. A better-than-average Irish pub, it tends to be filled with neighborhood regulars and hospital employees winding down after long shifts. The bar has been around for about 70 years but it was previously the Recovery Room and What Ales You. In addition to having 11 beers on tap, it also boasts a full menu ($7-$11 entrees) served beside hand-painted murals.

## P.J.Carney's (a.k.a Murray Hill Tavern)

591 3rd Ave. (@ 39th St.)
212-684-4421

CHEAP DRINKS, great specials and free munchies are all good reasons to visit the Murray Hill Tavern. They are also probably the only ones if you don't happen to be a local. Sports show regularly on a big screen TV, but the real draw is the 5-7p.m. cocktail hour with free pub food and $3 drinks. The pleasant bar staff serves $4.50 pints and hi-balls after 7p.m. Enjoy their homemade potato chips while the locals serenade you with their versions of Roy Orbison tunes from the jukebox.

## Musical Box

219 Ave. B (13th & 14th Sts.)
212-254-1731

THE MUSICAL BOX is well hidden; not only is there no sign, it seems as if there's no place. But don't think it's empty inside; behind the hidden doorway lies a beautiful space decorated with dim candlelight, classic rock photos and overstuffed lounge chairs. This is a great place for a date, a party or even a night out with mom. Weather permitting; a back patio space is open to midnight loungers. Drinks are moderately priced and the staff is super friendly. Of course you can't mention the Musical box without mentioning the music; depending on the night's bartender/music-pharaoh, you'll hear anything from the Verve and Cornershop to Jimi Hendrix and Bob Dylan.

## Mustang

1633 2nd Ave. (85th & 84th Sts.)
212-744-9194

THIS POPULAR TEX-MEX bar and restaurant is a solid summer hangout and busy evening pick-up spot. A casual crowd of suits and professionals flocks here on weekends for the Tequila and some light flirting. The happy hour is not very impressive and the $8 margaritas are pricey, but the prices keep the kids away. The attractive back lounge is marred only by the $50 minimum required to sit there. A cigar bar keeps the yuppies feeling important, while the constant flow of frozen drinks keeps the girls feeling attractive. Come to pick up some nachos, or perhaps just someone cheesy.

## Mustang Harry's

352 7th Ave. (29th & 30th Sts.)
212-268-8930

UNDER THE SAME management as its neighbor, Mustang Sally's, this Madison Square Garden area bar is brighter, cleaner, and a touch more antiseptic than its more comfortable sister. The long bar opens into a dining area where patrons can enjoy a full menu of straightforward meals and select pub favorites. Harry's can get pretty crowded after work or a big Garden event, and an upstairs bar is opened on busy nights. Eight beers on tap and a few good wines help to make this bar casual, yet civilized.

## Mustang Sally's

324 7th Ave. (28th & 29th Sts.)
212-695-3806

THIS DARKER AND dustier sister bar of nearby Mustang Harry's offers 12 beers on tap, a full menu and a large projection TV. We were told that, at Sally's, "every hour is happy hour," which means they don't have one, but the drinks are reasonably priced and its proximity to the Garden makes it a good post-event watering hole. Large crowds come in after work to chat, drink and enjoy the atmosphere decorated mainly with many strangely out-of-place movie and Broadway show posters.

## ñ

33 Crosby St. (Broome & Grand Sts.)
212-219-8856

TUCKED AWAY ON a rather inconspicuous street in SoHo, ñ is a true find and the trailblazer of tapas bars in the city. The sangria is authentic and refreshing on summer afternoons. ñ also serves a wide variety of sherries and wines. Authentically Spanish, rustic and warm, ñ fills with groups of friends from area offices and locals. Come early. the bar is small and narrow, so having a seat is crucial to enjoying your time here.

## Naked Lunch

17 Thompson St. (@ Grand St.)
212-343-0828

THIS SOHO SPOT is lounge-sized but insists on being a club. So dance club it is then, with the kind of space where everyone is so mashed together the crowd just kind of shifts back and forth like one giant sweaty pelvis. While perched on one of the semi-circular sofas, you can peer through the patches of shadow and make out the unmistakable silhouettes of slicked down yuppies and spiked up artists. There's a DJ every night and a $5 cover when the owner gives the nod to the doorman. Kick back, enjoy the variety of wines and the house specialty Tanqueray tea and dance the night away.

## Nancy Whiskey Pub

1 Lispenard St. (@ W. Broadway)
212-226-9943

ONE OF PERHAPS only two bars in the city to offer the wonderful, yet not oft appreciated game of shuffleboard. Beyond that, the Nancy is really just another hole in the wall bar that just happened to open in the days before the land below Canal St. became noteworthy. So what we have is a dinosaur of sorts that fills with locals and blue-collar workers from the municipal buildings in the area.

## Nassau Bar & Lounge

118 Nassau St. (@ Ann St.)
212-962-0011

SITTING IN THE lobby of Pace University, I overheard a tale about bikini clad bartenders, air conditioning, and strong drinks. Down Nassau St. I wandered, and somewhere between Pace and Fulton street I came to Nassau Bar & Lounge. The novelty of barely dressed females was quickly cut short, when the "man in charge," sitting next to his "bouncer," was kind enough to give me a quote, "We don't want to be in any F*!#king review guide. Now get out!" From the 129 seconds I was in the place, a few things struck me as odd. The people at the far end of the bar had their own bikini-tender. I wasn't allowed to walk beyond the men who kicked me out. I started asking questions, I was promptly escorted from the premises and when I stayed outside peering in the window, the henchman came out, threatening bodily harm. All this secrecy and hassle for a few skanky girls in a dingy, over air-conditioned bar.

## Nathan Hale's Bar & Grill

6 Murray St. (@ Broadway)
212-571-0776

NATHAN HALE'S IS a good bar on the edge of the Financial District that also has equally good, cheap eats (cooked by former Hilton Las Vegas head chef, Mike Tahoun). Word of mouth, rather than flashy advertising, has led to Hale's gradual expansion, which now includes a take-out menu and delivery service. Guest bartenders and beer company promotions always seem to pop up here. If Nathan Hale were alive, he surely would have hollered: "I regret that I have but one meal to fill up my tummy." Er, or something like that.

## Neary's

358 E. 57th St. (@ 1st Ave.)
212-751-1434

IT'S JUST ANOTHER ONE of those typical Midtown Irish pubs that offers nothing particularly noteworthy except a friendly spot to grab an after work drink and catch up with friends. Don't mistake this for one of the popular pick-up spots in the area, Neary's crowds are generally on the older side.

## Negril

362 W. 23rd St. (8th & 9th Aves.)
212-807-6411

KNOWN FOR ITS incredible Caribbean fare and fruity drinks, Negril is a great place to bring a date or close friends for an island getaway experience. Their $5 piña coladas are the best in the neighborhood. And they're served by a staff decked out in shirts that make you want to say "Ya Mon!" So if you're looking to "lively up" yourself to the reggae beat, which is just what '80s sitcom star Malcolm-Jamal Warner was doing when we visited, Negril may be the tropical paradise for you.

## Nell's

246 W. 14th St. (7th & 8th Aves.)
212-675-1567

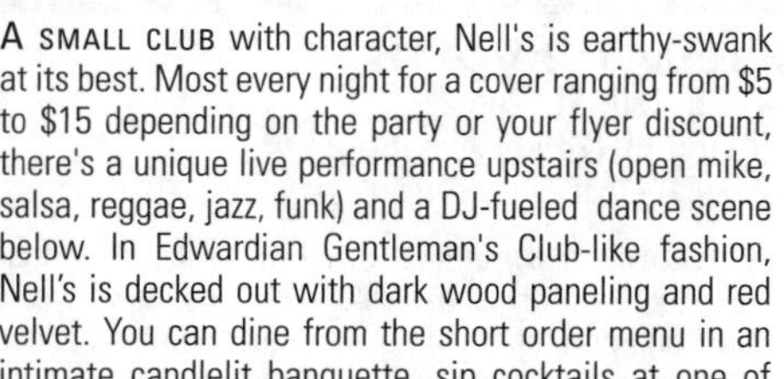

A SMALL CLUB with character, Nell's is earthy-swank at its best. Most every night for a cover ranging from $5 to $15 depending on the party or your flyer discount, there's a unique live performance upstairs (open mike, salsa, reggae, jazz, funk) and a DJ-fueled dance scene below. In Edwardian Gentleman's Club-like fashion, Nell's is decked out with dark wood paneling and red velvet. You can dine from the short order menu in an intimate candlelit banquette, sip cocktails at one of three full bars, get a rubdown from the masseuse occasionally stationed up front, chill in a downstairs couchy nook or just hide in the spacious bathrooms.

## Neva

28 7th Ave. So. (Leroy & Morton Sts.)
212-243-3166

THIS TRIPPED OUT, psychedelic, confused mess of tables, chairs, mirrors and loud throbbing music unfortunately exists. Fortunately, it's on a rather desolate stretch of 7th Ave., so you probably won't accidentally wander in . An older, ethnically diverse crowd huddles around the bar straining their voice boxes to shout above the pumping hip-hop music. Food is available in the form of any type of kebab you can imagine, but that's just about the extent of it. There are also poetry readings and dancing (call for show times and cover).

## Nevada Smith's

74 3rd Ave. (11th & 12th Sts.)
212-982-2591

LOCATED IN THE East Village, Nevada Smith's is considered one of the biggest soccer bars in the country and also serves as the U.S. headquarters for Manchester United, Britain's famed soccer team. Fans come from all over to watch the games on the huge televisions and drink the $5 import ales. The bar attracts a college and local crowd who enjoy the cheap mixed drinks and the DJ's on weekends. If the bar crowd gets too noisy, try the downstairs lounge which is filled with antique couches and chairs. Happy hour runs from 11a.m. to 7p.m. everyday. If you plan on catching a soccer match, go early in the morning because they tend to sell out.

## New Tokyo 18

113 E. 18th St., 2nd Fl.
(Irving Pl. & Park Ave. So.)
212-477-7516

ABOVE THE RESTAURANT Sushi-Desse lies a virtual cross-section of Japanese culture. The bar area is carpeted and decorated with a salt water fish tank and a baby grand piano. Around the corner and through the almost soundproof door is a room filled with monitors broadcasting the karaoke choices of the clients. If you're looking for a unique experience and an insiders look at Japan without shelling out airfare, come sing, watch and listen for a cover charge of $18 and a $12 per person minimum on weekends During the week there is no cover.

## New York Comedy Club

241 E. 24th St. (2nd & 3rd Aves.)
212-696-5233

THE DUMP TO end all dumps. You'd have an easier time proving God exists than trying to figure out how this place stays in business. On any given night you can see one of the worst displays of entertainment this side of a yodeling competition. And it's not even the kind of bad that's funny. It's worse. The drinks are overpriced, the ventilation sucks and the décor is more suited for a rape then a comedy show. It has the feel of an open mike, but it's not. When real comedians actually perform, the pain of sitting through the other acts is so great that it's not even worth it. There are definitely better choices out there for comedy.

## Niagara

112 Ave. A (@ 7th St.)
212-420-9517

NIAGARA'S SWANKY INTERIOR and '50s style bar transports you to the classic days of zoot suits and wallet chains. Don't be deceived by the table-filled space on the ground floor, because there is a completely different vibe going on downstairs. Once you enter the basement's Tiki Room, bask in the warm atmosphere of palm trees, fish tanks even the occasional dancing girl. There is a VIP room (entrance on 7th St.) that hosts parties such as "Greendoor NYC" and a gay night called "Fag Hag & Sleazebag." Both parties charge covers. The crowd varies: yuppies and local newcomers rub shoulders with locals, rockers and the tattooed set.

## Nice Guy Eddies

5 Ave. A (@ Houston St.)
212-253-1666

DON'T BRING THE frills here because they don't want 'em. The combination of the generation-spanning music on the jukebox and plenty of cheap goodness served in the kitchen and at the bar, Nice Guy's might be the place to stop before you go out, or the place you choose for Sunday brunch. With all the grace of a three-legged dog, this neighborhood bar will fill you up one way or the other.

## 9C

700 E. 9th St. (@ Ave. C)
212-358-0048

IT'S LOUD. IT'S SMALL. It's hot. It's sleazy. It's red. 9C offers something different on this strip of recent renovations and boring additions. This is one place where the squatters definitely outnumber the yuppies. Maybe it's the volume (just how loud can you listen to The Stooges "Raw Power"? ...LET'S MAKE SOME EARS BLEED!. Bust out the devil horns 'cause it's always steamy in here and if you stick around long enough, you're sure to start feling sleazy. With a 2 for 1 happy hour and fairly priced bottled beer afterwards, you can get as lacivious as you want.

## 19th Hole

322 2nd Ave. (@ 19th St.)
212-673-2023

ON A COURSE of 19 bars, this bar would be the last to be visited. Such an unassuming place, it just seems to exist. It's never crowded and leaves no lasting impression. Frequented by neighborhood regulars, it's not offensive in any way, but it doesn't exude a welcoming feeling. Perhaps it serves as an extension of the living rooms of the folks who choose to drink here. Certainly nobody goes out of his or her way to end up here.

## Niva

188 Allen St. (Houston & Stanton Sts.)
212-254-9360

A BRAND NEW bar tucked into what seems like the storage closet of a vast, past-its-prime dance club, Niva snubs its nose at size and keeps the party going. So small and simple, with a tiny copper bar and assorted, crammed together couches, this place will have a hard time ever becoming pretentious. It's around the corner from Lounge Ground Zero on Orchard St., so it can be chill and happening at the same time. The front opens onto the sidewalk, meaning the young crowd can groove to the drum-n-bass spinning indoors while feeling the vibe of the street outside.

## No Idea

30 E. 20th St. (Broadway S. Park Ave. So.)
212-777-0100

THIS POPULAR Gramercy Park watering hole is the stomping ground for Flatiron suits and students of the NY Film Academy. A friendly crowd packs in here nightly for happy hour and to play darts and pool. Not fully dedicated to being a sports bar, a singles place or any other specific type of bar, so the name is quite accurate. If your name and their "name of the day" match you'll get a free drink! Yippee!!! The atmosphere is friendly, but there really isn't a whole lot going on here during the weekends.

## No Malice Palace

197 E. 3rd St. (Aves. A & B)
212-254-9184

HAVING REPLACED THE once-grand Delia's Supper Club (and still bearing the same black awning), No Malice has quickly gained a loyal following of artists, trendoids and model types. It's also one of the few cool places in the East Village that sports a dog friendly patio and crowd. If Lassie isn't your first choice for a date, you can probably score some digits from one of the many hotties lounging on the beat-up couches lining the walls. The drinks cost a little more than you would expect, but the good vibe makes it worth the extra sheckels. Dim lighting, old furniture and cute chicks seems to be the right formula for a popular bar in New York City. We're still waiting for the trend to turn to a generic crowd, expensive drinks and conversation so dull that it makes watching paint dry seem exciting. Oh wait, that's the Upper East Side.

## No Moore

234 W. Broadway (White & N. Moore Sts.)
212-925-2595

"IF I CAN'T SEE IT, I don't want to own it," says owner Chuck, who lives across the street. First came the local artists' haunt Liquor Store Bar across the street, then it

was time to throw the suits a bone. But, what can start off as a Smith Barney scene gets much more interesting when the lower level gets going. Dance to live music from Afrobeat to East Coast swing or get lessons on salsa night for a minimal cover on certain days. Or, you can stay upstairs at no charge to drink quality cocktails from old-time bartenders in the simple brick-wood-and-windows main room. This is definately one of the best neighborhood hangouts in TriBeCa.

## North Star Pub

93 South St. (@ Fulton St.)
212-509-FOOD

AFTER DIZZYING DAYS on the seas of investment banking, Wall Street mariners pop into this truly British pub across from the South St. Seaport. No American beers are served in the establishment, but a good selection of English ales are on tap. Although it's always loud and smoky, North Star is a great place to get a drink before jumping on the ferry to Shea Stadium.

## North West

392 Columbus Ave. (@ 79th St.)
212-799-4530

ONE OF THE most attractive and classy places to hit the Upper West Side in recent history, North West doubles as a romantic restaurant and sexy lounge. The plush couches in the aesthetically pleasing upstairs cigar bar beckon the "Sex and the City" neighborhood set to bask in the clubroom. Attentive bartenders expertly prepare generous martinis and make you feel like a regular no matter who you are. Located across from the American Museum of Natural History, it's understandable that prices are steep; someone's got to pay the hefty rent.

## North River Bar

145 Hudson St. (@ Hubert St.)
212-226-9411
Temporarily closed for renovations.

## Novecento

343 W. Broadway (Grand & Broome Sts.)
212-925-4706

FRAN DRESCHER isn't Argentinean, but she might

apply for honorary citizenship should she visit Novecento. There is no shortage of loud clothing and big belts in this Argentinean owned bi-level lounge that used to hold an upstairs dance club. The happening upstairs dance party came to a screeching halt when Giuliani's regime lifted Novecento's cabaret license. The top floor now caters to a calmer dining crowd. The bar itself is pretty small with relatively little seating, but the surrounding tables provide adequate space for those who want to indulge in an extensive wine list and eclectic appetizers. The singles scene is evident and people are here to impress.

## Nowbar

22 7th Ave. So. (@ Leroy St.)
212-293-0323

IF YOU LOVE DEEP, dark kinky lounges, this is the perfect spot for you! Every Friday you will find a different fetish to tickle your curiosity; for example women or transvestites will flog you senseless if you ask them nicely. Or, how about a good, old fashioned game slap and tickle? Cough up the $20, you will definitely get your money's worth. Parties are Wed-Thurs from 11p.m.-4a.m. and Fri-Sat from 10p.m.-4a.m. With some advanced notice, this place can be rented for private parties. Come to Nowbar, kneel down and get what you deserve.

## NV

289 Spring St. (Hudson & Varick Sts.)
212-929-6868

UNCHARACTERISTIC OF THE trendy bars in SoHo, NV is neither chichi, trendy nor secret. The two levels are completely different micro-cosms. Hit the downstairs hip-hop room for a night of serious dancing. The more you drink, the easier it is to decipher the optical illusion paintings of celebrity faces hiding in pastoral scenes. Around the sleek, cushy interior of the main level (where Top 40 tunes rule), you'll spot an overload of yuppie couples, products of the ridiculous door policy that does not allow a man to enter unaccompanied by a chick with huge boobs. Recruit your own crowd for the evening, because the patrons here are about as exciting as a yawning festival. Drinks, if expensive and small, are at least quickly obtainained at both the upstairs and downstairs bars.

## NW3

242 E. 10th St. (1st & 2nd Aves.)
212-260-0891

NW3 BOASTS A multitude of DJ's spinning every night of the week. Whether it's drum-n-bass, jungle, house or trance, it's always an electronica experience. Attracting more of a "word of mouth" crowd than regular patrons, one bartender described it: "like throwing a party at your house and inviting fifty friends." This easy-going attitude has lead to perpetually soiled bathrooms, sorry ladies. The floors are black and white checked tile and the rest is a study in red velvet from the benches to the stapled ceiling. NW3 is one sexy little hangout.

## Oak Room

768 5th Ave. (@ 59th St.)
212-546-5330

LOCATED IN THE Plaza Hotel on Central Park South,this is the best spot we can think of to pick up an expensive, foreign, 19 year old hooker, if you are an American, 200 year old man. If this not your cup of overpriced mylanta, try one of the many single malts they offer, along with the tasty edibles. Not the hippest place to drink, but certainly convenient if you are stuck in Midtown.

## The Oasis Lounge

121 St. Marks Pl. (1st Ave. & Ave. A)
212-598-4968

THIS PLACE HAS the makings of a hoppin' little lounge, but on a street peppered with neon signs, tourist traps and grungy freaks, it gets lost in the scenery. Hence the name; it truly is an oasis. There is a spacious back room, live music pumps four days a week and the walls are an open platform for local artwork The jukebox has a spirit of its own, and if you look hard enough you'll find board games and coloring books, complete with crayons. Drinks are cheap and during the 5-8p.m. happy hour, you'll catch $2 wells and drafts.

## Obeca Li

62 Thomas St. (W. Broadway & Church St.)
212-393-9887

OBECA LI IS a huge beautiful space tucked away on a quiet street in one of the city's more upscale neighbor-

hoods, which may be its biggest problem. The upstairs is a well-thought-out sake bar with a reputation for good food and service. When the downstairs bar opened two years ago, it was a promising spot for up-scale club types, meeting over expensive drinks and DJ beats. But after too many noise complaints from the locals, the nights here now end early.

## O'Connor's Bar

**39 5th Ave. (Bergen & Dean Sts.) Brooklyn**
**718-783-9721**

STEPPING INTO O'CONNOR'S you're liable to stumble over somebody's unsupervised hound. On your way out, seven or so drinks later, you'll probably be tripping over your own feet. This is a simple, hard drinking bar. As local loyals insist, O'Connor's may be "The Best Bar in Brooklyn" and it's certainly got a shot at being the oldest. The bar was opened by Dale O'Connor in 1933 in what had been a speakeasy and moved to its present location on Fifth Ave. Back then its doors opened at 7 a.m. so that workers could stop in and add a little tipple to their morning coffee. Now, the thirsty have to wait until 8 a.m. for the current O'Connor's to open up. Neither times nor the decor have changed much at O'Connor's since the '30s. There are no ritzy themes or yuppie beers here, just good, honest drinking.

## The Odeon/Bar Odeon

**145 W. Broadway (Thomas & Duane Sts.)**
**212-233-0507/233-6436**

AN INSTITUTION OF SORTS in the TriBeCa area, the Odeon has been around since before DeNiro was cool. Deco décor and a satisfying menu keeps the locals coming back for seconds. Should you find the wait a bit tedious, wander across the street to its child, Bar Odeon. It's a smaller, bistro version of the original that captures the neighborhood vibe and has a much shorter wait. Great people watching.

## Odessa

**119 Ave. A (7th & 8th Sts.)**
**212-253-1470**

KOOKY YET COMFORTABLE, bold yet secretive. Odessa offers affordable drinks and great diner food (same kitchen as the popular diner next door) in a wacky setting. Red stucco ceilings from which lacquered gourds hang (looks like a shag carpet sprouting veggies), red vinyl booths and artwork you'd swear you saw at a Holiday Inn Art Show give this place quite a different touch. But don't fret; the people inside aren't as crazy as the decor. The customers are cool, young, East Village types who come here to hide out, chill, drink and eat with other no-nonsense locals. Waitresses will take your food orders but you gotta get to the bar for your own drink here, buddy!

## Off The Wagon

109 MacDougal St. (3rd & Bleecker Sts.)
212-533-4487

THE BEST THING about "Off the Wagon" is the humor of its name, suggesting a place where people who failed AA can have a beer without having to do contrition. This is not the case. What you get instead is a bunch of aging fraternity brothers who, in the absence of keg stands, resort to cheering over their foosball, pool, darts or satellite sports games. It's like watching a bunch of horny dogs that, in the absence of any available bitches, have resorted to humping each others legs.

## O'Flaherty's Ale House

334-36 W. 46th St. (8th & 9th Aves.)
212-581-9366

LIVE MUSIC NIGHTLY, a huge central bar, free Irish grub, 12 beers on tap ($3 during happy hour, 3p.m.-6p.m.), pool tables, a garden, a romantic fireplace, darts and real books lining the shelves, attract a far more diverse crowd than the than just the pre and post-theater throngs. There are even enough artists themselves in the midst to merit Wednesday night "actor's night."

## O'Flanagan's

1215 1st Ave. (65th & 66th Sts.)
212-439-0660

HUNTING LODGE MEETS pseudo dance club at O'Flanagan's. With a cover band Tuesday-Saturday rocking the house, this is not your ordinary Irish bar. People in their 20's and 30's stumble out to the dance floor when the place gets heated up. If you're not a Solid Gold dancer, then park yourself in front of one of the seven TVs and concentrate on drinking up the nerve to hit the dance floor.

## O'Flannagan's Old Ale

**1591 2nd Ave. (82nd & 83rd Sts.)**
**212-472-2800**

THIS IS ONE of the nicer Irish pubs on the Upper East Side. There is a small restaurant in the back that serves bar food until 1 a.m., there are 10 beers on tap, house wine and a fairly large liquor selection. The prices are average and there is a happy hour Mon.-Fri. from 4p.m.-7p.m. when domestic pints, bottled beer and well-drinks are $2.50. The bartender is friendly, but try to keep track of your own tab. A young, fratty crowd gathers here to chill out.

## Ohm

**16 W. 22nd St. (5th & 6th Aves.)**
**212-229-2000**

ANOTHER ENTRY IN the highly profitable Flatiron megaplexes, Ohm provides the backdrop for meeting someone to use for sex and money. That's the long and short of it. Granted, the music is kickin', but the dance floors in this multi-level mega club are so crowded you feel like 12-inch penis is a 6-inch condom. The drinks are too expensive to enjoy, especially since you'll be reeling from the $20 cover charge you paid to enter. The couches are littered with people, which leave you wandering around striking up random one-sided conversations with people as interesting as a jar of hair.

## Okie-Dokie

**307 E. 84th St. (1st & 2nd Aves.)**
**212-650-9424**

IN 1950, AFTER working as a telephone operator for 18 years, Elsie opened the Okie Dokie. It has since become legendary for its owner's no-nonsense attitude (there's a $5 fine for cursing) and eccentric door policy (If she doesn't know you, you don't get in.) Patrons must knock on the glass and--depending on if they come "recommended" and how much Jaegermeister the 85-yr old has in her--she may or may not allow admittance. Those lucky enough to find themselves inside Elsie's must expect neither steel nor glass; the decor is well used to put it mildly. There are a few old, ripped barstools. (other wise it's standing room only). There's a jukebox hat's not getting any younger either--in fact, it plays Edith Piaf and Peter Duchin 45's. That's the beauty of the place: it's a classic.

## Old Homestead Inn

102 1st Ave. (6th & 7th Sts.)
212-420-9668

DON'T LOOK FOR the name of this place anywhere, it's not posted. You may even miss it the first couple of times you walk by. There is nothing remotely special here except for the autographed picture of Kaity Tong on the wall and the fact they offer beer nuts. But if you do spot the creaky old door, fear not. Enter, and you'll find a decent dive where you and your posse can get tanked for dirt-cheap. And in New York, in this day and age, that may be something special after all.

## The Old Stand

914 3rd Ave. (@ 55th St.)
212-759-4836

IF YOU'RE A sports fan you'll really appreciate the knowledgeable, friendly staff at The Old Stand who seem to know everythng thre is to know about baseball. Its walls are plastered with photographs of famous sports stars, which make the predominantly male clientele feel right at home. There isn't much in the way of decor except the TV and a sign that informs you that there's no dancing allowed.

## Old Town Bar

45 E. 18th St. (Park Ave. & Broadway)
212-529-6732

THIS FIXTURE ON 18th St. is a dark, primitive saloon. With 14' ceilings and stained glass, Old Town has retained its original character since it opened in 1892. Families, trendy locals and Bowery bums can be spotted here, as well as an occasional celeb. The chatter of the crowd and one small TV fills the quiet void that would normally be filled with music (there is none). A brass rail bar runs the entire length of the restaurant and guards the 2-ton, original cash registers. Dark wooden booths are separated by high wood and glass dividers each adorned with their own charming stained glass tulip lamps. Bar fare is served until closing at 1:30a.m.

## Oliva

161 Houston St. (@ Allen St.)
212-228-4143

FASHIONED AFTER SOME rustic wine cellar tucked away in the Spanish Pyrenees, Oliva appears far too quaint to withstand the bustling traffic on one of the city's most active intersections. For that reason, the windows are frosted over, blocking out the chaos from the eyes of the stylish clientele working away at plates of appetizing Basque-influenced seafood entrees. Although Oliva is ostensibly a restaurant, its delicately vaulted stucco ceilings and tasteful lighting make the bar an ideal place to have either a glass of sangria or their pricey, but ecstasy-inducing, mojitos.

## Olive Garden

201 W. 47th St. (Broadway & 7th Ave.)
212-333-3254

THE OLIVE GARDEN is a faux-Italian corporate restaurant; a three-tiered beacon to the out-of-towner in Midtown. But the view from within is singular. The main bar is on the second floor and massive windows on three sides afford a Caesar's eye perspective of the glittering coliseum of Times Square. The vibe is mass-market tourist, the décor is nondescript and the squawking P.A. announcing parties' reservations spoils the convivial mood a bit. The Garden boasts the Italian margarita, a dangerously potent cocktail to sip while gazing at the throngs below.

## The Olympic Lounge

654 W. 49th St. (@ 12th Ave.)
212-489-6088

THIS BAR IS open Wednesday-Sunday and features their very special "Papi Chulo" dancers, which translates as, "young, well-hung Latin men shaking da booty." This is one of the most interesting gay lounges you will encounter because the dancers work hard to please the crowd and earn their tips. Located on 12th Ave., this is not the place to bring your mother or religious friends. If you've never been to the Olympic, enter at your own risk.

## One & One

76 E. 1st St. (@ 1st Ave.)
212-260-9950

IF YOU'RE FEELING "clean as a whistle" check out this Irish pub and café for some down-home fish and chips with vinegar and a tall glass of Woodpecker Cider. One & One the kind of place where you can come alone, sit at the bar and drink stouts 'till the giant fishing mural comes alive, and never get hit on. The traditional Irish food is moderately priced, and, during happy hour, $10 will get you an order of chips with curry and two cocktails.

## One 51

151 E. 50th St. (3rd & Lexington Aves.)
212-753-1144

THE FORMER "TATOU" is now home to a younger crowd in their late 20's who enjoy sitting back and smoking cigars. Some come for dinner, some to drink, and the weekend crowd dance all night to contemporary tunes. Although it hasn't yet established itself as a mid-week after work place like its neighbor, Whiskey Blue, it's only a matter of time until it becomes a regular every-day home to Midtown workers. One 51 is worth checking out, but be prepared for some picky bouncers

## 147 (Man Ray)

147 W. 15th St. (5th & 6th Sts.)
212-929-5000

NOW OVER 2 years old, 147 has become a staple in Chelsea. The huge bar area and good food have kept a good looking, but not too trendy crowd coming back again and again. The drinks can be a little pricey, but the great looking staff, potent cocktails and quick service will distract you enough that you won't notice the bill.

## 101

101 7th Ave. So. (@ W. 4th St.)
212-620-4000

DON'T WALK TOO close, you may be pulled in by a few pushy guys to this live funk and R&B bar. Its clientele is an ethnically mixed crowd, due in part to the bar's location directly across the street from the Christopher St. subway stop. At the end of a long narrow bar there are a few tightly packed tables grooving to the free music. No beers on tap, bottles are $5.50, and mixed drinks, $6.50. Since there is no cover, 101 is a good spot to go to if you want to hear live music for cheap.

## One If By Land Two If By Sea

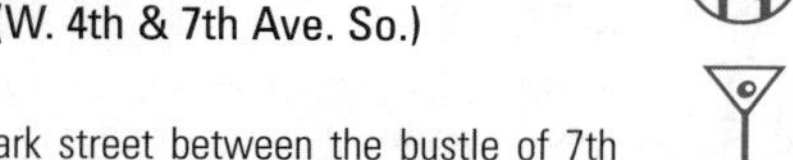

17 Barrow St. (W. 4th & 7th Ave. So.)
212-228-0822

HIDDEN ON A dark street between the bustle of 7th Ave. and the throngs of W. 4th St. and touted as New York's most romantic setting, OIBL sets the stage for a totally transporting experience. Expensive American food is served in the 18th century carriage house filled with fireplaces, flowers, candles, pastoral artwork and an over-40 set of Long Islanders basking in the glow. If you can't afford the $56 prix-fixe menu but are still interested in impressing a date, the bar will do the trick perfectly. Grab a seat close to the baby-grand piano and let the mood take over.

## 119 Bar

119 E. 15th St. (Irving Pl. & Union Sq. E.)
212-777-6158

EVEN THOUGH 119 BAR is a dirty dive bar, it's still one hundred times better than the overrated Belmont Lounge next door. The drinks are small but strong and the bartenders are friendly and quick. The pool table is very competitive, so if you feel like teaching your girlfriend how to shoot, this isn't the place for her to be cute. Usually groups of friends gather here before and after shows at Irving Plaza. The bathrooms are nasty, but if you gotta go, you gotta go.

## 169 Bar

169 E. Broadway (Rutgers & Jefferson Sts.)
212-473-8866

DEEPLY ENTRENCHED IN Lower East Side history, 169 Bar was known to locals as "The Bloody Bucket." Not that enticing by today's standards, but then again this place has been around for over 50 years. The joint is actually a good, down-to-earth party bar, with DJ's and live music almost every night of the week attracting local musicians and artsy types. The bar is decorated in reds and blacks; a large open space that allows patrons to mingle and dance. The bar features a lot of different music parties, so call head to see about cover charges.

## O'Nieals

174 Grand St. (Centre & Mulberry Sts.)
212-941-9119

THIS CIGAR FRIENDLY Little Italy lounge serves eclectic food in a sexy clubroom filled with black and white photographs of yesteryear New York. The helpful bartenders will never fail to light your cigarette or offer suggestions on the perfect glass of wine to start your evening. Hip trance and mood music plays at a level that won't burst your eardrums or force you to shout your conversations, making this a perfect spot for a date or a drink with a few friends on a weeknight. Get here early on weekends before the throngs of locals grab the seats.

## Opal

251 E. 52nd St. (@ 2nd Ave.)
212-593-4321

OPAL TRIES VERY hard to be the cool kid on the block and it passes the test with flying colors. Very swank and lively, Opal's ambiance is that of blue, glowing candlelight and jazz music. The only quasi-problem with Opal is that it's a difficult place to go with friends since it's so intimate. You won't have any luck picking-up here since most folks are on a date in the first place.

## Opaline

85 Ave. A (5th & 6th Sts.)
212-475-5050

WHY IS OPALINE so beloved? Is it the speakeasy feel of the smoky, couch-filled lounge, or the way it opens onto a large, airy dining area complete with slow ceiling fans and 19th century French posters? Is it the French/American menu that delivers on its gushing gustatory promises? Is it the pyramid of TVs above the bar displaying locally-made films? The attractive clientele? The polished, well-stocked bar? Sure, but, all said, it's really the undeniable references Opaline makes to absinthe -- that elusive, illegal tincture of wormwood and grain alcohol that served as muse to poets and artists for over a 100 years. Okay, so they don't serve it, but they do, however, offer tastings of a green-tinged, baby wormwood-infused drink whose commercial name is "Absente." Hmmm.

## Opium Den

29 E. 3rd St. (2nd Ave. & Bowery)
212-505-7344

THIS DARK gothic cave has served as one of the original cool lounges in the East Village for over 5 years. With dark Mission style furniture, the ever essential red velvet and a good looking bar staff, it's no wonder this place has stood the test of time in a lounge scene that is usually shorter than a midget in sandles.

## Orchard Bar

200 Orchard St. (@ Houston St.)
212-673-5350

THIS BAR REMAINS the créme de la créme of the ever-expanding Orchard Street bar stretch with its unique and slick décor including partial wall aquarium installments and a wooden wine cellar ceiling. Shecky's loves the cool vibe exuded by Orchard. As the hours wear on, the swankier the scene of black wearing beautiful and successful artsy types gets. Every night there is a live DJ showing off their turntable moves mixing mainly jungle and trip hop,.

## Oscar's (@ The Waldorf Astoria)

301 Park Ave. (49th & 50th Sts.)
212-872-4920

THE BAR AT Oscar's restaurant plays host to an appealing after-work crowd. There are two for one happy hour specials daily, peanuts, potato chips, frequent drink promotions and a complimentary hors d'oeuvres buffet. Oscars amounts to an upscale neighborhood bar that just happens to be in a hotel. It's dignified without being pretentious, and it's friendly without encouraging the drunken carousing of most local pubs. However, this doesn't mean you can't leave in a stupor!

## Oscar Wilde's

221 E. 58th St. (@ 2nd Ave.)
212-486-7309

THIS EAST SIDE gay bar with its oversized couches and very long narrow bar will make you feel like you're at Continental's One Pass airport lounge with the exception of the extension cords covered in electrical tape. The diverse crowd of older locals, East Side yuppies and your very occasional muscle boy, all sit around drinking amiably while patrons select tunes (Whitney Houston & Cher play all night) on the jukebox. This place, unlike the name, is not a classic or even memorable.

## Other Room

143 Perry St. (Greenwich & Washington Sts.)
212-645-9758

THIS SISTER BAR to the Room & Another Room is definitely the cream of the three bar crop. Hosting a selection of over 40 beers at any given time and more than 10 wines, the Other Room is one of the best bets in this beautiful West Village neighborhood. The crowd is young, good looking, friendly, straight and not full of guys just looking to score (a nice change of pace for any bar). The modern décor and friendly bartenders make this small gem a great retreat for a date, or just a comfortable spot to hang out with a small group of friends.

## Otis

754 9th Ave. (50th & 51st St.)
212-246-4417

OTIS IS A slice of Soho in Hell's Kitchen. You get the feeling that Quentin Tarantino will film a scene here for Pulp Fiction II. A funky place to hang out, you get the Huggy Bear and James Brown vibe all in one. People flock here to chill amongst the vinyl, velvet and dim lighting. Come just for drinks or to groove to the jukebox, live music or just to grab a bite to eat.

## Oyster Bar & Restaurant

Grand Central Station, Lower Level (42nd St. & Vanderbilt Ave.) 212-490-6650

GRAB A SOOTHING glass of wine after a hard day's work and suck down some oysters at the dining counters and raw bar. Not your usual train station bar, this is a more upscale haven for commuters. During the day the clientele mainly consists people conducting business who have no problem picking up the steep check. The Oyster Bar is classy, and if you are into oysters, this is the place to go.

## Ozone

1720 2nd Ave. (89th & 90th Sts.)
212-860-8950

WHAT COULD HAVE been a pretentious scene has become a truly low-key and swanky spot on the rarely hip Upper East Side. Put your head between your knees and breathe normally, everything will be okay. Dark and moody, Ozone is divided in two parts by a tent. Try their sweet concoction, the Ozone bubbilicious, which got raves from the Food Network. You can select a cigar from their stock then wander past the bathrooms, through a long tent curtain to the ultra-cool lounge to smoke it. Get there early to snag an antique couch and enjoy the acid jazz and hip-hop spinning regularly. Now that the shock has worn off, why are you still home?

## P&G Café

279 Amsterdam Ave. (@ 73rd St.)
212-874-8568

YOU WON'T CROSS town to come here, but you will thank your lucky stars that it's in your neighborhood. It's got all the workings of an old school corner bar: ample draft choices available by the pint or pitcher, bartenders who pour with a generous hand, a jukebox selection that stretches back to the beginning of time (when they opened) and a Cheers-like crowd. Nothing fancy here folks, but nothing to be scared of either. Next time Grandpa comes to visit, you might want to end up here, you're both likely to be equally at ease.

## Paddy Maguire's

237 3rd Ave. (19th & 20th Sts.)
212-473-8407

THIS CUTE NEIGHBORHOOD pub is decorated with a forest of white branches twinkling with Christmas lights that never come down. The long bar leads into a back area with two pool tables and darts. Refreshingly uncrowded, this local watering hole is home to sports enthusiasts and a good after work crowd.

## Paddy Reilly's

519 2nd Ave. (@ 29th St.)
212-686-1210

LOOKING FOR A little slice of Dublin in the city? Paddy Reilly's may be the quintessential East Side Irish pub. A mixed clientele of New Yorkers and those fresh from the homeland convene in the cozy, cottage-loke atmosphere for Guiness and friendly conversation. Paddy Reilly's always has well known Irish bands on weekends for only a $5 cover charge. It's worth every penny to hear traditional music while catching young lasses doing gigs. And it is certainly a nice change of pace from the usual shouting over the Dave Matthews CD that seems to be playing on an infinite loop. Paddy Reilly's ought not to be confused with the slew of Irish bars that pepper this area as it has a charm all its own..

## Pageant

109 E. 9th St. (3rd & 4th Aves.)
212-529-5333

Gold chains, hairspray and wife beater tee-shirts. What do all of these have in common? Pageant. If you yelled out, "who dropped their EZ pass", odds are with it, there would be a full out- cry to regain the valued pass back to the bouroughs. This is the definition of a nice space gone terribly wrong. Pageant's music is hip, but when it gets crowded the scene morphs into sleaze ball pick up central and loses any chance it ever had to be cool. This is still a favorite among NYU co-eds.

## Palio

151 W. 51st St. (6th & 7th Aves.)
212-245-4850

THIS MIDTOWN MAIN stay is a perfect spot to grab a drink in a beautiful deco setting with impeccable service and a creative cocktail selection. After work this spot fills up with business folk making deals and trying to weasel their way up the proverbial corporate ladder. The restaurant offers top food at expense account prices, but this spot is worth the cash.

## Panache

470 6th Ave. (11th & 12th Sts.)
212-243-2222

DON'T BE INTIMIDATED by the blazing red exterior and ultra trendy patrons of this little West Village café. It was formerly known as L'Atitude and was recently renamed Panache after their specialty, a tasty little concoction of beer and lemonade. This bistro offers comfortable, affordable dining with its non-intrusive interior, down to earth, attentive staff and savory, French meals. It's obvious the owners put a lot of thought into the overall experience; Panache certainly lives up to its name.

## Pangea

178 2nd Ave. (@ 11th St.)
212-995-0900

OH BOY, ANOTHER "haute-whatever"; snore. There's nothing to distinguish Pangea from any other high-on-itself East Village spot. Well, the menu does aggressively strive for new heights of exoticness, and with some success, but it does so at terrifying prices. The crowd flaunts their supposed intellects, while the waitstaff, however friendly, could use just a smidgen more.

## Papa Joe's Original

413 E. 70th St. (York & 1st Ave.)
212-650-9687

THIS PLACE, FORMERLY known as Nimrods, is small and hidden but worth the find. This Jamaican theme bar has a selection of Czech and Jamaican beer at a refreshing $4 a pop. Ya mon, pull up a stool and order some "eyrie" (fries and jerk chicken). Smoke a fatty and mellow out with the live reggae and jazz bands. Chill out in the exotic bamboo laden décor and let the friendly bartenders melt those troubles away. This is a refreshing change from the multitude of frat bars on the Upper East Side so stop in for a little of that Jamaican hospitality. Open all day everyday until 4a.m.

## Paris Café

119 South St. (@ Peck Slip)
212-240-9797

SINCE 1873 PARIS CAFÉ has been serving New Yorkers in the seaport/Fulton St. Fish Market area.

Steeped in tradition and history, the café serves drinks and dinner to a mixed crowd of business people and tourists until 4a.m.

## Park Avalon

225 Park Ave. So. (18th & 19th Sts.)
212-533-2500

PARK AVALON IS another successful venture of Steve Hanson, owner of the Blue Water Grill and Ruby Foo's empire. This large airy space is very popular with good-looking suits and fashionable women that have tired of the Angelo & Maxie's scene. The candles are inviting in winter and in summer the open windows beckon passersby. Come to pick up a date or dine on the consistently good food.

## Park Avenue Country Club

381 Park Ave. So. (@ 27th St.)
212-685-3636

CALLING ALL SPORTS fans, enthusiasts, supporters and admirers! Park Avenue is the place for all spectators. Five big-screen and 25 TVs of different sizes make this place the hot spot for New York City's sports scene no matter what game you're craving. It's crazy during football games, so you best reserve a space. Party planning is also an option for those arranging a large get-together.

## Park Bar

15 E. 15th St. (Union Sq. W. & 5th Ave.)
212-367-9085

THIS UNION SQUARE newcomer has quickly built a loyal following with its small and cozy space, friendly staff and reasonably priced drinks. The crowd is a nice mix of Silicon Alley dot com'ers and the Wall Street set. This is a nice place to stop in for a drink before grabbing some food at the adjoining restaurant, Tocqueville.

## Park Slope Brewing Co.

(Brooklyn Heights Annex)
62 Henry St. (Cranberry & Orange Sts.) Brooklyn
718-522-4801

FOR FIVE YEARS NOW, the Park Slope Brewing Company has been serving a neighborhood crowd of ex-frat boys, yuppies and everything in between. You can find decent American food here at a fair price; but it's nothing to rave about. The bar seems to keep the locals satisfied, but we at Shecky's won't be rushing here any time soon.

## Parkside Lounge

317 E. Houston St. (Aves. B & C)
212-673-6270

SOMETIMES A BAR does well to just sit and wait for people to discover the allure. Such is the case with this friendly E. Houston mainstay; a place that has catered to a solid neighborhood crowd for years and now finds itself on the verge of being absorbed into the Lower East Side maw of gentrification. Housed in a classic fifty-year old corner bar and grill space, The Parkside resides east of almost everything that's happening. All manner of recreation is available inside, from pool and pinball to the best of all indoor diversions, happy hour. Though the kitchen is long gone, the owner has added a stage in the back room where bands (Latin on Fridays) and comedians can entertain the old timers and their new neighbors. Thank God there is still a cheap good time to be had just outside the lounge belt.

## Parlay Lounge

206 Ave. A (12th & 13th Sts.)
212-228-6231

THE GENTRIFICATION BOMB has hit and destroyed an East Village relic called Z-Bar and left in its place a big fat, pretentious, velvet roped, super clean lounge. Minimally decorated in dim lighting, retro white leather booths and Knoll-style designed bar stools, Parlay lounge has achieved a very cool 2001 Space Odyssey look. The sour apple and chocolate martinis taste great. The DJ spins decent R&B, hip-hop and house music, but what makes this lounge ultra-beat is the velvet rope and the hulky doormen who selectively allow people inside. Let's face it, the velvet rope should simply be replaced by a big sign that reads, "WE SUCK!"

## The Parlour

250 W. 86th St. (Broadway & West End)
212-580-8923

IF YOU'RE LOOKING for a more comfortable alternative to the cramped meat market quarters on Columbus and

Amsterdam, step off the beaten path and into The Parlour. Its strongest selling point - apart from the occasional Carson Daly sighting - is a super friendly barstaff serving up a healthy selection of beer. A good spot any night of the week to meet up with friends for some Irish-American fare and put a couple bucks in the jukebox upstairs. On the weekends, dance the night away with twentysomethings to live music. Although the Parlour doesn't quite live up to its self-appointed label of "Authentic Irish Pub" (Duran Duran cover band?), chances are, you won't care.

## Passerby

436 W. 15th St. (9th & 10th Aves.)
212-206-7321

Attached to the Gavin Brown gallery, Passerby is the coolest little bar in the city. With a lighted disco floor, (not for dancing) a hidden location and an attitude free staff, it's no wonder this little gem has become so popular amongst the local artists and gallery geeks. With great tunes and a fashionable crowd, it's almost a shame that there's only enough room here for you, a date and a mini-dachshund.

## Pastis

9-11 Little W. 12th St. (@ 9th Ave.)
212-929-4844

Is it possible to open a French bistro in Manhattan and not have it become a scene? Apparently not. Pastis is far and away the scene of scenes in the West Village and consists of the best looking crowd. With a large, open, airy dining room and traditional French fare, Pastis and all of the McNally family of bistri, have touched a Francophile nerve and palette. Be prepared to wait for a table since they do not take reservations. Great people watching and a surprisingly attitude-free staff make this a welcome addition to the new French packing district.

## Patria

250 Park Ave. So. (@ 20th St.)
212-777-6211

Patria is a swanky Latino-American restaurant and bar. Popular with the corporate and jet-set crowd, it's a festive environment where patrons can sip Cuban cocktails and relax to the Latin rhythms that seep under the fashionable patrons' skin. Sample the mojito or check out the vast wine list that complements the Nuevo Latino cuisine concocted by Chef Andrew DiCatldo. Colorful tile mosaics, warm light and an abundance of dark wood offset the open space and high ceilings creating an inviting and comfortable atmosphere.

## Patrick Kavanagh's

497 3rd Ave. (33rd & 34th Sts.)
212-889-4304

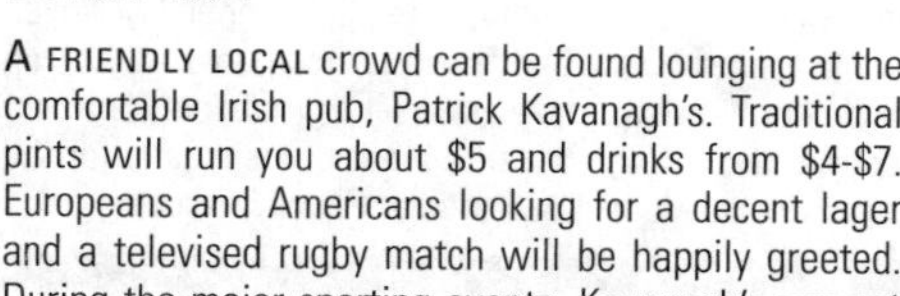

A FRIENDLY LOCAL crowd can be found lounging at the comfortable Irish pub, Patrick Kavanagh's. Traditional pints will run you about $5 and drinks from $4-$7. Europeans and Americans looking for a decent lager and a televised rugby match will be happily greeted. During the major sporting events, Kavanagh's can get rowdy and packed. A kitchen serves up pub grub till 11p.m. on weekdays, and 1a.m. on weekends.

## P.D. O'Hurley's Bar & Grill

174 W. 72nd St. (Columbus Ave. & Broadway)
212-874-9304

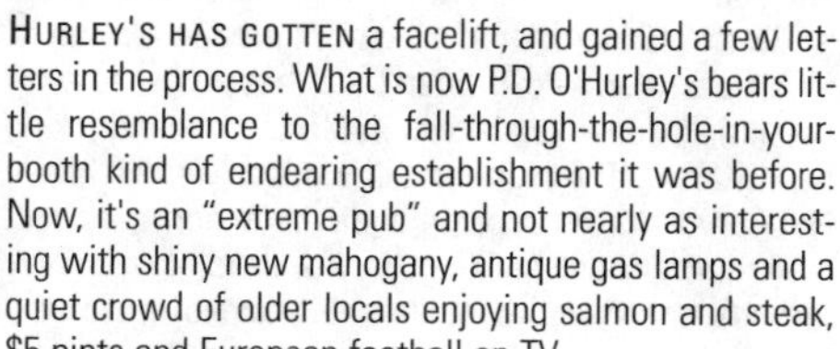

HURLEY'S HAS GOTTEN a facelift, and gained a few letters in the process. What is now P.D. O'Hurley's bears little resemblance to the fall-through-the-hole-in-your-booth kind of endearing establishment it was before. Now, it's an "extreme pub" and not nearly as interesting with shiny new mahogany, antique gas lamps and a quiet crowd of older locals enjoying salmon and steak, $5 pints and European football on TV.

## Pearl Oyster Bar

18 Cornelia St. (4th & Bleecker Sts.)
212-691-8211

EVER IN THE mood for a quick oyster? Probably not, but Pearl Oyster Bar seems to have been designed on the principle that everybody is just looking for a spot where they can stop and down a quick plate of seafood. Designed like a post-modern industrialist snack bar (think exposed light bulbs in expensive lamps designed to look cheap), the main area consists of two long marble bars that give as much intimacy and comfort as

Grand Central Station. It's something different. Not different and fun, just different.

## Peasant

194 Elizabeth St. (Prince & Spring Sts.)
212-965-9511

IT'S A GOOD thing they wrote their menu in Italian; if they had written it in English, I might've been able to read it. Despite this unnecessary hurdle, the food and ambiance at this new Italian eatery/bar are top notch and a welcome addition to Little italy. Although the bar serves mostly as a pre-dinner hang, the open brick oven kitchen in the back and flowersplaced around this hip and unpretentious place makes it a great spot for a first date in this lounge infested area. Come mostly for the food, but this is is an all around Shecky's pick.

## Peculier Pub

145 Bleecker St. (LaGuardia Pl.& Thompson St.)
212-353-1327

ADOLPH COORS WOULD definitely be impressed by Peculier Pub, noted for having the best beer selection in NYC. With over 430 different beers from 49 different countries and 20 states, ranging in price from $3.25 to $13 per bottle, 19 different beers on tap at $7.50 per liter, and 9 beer tails (beer crossed with liqueur), Peculier Pub is a great place for beer drinking hands-down. The high-backed wooden booths house NYU students broadening their beer horizons from their high school swilling Schlitz days. The groovy jukebox, mood and beer definitely make up for the lack of decor.

## Pegasus

119 E. 60th St. (@ Lexington Ave.)
212-888-4702

EXCELLENT PIANO PLAYERS entertain with a mix of show tunes and pop music while a distinguished, mature crowd lounges in this tastefully decorated gay men's lounge. The popular bar fills up with a predominantly Asian crowd that frolics in the garden during seasonable weather. Wacky drag shows and karaoke in multiple languages are a fantastic way to pass weekend evenings.

## Penang

240 Columbus Ave. (@ 71st St.)
212-769-3988
109 Spring St. (Greene & Mercer Sts.)
212-274-8883
1596 2nd Ave. (@ 83rd St.)
212-585-3838
64 3rd Ave. (@ 11th St.)
212-228-7888

PENANG'S SUBTERRANEAN LOUNGE has witnessed its share of canoodling couples. "I don't know what it is," one employee says, "but there can be a lot of making out going on." Maybe it's the wine cellar-like digs, dark as a vat, that get couples all hot and bothered. A young crowd samples the Sarang Burung, $5 Asian beers, and love-inducing cocktails in a brick-and-wood setting (enhanced by live jazz on Tuesday and Sunday nights).

## Pentop Bar Terrace

(@ The Peninsula Hotel)
700 5th Ave. (@ 55th St.)
212-903-3097

LOCATED AT THE top of the Peninsula Hotel, this bar draws mainly businessmen and tourists. The views of midtown Manhattan are unparallel, although the Astroturf outdoor carpeting does detract a little from the quality of the experience. Apparently it costs a lot to get alcohol up to the top of the building because beers here are $10 and mixed drinks are $14. But if it's on your company... who cares right? Come early during the summer because tables fill up quickly.

## Peter McManus

152 7th Ave. (@ 19th St.)
212-929-9691

OPEN SINCE 1936, this obligatory stop is best described as a saloon. Not in the swinging door sense, mind you, but certainly in the manner of the modern-day cowboy clientele, savvy barkeep and dirt-cheap drinks ($2 Buds). A perfect spot for tying one on at high noon (they start slinging 'em at 11a.m.) you can also enjoy a hearty burger or fresh roast beef to temper that drinker's stomach. Full of middle-aged locals who all know each other by name, McManus is always ready to welcome in a new face of any age.

## Pete's Candy Shop

709 Lorimer St. (Frost & Richardson Sts.)
Brooklyn
718-302-3770

IF THERE IS one bar in Williamsburg that best exemplifies the qualities and personalities of the people who have spearheaded this Brooklyn neighborhood renaissance, it's Pete's Candy Shop. Attracting a slightly older crowd than its neighbor Enid's, Pete's is an enchanting bar. The majority of its patrons seem to be working artists who have left self- importance in their younger years, traded in their Cure shirts for tennis shoes and gotten on with their lives. In the back of the bar is a small lounge with a small stage where Beth Orton recently gave a surprise performance while in town.

## Pete's Tavern

129 E. 18th St. (@ Irving Pl.)
212-473-7676

ANY LITERARY BARHOPPING tour of New York should include a stop at Pete's Tavern, where O. Henry supposedly turned out "The Gift of the Magi." Established in 1864, Pete's is the city's oldest original bar and restaurant, though it doubled as a florist shop during the Prohibition years. Aside from its interesting history, the place doesn't have a lot to offer. There are old saloon-style wooden booths, original moldings and low light; but the food is only so-so (why would a place like this serve Italian, anyway?) and the jukebox is full of Steve Miller. Pete's is perfect for the ultimate combo: a beer, a quick bite and the game du jour. Just stay away from the eggplant parmigiana.

## Peter's

182 Columbus Ave. (68th & 69th Sts.)
212-877-4747

AS YOU WALK through the mixed crowd of conservative thirtysomethings, your eyes and ears get lost between the naked statues, the top 40 jukebox, the big screen TV playing sports and the decision between the front and back bar where there are plenty of single men and women looking for that special someone to go home with at the end of the night. During the week, people come in to celebrate that night's big softball game and on the weekend the crowd gets heavy. In case you think someone next to you farted at the front bar, don't think twice about it, it's just the soft-boiled eggs being offered up as a bar treat.

## Phebe's

359 Bowery (@ 4th St.)
212-473-9008

NEW OWNERS RECENTLY remodeled this former underage NYU dive and gave it a much-needed facelift. Thankfully, the drink prices are still reasonable. The crowd is a mix of twentysomethings who probably couldn't pass the bouncer at B-Bar. There is a crowded pool table and a good amount of lounge seating. If you want the "feel" of being at a trendy bar without dropping a ton of cash you've landed in the right spot.

## The Phoenix

447 E. 13th St. (1st Ave. & Ave. A)
212-477-9979

YET ANOTHER GAY bar to sprout up in the East Village, The Phoenix is the best new kid on the block. This comfortable and spacious bar exudes a calm familiarity that can make anybody become a regular. The exposed brick walls, gentle red lighting and immense mirror over the bar ooze a medieval retro feel. A great jukebox plays everything from the Stooges to the Chemical Brothers unobtrusively in the background, making conversation effortless. A pool table and pinball machine provide some entertainment while live performances take place on Thursday nights with an occasional cover charge. Whether you're on a date, looking for a date or want a comfortable alternative to home, the Phoenix is definitely a great East Village hotspot.

## Pieces

8 Christopher St. (@ Greenwich Ave.)
212-929-9291

PIECES IS A festive gay bar for locals and outer borough boys, minus the attitude that runs rampant at other bars. With 6-hour happy hours from Mon-Fri., it's no wonder why everyone is so friendly. If you're the shy type, try Post Office Personal Thursday's when you can hear the popular drag queen/recording artist Jimmy James perform his legendary show at 10p.m.

## Pierrot

28 Ave. B (2nd & 3rd Sts.)
212-673-1999

WE'RE ALL FAMILIAR with American camp consisting of Howdy-Doody memorabilia, bowling-pin table lamps and fin-tailed DeSotos. Check out Pierrot's Parisian take featuring porcelain harlequin statues, barstools topped with rustic steel tractor seats, faux middle-eastern pottery and a bizarre oil painting of a half-cheetah half-battle tank wearing a caftan. The selection of giddily named specialty cocktails, such as the Holly go lightly and dreamsicle martini, are delightful, and the menu offers tasty dishes like duck and chorizo pizza. Pierrot is a swell place for appetizers and a festive tipple, but those of more austere aesthetics may feel a tad uneasy in this freewheeling kitsch-riot.

## Pig 'n' Whistle

365 Greenwich St. (Franklin & Harrison Sts.)
212-941-1771
165 W. 47th St. ( 6th & 7th Aves.)
212-302-0110

922 3rd Ave. (55th & 56th Sts.)
212-688-4646

NOT MUCH GOES on in this 11-year-old off-the-beaten-track bar-restaurant and everyone seems to like it that way. Which is why this is a good after-work alternative for those who work on the lower end of the island but want to avoid rowdy Wall Streeters. The classic rock and pop jukebox plays at a comfortable, conversation friendly level, the drink prices are fair and the bartenders graciously understand the idea of buy-backs. Plus there's a decent bar-food selection with a steak and fries special, which lets you stuff yourself for a mere $8.50.

## P.J. Clarke's

915 3rd Ave. (@ 55th St.)
212-759-1650

THE ONLY THING that shut P.J. Clarke's down was prohibition, and even that little piece of nonsense legislation could not keep it closed long. As one of the oldest bars in the city, you'll get a piece of New York history every time you grab a beer at the large wooden bar, making P.J. Clarke's a great place to bring tourists. It has retained a low-key, friendly atmosphere, (not to mention cheap beer and a great burger), which makes it an appealing place to hang out and watch a game.

## Planet Sushi

380 Amsterdam Ave. (@ 78th St.)
212-712-2162

As the name suggests, Planet Sushi is a fish joint first and foremost. But come later in the night (they're open daily until 2a.m. at the earliest) and the staff won't mind at all if you use one of their popular patio or indoor tables to sit and drink your fill. Six sake varieties at $5 to $7 grace the menu along with Sapporo, Asahi and other popular Japanese beers. There's a full bar in back offering the planet's other beverages.

## Planet Thailand

141 N. 7th St. (Bedford & Berry Aves.)
Brooklyn
718-599-5758

Formerly located on Bedford Ave., this restaurant was heralded as a staple for good Thai food at cheap prices. It's gotten even better. The lofty space is four times the size of its predecessor; three bars have been added, one for sushi, two for cocktails and DJ's spin low-key grooves deep into the night for Williamsburg lounge hounds. The Planet's ceilings are vast enough to suspend some very unusual water fountain/mobile hybrids overhead. (Check out the leaking row boat paddling by.) Its expansive walls showcase local artists' work. But the bars are not as entertaining as the food, so do yourself (and your date) a favor and sit down for some of the best Thai food this side of the East River.

## Plant

217 E. 3rd St. (Aves. B & C)
212-375-9066

Opened at press time,, August 2000, so we haven't had a chance to stop by. Plant plans on having DJ's spinning lounge music to create a grooveilicious vibe.

## Plug Uglies

257 3rd Ave (20th & 21st Sts.)
212-780-1944

THE ONLY REASONS to visit Plug Uglies are to play shuffleboard, pool or darts and drink cheap beer. The clientele consists mainly of off duty cops talking shop and local guys who are privy to the most available pool table and shuffleboard in the area. If you need a place to hang out with friends and not be bothered by the pushing and shoving, this is by no means a bad choice. Wednesday nights 50-cent draught beers make this odd place that much sweeter. You will leave wondering how they pay their bills!

## Polly Esther's

186 W. 4th St. (Barrow & Jones Sts.)
212-924-5707

LIKE ITS faux-fabric namesake, Polly Esther's is a place you'll quickly develop a love-hate relationship with. At this cheesy establishment, you and the bachelorettes can belt out "I Will Survive;" on the sweaty dance floor after downing house drinks named the afro-disiac and Brady punch. Up the ante a bit, and you'll be gyrating obscenely with the Jersey girls on top of the bar. You may not admit you ever came here, but someday, in the throes of a drunken wander, you will be back.

## Poolbeg Street Pub

304 3rd Ave. (23rd & 24th Sts.)
212-253-6848

POOLBEG IS THE former home of the seediest bar for many blocks, Gloccamorra. They took this diamond in the rough and miraculously transformed it into a stereotypical Irish Pub right down to the Guinness advertisements on the walls and the ornate wooden bar. Poolbeg is a welcome addition for the young local mainly male crowds who play pool, darts, video games or just watch one of the four TV's. If the games get boring come on the two nights they have live music.

## Pop

127 4th Ave. (12th & 13th Sts.)
212-674-8713

POP IS A whole lotta nothing special wrapped up in really nice paper. This trendy and sterile space station atmosphere serves those who try so hard to be hip but always fall short by a hair. The scene is filled with good-looking people who think nothing of dropping bundles of cash for drinks. The one thing that can't be denied about Pop is its retro-hip Warhol feel and friendly service by lovely bartenders. But if you plan on making conversation with the beautiful folks, you'd spend less money and have more luck going to a strip club.

## Porter's

216 7th Ave. (22nd & 23rd Sts.)
212-242-7900

PORTER'S IS THE creation of Mirso Lekic, the man behind the legendary Il Valentino and Sutton Hotel. It is an ostensibly chic wine bar with an extensive cellar and decent prices, but Porter's falls a bit short in the hip department. The decor feels like a Staten Island dining room circa 1980 - teal, lilac and gold are everywhere. The attractive staff will cater to all your needs if they catch a whiff of expense account on your Prada threads. This popular after-work haunt closes early, so warm up your charge cards and snag a table before the sun goes down.

## Potion Lounge

370 Columbus Ave. (77th & 78th Sts.)
212-721-4386

ACROSS THE STREET from The American Museum of Natural History, you will discover some of the most wonderfully unnatural cocktails in the history of NYC, Potion's signature layered cocktails. Try their "love potion" and then meander with the object of your affection out of circulation to one of the sofas. Watch your intake of all of the chemical concoctions because the trip to the bathroom may end up being a rendezvous with the Bubble Wall instead. Friday and Saturday nights DJ's spin a good mix to get ALL of your juices flowing.

## The Pour House

1710 2nd Ave. (88th & 89th Sts.)
212-987-3790

THIS FRIENDLY DIVE caters to shot-happy locals on weekdays and partying neighborhood kids on weekends. But mostly it's home to dart sharks, especially during the 4-7p.m. happy hours. In fact, its back room is a dart-only zone and the site of the New York Dart Association competition. A healthy jukebox of classic rock appeases a mixed lot sipping on $4-$5 drinks and beers.

## Pourhouse

790 Metropolitan Ave. (@ Humboldt St.) Brooklyn
718-599-0697

ASK ANY OLD-SCHOOL Williamsburger what they think of all the new establishments popping up in the neighborhood and they're likely to respond with a morose groan. But a little over a year ago, Metropolitan Ave. was blessed with Pourhouse, and nobody groused. Hordes of locals frequent this place to shoot the breeze (or pool), but that ain't the only thing offered. Step into the backroom on a Wednesday and check out some local film makers' 16mm flicks (popcorn included). Tuesday nights feature an open mic, Saturdays are known as "Funk & Junk," when a DJ spins old-school funk and trashy rock and on Sundays you can catch live jazz. (A rockabilly band is in the works.) Happy hour runs from 4-9p.m. with $2 bottles and $3 drinks.

## Pravda

281 Lafayette St. (Houston & Prince Sts.)
212-226-4696

WHAT GOES UP must come down. After four years, the hype of a Keith McNally joint (the creator of The Odeon, Café Luxembourg, Lucky Strike, Balthazar, and Pastis) comes crashing down. The heavy, hidden door still suggests a secret society of elite, but the crowd has quieted down and now bask in the coziness of a Soviet-style rathskellar. On weeknights, Wall-Streeters dominate the lounge smoking Cuban cigars as the male/female ratio reaches infinity. Pravda continues to offer a variety of international luxuries including killer martinis and a world class selection of caviar. Yet...it's still a Shecky's pick.

## Prohibition

503 Columbus Ave. (84th & 85th Sts.)
212-579-3100

AFTER FIVE SUCCESSFUL YEARS, Prohibition remains a resilient hallmark of untailored elegance and promises to shine like the diamond in the rough for many years to come. Having earned a solid reputation as a comfortably sensual meeting ground for casual sophisticates due to the thoughtful and provocative period décor, extensive wine list and creative martini menu, it's busiest later in the evening, when a jazz, funk or soul band takes to the stage. And let's not forget the delicious eye candy provided by both patrons and staff.

## Puck Fair

298 Lafayette St. (@ Houston St.)
212-431-1200

NAMED AFTER THE Irish celebration of male fertility, the Puck Fair has that indefinable quality that many bars strive for. When you enter, you feel like you've been transported somewhere magical. Everything here is state of the art. The walls are covered with a visual montage and written history of the Puck Fair. The mezzanine, where the DJ spins everything from Brit Pop to Acid Jazz, is also a sound stage for bands. Each tap is independently chilled and gas-regulated, and you can taste the difference. The bartenders also happen to be some of the best mixologists in the city. True perfection may be impossible, but this place comes close.

## Puffy's Tavern

81 Hudson St. (@ Harrison St.)
212-766-9159

THIS 52-YEAR-OLD neighborhood staple is everything a bar should be. Completely devoid of pretension and gimmicks, Puffy's represents what TriBeCa was prior to its recent "hip-ification." The locals keep the conversation interesting and inclusive, while respecting those who want to be alone. And while you may meet your match at the dart-board in the back of the room, save money for the excellent jukebox that features music ranging from James Brown to Marlene Dietrich. This spot is definitely worth the trip if you're sick of the new "super lounges" invading this area.

## Push Café

294 3rd Ave. (22nd & 23rd Sts.)
212-477-8100

SINCE THE PROLIFERATION of Starbucks and Xando, it has become nearly impossible to find a cool place to sit, smoke, talk, hang out, and basically just have a home away from home. Thankfully, Push opened its doors (next to Starbucks) to welcoming throngs of twentysomethings, neighborhood folks and SVA students. The brick walls are covered in rotating original artwork and colorful track lighting hangs over the barista area. For more privacy there is an awesome sunroom in the back separated from the rest of the café by a glass door. A large selection of bottled beers is served, 23 in all, at $3.75 a piece.

## Pyramid Club

101 Ave. A (6th & 7th Aves.)
212-473-7184

THE BEST '80s new wave dance party (aptly named "1984") takes place here every Friday night for only a $5 cover. Usually Pyramid fills up with young gay guys and a mixed Village contingent. This dark smoky cave also serves as a second home for goth and punk kids who come to dance on Saturday. There's no doubt about it, the weirdo factor is high, but this place never fails to entertain. And...rumor has it RuPaul was discovered here.

## The Quiet Man

1768 2nd Ave. (@ 92nd St.)
212-348-0879

BOYS IN KHAKIS on the prowl line the winding bar of this Upper East Side training ground for frat boys on their way up to become suits. Upon entering The Quiet Man, a patron uttered, "There's so much dick in here, it's ridiculous." We agree. Weekdays locals throw down $5 beers and dance. Although there's lots of room for dancing in the back of the bar, there's no cabaret license, so keep that boogie to yourself. If you want, go back to your college days: $15 will get you all you can drink from 8p.m. to 11p.m. Thursdays thru Saturdays.

## Raccoon Lodge

1439 York Ave. (76th & 77th Sts.)
212-650-1775
480 Amsterdam Ave. (@ 83rd St.)
212-874-9984

GOOD THING THERE is a Raccoon Lodge in three parts of town so you don't have to travel far to get down and dirty. Frat boys come here to guzzle beer with the rough and tumble Harley set. Don't be fooled by the moose head on the wall or the pony-tailed guy with a hand full of finger armour. The Raccoon Lodge is a bar for anyone who is ready to get pissed drunk and have fun.

## Raccoon Lodge

59 Warren St. (@ W. Broadway)
212-766-9656

"THIS IS AMERICA, and I want three shots of Tequila at once." Man, dive bars are the bomb, but the people make this one particularly extraordinary. Squeezed into the south side of TriBeCa, this Lodge is by far the best one, offering a frightening cross section of people. You have homeless junkies buying drinks for lawyers sitting next to hookers, millionaires and whiskey swilling celebrities. Granted, "a few more chokeholds are put on people here than in other places," but you know what you're getting into at the door.

## Radio Perfecto

190 Ave. B (11th & 12th Sts.)
212-477-3366

THE ILLUSTRIOUS PROPRIETORS of Opaline tried their luck further northeast last year and have been met with great responses. Radio Perfecto's theme is derived from the owner's own quest for the perfect vintage radio. The spoils of his quest adorn the unoffensive interior and add a bit of quirk to the "adaptive American" fare. Beers on tap and a selection of wines keep you busy while you wait for a table on their summer patio. But to really appreciate Radio's presence in the neighborhood, head here in the winter for a glass of Merlot and a cure-all chicken dumpling soup Mom would be proud of.

## Rain

1059 3rd Ave. (62nd & 63rd Sts.)
212-223-3669
100 W. 82nd St. (Amsterdam & Columbus Aves.)
212-501-0776

RAIN'S TWO LOCATIONS are unique changes of pace from the divey frat bars that litter their neighborhoods. This eclectic Asian bar/restaurant appeals to a younger, more discrimination crowd. No longer satisfied with sawdust covered floors, young men try to impress dates and groups friends after work by ordering wines by the glass or one of 20 bottled beers at this casually elegant spot.

## Raoul's

180 Prince St. (Sullivan & Thompson Sts.)
212-966-3518

OOH LA LA, tres chic. Raoul's never fails to deliver an authentic French experience. From the posters on the walls to the smoke filled bar to the wonderful food and drinks, this bar/restaurant serves its purpose well. The small bar area is perennially jammed with a thirtysomething crowd of professionals, models and locals all looking for and having a great time.

## Rathbones

1702 2nd Ave. (@ 88th St.)
212-369-7361

GIRLS, WE DON'T suggest you wear Manolo Blahniks to Rathbones, not due to casual atmosphere but the mounds of sawdust on the floor. This Irish bar has been serving beers to a devoted crowd for 27 years. Permanently packed with older regulars catching whatever game is on, eating shepherd's pie and drinking beers, Rathbones is a mellow hang.

## Raven Café

194 Ave. A (@12th St.)
212-529-4712

THE RAVEN HAS clearly grown up, and in the process, has not lost its way. Its awesome juke box and cozy couch filled "living room" still draws an eclectic East Village crowd and makes it an excellent place to frolic with a few friends. Owner, Harold Kramer, keeps it pumping with a nightly line up of slamming DJ's and live music events. Check in for the latest line up.

## Rawhide

212 8th Ave. (@ 21st St.)
212-243-9688

A CHELSEA LANDMARK for years, and a leather lover's delight with all the accoutrements, Rawhide packs in an interesting mix of gay Chelsea men. It opens at 8 a.m., perfect for a drink on your way to work or if you're still out from the previous night. The bunk house look serves as a standard watering hole the aging gay set.

## Rebar

127 8th Ave. (@ 16th St.)
212-627-1680

REBAR MAKES ITS own hours and plays by its own rules. It's known to host happening hip-hop parties and comedy/spoken-word nights, so call ahead before trekking to the two-floor den of debauchery. The tile bar and comfortable seating makes for a cozy environment, but getting a drink on a crowded night is not easy. Cover charge is $10-$15, depending on your gender and the evening.

## Recess

310 Spring St. (Greenwich & Renwick Sts.)
212-590-6050

A KINDER, GENTLER alternative to the pseudo-swank of nearby Sway, Recess is a mom-and-pop kind of homey establishment, New York-style. Run by a welcoming, hip couple and designed like an apartment too big to be your own, Recess offers free snacks, board games and cool cocktails like the milky smooth velvet hammer, and the requisite old couches to enjoy them on.

## Red Bench

107 Sullivan St. (Prince & Spring Sts.)
212-274-9120

DON'T BLINK OR you may miss this tiny bar. Loyal regulars relish the tranquility of this cozy SoHo find. Mingle up front if you can squeeze in, but your best bet is to grab a seat in the back and check out the model-types who hang here. Red Bench is pricy, but the sexy lounge music, candles and low lighting make for a great seduction scene, and you can't put a price on a good lay.

## Redeye Grill

890 7th Ave. (@ 56th St.)
212-541-9000

WHETHER PRE-DINNER or post-Carnegie Hall, the somewhat older crowd at Redeye Grill's bar is probably not hunkering down for long. The simple, understated bar area alludes to the seafood preferences of the patrons - a large metallic shrimp twirls at one end of the bar. Whether or not they are here for the famous "dancing shrimp" (skewered on a bed of pineapple), drinkers must shell out $14 for cosmos and martinis, $9 for a draft beer, and $14 for a glass of wine. Companies picking up the bill for business entertaining don't seem to mind; they're here to impress.

## The Red Lion

151 Bleecker St. (Thompson & LaGuardia Sts.)
212-260-9797

THE MAIN ATTRACTION of The Red Lion is the excellent cover bands doing all the classic rock songs you can't help but sing along to. Well, that and the hot college girls who come in when NYU is in session. Other than that, The Red Lion is indistinguishable from any other bar along the Bleecker Street strip. The food is average, the waitstaff friendly and hospitable. There's a nice selection of beers on tap, some funky bottle cap decorations along the back wall and an inconvenient $5 cover charge every Friday and Saturday night.

## Red Rock West

457 W. 17th St. (@ 10th Ave.)
212-366-5359

THIS WILDLY OUTRAGEOUS and unparalleled drinking man's saloon deserves to be nominated in the category of "Most Outrageously Fun" bars in the city. This complete dump has a special charm that extends to those lucky enough to have been here. Leave your attitude at home and let the bartenders-cum emcee's lick some whipped cream off your stomach. Girls should be prepared for a night of dancing on the bar and lots of shots. Be prepared to call in sick: the hangovers are killer!

## The Ref's Corner

302 E. 92nd St. (1st & 2nd Aves.)
212-722-9778

SINCE 1948, the Ref's Corner had been a refuge for Archie Bunker types who like to fight. About six years ago the Corner got a minor facelift and the passiveaggessive are now welcome. A tiny bar area gives way to a back room, which houses a pool table. The back porch is open for a very friendly bring-your-own bar-beque, or you can buy a microwave White Castle burger behind the bar; two grills, no waiting. A fine local dive, the staff and patrons are content to drink and watch the Yankee game while grilling.

## Regents

317 E. 53rd St. (1st & 2nd Aves.)
212-593-3091

THIS IS A gay man's English pub with live piano entertainment nightly. The lounge area tends to get "cruisy"; with young things looking for sugar daddies. Friday nights bring a younger and hipper crowd looking for some action and live entertainment. There is never a cover charge and weekday happy hours are lively.

## Relish

225 Wythe Ave. (3rd St. & Metropolitan Ave.)
718-963-4546 (Brooklyn)

ONLY 2 MONTHS OLD and Relish has already made a name for itself. This classic, all original diner car was manufactured in the '40s, and its beautiful chrome decor still shines. The red and gold walls of the super swanky lounge in back are bathed in candlelight. Head downstairs to see "the sexiest bathrooms in Williamsburg." The bar is open until 4 a.m. serving an extensive drink menu. You can sit in a booth and have a quiet romantic meal or at the counter/bar and chat it up with the attractive staff.

## Reservoir

70 University Pl. (10th & 11th Sts.)
212-475-0770

WARNING: SERIOUSLY CHEAP DRINKS. One of the only bars in New York where you can get a beer for $2.50 any time without the stipulation of happy hours, it's no wonder local patrons never leave. If you haven't met your neighbors yet, don't be surprised if you wind up playing against them in a game of pool. Tables in the back area are great for larger groups indulging in artery clogging joy like nachos and wings. The jukebox plays classic rock and nobody is afraid to sing along.

## Revival

129 E. 15th St. (Irving Pl. & 3rd Ave.)
212-253-8061

THE GOOD NEWS: Revival has a swanky upstairs lounge with comfortable 1920's style furniture and a spacious back patio that is wonderful on a summer's night. The bad news: These spaces are so often rented out for private parties that they might as well not exist. For most customers, the only place to go is the tiny, cramped front bar space that feels more like a hallway than a place to hang out. So while Revival is an excellent, economical spot to throw a party, if you're not invited, you'll end up feeling left out.

## Revolution

611 9th Ave. (43rd & 44th Sts.)
212-489-8451

THIS LARGE LOFT space in Hell's Kitchen invites a thirtysomething crowd in for dinner, some tunes and great, friendly service. A comfy lounge nook warmed by an exposed brick fireplace provides the neighborhood crowd a lounge to shoot the breeze in and a place to chill late night. The majority of the vast space is occupied with a long bar and tables that serve American fare. While the frozen margarita is Revolution's specialty drink, there are 8 beers on tap, wine and mixed drinks.

## Rhone

63 Gansevoort St. (Greenwich & Washington Sts.)
212-367-8440

THIS NEW WINE BAR in The Meat Packing District is Shecky's choice for best new Downtown bar. A great wine selection, (all Rhone, of course) a huge, loft-like space and a wonderful, modern decor has quickly attracted a very stylish and un-pretentious crowd. The large open doors and the authentic French food adds to the appeal. Definitely worth going out of your way for, especially if you're trying to impress a date.

## Rice

227 Mott St. (Prince & Spring Sts.)
212-226 5775

IF YOU ALWAYS wanted to be an alchemist or a painter, but ended up with a banking/consulting career, Rice is the place to express your creativity. Choose a rice (Bhutanese red, Thai Black, Basmati, Sticky or Japanese), and match it with one of the exotic Asian toppings. To match your exotic dinner, try one of one the international beers they serve. But no worries, there are no bankers in this Nolita neighborhood hang-out; it's purely downtown, artsy intellectuals.

## Richter's Bar

1608 3rd Ave. (90th & 91st Sts.)
212-722-6405

An older frat crowd assembles in this small, low-lit, neighborhood hangout. Hardcore locals followed Richter's when it moved to this location from 86th St. 10 years ago. Your best bet is their week-long happy hour from 4p.m. to 7p.m. which features $2 Bud, Bud Light and well drinks. You'll be entertained by pinball, shuffle bowling and darts and the bartender will match you shot for shot of Jagermeister just because she can.

## Right Bank Café

409 Kent St. (@ Broadway) Brooklyn
718-388-3929

Around for almost 10 years this fantastic bar deserves some long overdue credit. This Café is one block from the water, has an enormous outside space with breathtaking views of the Manhattan skyline and a hammock! There's great live jazz every Tuesday at 10 p.m. This space is also great in the off season when you can enjoy a game or sit upstairs in the newly renovated lounge where there are spectacular views of the city. Include the friendly staff and customers and Right Bank Café is the right place to come.

## Rink Bar

1 Rockerfeller Plaza (49th & 50th Sts.)
212-332-7620

If you can get past the crowds of gawking tourists who swarm the perimeter of Rockefeller center, this is actually a nice after work drink or dinner spot. During the winter, come watch and laugh at all of the amateur skaters face-planting on the rink. The atmosphere here is laid-back and the drinks are reasonably priced for midtown. This is one of the few touristy places where they will put on CNN instead of a Yankees game. If you're looking for a scrumptious snack, try the fried calamari with wasabi sauce at the bar.

## Rio Mar

7 9th Ave. (Little W. 12th St.)
212-242-1623

ON A COBBLESTONE SQUARE, Rio Mar is a charming little Mexican restaurant with a bar that feels straight out of a border town. With its odd decorations and candles, it's funky enough for friends and romantic enough for dates. Fortunately, it's set up for both: fantastic, inexpensive tapas served until 6p.m. make it a good after work spot, and the courteous, professional waiters will make any date that much more pleasant. Just remember to bring cash or your Amex.

## Rising Café

186 5th Ave. (@ Sackett St.) Brooklyn
718-622-5072

THOUGH IT HAS recently come under new management, Rising Café was and continues to be one of the hottest lesbian bars on Brooklyn's side of the river. At almost any given hour of the day or night you can stop in grab a coffee, beer or a mixed drink and join in on the fun. The bar itself is sparse and some what minimalist, giving the impression of a San Francisco style coffee house that someone gave up decorating midway through. Still, no one comes here for a crash course in interior design. Instead they come to flirt with the cute tattoo-sporting, tank top clad, girls behind the bar and chat with the equally bohemian clientele. Lesbian rock is the music of choice and there are always scheduled bands and performances; though the caliber can vary from the extremely interesting to the god-awful. Whatever the night, the bar is always packed with local girls and new faces looking to enjoy some female company.

## Rivertown Lounge

187 Orchard St. (Houston & Stanton Sts.)
212-388-1288

RIVERTOWN LOUNGE HAS maintained calm, mellow balance with its oh-so-hip neighbors over the years.

You won't see as many hipsters running around here as you would at Orchard Bar across the street. Great jukebox, pool tables in the back and eclectic mixture of people are good reasons to get your ass off the couch and go mingle. There is a DJ that begins at 9p.m. Thursday through Saturday which tends to bring in a bridge and tunnel crew, but the space is huge and those leopard skin and velour sofas are comfy enough to stake your claim and avoid the dancing if you so desire.

## Riviera Café & Sports Bar

225 W. 4th St. (@ 7th Ave. So.)
212-929-3250

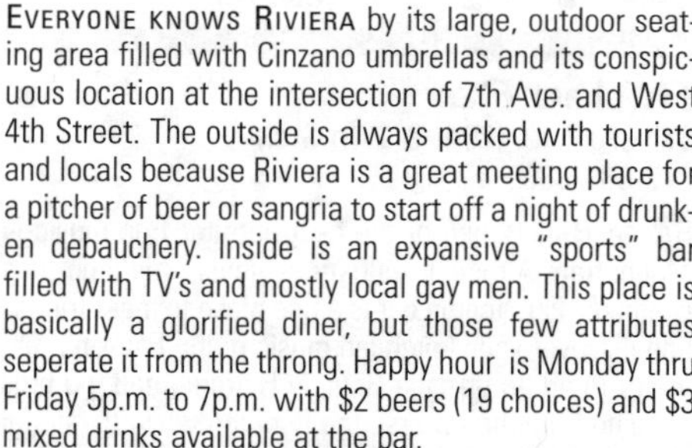

EVERYONE KNOWS RIVIERA by its large, outdoor seating area filled with Cinzano umbrellas and its conspicuous location at the intersection of 7th Ave. and West 4th Street. The outside is always packed with tourists and locals because Riviera is a great meeting place for a pitcher of beer or sangria to start off a night of drunken debauchery. Inside is an expansive "sports" bar filled with TV's and mostly local gay men. This place is basically a glorified diner, but those few attributes seperate it from the throng. Happy hour is Monday thru Friday 5p.m. to 7p.m. with $2 beers (19 choices) and $3 mixed drinks available at the bar.

## Rocking Horse

182 8th Ave. (19th & 20th Sts.)
463-9511

THIS CLASSIC CHELSEA HANGOUT has undergone many changes in its 12 years on the block. Its most recent incarnation, Café Mexicano, is about to be phased out in favor of a more modern motif (think glass bar and sprawling skylight) with an expanded dining room. For now, though, Rocking Horse boasts one of the most impressive selections of tequila around (over 50 varieties ranging from $6-$28 a glass). The delightful, health conscious cuisine is nothing to scoff at either, but the main attraction at this after work/movie spot are the outstanding margaritas. These are likely to remain a staple as the management redesigns and possibly extends the hours. Do yourself the service of seeing the Rocking Horse before and after its curent evolution.

## Rocky Sullivan's

129 Lexington Ave. (28th & 29th Sts.)
212-725-3871

WELCOME TO ROCKY SULLIVAN'S, home of Irish authors and thinkers alike. Don't misunderstand, just because they read doesn't mean they can't put 'em away. A steady stream of Guinness and Harp pours from the taps at this cerebral, Gaelic hall where the famous and the not-so-famous come to meet and drink. Frank McCourt, Barbara Fischkin and even Kurt Vonnegut have all dropped by to pontificate and make everyone else feel like taking the small bus home. Weekly events include comedy, musicians, trivia and readings. The schedules change, but the one constant is the steady stream of after work crowds.

## Rodeo Bar

375 3rd Ave. (26th & 27th Sts.)
212-683-6500

RODEO BAR IS one of the best bets for free music in Manhattan. Although touristy at times, this long-time Gramercy Park theme bar is a fine place to meet friends and discover your American music roots. Enter the bar area to find an upscale Hogs & Heifers (read: no bras hanging from the rafters), the floor strewn with peanut shells from the complimentary baskets on the tables. The total effect is "Candlelit Hillbilly." Expect a strong after-work crowd on the weekdays and a packed local crowd on the weekends. Come and listen to a fresh mix of rockabilly, country, and roots rock. If you're looking for a true redneck bar, leave Manhattan. But if you're happy pretending, you'll be welcome at the Rodeo. Note: Beware the killer margaritas!

## The Room

144 Sullivan St. (Houston & Prince Sts.)
212-477-2102

THE ROOM is a teeny-weenie, unpretentious lounge perfect for getting away from the maddening crowds of other SoHo bars during the week. The narrow two-room lounge is candlelit and quite sexy in an innocent way. Weekends tend to draw a non-local group of patrons who make it nearly impossible to grab a seat and hold a conversation. A wide variety of beer and wine from around the world makes this a nice change from the ordinary. The Room is absolutely worth a visit, but come early, stake out a seat and enjoy the cool scene.

## Rosa Mexicano

1063 1st Ave. (@ 58th St.)
212-753-7407
61 Columbus Ave. (@ 62nd St.)
212-977-7700

THIS CLASSY, EXPENSIVE Mexican restaurant and bar is a hot spot every night and considered by many to be the best Mexican food in the city. And now you can enjoy this place on both sides of the park. The West Side is brand new with the interior designed by David Rockwell of Nobu and Vong complete with an impressive water wall, while The East Side remains warm and traditional in pink stucco. The margaritas and fresh guacamole prepared tableside is an extra-added bonus to this pleasurable dining and cocktail experience.

## Rose Mary's Greenpoint Tavern

188 Bedford Ave. (N. 6th & 7th Sts.) Brooklyn
718-384-9539

ROSE MARY'S IS everyone's bar everyday, and that's no lie. Rose Mary has owned this landmark for over 40 years. And even with the recent Williamsburg-buzz, things are still just the way she wants them...if it ain't broken, don't fix it. With an amazing flair for decorating and an obvious love for the holidays, Rose Mary transforms this local hang into pure eye candy around Christmas time or Easter. Belly up to the bar and order yourself a Super-Size styrofoam cup of domestic brew that will put any Big-Gulp to shame for a mere $3.50! Play some Backgammon with a real old school local and hear a tale about the neighborhood. Throw on some Sinatra in the jukebox, sit back, watch the game and settle in. Rose Mary's happy to have ya!

## Rose's Turn

55 Grove St. (@ 7th Ave.)
212-366-5438

ROSE'S TURN IS an excellent piano bar with efficient and friendly service. Sunday nights fill up with groups of men belting out show tunes. It's amazing how everyone seems to know every word to every song! These singers are serious and they are not asking the piano player for Annie or The Sound of Music, they're singing complete scores from the best of Broadway. Happy hour offers half price drinks; those Absolut martinis go down easy when they're only $3.75! What will keep you coming back to Rose's Turn is the relaxed ambiance, the rustic interior and the clientele's remarkable ability to keep to octane level high while remembering all of the words. Whatever your pleasure, Rose's Turn is sure to please.

## Rosie Too!

640 10th Ave. (45th & 46th Sts.)
212-245-9566

THIS IS ONE of New York City's most popular piano bars where people who love show tunes come to sing, sing, sing. Upon entering, the bartenders stop singing just long enough to take your order. They like to belt them out here, so if you're a shy, closet show tune queen and you're a little off key, feel free to join in, no one will notice. But if you fancy yourself a virtuoso, you'll certaibly have your competition cut out for you. The drinks start at $5 and are nothing to write home about, but let's face it; chances are you're not here just for a drink.

## The Round Bar (@ Royalton Hotel)

44 W. 44th St. (5th & 6th Aves.)
212-944-8844

HIDDEN AROUND A corner inside The Royalton Hotel is The Round Bar, a vodka and champagne bar serving expensive cocktails since 1989. Late at night this small, padded round room fills up with thirsty twenty and thirtysomethings drinking and canoodling. Expect to endure hostile stares until you prove yourself worthy to drink among this merry band of the self-anointed.

## Route 85A

85 Ave. A (5th & 6th Sts.)
212 673-1775

HIDDEN BELOW KIM'S Video is a great old school East Village hangout devoid of cell phones, Prada and attitude. Super friendly bartenders pour cheap drinks and treat you like a friend. Dark red walls, old hubcaps and license plates adorn the walls while a jukebox spits out local favorites from the Kill Van Kull, Nashville Pussy and the Pristeens. A DJ spins on most nights including Fridays when retro '40s tunes attract a decked out 1940's style crowd, while Saturday nights' new wave and disco will bring you back to the '70's and '80's. Route 85A maintains a great, low key, East Village vibe making it a hidden jewel amongst the mad gentrification of Ave A.

## The Roxy

515 W. 18th St. (10th & 11th Aves.)
212-645-5156

THIS MEGA CLUB hit NYC in the early '80s and still packs them in with mad dancers and techno heads. Leave your piece at home (yes, that means you too, Puff Daddy) because you will be frisked before walking through metal detectors. Each night boasts a different event, such as Roller Derby Wednesdays. (call for details.) The DJ's rotate and play a variety of music. Expect a hefty cover charge and strict door policy.

## Ruby Foo's

2182 Broadway (77th & 78th St.)
212-724-6700
1626 Broadway (@ 49th St.)
212-489-5600

THIS DUO of self-described dim sum and sushi palaces also offers a royal good time. Both locations are doused in shiny reds and blacks, Chinese lanterns, golden Buddhas and packed with those waiting to try succulent Pan-Asian cuisine to compliament the buzz from one of the kitschy house specialties like the Asian margarita and the fruity Ruby Foo. Stumpy martini glasses make for a less precarious trek through the throngs, and there's a refill or two for you left in the shaker; never a bad thing.

## Ruby's Tap House

1754 2nd Ave. (91st & 92nd Sts.)
212-987-8179

BESIDES A NICE sampling of international beers, Rudy's feels like an out-of-place ski-lodge without the ski bunnies. For over 7 years, Rudy's has been serving locals with a decent bar menu and a 4p.m.-7p.m. happy hour. Rudy's is home to a slew of local clubs and teams: pool, darts, softball and drinking (mandatory meetings nightly), but offers little to non-locals. A DJ spins Wednesday through Saturday. Get jiggy with it.

## Rubyfruit

531 Hudson St. (Charles & 10th Sts.)
212-929-3343

LOCATED IN THE heart of the West Village, Rubyfruit serves inexpensive food in its downstairs restaurant (Monday lobsterfests are a big draw) and cheap drinks in the civilized, comfortable and cozy upstairs lounge. An excellent pick-up spot for lesbians, the parlor atmosphere of Rubyfruit is lively and conversational without being overbearing and pretentious.

## Rudy's

627 9th Ave. (44th & 45th Sts.)
212-974-9169

DIVING IT UP in Hell's Kitchen for 50 years, Rudy's packs it in with everyone under the sun looking for cheap drinks, hotdogs and a large back garden. Decorated with old retro style booths, hanging neon signs and even a handmade front door reading "Rudy's," this dive serves up an early bird special where a pint of Bud is $1.50. Otherwise, drinks are cheap as hell; liquor is $2.75 during the day and $3 at night. Not the greatest place for a date, unless she is very easily impressed or been living under a rock.

## Rue B

188 Ave. B (11th & 12th Sts.)
212-358-1700

NEXT DOOR TO its sister spot Radio Perfecto, this cozy café is the new kid on the block. But don't be fooled: the partners are veteran bar/restauranteurs with a knack for service and class. Try their delicious array of gourmet French/Italian fare while sipping aperitifs or sparkling wines. With or without the jazz, the exposed-brick Jordan Jacobs interior, reasonably priced beer and unpretentious charm will entrance you. Just don't expect to get wild: hard liquor is as scarce as the coffee is black.

## Russian Vodka Room

265 W. 52nd St. (Broadway & 8th Ave.)
212-307-5835

THE NAME OF this bar gives the element of surprise away. But, not only do they boast over 70 vodkas of exotic flavors, the place is actually staffed with real Russians. Don't be put off by the hole in the wall entrance, come in and take delight in the stunning martinis and caviar that rivals Petrossian's. The vibe is international (but not pretentious), with a wide range of people from all generations. Good for after work or a late night with friends, the RVR makes us happy to see the Cold War is a thing of the past.

## Ryan's Daughter

350 E. 85th St. (@ 1st Ave.)
212-628-2613

A NICE LITTLE neighborhood bar, Ryan's Daughter is a pleasant place to kill a couple hours sucking down beer, watching sports and bullshitting with the guys. Watch out, though, the friendly Irish bartenders have a smart answer for everything. The crowd of regulars are more than happy to sit and chat with you about anything under the sun, and before you know it, you'll be sucked into the warmth of Ryan's Daughter. College students flock to Ryan's to party before the parties, which makes this a primo pick up joint for horny, carousing co-eds.

## Ryan's Irish Pub

151 2nd Ave. (9th & 10th Sts.)
212-979-9511

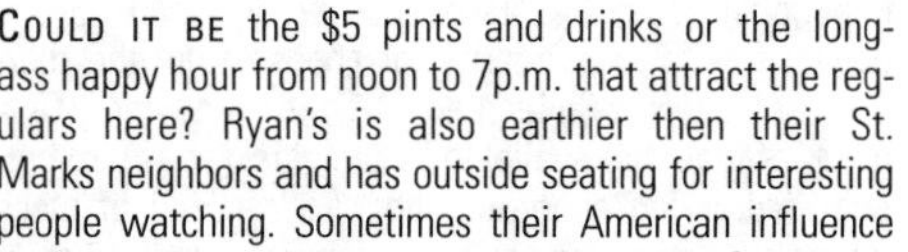

COULD IT BE the $5 pints and drinks or the long-ass happy hour from noon to 7p.m. that attract the regulars here? Ryan's is also earthier then their St. Marks neighbors and has outside seating for interesting people watching. Sometimes their American influence overshadows the "pub" atmosphere, but they do serve Guinness in pie form, which wins them back many points.

## Ryan's Sports Bar

46 Gold St. (John & Fulton Sts.)
212-385-6044

COMFORTABLE GREEN LEATHER chairs and white Christmas lights surround this Wall Street area sports bar. Usually filled with a business crowd sipping cheap drinks after a long day at the office and always reliable for a quick drink and watching a game, Ryan's Sports Bar serves its purpose well.

## S & T Bar

587 3rd Ave. (38th & 39th Sts.)
212-661-3181

THIS 4 YEAR-OLD Murray Hill spot hosts a crowd of young professionals for after work drinks. If you can manage to navigate your way through the tasteful bar area, you can score a back table with friends and enjoy a good selection of tap beers at $5 a pint, or sample a martini special for around $8. Towards the back is a casual dining area, and down a flight of rickety steps is a second outdoor/indoor heated bar area which looks like a ski lodge cabin, complete with a real tree growing in the middle. It can get packed in the summer, so your best bet is to relax at a table and soak in the E-Z listening rock.

## Sabor

462 Amsterdam Ave. (82nd & 83rd Sts.)
212-579-2929

SABOR OPENED EARLY summer 2000 to a warm reception and promises to be fierce competition for Calle Ocho. Its unfair advantage is its spectator friendly dÈcor that allows passersby to view the open air dining room and bar. The place is always filled with people waiting for tables where they will dine on tiny portions of tasty Spanish cuisine with Caribbean infusions (mango all over the place). For $7, you can have a decent mojito or margarita, or choose from the thorough selection of Chilean and Argentinean wines. Only a few of them are available by the glass, so you're better off ordering a bottle. Sabor is the kind of place where how much fun you have is in direct proportion to how much money you're willing to spend.

## Saints

922 Amsterdam Ave. (@ 109th St.)
212-961-0599

A FABULOUS CROSS-SECTION of gay New York, the crowd at Saints represents every color of the rainbow.

Hop on the 1/9 and you will experience a new kind of bar where the Upper West Side meets hip downtown for mutually pleasurable results. Bartenders randomly call out happy hours during the night, so it's hard to leave here without a significant buzz. Gregarious groups of friends congregate at the long bar or in the booths always ready to meet someone new.

## Sala

344 Bowery (@ Great Jones St.)
212-979-6606

IF YOU WANT to impress a date, take her to dinner at Sala. If you want a date, you should still go to Sala; just a little later. Sala, espanol for living room, is a well-thought-out Spanish-style restaurant that transforms to a bar after dinner. The food is traditional Spanish, and you may find yourself receiving a lecture if you commit the faux pas of ordering sangria with dinner. The crowd is older, and on weekends, the DJ spins house music for the yuppie-ish crowd. There isn't really a dress code, but bust out the snazzy threads if you plan to snag Mr. Right Enough.

## The Saloon

1920 Broadway (@ 64th St.)
212-874-1500

A FAIR SIZED bar occupies one corner of this large, crowded Lincoln Center restaurant. Not the most exciting or picturesque location to spend an evening, but reasonable prices, friendly bartenders and a lively atmosphere make this a descent place to hang out with friends and co-workers. Most of the regulars work in the area and congregate here to wind down.

## Sam Beckett's

1373 1st Ave. (@ 74th St.)
212-717-8177

THIS NEIGHBORHOOD PUB has the power to grow on you. It's totally free of pretension, if a little rough around the edges. You won't be dazzled by the decor, but darts and a pool table will divert your attention from your busy day. Scratch beneath the surface a bit and you're more than likely to discover that Sam Beckett's is a friendly place that will keep you coming back.

## Sapphire Lounge

249 Eldridge St. (Houston & Stanton Sts.)
212-777-5153

Remember the scene in Animal House when the the extremly white frat guys walk into an all black club? Similar, but not as drastic, Sapphire serves as a stomping ground of white chicks lookin for Mocha love. Still one of the more entertaining and energetic spots to boogie on the weekend, Sapphires one short cumming, (spelled intentionally) is it's size. Sometimes size does matter. With a cover charge ranging from 3-5 dollars, this little hot spot is still one of your best dancing bangs for your buck. Getting served at the bar is nearly impossible with the packed dance floor, but fuck, do you really need a gin and tonic while you're pretending that you're pretty fly for a white guy? A good spot, a fun time and the next best way to burn some calories. Now rock on with your bad self.

## Savoy

70 Prince St. (@ Crosby St.)
212-219-8570

THE LOUNGE UPSTAIRS at the familiar Savoy restaurant has an unusual, slightly disconcerting atmosphere. The tiny bar is surrounded by a larger area that has the feel of a Park Avenue doctor's office with small end tables and chairs lined up against the wall, all facing a beautiful candlelit fireplace. The moderately priced liquor selection here is anything but standard, with an emphasis on quality over quantity. The condensed lounge menu is delectable and eclectic. The dining room is startlingly romantic and comfortably sophisticated. In short, this is not the place for a bachelorette party, but it's a perfect spot to pop the question.

## Savoy Lounge

355 W. 41st St. (@ 9th Ave.)
212-947-5255

THIS HELL'S KITCHEN dive was previously home to young, gay hustlers until they turned it into a jazz and blues joint. Savoy Lounge is a great local dive which serves up cheap drinks for die hard drinkers from 8 a.m. to 4a.m. There is nightly live jazz with a cover only on Fridays and Saturdays and one of the best jazz jukeboxes in the city.

## Scandal

359 W. 54th St. (8th & 9th Aves.)
212-582-2200

THIS VERY TRENDY gay bar just opened this year on West 54th Street. Brougt to you by the same owners of the more fabulous and interesting Chase, Scandal doesn't really live up to its name, though it's beautifully decorated with chandeliers and mirrors and packed with gay "trendoids." The music is the standard gay lounge/club mix smattered with Madonna, Pet Shop Boys and George Michael but the service is friendly and efficient, making Scandal a good neighborhood find.

## Scharmann's

386 W. Broadway (Spring & Broome Sts.)
212-219-2561

HOW IN THE WORLD did they come across this much space in SoHo? And, where did they get all of this furniture? A coffee shop by day and a bar at night, Scharmann's is one of the roomiest places in town. Filled with mix and match sofas and chairs, Scharmann's looks like an upscale thrift store down to the huge, low hanging chandelier in the center of the room. For people watching, they have a nice outdoor terrace on SoHo's scenic streets. Unfortunately, this place attracts more than its share of fanny-packed tourists--but that's SoHo. The waiters tend to get lost in this warehouse-sized spot, but once you find them, they're pretty accommodating. Scharmann's is a better group place than pick up spot.

## The Scratcher

209 E. 5th St. (2nd & 3rd Aves.)
212-477-0030

THE LITTLE WALK down into the comfort zone is like a portal to Brigadoon. In a city peppered with Irish hangouts, Scratcher possesses indefinable charm. It could be the dimly lit, basement location and live traditional music that makes it charming. Or maybe it's the East Village attitude. You come here, it feels natural, you get something to eat and it's almost like being home. Whether, you're from Ireland, Manhattan or Timbuktu, you'll be comfortable here.

## Screening Room

54 Varick St. (@ Canal St.)
212-334-2100

IF YOU WANT to feel like a character in an F. Scott Fitzgerald novel, then come to the Screening Room. This art deco space is reminiscent of the time when dinner and a movie was the ultimate evening out. On Mondays you can catch the live jazz band on the open mezzanine while sipping oversized martinis at the spacious bar area. Enjoy dinner in the velvet-draped dining room, and top your evening off with an indie film in one of the cozy theaters equipped with love seats down the hall. You can also come by for a brunch and screening of Breakfast at Tiffany's on the weekend. Prices run on the high side, but they offer an excellent prix-fixe that includes movie tickets.

## Seaport Café

89 South St., South Street Seaport, (@ Pier 17)
212-964-1120

LAID-BACK, chilled-out people enjoy a fine view of the harbor and Lower Manhattan's skyscrapers from this cafe. Stop in for a hamburger, specialty sandwich or pasta with a domestic draft or glass of wine on your way back uptown. For a quick snack, the flaky French and Indian pastries are delightful. Open 'til 4a.m.

## Sequoia

South Street Seaport (@ Pier 17)
212-732-9090

NO TEARS WOULD be shed if Sequoia shut its doors to the throngs of classless tourists who visit the seaport thinking it's a "real" New York thing to do. There is outside seating that serves as a nice spot for happy hour if you work in the Financial District. Happy hour features beer and frozen margaritas for $3, Monday thru Friday.

## Serena

222 W. 23rd St. (7th & 8th Aves)
212-255-4646

ANYTHING HOUSED IN the basement of the Chelsea Hotel is bound to have its own share of infamy. Sexy Serena, created by ex-Details mag man Sam Shaffer (and named after his well-connected mom) had to get a nearby synagogue desanctified in order to get its liquor license. One year later, the red, Moroccanesque lounge is still hot with glamorpusses galore and cocktails like the popular, and promising, passionate screw.

## Session 73

1359 1st Ave. (@ 73rd St.)
212-517-4445

AN INFUSION OF something funkier than normal in the otherwise bland Upper East Side, Session 73 quickly established itself as one of the top music bars in Manhattan. This distinction is not undeserved since top quality bands play every night of week free of charge. Groups of well-dressed cosmopolitan twentysomethings chill out and groove to the funky vibes and mingle at the long bar. Session 73's only problem is that it's too corporate; it's true colors are not shining yet.

## 7A

109 Ave. A (@ 7th St.)
212-673-6583

YOU KNOW IT, you love it, and it's open 24/7. 7A is about as East Village as you can get. "It's not trendy, it's not cliquey, it's not trying to be something it's not; it's just 7A." The crowds move through here quicker than the clanging of the kitchen bell, but it's always packed. The menu ranges from vegetarian to burgers and burritos to pasta. Breakfast is served 4a.m.-5 p.m. daily and the challah French toast during Sunday brunch is delicious. Eats and drinks, punks and drunks...7A has got it all.

## 7B (a.k.a Vazac's)

108 Ave. B (@ 7th St.)
212-473-8840

THIS LOCAL DIVE has witnessed a lot of change in the neighborhood over the last 15 years. From the tattooed, East Village derelicts and bikers of yesteryear that still reign over the bar, to the shameless frat boys and uptown edge-seekers that now crowd the doorway on weekends, it seems everyone has called this their "spot" (just ask Jeanine Garafolo). But the dimly-lit horseshoe bar with solid stools and rickety tables will not cave to the times. The down-to-earth rocker staff is sympathetic to all of your alcohol needs and the pinball machines help you kill time to the tunes from the kick-ass jukebox. Grab a cold one for $3 to $5 or a pitcher of Rolling Rock for $8, and set up the Wild Turkeys, boys, 'cuz you're in for a ride.

## Shade

241 Sullivan St. (@ 3rd St.)
212-982-6275

NOT JUST SHADY, but pitch black, Shade is a romantic candlelit cave filled with Japanese fans, giant velvet curtains and the soft screeching of Bjork. They serve good, inexpensive food, including awesome crepes, until 3 a.m., and the wine list is interesting and varied, especially a selection of 20-year-old ports for that post-meal afterglow. Shade isn't a ton of fun without a date, but perfect if you don't want your attention to wander from that special someone.

## Shades of Green

125 E. 15th St. (Irving Pl. & 3rd Ave.)
212-674-1394

"SHADES OF GREEN," is that just a clever name for an Irish bar, or does it represent the hues patrons turn after too much Guinness? You be the judge. But for a joint located near a major university, Shades of Green is surprisingly relaxed and pleasant. It has a clean polished bar, an enormous back room and a respectable selection of beer. The kitchen serves primarily Irish food, but there are veggie offerings and ambitious daily specials. Even if you're long past the age where you have to worry about mid-terms, Shades is a decent place to be a regular.

## Shampu

9 Ave. A (Houston & 2nd Sts.)
646-602-2590

HERE LIES THE perfect Upper East Side lounge; unfortunately it's in the East Village. Besides its dangerously dim interior, your wait at the bar will not be adequately rewarded with a good drink and the DJ's acid jazz spinnings are ordinary at best. The only saving grace for Shampu is its tapas menu. It may be a stop off, but it's no destination.

## Shark Bar

307 Amsterdam Ave. (74th & 75th Sts.)
212-874-8500

A LAID BACK after work hangout during the week, this predominantly African-American bar comes to life on the weekends when there is often a line to get in. Explaination? The great soul food, the groovin' tunes and the "not so" subtle pick-up scene. Catering to a mostly twenty to thirtysomething professional crowd, Shark bar has been an Upper West Side staple for years and a favorite of the New York Knicks. One of the best bars in this 'hood.

## Shine

285 W. Broadway (@ Canal St.)
212-941-0900

TO THE NAKED EYE, this seems like just another mega-club/lounge with a velvet rope, great DJ's and painful waits for the bartender's attention. Wrong. It is all that PLUS a hefty cover charge. Occasional live music performances are a refreshing treat since the artists are at an arms length away, making everyone feel like a VIP. A healthy group of young Manhattanites come here to mix, mingle and work it all out. Since you won't bump into any of the Victoria's Secret models here, you'll be able to get past the door guys without a lot of shitty attitude.

## Ship of Fools

1590 2nd Ave. (82nd & 83rd Sts.)
212-570-2651

THERE'S NO SHORTAGE of sports bars in New York, but even if you're downtown and want to watch a game, it's worthwhile to pull out your Metrocard and trek to the Upper East Side to check out Ship of Fools. The bar boasts 21 TV's (six of which are large screen), darts, two pool tables, two bars and three large rooms, the last of which can be rented out for private "sports" parties. This is incontrovertibly one of the best sports bars in NYC.

## Ship's Mast

351 Kent St. (@ So. 5th St.) Brooklyn
718-599-1936

RIGHT BELOW THE North side of the bridge, and one block from the water, this place serves as a watering hole to the factory workers of Domino's sugar. Behind the large circular bar are two huge mermaids from the crests of old ships, and a great little niche called "The Cave" that looks like a giant piece of fish tank decoration. Free hot dogs are served along with a menu of basic pub food. Drink prices are pretty cheap and the bar is open till 4a.m.

## Siberia

1627 Broadway (@ 50th St.)
212-333-4141
(In the downtown 1/9 Subway Station)

THE DARK AND well-hidden underground Siberia provides New Yorkers with a surefire change from the ordinary. Add walls covered in graffiti and random Russian gewgaws to the mix and you'll come up with the best dive scene in the city. This tiny bar opened a large back lounge where bands play on certain nights of the week. Super friendly bartenders make you feel at home while pouring dirt cheap drinks and lots of potent Russian vodka shots. European tourists, cool regulars, writers and theatre types gather here to booze while listening to an excellent jukebox. It's not a pick up bar, just a warm and friendly gem hidden in the underbelly of New York City.

## Sidewalk Café

94 Ave. A (@ 6th St.)
212-253-8080

SIDEWALK CAFÉ GETS a big fat A+ in keeping the trendoids away from the front door. This East Village landmark definitely caters to the anti-Soho, non-conformist types who like cheap drinks, good live music and a game of pool. The café serves up cheap American fare 24 hours a day while the sounds of Helmut and The Ramones rock through the smoke filled air. A great happy hour seduces drinkers into a place that many old-school locals still call home.

## Simone

134 1st Ave. (@ St. Mark's Pl.)
212-982-6665

YOU CAN'T MISS SIMONE...the owner's portrait is plastered on the building. This beautiful cafe/bar has become a neighborhood staple for young, hip East

Villagers who want the vibe of a bar, the intimacy of a local coffee house and the decor of sleek Asian restaurant. Cool jazz and low lighting has also made this a favorite date spot for people not looking to break their bank accounts, just to swap a little spit. Good snack food, great drinks and a very accomodating staff has kept this place going for over 2 years now, which just goes to show that you don't have to be a trendy lounge with ratty couches to gain a following in the East Village.

## Sin Sin (Leopard Lounge)

85 2nd Ave. (@ E. 5th St.)
212-253-2222

THIS LOW-LIT, leopard-clad lounge atop Sin-Sin bar and restaurant is a meeting place for the hip and beautiful. The music level allows for easy conversation and a casual pick-up scene. Try the leopard tartini, it's to die for. If the luck of the Irish is with you, the generator from the bar downstairs will kick in causing your couch to vibrate uncontrollably like the coin-operated heart shaped beds in Niagara Falls. Leopard Lounge is one of those places that fits the bill on every level: good date spot, good pick-up spot and good meeting spot. The Celtic artwork hanging under the disco ball describes this bar eloquently and truthfully, "Heart and Soul."

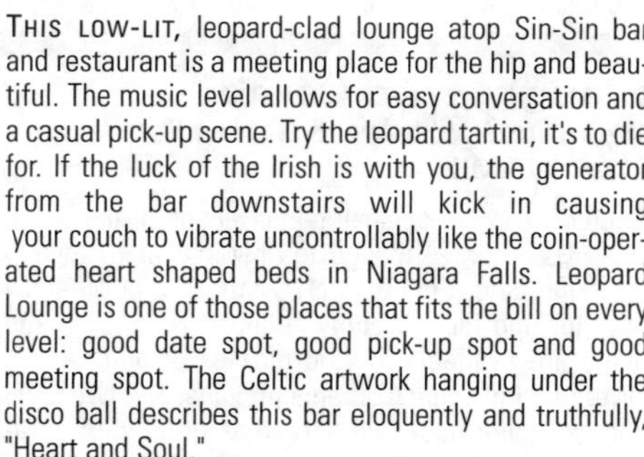

## Sin Sin

248 E. 5th St. (@ 2nd Ave.)
212-253-2222

SIN SIN, PRONOUNCED Shin Shin, possesses a discrete duality. Although it houses the overflow from the upstairs Leopard Lounge, it has its own following of sophisticated customers that run the drinking gamut from mafioso and working class to frou-frou SoHo types in Daryl K. Pinball and a Mega Touch Max game machines juxtaposed against the ornate light coverings and animal print on the couches, lend to the eclectic feel that is also reflected in the patrons. One young lady summed it up beautifully, "I'm not high maintenance, but I'm a high maintenance drinker." Indulge in a "burger and fries break" if you get bored of mingling with the eye candy that usually hang here. As long as you've got 23 chromosomes, you'll feel comfortable in this joint.

## SJ South & Sons

273 Church St. (White & Franklin Sts.)
212-219-0640

THE CLASSY AND BEAUTIFUL arched plate glass windows bring light into this brick-walled pub owned by one Irish guy and one Texan who have been too busy drinking to rename the place since it changed hands. A friendly vibe permeates the crowd that consists of locals and happy hour revelers.The Grandfather clock on the wall is stuck on 10p.m., so enjoy the illusion and ask the bartender to keep 'em coming. Bottom line: a neighborhood joint that can always be relied upon for a friendly smile and a cold brew.

## Slaughtered Lamb

182 W. 4th St. (6th Ave. & Barrow St.)
212-627-LAMB

THE LAMB IS the original mad invention of the Jekyll and Hyde crew. Although terribly similar in theme, the lamb caters more to NYU students and Jersey boys looking for "da booty" than tourists. Over 250 beers are available in yard glasses or pints and a "Werewolf in London" theme prevails. The two level pub has quiet nooks and crannies filled with paraphernalia relating to its theme. Outside seating is available in the summer but not recommended since the high volume of pedestrian traffic is sure to eat away at your nerves.

## Slipper Room

167 Orchard St. (@ Stanton St.)
212-253-7246

SWANKY IS THE best way to describe this recent addition to the Lower East Side. A swinging retro-style lounge that offers fine cocktails in a relaxed atmosphere, The Slipper Room is the type of place one would expect to find Hef and his playboy bunnies. You can enjoy something stiff off the specialty drink menu while checking out the burlesque shows that feature singing, dancing and an occasional saucy striptease. Or you can just kick back at one of the many tables and try your luck with the ladies that pack the place on the weekends. There is no door policy yet, but if you plan on getting into the VIP lounge you better do some primping.

## Sliver Wine Bar

337 W. Broadway (@ Grand St.)
212-226-6644

THE OPEN AIR SPACE invites passersby into the newest bar on this strip, but the friendly owner behind the bar and the eclectic high-end wine list will keep you coming back. A good selection of foreign beers and special fruity martinis are a nice touch. Fish tanks are so eighties, but the impressive salt-water tank perched next to the dining area is totally cool. Check out the baby shark before he grows up and goes back to the Dead Sea.

## Smalls

183 10th St. (@ 7th Ave. So.)
212-929-7565

STILL THE BEST jazz value in New York, Smalls has sustained their intimate feel and solid roster of talent by leaving their six year-old format untouched. Here's how it works: They open at 10p.m. at which point you shell out $10 for ten hours of jazz. True to its name, Smalls occupies a basement nook in the West Village and features nightly some of the finest unsigned and emerging talent in New York. Mitch Borden, the owner and sole employee, sits at the front of the long line, and will be happy to discuss anything from Monk to Kafka while you wait. Smalls is BYOB, maintaining an ultra-casual atmosphere within the smoky walls. The low price brings in a varied crowd from NYU music students to Upper East Side professionals. Many of the bands share musicians and famous faces sometimes show up for the 2 a.m jam session.

## SMF

126 St. Marks Pl. (1st Ave. & Ave. A)
212 473-1620

PROPRIETOR FRANK Giresi could try any number of shenanigans to attract the thuggish herds of weekend wassailers traipsing up and down the Ave. A tavern strip and make a killing. But that would be casting pearls before swine. He continues to serve up well-selected and well-priced wines to a small crowd of enthusiasts. Were this homey and unpretentious boite located somewhere more chic, say, smack-dab in the middle of NoLita (find Giresi's wine store, Elizabeth & Vine, there), SMF would be booming. But Giresi, intent on snatching goblets from the "monocle'd wine snobs" and placing them in the hands of the people, seems on a mission more exalted than making a fast buck.

## Smith's

701 8th Ave. (@ 44th St.)
212-246-3268

THIS PLACE HAS "David Lynch location spot" written all over it! Open since 1910, this New York institution (literally), with its half burned-out neon sign, is downright depressing. Harboring a bus station mosaic of patrons, here you'll find the people the Beatle's were talking about in their song "All the Lonely People." In the early '20s it was probably a really rockin' spot, but check your calendars people, we're in a new century. The bartender's friendliness and willingness to do shots with the patrons makes it an above average place to hang out.

## Sneakers

392 West St. (@ Christopher St.)
212-242-9830

THIS SMALL, GAY NEIGHBORHOOD dive bar has been serving drinks to a devoted clientele for the past twenty years. A mixed (male/female) crowd come here to schmooze and booze. The cheap drinks and friendly atmosphere make this an exceptional shithole.

## SOB's (Sounds of Brazil)

204 Varick St. (Houston & King Sts.)
212-243-4940

DECORATED IN BAMBOO, palm trees and a tropical motif that feels like a small, Brazilian roadside dance hut, SOB's serves up the hottest salsa parties in NYC. A hefty cover charge (usually upwards of $20) and steep drink prices are some the things you will have to work through, however there is enough energy in this hot-spot to help NYC get through the next Arab oil embargo.

## Soho Kitchen & Bar

103 Greene St. (Prince & Spring Sts.)
212-925-1866

COMMONLY CONSIDERED THE most extensive wine bar

in the city, this SoHo space is as popular with tourists as it is with young professionals. In a large, lofty room with dangling planes overhead, amateurs and connoisseurs can feel equally comfortable sampling from the 100 wines, ranging from $4.50-$20 per glass, or the 40 beers. Surrounding the huge central bar are simple tables where hearty American bistro fare may be sampled.

## Solas

232 9th St. (2nd & 3rd Aves.)
212-375-0297

TRANSPORTED BACK TO the 1930's decadence, Solas has a good vibe and a cool scene. You won't find any midgets selling cotton candy in here, but they do have a DJ every night.This chic two-story lounge always has a smart looking group of people lounging around. The billiards room is fantastic with unusual lighting and original artwork. Even though people seem to compare the difficulty quoitient of pouring a Guinness to mapping the human genome, it's not, but still, bartenders here serve a nice brew.

## Sophie's

507 E. 5th St. (Aves. A & B)
212-228-5680

COME ONE, COME ALL to Mona's ugly sister, Sophie's. Crowded with world travelers, musicians and those straying from the path of Jesus, this East Village dive has a warm inviting vibe. Rickety wooden chairs and tables fill the bar next to the pool table, and vintage beer signs clutter the walls along with featured new works from the artist of the month. The jukebox has a great selection of classic rock, punk, oldies and reserved spots for local bands that hang out here. Domestic beers are a mere $2.75 a bottle and $7 a pitcher. Caution: Walking into Sophie's may leave you stumbling out in a stupor.

## Spa

76 E. 13th St. (Broadway & 4th Ave.)
212-388-1060

BREAK OUT YOUR Bedazzler and spike up the 'do and call your Columbian drug dealer friends. Welcome back to '80s decadence with a modern facade. This newly opened lounge/club sprouted from the ashes of the old Key Club and now caters to a hipper, trendier crowd of hedonists. If you manage to circumvent the fashion police and know the right names (or shell out a steep $20 cover), you're in for a night of go-go dancing and fun. Bar one sports a cascading wall of water behind the model bartenders and sleek brushed steel hardware. Bar two is the perfect outpost for checking out the considerable dance floor and sipping your pricey cocktail to the best of Brit pop, big beat, house and soul classics. Bar three is tucked into what used to be Key's swanky VIP lounge and is lined with translucent plexiglass sheets and white banquets. One would expect nothing less from Steve Lewis, promoter for Life and Limelight in their glory days. The door policy is strict, but it has to be in order to keep attracting celebrities. Your best bet is on a Wednesday or Thursday when friendly and attractive clubbers run the show.

## Spaghetti Western

59 Reade St. (Broadway & Church St.)
212-513-1333

ALTHOUGH THE MANAGER claims that this place is busy for lunch and dinner, especially when jury-duty sufferers pour out of the nearby courthouses for quick sustenance, Spaghetti Western on a Friday night is as dead as the OK Corral after the shoot-out. And not without reason. Although the space itself is not unattractive, the Wild-West decor is cheesy and repellent. The liquor selection, though sufficient, offers nothing interesting; hell, not even a few good tequilas. The Atomic Wings might deliver the Donner Party from more grisly suppers, but they wouldn't be exactly licking their collective chops in anticipation. Some of the clientele might fire up the loins of the loneliest of prospectors, but he'd still be arguing down the price with the house madam 'till the cows come home.

## The Spike

120 11th Ave. (@ W. 20th St.)
212-415-3100

CALL THE HISTORICAL Society because they missed one of New York City's most famous leather bars and a true gay staple. Big men with tattoos, piercings, tight Levi's, and flannel shirts flirt with the tourists who can't get enough of them. This pick-up bar is a perfect spot to meet a rough and tumble character.

## Splash

50 W. 17th St. (5th & 6th Aves.)
212-691-0073

STRAIGHT OUT OF the movie "Cocktail", the upstairs of Splash is all shiny metal complemented by small candlelit tables and railings, railings, railings. The downstairs dance floor gets packed with sweaty and shirtless gyrating men. A rather odd and intriguing door free bathroom allows for good views of patrons, along with their cocks, pissing into the trough. That along with the awesome dance music makes this a teriffic gay pick-up spot. A sexy crowd packs the place on weekends when there is a $10 cover charge.

## Splitzzz

625 8th Ave. (@ 42nd St.)
Port Authority, 2nd Floor, South Wing
212-268-2822

SPLITZZZ IS UNDOUBTEDLY the TGI Fridays of the Port Authority. Located next door to the Leisure Time Bowling Alley, Splitzzz welcomes commuters, bowlers and sad to say, regulars. A large oval bar occupies most of the room and the main visual attractions are the huge tropical fish tank and a big screen TV playing all sports. The older 40's crowd munch on burgers and fries while chugging cheap drinks and listening to a top 40 jukebox. You probably won't meet your Knight in Shining Armour here, but hell, it beats waiting for a bus in the skanky hallways of Port Authority.

## The Sporting Club

99 Hudson St. (Franklin & Leonard Sts.)
212-219-0900

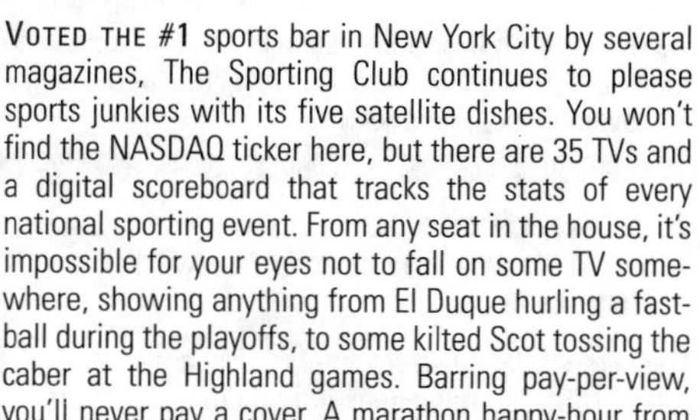

VOTED THE #1 sports bar in New York City by several magazines, The Sporting Club continues to please sports junkies with its five satellite dishes. You won't find the NASDAQ ticker here, but there are 35 TVs and a digital scoreboard that tracks the stats of every national sporting event. From any seat in the house, it's impossible for your eyes not to fall on some TV somewhere, showing anything from El Duque hurling a fastball during the playoffs, to some kilted Scot tossing the caber at the Highland games. Barring pay-per-view, you'll never pay a cover. A marathon happy-hour from noon to 7p.m. will thrill any lover of American beers and kamikaze shots.

## Spring Lounge

48 Spring St. (@ Mulberry St.)
212-964-1774

THIS CORNER JOINT attracts an after work crowd, street bums and some frat boys. The patrons generally get shit-faced and rowdy at this local bar that hasn't yet conformed to the style of the other trendy bars in the area. If you happen to stop by on a late night, don't expect to have an intimate conversation or be coddled by the bartender. Keep your eyes peeled for staggering drunks who have a tendency to spill beers on unsuspecting laps.

## Spy

101 Greene St. (Spring & Prince Sts.)
212-343-9000

SPY AND BE SPIED at this lush lounge. Operatic in spirit, this chandeliered, oil-painted and blood red two-tiered space caters to the fashionable set. Drinks are pricey, the menu's laced with lobster and Beluga, and you may have to know someone to get past the doorman. Once inside, though, you'll feel you've arrived...even if it does require binoculars to see where.

## Square Rigger Pub

163 Front St. (John St. & Maiden Ln.)
212-422-0188

THIS OLD WESTERN saloon-style sports bar features karaoke on Thursday nights from 6-10p.m., a free, hot buffet and beer and drink specials. There is only Sam Adams and Budweiser on tap, but they have all sorts of liquor, wines and cocktails in stock. This bar appeals to the Wall Street crowd craving to have fun for a change. The average meal runs $8-$10.

## St. Andrew's

120 W. 44th St. (Broadway & 6th Ave.)
212-840-8413

DESPITE ITS "Scottish-theme-bar" appearance and kilted host, St. Andrews does not bludgeon you with its kitsch. The international selection of over 100 scotches is staggering, not mention over 20 beers on tap and over 100 bottled. The decor is low-key pub with a comfortable bar and tables in the front for drinking and noshing on the raw bar, Brit chips, Scottish eggs, etc. Attracting mostly an after-work crowd, later in the evening the bar houses the restaurant staff of other Midtown establishments. A pleasant alternative to the tourist-geared, flashy bars of Times Square.

## St. Dymphna's

118 St. Marks Pl. (1st Ave. & Ave. A)
212-254-6636

THERE'S A REASON this authentic Irish pub was named after the patron saint of mental illness. You'd have to be crazy to come here. The back garden and walls of chipped paint do add character, but other than that, it's just a room that serves Guinness, where you sit wondering why you stopped here and where you're going next. The only reason to visit deliberately is the authentic Irish cuisine, served breakfast, lunch and dinner, which includes everything from "crisps" to imported Irish chocolate bars. Saint Marks has lots of things going on; this isn't one of them.

## St. Mark's Ale House

2 St. Marks Pl. (@ 2nd Ave.)
212-260-9762

I HAVE DIED and gone to sports heaven...9 satellite TVs playing sports, a 100" pull down screen for big games and 24 beers on tap. What else could you want? They have a 2 for 1 happy hour weekdays from 5-7p.m. and for the hungry man, 2 for 1 pasta noon to 5p.m. If you don't like Imported German, Belgium and microbrew beers on tap, they also have 15 domestic bottles. Drinks and food are cheap. The kitchen is open as long as the bar is and the bar is open as long as there are athletes sweating somewhere in the world. Hands down, this place rocks.

## The Standard

158 1st Ave. (9th & 10th Sts.)
212-387-0239

WHAT DO get when you mix a layed back crowd, friendly bartenders, a great DJ and a chic, minimalist space?

Hopefully it's an orgy. But more than likely, it's Standard. Pleasing East Villagers for over 2 years now, this spot has managed to stay hip and not have a door goon in an area that has been over-run with velvet ropes and lousy attitudes. The drinks are strong, the crowd is fairly easy to look at and the vibe is always right on the money. With this combination, we're still hoping for the orgy to break out.

## Standard Notions

161 Ludlow St. (@ Stanton St.)
212-473-3535

THE NAME REMAINS the same, but the definition of "standard" has changed at this Ludlow St. nouveau pub. Given a recent facelift to keep up with the suddenly chic block it's on, Notions has finally found a niche. Where before it seemed simply utilitarian, with a conventional menu and reliable bartenders, now it's one of the best joints in the area for a night of food, drinks and music. The new Caribbean theme menu is flashy and satisfying and the subtly futuristic décor complements the DJ set up in the corner. Comfort is still key here, however. The covered back garden is a fresh air paradise and the staff is reliable and friendly.

## Starlight

167 Ave. A (10th & 11th Sts.)
212-475-2172

THIS COZY BAR/LOUNGE caters to a working class gay clientele in their 30's. The front bar transports you to a kinder, friendlier time with a romantic '60s vibe complete wih people hanging out and picking up the mate o' the night. The back lounge has comfortable seating with candlelight and overhead lights. A DJ spins soft house music while friendly waiters scurry around with trays of drinks. Overall, this is a relaxing, neighborhood spot.

## Stellas

266 W. 47th St. (Broadway & 8th Ave.)
212-575-1680

THIS IS ANOTHER West Side gay strip hangout much like the Olympic Lounge with go-go boys every night after 11:30 p.m. except Wednesday. What else can you say about a manly-man's bar whose main attraction are boys in their underwear gyrating their "hey-nanny-nanny's" on the stage? The bar itself is large and always crowded with an interesting mix of locals, Chelsea boys and older men who enjoy sipping scotch while watching young studs slither around half naked.

## Stinger

541 Grand St. (Roebling & Driggs Sts.)
Brooklyn 718-218-6662

THIS DARK LOUNGE stepped right out of the '70s with a black and red vengeance, to house the local trendoids and thrift store stylists. Stick around and the decor will make you feel like you're in a David Lynch film. If you're not a Blue Ribbon fan, get a well-drink from a vast selection of liquor for around four bucks. This little hot spot has got a great dive feel, and you'll surely meet someone interesting in this dark seedy lounge. Stinger has DJ's on Wednesday and Saturday, and live music on Friday and Sunday. Ask the bartender to show you how the bar got it's name.

## Stingy Lulu's

129 St. Marks Pl. (1st Ave. & Ave. A)
212-674-3545

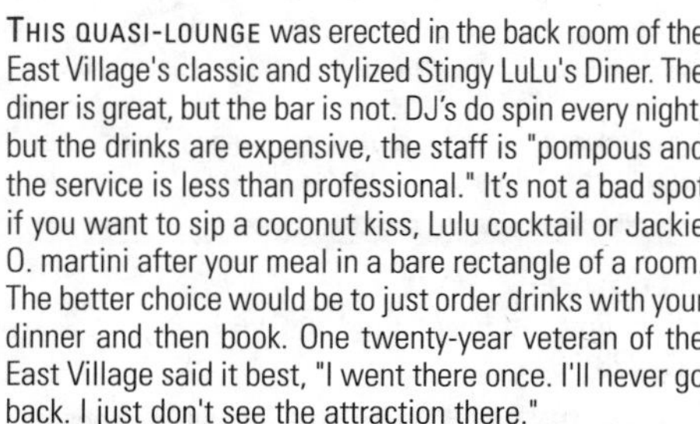

THIS QUASI-LOUNGE was erected in the back room of the East Village's classic and stylized Stingy LuLu's Diner. The diner is great, but the bar is not. DJ's do spin every night, but the drinks are expensive, the staff is "pompous and the service is less than professional." It's not a bad spot if you want to sip a coconut kiss, Lulu cocktail or Jackie O. martini after your meal in a bare rectangle of a room. The better choice would be to just order drinks with your dinner and then book. One twenty-year veteran of the East Village said it best, "I went there once. I'll never go back. I just don't see the attraction there."

## Stoned Crow

85 Washington Pl.
(6th Ave. & Washington Sq. W.)
212-677-4022

FOR SOME REASON, Stoned Crow attracts a lot of single women to its bar area. This is despite the fact that the place boasts not one but two video car racing games, a pool table, walls plastered with photographs of macho, male movie stars and a rock 'n' roll jukebox. Nevertheless, for reasons unknown, the bar area is crammed every night with loads of single women. Guys, if you're lookin' for love, start here.

## Stonewall

53 Christopher St. (Sheridan Sq. & 7th Ave.)
212-463-0950

On the sight of the legendary Stonewall riots, this gay bar is newly renovated and looking quite hip. This neighborhood spot is on the itinerary of every gay tourist and bridge and tunneler. While waxing nostalgic about the first gay civil rights victory, remember Judy Garland died on the day the Stonewall riots broke out! Monday is bingo night and cheap drink specials lure in a large crowd.

## Street Car Café

370 W. 46th St. (8th & 9th Aves.)
212-262-1452

Located in the heart of the Theater District, you might expect to find Blanche Dubois sitting here lamenting. The understated, yet classy French decor make it a great spot to come after work or after the theater and lounge in the comfortable seats. Happy hour prices are $2-$3.50 until 9p.m. and martinis and margaritas are $5.50. This brand new café is not yet crowded, but the relaxed atmosphere and friendly service will catch on sooner or later.

## Subway Inn

143 E. 60th St. (@ Lexington Ave.)
212-223-8929

Subway Inn represents stability in this dangerous era of Guiliani gentrification. If you went 50 years ago to this neighborhood dive, chances are the only thing that has changed is the level of the dust that clings to just about everything. It is a hole some celebrities have chosen to hide in. Others tend to get too drunk on the cheap pints and cause a melee -- there are bullet holes in the back from a mob shooting and weekly bar brawls. Never a dull moment.

## Sushi Generation

1571 2nd Ave. (81st & 82nd Sts.)
212-249-2222

SUSHI GENERATION (WHO are these people?) finally links our nation's two favorite pastimes: watching sports and eating raw fish. This Yorkville establishment is a great place to watch a game as long as you really don't like sports (they have yet to learn that six TVs does not a sports bar make). This restaurant/bar has plenty of seating, both inside and out, for its largely professional, post-work patrons. The large copper bar is kept spotless, which isn't difficult considering the speed at which the drinks are poured leaves many a bit parched.

## Suspenders

111 Broadway (@ Thames Pl.)
212-732-5005

THIS WALL STREET bar comes as close as you'll get to a home away from home, that is if you work in the area. A large spacious drinking area fills up every night with groups of friends gossiping and talking shop with each other. The bartenders never seem to change and are always friendly. Don't forget it's underground, next to the subway station.

## Sutton Grill

209 E. 56th St. (@ 3rd Ave.)
212-355-6868

LOCATED RIGHT IN the middle of one of the busiest districts in the Big Apple, Sutton Grill boasts a low-key, (i.e. boring) atmosphere. Recently under new management, the bar offers a full menu in the sandwich and salad spirit. The best parts about this spot are the glass window of flora and fauna in back and the selection of twenty-eight beers. Not to be confused with the nearby Sutton Place, this smaller bar/restaurant hosts a bit of an older crowd more into socializing in groups than mastering the pick-up game.

## Sutton Place

1015 2nd Ave. (53rd & 54th Sts.)
212-207-3777

THIS TRULY IS a frat bar, but there's something oddly charming about the way "SP" presents itself that tempts you to think it's trying to be something more. Is it the bouncer that gives you a very minimal hard time to create an air of exclusivity, even if for a second? Or the pricey drinks, which are supposed to make your subconscious think this place is actually worth it? Despite the "wannabe" identity status of this sports pub, it's a good place to meet up with some friends and down a few while listening to the top 40 hits. The crowd is so enormous and homogenous that chances are you'll see someone from college, or even worse, high school.

## Swan's Bar & Grill

213 Pearl St. (John & Fletcher Sts.)
212-952-0266

SWAN'S BAR IS one of those old drunk hangouts that get you imagining some Bowery wino hobbling in, waving a wrinkled double sawbuck (found in some bus depot somewhere) above his sparsely-haired head, and hollering for Rhinegolds on the house. His buddies from the El Dorado flophouse file in after him, drink up the tab in four minutes, and pester all of the Wall-Streeters who have, until now, quietly sipped away at their $5 cocktails.

## Sway

305 Spring St. (Greenwich & Hudson Sts.)
212-620-5220

SWAY WAS SUBDUED swank for a week or so. Unfortunately, in the tradition of all-things-discovered, it's now a velvet-roped, who-do-you-know-to-get-in kind of place. When you get shafted, just go across the street to the oasis for Sway-exiles, Recess. It's worth trying again on a weeknight after 10p.m. Once inside this Moroccan themed lounge that's mysteriously situated under the sign of its pub predecessor, McGovern's, you'll be able to kick back in a banquette with the cool crowd and a killer Long Island iced tea. You earned it.

## Sweet & Vicious

5 Spring St. (Bowery & Elizabeth St.)
212-334-7915

THIS NOLITA NEIGHBORHOOD bar is simply and tastefully designed making it a favorite for those in the know. The intimate décor and exposed brick walls make anyone feel at home. No food is served, but the owners encourage hungry bar-hoppers to order in a pizza when needed. This Turkish theme bar gets crowded on weekends so there are usually friendly doormen checking ID's and keeping out the riff-raff.

## Sweet Basil

88 7th Ave. So. (@ Bleecker St.)
212-242-1785

GRANTED IT'S A village institution well known for it's great jazz performances, but the folks at Sweet Basil take themselves too seriously. After paying a $20 cover charge, it's quite off-putting to then shell out $5 for a little bottle of water. The audience sits quietly during the sets, almost afraid to get of their seats for fear of being chastised by the anal retentive crowd. The head wagging mix of Ginsburg types focus intently on the dissonant music and appear pensive. If you're not a true jazz lover, this is probably not the vibe you're looking for on a weekend night.

## Sweetwater Tavern

105 N. 6th St. (Berry & Wythe Aves.) Brooklyn
718-963-0608

CHEAP BROOKLYN PINTS, best jukebox known to any punk (including "Where's My Shoe?"- Sweetwater's own compilation of local punk bands), a pool table and pinball machine are the things that set this bar apart. If you can stomach the atmosphere, Sweetwater is a great left of center place. Shut up and drink, punk!!!

## Swift Hibernian Lounge

34 E. 4th St. (Bowery & Lafayette Sts.)
212-260-3600/212-22-SWIFT

SWIFT TAKES the mold of the typical Irish pub and smashes it to pieces. Jonathan Swift, the author of "Gulliver's Travels," is this cozy bar's inspiration. Its castle-like environment transports you to the 17th century, yet the bar has only been here for four years. There are 23 different drafts and over 50 bottles of beer to choose from. Even the most introverted folks can make friends in this warm, lively and friendly atmosphere. On Tuesdays, Swift has live traditional

Irish music and Thursday through Saturday has a DJ spinning (from the pulpit) some eclectic and happy tunes.

## Swim

146 Orchard (Rivington & Stanton Sts.)
212 673-0799

THIS LOWER EAST Side neighborhood bar has recently taken a more mellow tone. Since June '99, when the Fire Department shut down the "hazardous" sushi restaurant on the second floor, Swim has grown smaller (only the first floor bar), and cozier (no more bridge and tunnelers!). The décor is classic Lower East Side with wooden tables and benches and some funky art doodle-displays embedded in the walls that raise a million questions. Every night a different DJ spins, and on weekends the grungy artist crowd gets a nice dance scene going.

## Swine on Nine

693 9th Ave. (47th & 48th Sts.)
212-397-8356

THE HUGE PIG statue sitting on the sidewalk in front of Swine on Nine foreshadows what to expect once you walk into this Hell's Kitchen watering hole. Plenty o' pigs adorn this tiny bar, from the neon pigs on the walls, to the porcelain pigs lined up above the bar to the pig that oinks hourly. If you have an aversion to pigs, then go snort some place else. This small dive serves up cheap drinks to yuppies, locals and older transient Port Authority types. The friendliest doorman around checks ID's at the front due to the up-and-coming trendiness of Hell's Kitchen; much to the chagrin of the old timers. If you have a penchant for cheap drinks and pigs, then Swine On Nine is the place for you.

## Tall Ships (@ The Marriott WTC)

3 World Trade Center (Liberty & West Sts.)
212-444-4025

BEAUTIFUL HARDWOOD FLOORS, tables and gigantic black and white chandeliers decorate this after work hotel bar. It's a safe place to meet and grab drink, but not the kind of place where one would spend the whole evening. Wines range from $8-$10, and snacks get a little on the pricey side. Although the spot is cigar-friendly, there are definitely more interesting bars in this area that'll let you suck on a stogie with your scotch.

## Tammany Hall

218 E. 53rd St. (2nd & 3rd Aves.)
212-355-6607

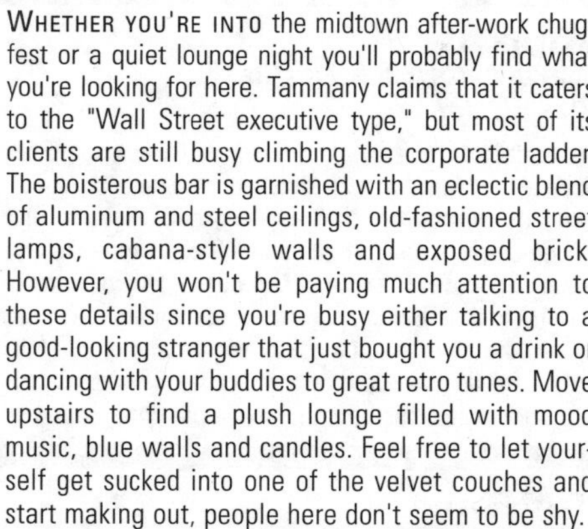

WHETHER YOU'RE INTO the midtown after-work chug-fest or a quiet lounge night you'll probably find what you're looking for here. Tammany claims that it caters to the "Wall Street executive type," but most of its clients are still busy climbing the corporate ladder. The boisterous bar is garnished with an eclectic blend of aluminum and steel ceilings, old-fashioned street lamps, cabana-style walls and exposed brick. However, you won't be paying much attention to these details since you're busy either talking to a good-looking stranger that just bought you a drink or dancing with your buddies to great retro tunes. Move upstairs to find a plush lounge filled with mood music, blue walls and candles. Feel free to let yourself get sucked into one of the velvet couches and start making out, people here don't seem to be shy.

## Tapas Lounge

1078 1st Ave. (@ 59th St.)
212-421-8282

SITTING IN THIS medieval-mess-hall-meets-gold-lame-pillowed space means fulfilling the two-per-person tapas rule. Add this your selection from the Spanish wine list ($30 to $80), a seemingly bottomless pitcher of Sangria ($45 for a large), or an orangey margarita ($10), and things can get pretty pricey. But, once you settle into this dark and funky space and the attentive wait staff brings on the olives, you might not mind.

## Taperia Madrid

1471 2nd Ave. (76th & 77th Sts.)
212-794-2923

THIS UP BEAT authentic Spanish restaurant and bar is a real Upper East Side hotspot. The fairly large restaurant has a small "J" shaped bar that is always hopping with a young area crowd sharing tapas and sangria. The music is fun, but very loud; so don't bring a first date here. The tables are communal (and uncomfortable) which add to the true Spanish charm of the place. There is a large and exotic selection of beer from more than six different countries. If you're looking for a loud, lively evening with a mixed upscale crowd, this is a must see.

## Tapika

950 8th Ave. (76th & 77th Sts.)
212-397-3737

PERFECT FOR THE semi-grownup after work crowd, Tapika is a fun place to throw back a few cocktails. With its attractively simple decor, good lighting and adobe-colored walls, it has enough class to make you want to behave. But after a few of the delicious drinks go down, that will change. Try a tasty margarita with one of the 34 different kinds of tequila and grab a bite to eat (to absorb some of that booze). This is a good place for casual clients, friends or a pre-date drink.

## Tar Bar

1412 1st Ave. (74th & 75th Sts.)
212-570-5704

THERE'S SOMETHING VERY creepy about the dark black walls, the unique bouquet of dead flowers in the corner and the staring eyes of the bar staff. However, Tar Bar is not without its charms. A very cool poolroom in the back has a comfortable seating area for those who are waiting their turn. The ambiance is just pleasant enough to be romantic, but too intimate to be friendly.

## Tavern on Jane

31 8th Ave. (@ Jane St.)
212-675-2526

THIS COZY EATERY plays host to a pleasant collection of oddballs, neighborhood regulars and the friendly owners who will most likely be perched on the stool next to yours. The paper tablecloths are topped with crayon centerpieces, should you feel the sudden urge to scrawl. Catch the Yankees on one of the two TV's above the bar or just mellow out to Paul Simon or The

Stones (or whatever other CD your waitress feels like popping in). There is a decent selection of both beer and wine, and it's the kind of place where you'll feel OK refreshing your own coffee at the server's station.

## Tavern on the Green

Central Park West (66th & 67th Sts.)
212-873-3200

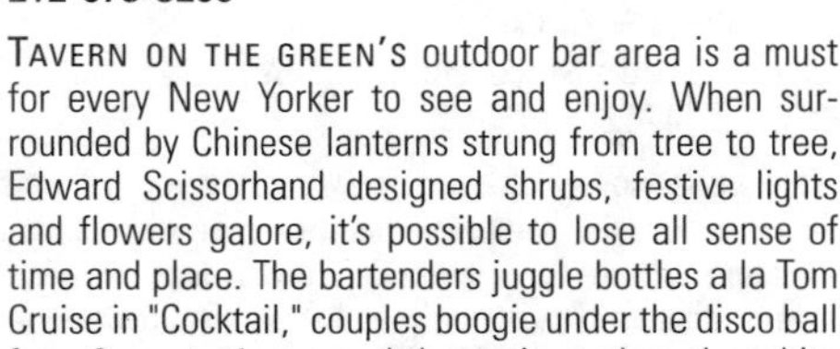

TAVERN ON THE GREEN'S outdoor bar area is a must for every New Yorker to see and enjoy. When surrounded by Chinese lanterns strung from tree to tree, Edward Scissorhand designed shrubs, festive lights and flowers galore, it's possible to lose all sense of time and place. The bartenders juggle bottles a la Tom Cruise in "Cocktail," couples boogie under the disco ball from 9p.m. to 1a.m., and those situated on the white cast iron patio chairs and stools forge their way through the 900 bottle wine list, or opt for a $9 Tavern or a Strawberry Fields martini. When the weather outside is frightful, take refuge in the bar upstairs, it's a comfortable indoor alternative equally charming and lovely.

## Teddy's

96 Berry St. (@ N. 8th St.) Brooklyn
718-384-9787

COME TAKE A step back into the late 19th century, into a bar that's 113 years old. Established in 1887, this historic bar and restaurant which was originally "Peter Doelgers," named after a local brew at the time. It has been Teddy's for over 50 years and still has the beautiful stained glass window that bears the Doelgers name. Teddy's has the classic feel of your perfect neighborhood bar. With all of the original decorations from the immense wooden bar and tin ceilings, right down to the tiled floors. The warm setting is the perfect place to grab a beer and watch the game. Come see live Jazz on Tuesday and Wednesday or a free form DJ spinning Thursday thru Saturday.

## Telephone Bar

149 2nd Ave. (9th & 10th Sts.)
212-529-5000

IT'S NOT COVENT Gardens in London, but this East Village slice of Britain is comfy and serves "good

British food," usually an oxymoron. The back room hosts nightly events (poetry slams, open mikes and Tuesday night movies) for a good change of pace. A solid, unpretentious crowd frequents Telephone bar, although during the school year NYU students will often invade on the weekends, which increases the pick-up factor but slightly reduces the relaxed charm of Telephone Bar.

## Temple Bar

332 Lafayette St. (@ Bleecker St.)
212-925-4242

TEMPLE is worthy of adoration. Any day you go feels like a decadent event in this ten year old lounge. Snuggle up with your sweetie in this dimly lit oasis where popcorn flows freely and there's an occasional book or poetry reading. Delectable edibles like oysters and steak, pricey but perfect martinis and ambience extraordinaire make this place a real aphrodisiac.

## Tennessee Mountain

143 Spring St. (@ Wooster St.)
212-431-3993

WHERE'S THE 3 ARMED, 1 eyed, 2 nosed mutant playing the banjo with his tongue? This isn't Tennesee, this is SoHo's rendition of the state with thirteen year old brides and moonshine strong enough to burn a hole in your colon. This mutant-free eatery/wartering hole serves some of the best ribs and chicken south of the Flatiron-Dixon line. If you don't want to mortgage your trailer or have your overalls repossesed, stop in for some good cheap eats and drinks sans attitude.

## 10th Ave. Lounge

642 10th Ave. (45th & 46th St.)
212-245-9088

ROMANTIC doesn't even begin to describe this 10th Ave. hideaway. This dimly lit lounge has a very mysterious vibe that attracts both gay and straight couples. The Roman mural above the bar and contemporary pictures and statues make you feel like you're in several cities at once. Happy hour is from 6p.m.-8p.m. and you can enjoy 2 for 1 draft specials, well drinks and frozen cosmos. Bar food is served from 6p.m. - midnight and consists of colossal shrimp on ice and chicken fingers, to name a few. If you need a break from your usual

Hell's Kitchen pick-up spots, this lounge will definitely provide you with a very cool evening.

## Tenth Street Lounge

212 E. 10th St. (1st & 2nd Aves.)
212-473-5252

IF YOU'RE THE type of person who plasters your apartment with pictures of celebrities or hangs out with wannabe supermodels, you'll feel right at home here. This place has got all the makings of a hit, but somehow falls short. The owners deserve that high school principal speech. You know the one..."You have so much potential! Why do you insist on the pissing it all away?" Sadly, one finds more inspiration from the bum outside playing invisible drums than from the scene inside. What else? Overpriced drinks, a cranky, demanding staff and a $10 cover. No more explanation needed.

## Terra Blues

149 Bleecker St. (Thompson St. & LaGuardia Pl.)
212-777-7776

THE MUSIC is excellent and the atmosphere is comfortable and fun at this non-Bleecker St. bar on Bleecker St. On any given night you'll witness some of the greatest live blues guitar players in town for only a $5 cover charge. Arrive early on weekends because seating gets as tight as a virgin on prom night. Light on attitude and heavy on quality, Terra Blues is a Village landmark.

## T.G. Whitney's

244 E. 53rd St. (2nd & 3rd Aves.)
212-888-5772

SETTING THE STANDARD for after work spots, T.G. Whitney's provides a fun, lively place for the business community to blow off steam after a hard day's toil. Depending on the night, you can expect live music, a DJ or karaoke and whatever game is on the tube.

## Third and Long

523 3rd Ave. (@ 35th St.)
212-447-5711

YOU COULD PUT this bar anywhere in the country and

it would still be a nondescript, white bread sports bar. The decor consists of six televisions that show current games or previously taped games that were played while Mid-town, mid-level, mid-management patrons were shuffling papers in their nearby offices. A jukebox plays all of the latest hits with the big party songs encouraging frat house sing alongs (Macarena, Thong Song etc.). The people are generally pretty nice and there are ten beers on tap, all reasonably priced by midtown standards. If you long for those funneling, blacking out, waking up on your doorstep and puking all morning college days, Third and Long is a good place to reminisce.

## The Thirsty Scholar

155 2nd Ave. (9th & 10th Sts.)
212-777-6514

A NEW ENTRANT on the Second Ave. "strip," the Thirsty Scholar deserves a better clientele or it may turn into a de facto sports bar. Despite the Samuel Beckett picture, the wooden floor and the Irish artwork, the Thirsty Scholar attracts mostly goatee and baseball cap types who think Irish is a synonym for liquor rather than an actual ethnicity. The tap is what you'd expect (Guinness, Harp, etc.), the jukebox is average, and the television is tuned to the sport of the day. The crowd is relatively pedestrian, but the 2p.m.-8p.m. happy hour features a $3 cosmopolitan that makes everybody look better.

## 13

13 E. 13th St. (@ University Pl.)
212-979-6677

THIS MINI-CLUB offers a much needed change of pace from the average too-cool-to-be-fun downtown spot. Free from pretentious patrons and staff, on weekends this small upstairs space packs in young execs, hood rats and locals united in the goal of getting a groove on. While scene-ster friends may frown at its mention, the loyal clientele know there's no better place to dance without breaking the bank. DJ's will have you sweating to hip-hop, disco and a smattering of '80s favorites. In warm weather, walk up to the roof to save your eardrums for next week.

## 357

357 W. Broadway (Broome & Grand Sts.)
212-965-1491

ABOUT 3 DAYS out of the week there is some model agency party at this "So SoHo" lounge that used to be Magnum. Every night you will find young emaciated male and female models showing plenty of collarbone through their minimal clothing, chatting, giving looks and keeping dibs on who is the newest hot face. Kevin Conner, 357 owner (and cousin of Lenny Kravitz, who makes occasional guest appearances), makes sure his DJ's play tunes that are current, funky and groovy. The space is always packed, but remarkably, the crowd manages to throw in some dance moves as they gossip. There is no cover charge, just a style test at the velvet ropes in front of the anonymous entrance, so if you're told at the door "sorry, there's a private party going on tonight", that means you're just not cool enough for this young, fashion crowd.

## Three Of Cups Lounge

83 1st Ave. (@ 5th St.)
212-388-0059

SHHHH... CAN YOU keep a secret? Votive candles light the path into the basement lounge. Go ahead, pull open that door and walk into the red. But don't walk too far, you'll slam into the wall! Most bedrooms are bigger than this place, but who cares! That just means there's less room for those packs of annoying, loud, obnoxious bar-hoppers that we all want to boot right back over the Hudson River! Great bartenders play awesome music and serve cheap beer, $3-$4 a pint make this super-tiny spot really cool. Big things do come in small packages.

## Timboo's

477 5th Ave. (@ 11th St.) Brooklyn
718-788-9782

TIMBOO'S is a beacon in a wasteland of vapid lounges. It's rather like an ugly child only a regular could love and think is cute. Timboo's is a real Brooklyn local's bar. The kind of place where toothless old men stare menacingly at strangers and the jukebox plays Guns 'n' Roses' "Appetite for Destruction" all day. In true Americana style, the walls host a medley of baseball memorabilia and trophies from various pool, darts and bowling tournaments.

## Time Out

349 Amsterdam Ave. (76th & 77th Sts.)
212-362-5400

WITH A BANK of 25 TV's, 10 satellite dishes, and 12 cable boxes, Time Out offers a pumped up version of Boomer's, the bar previously in this space. Considered one of the best sports bars around, it offers a touch of class with Scotch and lobster gracing the menu, its dark interior and elegant, red bar. But, the "Dude, kegger!" atmosphere is inevitable and most customers prefer to go for the $7 bucket of Rolling Rocks and hot wings.

## Tivoli

515 3rd Ave. (34th & 35th Sts.)
212-532-3300

OCCUPYING A SPACE next door to The Joshua Tree, Tivoli is looking to attract a more upscale crowd than it's frat boy neighbor. With a continental menu, a hip-looking bar and football on a projection TV, this Greek-owned venture is perhaps a bit too eclectic. The simple, clean setting offers the after work suit crowd $3 drafts and free appetizers from 4-7p.m.

## Toad Hall

57 Grand St. (W.Broadway & Wooster St.)
212-431-8145

THIS IS YOUR typical neighborhood tavern, albeit in SoHo, which is not your average neighborhood. Blatantly less hip than most of its neighbors, (most notably Lucky Strike right next door), Toad Hall offers a nice alternative for thirty and fortysomethings who want to play pool, watch sports and have a couple of drinks among people who are more mature and well- to- do than typical sports bar types. They also make an outstanding bloody mary for those rough mornings. Definately a refreshing change from the glut of lounges that populate the area.

## Tom & Jerry's / 288 Bar

(a.k.a. Bar 288)
288 Elizabeth St. (@ Houston St.)
No Phone

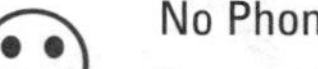

STILL ONE OF the best bars in NoHo. The crowd is always changing, as does the art on the walls. This spot always seems to feel like home. No pretense, no attitude and all bar. There's a subtle pick-up scene and a good vibe throughout the place. The bartenders are attentive and they offer one of the best Guinness pours in the city. You might even run into a friendly pooch as you sip cider.

## Tonic Bar

108 W. 18th St. (6th & 7th Aves.)
212-929-9755

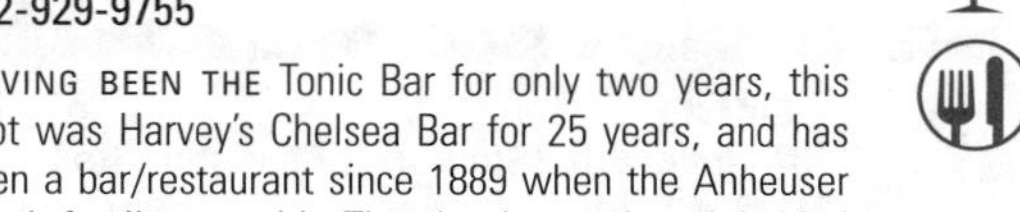

HAVING BEEN THE Tonic Bar for only two years, this spot was Harvey's Chelsea Bar for 25 years, and has been a bar/restaurant since 1889 when the Anheuser Busch family owned it. The classic wood work behind the bar is almost exactly as it was over a century ago, and the brass cash register on the counter is nearly a museum piece in its own right. The bar, which seems to be more of a complement to the restaurant than anything else, (two private dining rooms that seat over 300 people), does manage to attract after work locals as well as late night regulars. The staff are friendly and accommodating, and the dozen beers on tap at $7 a pint and general lack of activity make for a decent after work place, but offers little reason to visit if you hope to meet people or be entertained.

## Tonic/Subtonic Lounge

107 Norfolk St. (Rivington & Delancey Sts.)
212-358-7501

AS NYC's ONLY musician hosted club, Tonic is home to the best avant-garde, creative and experimental music in town. Shows will cost you anywhere from $8-$15 and are usually well worth the money. Below the main space is the Subtonic Lounge, open only from Thursday through Saturday. Years ago it served as an old winery, explaining the handful of very tall wine barrels which have now been cleverly designed into cozy booths. Resident DJ's spin assorted hip-hop/jazz/funk flavored beats nightly, which makes the hip, artistic, young music-enthusiasts very happy.

## Tool Box

1742 2nd Ave. (90th & 91st Sts.)
212-348-1288

QUITE POSSIBLY ONE of the sleaziest bars in Manhattan (gay or straight), Tool Box seems to keep their regular clients coming back due to a lack of options on the Upper East Side. Even though their drab decor sucks, they still manage to pack it on a regular basis. A small TV showing a loop of '80s porn from old, worn out tapes rivets the late nighters. They get crammed tight on the weekends, and although they claim not to be a pick-up bar, feel free to visit the downstairs lounge with a new friend for some one on one "conversation."

## Torch

137 Ludlow St. (Stanton & Rivington Sts.)
212-228-5151

OVER TWO-THIRDS of Torch's floor space is dedicated to numerous tables surrounding a small stage, the rostrum for nightly bands and crooners playing jazz standards. But the crowd that comes here pays no heed to the tables, opting instead to cram themselves into a small area around the bar, gulp down cape-codders and raise a general racket. Little do they realize, they're cheating themselves out of a most marvelous experience. Those in the know take a seat, order a professionally mixed cocktail from one of the striking, yet gracious, waitresses, select a few spectacular (and none too cheap) dinner items and revel in the music and atmosphere.

## Tortilla Flats

767 Washington St. (@ 12th St.)
212-243-1053

THE AMBIENCE IS anything but flat at this little bar that can hardly contain itself. So festive and fun, the patrons practically spill onto the street. Every night is a party whether it's your birthday, Door Prize Sunday or Tuesday Night Bingo. During the course of your Mexican feast and "Horny margarita" consumption, there's likely to be some sort of debaucherous entertainment from your saucy neighbors. Get happier on Friday and Saturday from 1a.m.-4 a.m. and weeknights from 4p.m.-7 p.m. with 2 for 1 Rolling Rocks and $5 off pitchers of margaritas.

## The Townhouse

236 E. 58th St. (2nd & 3rd Aves.)
212-754-4649

THIS ANGLOPHILE MULTI-LEVEL piano bar/lounge has something for everybody with three different bars on two floors. A mix of upscale professionals and their younger, yet classy admirers chat while sipping top shelf drinks in an extremely comfortable atmosphere. The front bar is lovely right after work with men clad in better suit selections than Barneys! Scope the club-room and do not forget to dress your best, they have a dress code and it is competitive.

## Tracy J's Watering Hole

106 E. 19th St. (Park Ave. So. & Irving Pl.)
212-674-5783

THE LONG NARROW bar owned by the ex-Knick Art Heyman is decorated with large wooden animal cutouts and remains an enigma. The bar crowd consists mainly of middle-aged men, staff from local area restaurants, and stragglers who diverted from Park Avenue South. The atmosphere is non-threatening and the drink prices are average. Happy hour (4 p.m.-7p.m.) attracts a spillover crowd from the nearby restaurants. A menu of BBQ items is served in a moderately sized dining area behind the bar. A good pit stop for a quickie on your way downtown.

## The Triad

158 W. 72nd St. (@ Broadway)
212-362-2590

TRIAD REMAINS HOT spot for live music on the Upper West Side hosting great jazz, blues and rock performances worth the $5 cover. Some of New York's best musical acts grace the cozy performance space downstairs, while a small dinner theater upstairs offers stand-up comedy and cabaret performances from $10 to $30. The crowd varies depending on the performer but is always laid back and composed of musicians and music lovers alike. Live music usually begins around midnight, which, not coincidently, is when the crowd starts to grow and the tables in front of the stage are snapped up.

## Tribe

132 1st Ave. (@ St. Mark's Pl.)
212-979-8965

OK, IT'S BEEN a year and a half and we're over the fact that Tribe took over The St. Mark's Grill. Even though it may feel like a Euro-mess when you walk in, sit down order the $6 martini of your choice and get over it. The cocktails are strong and by the second one you'll be laughing out loud at the DJ who is shaking his maracas to the beat of his choice Euro-American music. By the third drink you're mesmerized by the colorful shapes projected on the wall and even making small talk with the mostly non-English speaking crowd. The crowd is mostly Millennium beatniks, but don't knock it till you've tried it.

## TriBeCa Grill

375 Greenwich St. (Moore & Franklin Sts.)
212-941-3900

TriBeCa Grill is the spawn of restaurateur Drew Nieporent and actor Robert DeNiro. For the longest time this spacious loft like dining room and bar were in the middle of nowhere NYC. Due to the recent demographic shift in this area from no class to all class, the bar is being given a chance to shine. A perfect spot to come on a date and enjoy the casual atmosphere decorated with large oil paintings, burnt orange walls and soft lighting. It's a great place to make a merger or two; both the business and romantic kind.

## Trilogy

1403 2nd Ave. (@ 73rd St.)
212-794-1870

This is definitely one of the nicer looking frat bars on the Upper East Side, catering to an older and classier group of boys. Reliving their college days, the khaki and oxford set mill around the pool table and bar area trying to pick up 21-year-old girls. Every night has a theme and drink specials that will hopefully attract more women to this spot. This is a good place to go for a few drinks after work or for a loud and crowded evening but, be prepared, the door policy is a tad stringent.

## Triple Crown

330 7th Ave. (28th & 29th Sts.)
212-736-1575

This Irish owned and operated pub caters mostly to the unimaginative businessmen that flock from their

Midtown offices each evening, and throngs of people overflowing from Madison Square Garden. The standard pub fare is not bad but the prices are slightly inflated. The tap selection includes twelve varieties of good imported and domestic brews.

## True

28 E. 23rd St. (Broadway & Madison Ave.)
212-654-6117

FORMERLY CALLED "VANITY", the new management of True wish to do away with their reputation as a label whore B&T club. The main bar and dance floor are tastefully done with stained glass, dark wood and candlelight. Tuesday is a Latin party that packs in music industry types. Thursday is the only night you can get in with sneakers and cargo pants, as it's reserved for drum-n-bass freaks. Fridays get a mixed NY and Jersey crowd, all packed in for the hip-hop and dance tracks that spin until 4a.m. It can get a little snobby, but considering the reasonable $5-$15 admission, it's certainly an alternative to the uber-clubs Roxy and Tunnel.

## Tunnel

220 12th Ave. (@ 27th St.)
212-695-4682

THIS PLACE IS HUGE, with three floors and enough light, smoke and glitz to host a Kiss concert. Remember how you imagined a dance club to be at age 13? This is it. With a candy concession stand, 11 bars and lounges that look like Willy Wonka's living room, this is a clubbers kingdom. The rabble is an eclectic mix of transvestites, ravers and pretty young things from all over the city. Though the best in DJ talent gets everybody writhing, this place seems just a little slow to the punch, and the crowd is pretty patchy until the wee hours roll around. The cover is $25, so if the New York club scene is what your itching for, slither on into the Tunnel.

## Turkey's Nest

94 Bedford Ave. (@ N. 10th St.) Brooklyn
718-384-9774

THE INTERVIEW with the proprietor was too funny not to print. SHECKY: "What are your hours? "TURKEY: "Ohhhh...normal hours, I guess [pause]...8 in the mornin' ta 4 in the mornin'?"SHECKY: "Are you 'Dog Friendly'?" TURKEY: "A lotta the guys in here are a bunch uh dawgs, yeah...but they ain't too friendly!"SHECKY: "How long has the bar been around?" TURKEY: "Well...Let's see...I been here a lil' over 20 years an' before that, a buncha whacked-out brothers owned the joint...They called 'em 'The Whizzz Brothers.' That's when it was called 'The Whizzz Bar'. Yeah, they were a buncha sickos [dramatic pause] but they all croaked." Well, that should give you a feel for this dive. Yeah, it's grungy and stuffed with old men, but it's real. So drop by at 8 in the morning, sit down next to a "dawg," and tell him The Whizzz Brothers sent ya.

## Turtle Bay

987 2nd Ave. (52nd & 53rd Sts.)
212-223-4224

YOU JUST GRADUATED college and took a job with Merrill Lynch, so where do you go? You got it, good ol' Turtle Bay. This crowded hangout offers a suit clad scene and cute girls during the week that provides a nice segue to the pick up scene on the weekends. Live music plays in the spacious rustic-style lounge upstairs on Tuesdays and Wednesdays while a DJ provides background music downstairs for those mingling and schmoozing. Come and watch the big screen TV, drink or grab a bite to eat, this is a fun scene.

## Twilo

503 W. 27th St. (10th & 11th Aves.)
212-268-1600

BE WARNED: You arrive at Twilo (former home of the legendary Sound Factory) well after midnight, the trance from some star international DJ like Carl Cox or Sasha & Digweed trembles through you from giant speakers situated throughout the dance space of one of the city's biggest clubs. Perhaps the X sets in, the beautiful male gay crowd comes fresh from their naps at 5a.m., and the next thing you know it's time for brunch. If the ATM in the lobby is any indication, this is serious clubbing for those with the wallets (it can cost up to $35 for entry), the style and the stamina.

# Twirl

201 W. 23rd St. (7th & 8th Aves.)
212-691-7685

THIS IS STILL one of Chelsea's hippist and hottest clubs even though it's closed it to the public on every night except Saturday. Private functions now reign supreme at this gay/straight club. Doors open at 10p.m. and the cover charge is $10. You can call ahead of time to see about getting on the list. The huge house party is worth every penny you spend for drinks in plastic cups.

# Twist Lounge

(@ The Ameritania Hotel)
230 W. 54th St. (@ Broadway)
212-247-5000

THIS HIP LOUNGE in the Ameritania Hotel is a great place for an after work cocktail or a pre-dinner hang. Although the space is modern, hip and tasteful, the feel is still hotel. Strong drinks, strong prices and a cool setting makes for a good quickie (so to speak...).

# 2A

27 Ave. A (@ 2nd St.)
212-505-2466

SIMPLY NAMED AFTER its coordinates, 2A is an understated, cool duplex experience. The first floor is a neighborhood bar where beer drinkers commune at stools and small black back tables. The second floor is a handsome lounge with a bar of its own and another wall of plate-glass windows overlooking the corner of 2nd St.

# 2i's

248 W. 14th St. (7th & 8th Aves)
212-807-1775

WHILE 2I'S DESERVES credit for establishing an African-American hip-hop scene in the mostly white West Village, its vibe so negative that one can only hope someone else will do a better job with the idea. The music is consistently good hip-hop/R&B and the decor is sleek and electric, but the doormen and employees are such complete assholes that nobody but street punks looking to get laid and/or fight bothers going in. With a sizable attitude adjustment, 2i's could be a decent place to go dancing. As it is, you'll just pay $15 to get angry.

## 205 Club

205 Christy St. (@ Stanton St.)
212-473-5816

THE PREMIERE HIP-HOP club for the Lower East side for 10 years, 205 Club, calls the mellow hipsters to its funky couches. The good time vibe creates the perfect place to grab a drink and dance the night away. Drinks are cheap, between $4 and $7, and happy hour features $2 Buds .The beer and wine list is small, but the bartenders know how to make a nice mixed drink. Call ahead for cover charge information.

## 212 Restaurant & Bar

133 E. 65th St. (Lexington & Park Aves.)
212-249-6565

YOUR CLIENTS ARE in from Japan and you want to impress them with an ultra swank and trendy NY scene; dial up 212 a month in advance. This restaurant/bar showcases the art of minimalism with its decor, but the clientele is maxed out in every respect. Beauty and class seem to be a requirement here. Saddle up to the bar and join in the flirtatious atmosphere for a tasty cocktail.

## Two Potato

143 Christopher St. (@ Greenwich St.)
212-255-0286

TWO POTATO IS a veritable gay landmark that caters to an Afro/Latino crowd and their admirers. Happy hours are Mon-Fri. from 4p.m.-9p.m. with $2 well pours and domestic beers. Drag shows and slinky go-go boys alike dance to the pumping hip-hop music.

## Typhoon Restaurant

22 E. 54th St. (Madison & 5th Aves.)
212-754-9006

TYPHOON RESTAURANT IS a bi-level restaurant/bar that offers 6 of their very own micro-beers and great dining in a relaxed, after work atmosphere. You know this is a microbrewery in NY and not Colorado because of the excellent Thai cuisine they serve rather then the standard burgers and "beer" battered onion rings. Plus, the Asian spice keeps the beer flowing faster than the Yangtze (we know this river is in China not Thailand!). The trend of micro-beers is dead, but Typhoon is alive and well and a great place to hang and admire the funky, warehouse decor that could only fly in this city.

## Ty's

114 Christopher St. (@ Bleecker St.)
212-741-9641

THERE'S NOTHING LIKE a friendly and "mature" gay neighborhood saloon where you, your mustache and you're flannel shirt will fit right in. If it has ever been your fantasy to muck it up with firemen, stop by the second Tuesday of every month for "Fire-FLAGEM'S night. Shut-up and put-up for Wednesday night's leather theme. Just teasing. Don't be scared, that look in his eyes is probably just lust.

## Union Bar

204 Park Ave. So. (17th & 18th Sts.)
212-674-2105

THE OWNERS OF the sleek Union Bar probably didn't realize that their biggest crowd would come from Hoboken, but they enjoy taking their money. This comfortable and loungey space becomes slightly less comfortable as the after-work yuppies and Wall-Street crowd pile in. The young money crowd relaxes to jazz and R&B while watching CNBC. The soft leather booths and the wrap around bar fill up quickly with folks enjoying $9 Big Apple martinis (but they sure are tasty). The testosterone levels get even higher Thursdays through Saturdays as the B&T contingent pile in and wonder where all the women are.

## Vandam

150 Varick St. (@ Vandam St.)
212-352-9090

HOW CAN A place this nice, packed with beautifully enhanced people, be so unappealing? Slightly off the beaten path, this vanilla yuppie spot offers a nice venue for entertaining clients and impressing your buddies, but does little else. Being in SoHo, the crowd and the clientele tend to be tanned, stair mastered and smiley. Though hosting a variety of people who might be in the entertainment industry, Vandam's caters more to the packaging and distribution crowd than the creating and performing set. You probably won't see Tom Cruise here, but his agent might buy you a $9 kremely chocolatini (Chocolate Vodka with a Hershey's kiss). If you're looking for an L.A. scene in NY, you've found it.

## Velvet Lounge

223 Mulberry St. (Prince & Spring Sts.)
212-965-0439

UNLESS YOU'RE A SoHo veteran or have explored less obvious nightlife offerings in the neighborhood, the name Velvet Lounge may seem misleading, since the emphasis is on its French and Asian food. The upstairs lounge is only open on weekends unless you've booked a private party. Check out the razmopolitan and white chocolate martini; they'll kick your ass right into the cozy velvet couches. Relax and enjoy the laid-back atmosphere and eclectic selections of the DJ (from Latin to hip-hop to scary jungle sounds). The staff is far hotter than the crowd, so you're not likely to find a date - but it's not a bad place to bring one.

## Venue & The Lava Lounge

505 Columbus Ave. (84th & 85th Sts.)
212-579-9463

OVERLOUD AND OVERCROWDED, Venue and the basement-located Lava Lounge do their best to play Downtown in a decidedly un-Downtown neighborhood. All drapery and darkness, the first-floor lounge and bar appears something of a sexy romper room where couples sprawl out on actual beds. Ahem. Downstairs is filled with all-things glowing and textured, with an occasional private party. A place with such a velvet rope atmosphere would charge a cover if it were Downtown; but here you can save the loot for an expensive cosmo.

## Venus Room

1074 1st Ave. (58th & 59th Sts.)
212-207-3858

BEING THAT VENUS is the goddess of love, you'll get to feeling amorous upon entering the Venus Room. This

'50s retro-designed bar keeps the large sidewalk windows thrown open to let in a cool, refreshong breeze. The drinks are fairly priced, but don't go ordering that Manhattan just yet; Venus Room's apple martini ($7) is famous, and with good reason, it's just plain excellent. Although only two years old, the atmosphere and gregarious barkeeps are certain to ensure Venus a long and prosperous future.

## Vera

88 2nd Ave. (@ 5th St.)
212-420-0202

AN ELEGANT LITTLE spot where beautiful women gather in pairs or trios to either ignore or actively mock earnest schlemiels trying to chat them up with phony Italian accents. But the locale itself doesn't front; Vera offers a nice wine selection, healthy gourmet nibbles, and a decor that is heavy on the frills. Definitely a romantic spot for dates, or perhaps a discreet pick-up. Just leave the "Ciao, bellissima!" shtick at home.

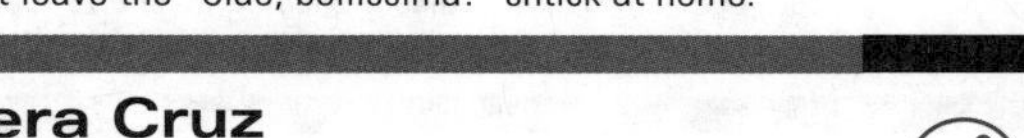

## Vera Cruz

195 Bedford Ave. (6th & 7th Sts.) Brooklyn
718-599-7914

WELCOME TO THE margarita capital of New York! People come from all five boroughs to this very agreeable Mexican bistro. On Friday nights the bar serves up to 35 gallons of the cocktail, extra salt. Vera Cruz has a deep, pleasantly dark storefront dining room and a full bar only feet from the sidewalk, serving wine and five kinds of Mexican bottled beer in addition to the staple beverage. The backyard is commodious and a year-round affair; in the winter, it is enclosed in heated tents. This is a robust, unpretentious neighborhood bistro with a definite touch of class. Put it this way: If Ernest Hemingway got lost somehow in modern day Williamsburg, he'd feel comfortable at Vera Cruz.

## Veritas

43 E. 20th St. (Park Ave. & Broadway)
212-353-3700

VERITAS IS A must for the devout oenophile. With an extensive wine cellar comprised of 3 personal collections containing over 1,300 selections, you will be overwhelmed. The sommelier will steer you in the right direction, whether you're dining on the delicious eclectic food or sitting at the bar. This elegant, classy, small 65-seater restaurant is a great bet for a date to impress or an expense account outing. Veritas is a hot spot at the moment so call now for a reservation next month. Or you might be lucky enough to get a seat at the bar where you can order from an a la carte bar menu.

## Vermouth

355 Amsterdam Ave. (@ 77th St.)
212-724-3600

IF ITS NAME and the glasses that are glued to the globe lights don't clue you in; this bar is clearly devoted to its martinis. Choose among 52 variations (from the fruity Paradise to the spicy Cajun). Vermouth is a popular chichi spot for Upper West Siders because the powerful concoctions are priced at $7; considerably lower than most other places on the same par. The dining room gets filled with folks munching eclectic American fare from Patria ex-pat, Michael Cressotti.

## Veruka

525 Broome St. (6th Ave. & Thompson St.)
212-625-1717

WHO ARE THEY trying to kid with those burly, pouty-faced masters of the universe, a.k.a. doormen, stationed behind the velvet ropes and passing judgment over the pathetic souls who mistakenly believe the party is here? There is no cover charge but Veruka tries so hard to be hip it just can't admit that its heyday on the Manhattan club circuit is way over. The bi-level lounge is decorated with low seating, (mainly reserved for friends of the owners and those who hemorrhage cash), sparse décor and tasteful dim lighting. The drinks are overpriced and served by an unfriendly staff. And as for the music, most people have bigger personal collections than the DJ. Simply put, this place is over.

## Vice Versa

325 W. 51st St. (8th & 9th Aves.)
212-399-9291

"EASY BREEZY COVER GIRL." That is how you'll feel as you step through the glass façade onto the front terrace of this fabulous bar/restaurant. Welcome to heaven all you pale, bitter New Yorkers! The Milan meets L.A. atmosphere of this subtle, sexy joint will have you running for Prada and a sunless tanner in no time. The décor is millennium chic with a stainless steel bar, white walls and ebony floors. The attractive professional staff serves up palate pleasing edibles and gorgeous cocktails in this attitude-free zone. Vice Versa has a pleasantly diverse mix of clientele and is suited for a date or drinks with friends. Definitely worth checking out.

## Viceroy

160 8th Ave. (@ 18th St.)
212-633-8484

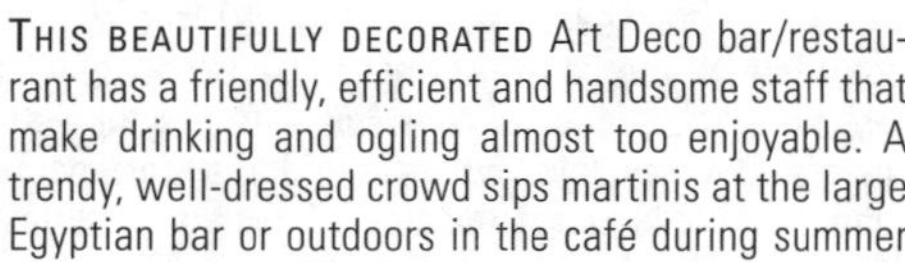

This beautifully decorated Art Deco bar/restaurant has a friendly, efficient and handsome staff that make drinking and ogling almost too enjoyable. A trendy, well-dressed crowd sips martinis at the large Egyptian bar or outdoors in the café during summer months.

## Victory Café

1604 3rd Ave. (@ 90th St.)
212-348-3650

A pleasant "Cheers"-like neighborhood bar and restaurant can be found at the Victory Café. Suits and locals enjoy the nostalgic setting and American/Italian menu with a few specials nightly. Since 1984, they have entertained their loyal crowd with a 4p.m.-7p.m. weekday happy hour. Local musicians and friends play light rock and jazz. The schedule is ultra-casual so when they play it's always a surprise. You can also enjoy their sidewalk café on nice nights. This is one of the few places Uptown where you and your pooch can enjoy a beer and bowl of water.

## Vig Bar

12 Spring St. (@ Elizabeth St.)
212-625-0011

This sleek, shadowy Little Italy lounge is a real treasure if you're looking for a swanky laid back environment where you can take a special date (or a few friends, if you don't have a date) to relax without giving yourself an aneurism trying to converse over the music. The smooth, art deco interior will soothe the savage beast with a variety of places to hang including a winding bar, a long leathery booth that lines the back wall and a very handsome, swank back room.

## The Village Idiot

355 W. 14th St. (8th & 9th Aves)
212-989-7334

"HEAR YE! HEAR YE! All ye drunken rednecks stranded in the township of Manhattan are hereby invited to gather this eventide at the Village Idiot!" With an awesome good ol' boy jukebox, a pool table, darts and hot sassy bartenders who'll let you do shots off their tits if you ask real nice (not really, but they sure seem like they would!), the Village Idiot has all the bait to attract those islanders who are tired of pretending to be smart. Unlike the self-aware Coyote Ugly, where the babe bartenders dance on the hour and the clever lines are all scripted, the Village Idiot bartenders dance 'cause they're shitfaced and the drunken rants only seem clever 'cause you are too.

## Village Lantern

167 Bleecker St. (Thompson & Sullivan Sts.)
212-260-7993

THE VILLAGE LANTERN is a sweetly romantic, mild-mannered sort of a bar, with half price bottles of wine after 10p.m. and excellent Italian food. Sunday through Tuesday there's live jazz starting at 10p.m., creating a lively atmosphere for a late dinner. On Wednesday and Thursday they have a DJ playing very mellow jazz standards. Most of the time The Village Lantern is the sort of place where single women can go to have a glass of wine in peace.

## Village Underground

130 W. 3rd St. (6th Ave. & MacDougal St.)
212-777-7745

OPENED IN JULY 2000, this performance space features live music every night and you never quite know what kind of crowd might show up. You enter upstairs in a bare room that seems to serve no purpose, but press on down the stairs to find a fun space with friendly staff and great music. The décor is smoky and sophisticated, but the music can be a bit loud at times, making conversation slightly difficult. A great spot for a night out but beware the sneaky cover charges which are sometimes collected well past the front door.

## Village Vanguard

178 7th Ave. So. (@ Perry St.)
212-255-4037

IF YOU'RE A jazz fan, the Village Vanguard will remind you why. If not, it might make you one. Unlike most jazz clubs, which are hot little rooms crammed with people, the Vanguard is comfortable and civilized. The music is of high quality, and while not everyone who plays here is a household name, they are all a pleasure to listen to and do justice to the club's rich history. As expensive as it is ($15 at the door) there's a $10 drink minimum the Village Vanguard is a luxury that can't be experienced enough.

## Virage

88 2nd Ave. (@ 7th St.)
212-420-0202

I CAN ONLY imagine that Virage is the outcome of one entrepreneur's amusing double dare to another; that dare being: how long could one run a restaurant/bar that absolutely sucks before bailing out to avoid financial devastation. But Virage's misguided attempts at swank are nothing but depressing for the customer. A few lost out-of-towners, decked out in turquoise jewelry and Daffy's basement bargains, haplessly poke at humdrum renditions of standards; such as fried calamari with chipotle, blah-blah, and endive and frisee with goat cheese, yaddah yaddah; among a haphazard, and nausea-inducing decoration scheme that meddles in every genre.

## Void

16 Mercer St. (@ Howard St.)
212-941-6492

WALK THROUGH A residential building on Howard St., down the dark door and you will find yourself enveloped in the trippy, cyber-funk, ambient music filled innards of Void. With the aid of five mini spotlights cutting through the darkness, you will notice the Gothic/New Age interior filled with random sofas and tables equipped with TV's. A huge screen continuously projects spacey images that grab your attention and don't let go. Weekday nights at 8p.m. hard-core artists and film enthusiasts gather for free film screenings, but the ultimate Void experience is the post-screening parties that involve D.J.'s mixing ambient grooves in collaboration with projectionists spinning video images on the walls.

## Von

3 Bleecker St. (@ Bowery)
212-473-3039

THIS COMFORTABLE VILLAGE bar began as an antique shop, but once it began started serving drinks, its owners realized its true calling. Located on a quiet stretch on Bleecker St., Von gets few bridge and tunnelers and the bartenders do a great job of keeping everyone happy. Everything about it is smart and subtle, including the patrons who leave their soap-boxes at home, the artists who realize there's more to life than discussing painting, and the young singles with too much dignity for the East Village pick-up scene.

## Vong

200 E. 54th St. (@ 3rd Ave.)
212-486-9592

VONG is a super-elegant, upscale restaurant featuring French-influenced Thai cuisine, but the bar alone is attractive enough for a visit. Big plants set off the curving wood walls while a large birdcage adds a touch of Far-East exotica. Toss your body into one of the plush burgundy and brown lounge chairs, cocktail in hand (try passion potion or Vong mar-tea-ni), and thrill to Vong's soundtrack of Buddhist chants and Balinese gamelan orchestras.

## Wakamba

543 8th Ave. (37th & 38th Sts.)
212-840-9273

WAKAMBA, LOOSELY TRANSLATING into "You will never get out of here alive," is a sketchy scene where you're buzzed in and out of the front door and the ten-sion is so thick you can slice it with one of the cut glass mirrors lining the walls of the bar. The predominately Latin, African American and Port Authority transient crowd live the vida loca on the dance floor to Latin, R&B, reggae and '70s disco blasting from the jukebox. The candlelit shrine set up outside for the recent civilian shot by a cop will hopefully make you think twice before being buzzed into this Hell's Kitchen watering hole.

## Wall Street Kitchen and Bar

70 Broad St. (@ Beaver St.)
212-797-7070

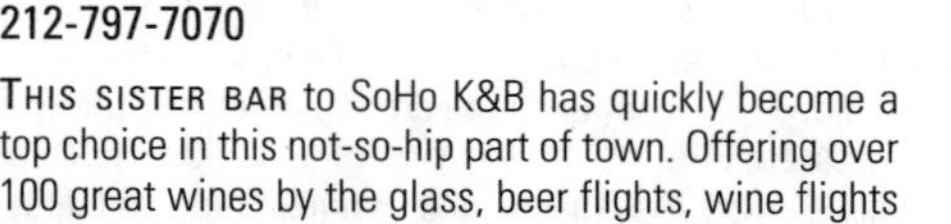

THIS SISTER BAR to SoHo K&B has quickly become a top choice in this not-so-hip part of town. Offering over 100 great wines by the glass, beer flights, wine flights and every liquor under the sun, it's no wonder this has become a favorite hangout for the near by investment bank clientele. Good food and good service make this bi-level "wine bar" one the best places to meet after work for a drink near the NYSE.

## Walker's

16 No. Moore St. (@ Varick St.)
212-941-0142

WALKER'S IS A triumphant and authentic neighborhood bar. This eleven-year old space (once a cop hangout called "Vics") has wisely preserved its ancient bar, untreated wood floors and hammered tin ceilings. Although they offer the splendid Hoegaarden on tap, don't overlook Walker's superb variety of single-malts, tequilas and cognacs. If you decide to seat yourself at one of the many tables (and there are two rooms full of them behind the main room), expect a menu full of food that will not exactly pitch you into throes of ecstasy, but does constitute a square meal.

## Waterfront Ale House

540 2nd Ave. (@ 30th St.)
212-696-4104

WATERFRONT ALE HOUSE is not close to the water but close to the new Kips Bay megaplex and shopping cen-

ter. The happy hour Monday-Friday 4p.m.-7p.m. is worth stopping for. Waterfront is usually filled with a middle-aged local crowd with a mix of NYU medical students and nurses, although lately the neighborhood feeling is being lost due to the influx of patrons coming here to grab a few drinks before or after the movies. The nice corner bar atmosphere makes everyone feel at home and keeps people coming back.

## Waterloo

145 Charles St. (@ Washington St.)
212-352-1119

HUGE GARAGE STYLE doors and a clean modern space makes this an absolute favorite in the West Village. The beer and food are top notch and the well dressed Euro-crowd could give Elsa Klench some style tips. The spectacular Belgian fare and great beer and wine selection only add to the appeal. A great place to take a date, pick up a date or just hang and people watch. Hands down, this is Shecky's favorite West Village spot.

## WCOU Radio (a.k.a. The Tile Bar)

115 1st Ave. (@ 7th St.)
212-254-4317

WCOU IS A room with bare walls, four tables, a jukebox, a long bar and not much else. Still, this 18-year-old neighborhood hangout draws a crowd, but stay away on weekends when the place is crawling with bridge and tunnel vermin. Happy hour is from 5-8p.m. when the drinks are half price and the draft Bass and Guinness is a-flowin' The wine selection consists "red" and "white" but they do have sake. This is a cool mellow hangout if you go at the right time, and if it's crowded, check out their West Side location

## The Web

40 E. 58th St. (5th & Madison Aves.)
212-308-1546

RECENTLY RENOVATED WITH a new sound system, The Web still holds its own as NYC's only gay, Asian disco. A young crowd gathers to dance to club and house mixes expertly spun by guest DJ's. Go-go boys dance

on two stages and in a metal cage above the dance floor. The Web has theme nights hosted by drag queens Sunday through Thursday. This club offers a fun and interesting alternative to the typical scene you'll find at the Roxy, Twirl, or Twilo.

## Webster Hall

125 E. 11th St. (3rd & 4th Aves.)
212-353-1600

A CIRCUS. Literally. When club-goers aren't transfixed and dilated on the main floor trapeze act, they wander four stories of something-for-everyone dance mixes and fleshy, R-rated scenery. This Mecca of clubbing calls to roving packs of ADD-enhanced pickup artists and all-nighter club kids from around the world, all broiling in a heat reminiscent of an Arizona summer when you can fry an egg on your fender. Take a deep breath and a deep drink and plunge in for an all-nighter you'll be sure to enjoy or sweat to death trying to.

## Welcome to the Johnsons

123 Rivington St. (Essex & Norfolk Sts.)
212-420-9911

IF YOU WANT to flashback to your youth then Welcome to The Johnsons, where the family portraits, the worn furniture and the old style fridge will take you back to that basement in the suburbs. A good mix of local down town hipsters play pool and drink relatively cheap drinks while listening to The Donnas, Boston, The Ramones and T-Rex on the cool jukebox. An unreasonably long daily happy hour from 3p.m.-9 p.m. serves up $1.50 PBR, $2 well drinks and $3 frozen margaritas. You can't miss The Johnson's - just look for the neighborly wooden sign that reads "Welcome to The Johnsons".

## Westside Brewing Co.

340 Amsterdam Ave. (@ 76th St.)
212-721-2161

A NAME CHANGE is in order since Westside no longer brews their own beer. Even though the golden kettles are long gone, this neighborhood standby still attracts a sizable, young, beer-swilling post-work crowd. Sitting along the lengthy mahogany bar inside, or at numerous tables on the wooden patio, patrons accompany their hamburgers and other bistro fare with various microbrewery heavy-hitters.

## Wetbar (@ W Hotel)

130 Lexington Ave. (38th & 39th Sts.)
212-592-8844

RANDY GERBER IS on a roll with the ultra swanky hotel bar scene, transforming hotels into places to see and be seen. Whether you're trying to get a glimpse of someone famous or setting your sights on someone to schmooze, you cannot overlook the roving stares of everybody checking each other out. The horny predators who frequent this bar for said hounding don't seem to notice the exorbitant drink prices or the stunning decor for the potential conquests. If you are looking for the quintissential NY people watching spot, you have hit the jackpot. It doesn't get any swankier than this. So don your best duds and join the show.

## Wetlands

161 Hudson St. (@ Laight St.)
212-386-3600

SINCE 1989, THIS hotspot has been supporting bands while strengthening the idea of Earth conciousness. A venue for Grateful Dead cover bands, as well as a mass of bands that are new, old, dead and alive, Wetlands has lent its wings to Pearl Jam, Dave Matthews Band, Oasis, Spin Doctors, Blues Traveler, etc. The spirit adheres to fun and activism in unison. The music is all inclusive from dance, rhythm, world beat, blues, rock to neopsychedelic, funk, fusion, punk and hardcore. Two levels rally with all types with a friendly staff. The crowd depends on the band so call for showings.

## The Whiskey(@ the Paramount Hotel)

235 W. 46th St. (8th Ave. & Broadway)
212-819-0404

THIS IS NOT your typical hotel bar. Owned by Randey Gerber, it's a trendy, chic bar catering to after work and late night crowds. Come early to grab one of the comfortable chairs and couches so you have an unobstructed view for people watching and eyeing the cocktail waitresses pranceing around in full body catsuits. Oh, my! The drinks are a bit steep but the titilating atmosphere more than makes up for your empty wallet.

## Whiskey Blue

541 Lexington Ave. (@ 49th St.)
212-407-2947

SIMILAR TO THE fate of its sister bar, the midtown W Hotel's Wetbar, the Whiskey Blue is a stomping ground for the beautiful, reconfigured, pretentious and trendy. If you make it past the door where the "bouncers" are hot babes and are a REAL threat, you'd better head for the only redeeming perk; the large, red velvet bed where you can lounge with your friends while sipping $10 cosmopolitans and avoiding the eyes of those on the prowl. Save this one for friends visiting from L.A.-they'll feel right at home.

## Whiskey Park

100 Central Park So. (@ 6th Ave.)
212-307-9222

IT'S NO WONDER that everyone at this neighborhood boite is dressed in haute couture as it's located on some of Manhattan's priciest real-estate. It's nice to walk into a bar with a doorman who greets you with a warm hello. Inside, you can expect to find crowds of young, rich and beautiful executives sipping Absolut martinis and excellent cosmopolitans ($10) while stretching out on comfortable modern chairs and couches. Offering views of Central Park and Sixth Ave., this very unassuming place with low lighting and sleek, extremely professional service is a superb ambiance shift from the arrogant and attitude ridden places.

## Whiskey Ward

121 Essex St. (Rivington & Essex Sts.)
212-477-2918

OPEN ONLY A few months, this clean unpretentious bar attracts a great mix of locals, hipsters and punks. Whiskey Ward really does live up to its name by serving an extensive variety of beer, whiskey and bourbon. The pool table and the jukebox (filled with old soul and punk) keep folks coming back for more. The service is awesome and the prices are reasonable and only get better during the half price happy hour every day from 5p.m.-8 p.m. One hell of a good bar!

## White Horse Tavern

567 Hudson St. (@ 11th St.)
212-243-9260

ESTABLISHED IN THE early 1800's, the White Horse Tavern dishes up a little slice of history. The old-fashioned, carved wooden benches and collection of Dylan Thomas paraphernalia on the walls hearkens back to the beatnik generation, a time when writers came to roost while slowly drinking away their angst. WHT remains a very popular New York staple and draws a mix of regulars and yuppies enjoying bar food, cheap pitchers and $2 draft happy hours. Weekends draw in the out-of-towners, but it's still a great bar in a beautiful part of town, especially in the summer when the outdoor tables emerge.

## Who's NYC

1683 1st Ave. (@ 87th St.)
212-410-2780

LOOKS LIKE A shoe, smells like a sneaker. No, just smells like a sneaker. With a floor reminiscent of porno movie theaters in the '70s, and a collection of everything that can be found in a closet hanging on the walls, it's no wonder the crowd screams class. The large space is filled with fratty twentysomethings looking for kind-of-cheap beer and a place to unofficially shake their beer bellies to the tasty, hip hop tunes being spun by the D.J. Why there's a cover on the weekend, baffles us.

## Wicked Wolf Restaurant

1442 1st Ave. (@ 75th St.)
212-861-4670

WICKED? THAT'S A HOWL. You're not going to find a bar with such friendly, hospitable and good-humored bartenders anywhere else And the regulars will treat you like an old friend. The $12.95 lobster special draws in the crowds on Monday and Saturday nights, but don't snub their everyday filet of sole and pasta dinners. 10 beers on tap and $4 cocktails.

## Willy's Bar and Grill

1538 2nd Ave. (@ 80th St.)
212-734-1888

ON ARRIVAL AT Willy's, one marvels at the beautiful and elegant colonial decor. The lovely wood-bordered walls and candles on every table make this a romantic and affordable spot for couples. The dinner recommendations of linguine primavera and roasted chicken are a mere $10, and cocktails run around $5. Willy's is a beautiful addition to the Upper East Side.

## Wilson's

201 W. 79th St. (Amsterdam Ave. & Broadway)
212-796-0100

WILSON'S IS A classy joint for a somewhat older live-music fans. Open daily until 4a.m., diners and drinkers can enjoy jazz, blues, Motown and R&B or experiment with Sunday's open mic night. With quality American cuisine, a cosmo with extra kick and the soulful Stingers performing Wednesdays and Fridays, it's a scene unique to its neighborhood.

## Windfall

23 W. 39th St. (5th & 6th Aves.)
212-869-4606

WINDFALL WELCOMES A large, young, after-work crowd to its spacious, attractive bar. Thirsty and horny young workers crowd around the 44-foot long bar discussing girls and dot-coms. Seventy years ago this bar was the private dining room of the Engineering Society. Today, you won't find any nerdy engineers wearing pocket protectors, you'll find cute Silicon Alley up-and comers and a fashion district crowd

## Wonder Bar

505 E. 6th St. (Aves. A & B)
212-777-9105

THIS CHARMING EAST Village art deco bungalow is the perfect spot for relaxing after work and into the wee hours. The dimly-lit lounge area is conducive for fondling that special person without getting thrown out. This trend-spoty and diverse bar has friendly bartenders that cater to New York's beautiful hip boy toys. A DJ spins out the funk while the relaxed clientele schmooze.

## The Works

428 Columbus Ave. (@ 81st St.)
212-799-7365

DEFINITELY 100 TIMES better than any gay bar rival on the East or West Side, encouraging the cute "guppies" cruise, play pool and drink very heavily. With a DJ, two-for-one happy hours and theme nights, you're sure to find something to get you going. On Tuesday all shirtless men can drink beer for $3. So take off your shirt, flex, sport some tattoos and piercings and let the good times roll.

## Wreck Room

116 MacDougal St. (Bleecker & 3rd Sts.)
212-253-1843

THERE'S NO GOOD time to go to Wreck Room. During the week it's empty, absolutely dead, not a single person in the tiny, dark, dirty place. A B & T crowd pay an obscene $10 cover charge on weekends to dance and listen to a crappy DJ in this sweaty, shitbox of a firetrap. The only redeeming thing about "Wreck Room" is that the girls are almost dumb enough to go home with you. Almost.

## WXOU Radio

558 Hudson St. (Perry & 11th Sts.)
212-206-0381

ANOTHER ONE OF those non-descript local bars that serves as a "safehouse" from the overcrowded bars in the area, this basic bar has a bunch of wooden tables and a decent jukebox. The crowd is a random mix of overflow from the White Horse and Corner Bistro looking for a quieter place to get a seat, hang out and drink. This total no frills spot serves its purpose well, just like any neighborhood bar.

## Xando Coffee & Bar

504 6th Ave. (@ 13th St.)
212-462-4188
257 Park Ave. So. (20th & 21st St.)
212-505-7978
2160 Broadway (@ 76th St)
212-595-5616

IF XANDO COULD somehow mange to snuff out Starbucks (a.k.a. "diet Xando") New Yorkers would be better off. This coffee shop-cum bar is a happening scene for hip young people who sometimes need a little more than caffeine and a cigarette to relax. They usually play everything from K.C. & the Sunshine Band to Chet Baker at a comfortable level. Although the atmosphere is quasi-suburban strip mall chain, they are large and roomy. Anyone with a laptop, a cell phone and no office could practically work out of here for free. So when you're looking for a place to read a book or hang out with friends, this is the perfect spot.

## XR Bar

128 W Houston St. (@ Sullivan St.)
212-674-4080

A PLACE TO see and be seen, XR Bar is a dark, low-lit bar with tiny tables and awkward seating. The brick and wood decor combined with red lights and glowing lanterns make you feel like you're in an otherworldly living room. The intimate atmosphere makes it a good place to bring a date, however it's not really the place to pick up. There's no kitchen, but they do have a delivery menus on hand. There is live music Sunday-Wednesday and DJ's spin dance beats Thursday-Saturday.

## Xunta

174 1st Ave. (10th & 11th Sts.)
212-614-0620

FIRST, IT'S PRONOUNCED "shoontah," and it's a TAPAS bar, not a TOPLESS one. Second, don't even sit at the bar because even their kalimoyxo (coke and red wine) can't numb the pain you will have in your knees from pressing up against the hard brick counter. But, for those who don't mind standing, Xunta is lively slice of Spain dripping with fishing nets and maps of the homeland. There are live Flamenco dancers on Mondays and Thursdays and Latin guitar on Tuesdays. As for liquor sorry, amigo, there's only five Spanish beers, a hearty wine list and a tasty sangria concoction.

## XVI

16 1st Ave. (1st & 2nd Sts.)
212-260-1549

FORMERLY A TURKISH Social Club, the theme of XVI (Bar 16) is artsy, mirrored and glamorous darkness. This lounge may or may not have a doorman positioned outside to collect the nominal $5 cover charge during weekends. DJ's keep the pulse strong on the downstairs dance floor. Monday through Wednesday drinks are $3 from 8-11 p.m., but the hefty $8 Long Island iced teas are what keep everyone going till 4a.m.

## Yabby

265 Bedford Ave. (Grand & N. 1st Sts.)
Brooklyn
718-384-1664

"YABBY"? MORE LIKE "Yuppie." Definitely not a place to bring your crazy uncle or funny-looking friends. See, Yabby caters to New-Williamsburg rather than Old-Williamsburg. Trendy young entrepreneurs posture and preen for one another lounging on the sofa. Others are attracted to its large outdoor space. A full menu is offered all day and all night, but many of the yabsters come for a 12-4p.m. Sunday brunch accompanied by live jazz. DJ's and experimental jazz outfits provide for a soothing lounge atmosphere for stressed-out, aspiring moguls.

## Yogi's

2156 Broadway (@ 76th St.)
212-873-9852

REJECTS AND LIBERTINES alike will delight in $5 pitchers of beer and $1.50 shots at this plebeian hole-in-the-wall hailed by its loyal constituency as "the pulse of the Upper West Side". Guzzle down MGD out of a dirty glass to the beat of Johnny Cash's "Ring of Fire" or slurp a shot of bottom-shelf tequila out of a barmaid's bellybutton. Every hour is happy hour, and every night is ladies night. All are welcome to donate a brassiere to the growing collection on the wall without fear of appearing immodest, because, after all, "nudity is not a problem" at this sister bar to the Village Idiot. Get ready to watch all hell break loose if you dare stay past midnight.

## Zanzibar

645 9th Ave. (@ 45th St.)
212-957-9197

THIS INTERIOR DESIGN-challenged bar is anything but ordinary. Named after a beautiful island off the coast of Africa, Zanzibar offers different specialty drinks everyday ranging from $8-$10. Because there is an eclectic crowd, anything goes. From a Euro crowd slumming in Hell's Kitchen to a bunch of frat dudes out trolling, you never know who you will run into. Much better than last year, but there are still a few kinks to work out.



## Zarela

953 2nd Ave. (50th & 51st Sts.)
212-644-6740

THIS COZY AND colorful Mexican restaurant is always a-bustle. On a busy night, there's hardly any standing room in the petite lounge area. The musicians themselves have to resort to playing from the staircase. The bar features Mexican beers and potent margaritas ($8.50), while the dinner menu offers tantalizing options such as roasted duck and striped bass.

## Zinc Bar

90 W. Houston St. (Thompson St. & LaGuardia Pl.)
212-477-8337

ONE OF THE coolest spots in the Village, Zinc Bar is a great place to relax, make conversation with gorgeous people and listen to some cool jazz. Designed like a funky cave, Zinc Bar can get pretty crowded on Friday and Saturday nights. The crowd is cool, un-pretentious, out to have a blast and bordering on (God forbid!) friendly. Drinks are reasonably priced ($5.75) when you consider that Zinc Bar feels trendy and offers live music. Casual dress is accepted, but it's more fun to wear something sexy.

## Zum Schneider

107 Ave. C (@ 7th St.)
212-598-1098

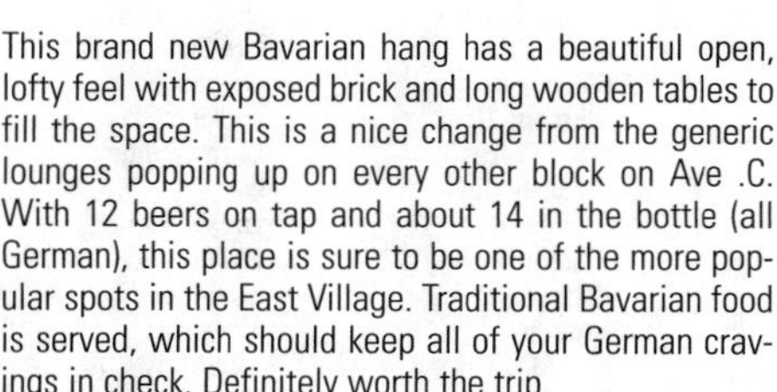

This brand new Bavarian hang has a beautiful open, lofty feel with exposed brick and long wooden tables to fill the space. This is a nice change from the generic lounges popping up on every other block on Ave .C. With 12 beers on tap and about 14 in the bottle (all German), this place is sure to be one of the more popular spots in the East Village. Traditional Bavarian food is served, which should keep all of your German cravings in check. Definitely worth the trip.

# LISTINGS BY NEIGHBORHOOD

## FLATIRON



## GRAMERCY



## GREENPOINT



## GREENWICH VILLAGE

Panache (formerly L'Attitude)
Peculier Pub
Village Underground
Wreck Room

## HELLS KITCHEN
Babalu
Bar 9
Bellevue Bar
Bongo
Bull Moose Saloon
Chaeira
Citron 47
Cleo's 9th Ave. Saloon
Collins Bar
Danny's Skylight Room
Dave's Tavern
Delta Grill
Don't Tell Mama
Druids
Film Center Café
FireBird Café, The
Gaf, The
Holland Bar
Jack Rose / Jack's Joint
Kevin St James
McDooley's
Mercury Bar
Mr. Bigg's Bar & Grill
Olympic Lounge
Otis
Revolution
Rosie Too!
Rudy's Bar & Grill
Savoy Lounge
Scandal
Smiths
Splitzzz
Stella's
Street Car Café
Swine on Nine
Wakamba
Xth Ave. Lounge
Zanzibar

## LITTLE ITALY
Chibi's Sake Bar
M&R Bar
Peasant
Rice
Sweet & Vicious
Velvet Lounge
Vig Bar, The

## MIDTOWN
44 (@ The Royalton)
53rd St. Cigar Bar
5757 (@ The Four Seasons Hotel)
Angelo & Maxie's
Annie Moore's
Aquavit
Asia De Cuba
Au Bar
B.B. King's Blues Club & Grill
Bar 54
Bar Code
Barclay's Bar & Grill
Barrymore's
Beekman Bar & Books
Beer Bar @ Café Centro
Bill's Gay Nineties
Birdland
Bistro Latino
Bliss Bar & Lounge
Brassierie 8 1/2
Brassierie Bit
Brassierie Centrale
Brew's
British Open
Broadway Lounge (Marriott Marquis)
Bryant Park Grill
Bull & Bear (@ The Waldorf Astoria)
C.J.'s Knockouts Sports Bar
Café Nicole Bar
Café Pierre
Calico Jacks Cantina
Carnegie Club, The
Caroline's Comedy Club
Catwalk
Chase
Chez Josephine
China Club
Club New York
Coco Pazzo Café
Commonwealth Brewery
Coopers Cars & Cigars
Copacabana
D Lounge
D.J. Reynold's
Dock's Oyster Bar
El Rio Grande
Escuelita
ESPN Zone
Etoile
Exit (formerly Carbon)
Faces & Names
Float
Flute
Fubar
Ginger Man, The
Guastavino's
Halcyon
Hallo Berlin
Hard Rock Café
Harley Davidson Café
Heartland Brewery
Hooters
Houston's
Howard Johnsons
Iguana
Irish Pub
Jameson's
Jekyll & Hyde
Jimmy's Corner
Judge Roy Bean
JUdson Grill
Kate Kearney's
Kennedy's
King Cole Bar (@ The St. Regis)
Le Colonial
Mars 2112
McFadden's
McGee's
Mica Bar & Lounge
Michael Jordon's Steak House
Mickey Mantle's
Monkey Bar
Morgans Bar
Morrell Wine Bar & Café
Motown Café
Muldoon's Irish Pub
Mulligan's
Mustang Harry's
Mustang Sally's
O'Flaherty's Ale House
Old Stand, The
Olive Garden
One 51
Oscar Wilde
Oscar's
Oyster Bar & Restaurant
Palio
Pegasus
PenTop Bar Terrace, The
Pig 'n' Whistle

P.J. Clarke's
Redeye Grill
Regents
Rink Bar, The
Rosa Mexicano
Round Bar, The (The Vodka Bar)
Ruby Foo's Dim Sum Sushi Palace (Midtown)
Russian Vodka Room
Siberia
St. Andrew's
Sutton Grill
Sutton Place Rest & Bar
Tapika
Tennesse Mountain
Townhouse, The
Turtle Bay
Twist Lounge
Typhoon Restaurant
Vice Versa
Vong
Web, The
Wet Bar
Whiskey Bar, The
Whiskey Blue
Whiskey Park
Zarela

**MURRAY HILL**

Bank Café, The
Black Sheep
Ellen O'Dees
Joshua Tree
New York Comedy Club
P.J. Carney's (formerly Murray Hill Tavern)
Paddy Maguire's Ale
Patrick Kavanagh's
S & T Bar (Stock & Tankard)
Third & Long
Tivoli

**NOHO**

288 Bar (Tom & Jerry's)
Acme Underground
Belgo Nieuw York
Bond Street
Fez
Five Points
Great Jones Café, The
Helena's
Joe's Pub
Marion's Continental
Sala
Swift Hibernian Lounge
Temple Bar
Von

**PARK SLOPE**

Blah Blah
Excelsior
Gate, The
Ginger (formerly Carry Nation)
Great Lakes
Loki Lounge
O'Connor's Bar
Park Slope Brewing Company
Rising Café
Timboo's

**SOHO**

357
Androgyny
Antartica
Aquagrill
Balthazar
Bar 89
Boston Comedy Club
Botanica
Café Gitane
Café Noir
Canteen
Casa La Femme
Circa Tabac
Cub Room
Denial
Diva
Don Hill's
Double Happiness
Ear Inn
Eight Mile Creek
Emerald Pub
Fanelli's
Grand Bar
Ideya
Jet Lounge
Kana Tapas Bar & Restaurant
Kavehaz
Ken's Broome St Bar
La Jumelle
L'Orange Bleu
Lounge at 203 Spring, The (formerly Lily's)
Lucky Strike
Merc Bar
Mercer Bar
Mexican Radio
Milady's
Milano's
n
Naked Lunch
Novecento
NV/289 Bar Lounge
Oliva
O'Nieal's Grand Street
Penang
Pravda
Puck Fair
Raoul's
Recess
Savoy
Scharmann's
Shine
Sliver
SOHO Kitchen & Bar
Spring Lounge
Spy
Sway
Toad Hall
Vandam
Veruka
Void

**TRIBECA**

Anotheroom
Baby Doll Lounge
Bar Odeon
Blarney Star
Bubble Lounge
Café Remy
Church Lounge (@ The Tribeca Grand Hotel)
City Hall
Due South
El Teddy's
Flor de Sol
Hudson B&B
i Restaurant & Lounge
Ice Bar
Independent, The
Juniper Café
Knitting Factory
Kori
Lafayette Grill & Bar
Layla
Liquor Store Bar
Lush
Mitch's Place
Mudville 9
Nancy Whiskey Pub
Nathan Hales
No Moore
Obeca Li
Odeon, The

Pig 'n' Whistle
Puffy's Tavern
Raccoon Lodge
S.J. South & Sons
Screening Room, The
Spaghetti Western
Sporting Club
Tribeca Grill
Walker's
Wetlands Preserve

**UPPER EAST SIDE**

212
American Spirits
American Trash
Arizona 206
Auction House
Back Page (formerly Entourage)
Bar East
Bear Bar
Bemelmans Bar (@ The Carlyle Hotel)
Big Sur
Bishops Lounge & Grill
Brady's Bar
Brandy's Piano Bar
Bridge Bar, The
Brother Jimmy's Bait Shack
Café Carlyle (@ The Carlyle Hotel)
Carnegie Hill Brewing Co.
Club Car, The
Club Macanudo
Cocktail Room, The (formerly Reminiscence)
Copper Lounge (formerly Sweet Melissa's)
Cowboy Bar
Dangerfield's
Decade
Divine Bar
Doc Watson's
Dorrian's Red Hand
DT/UT
Elaine's
Feinstein's
Finnegan's Wake
Fitzpatrick's
Flight 1668
Gaf, The
Great Hall Balcony (MET)
Hanratty's
Harry Cipriani
Headlines
Hi-Life
Hogs & Heifers
Hunter's American Bar & Grill
Iggy's Kick Ass Bar
Il Violino Rosso
J. G. Melon
Jimmy Walker's
Judge Crater's
Julie's
King's Carriage House
Kinsale Tavern
Le Bateau Ivre
Le Regence Bar
Library (@ The Regency)
L'Ivre
Luke's Bar & Grill
Luvbuzz
Mad River Bar & Grille
Madison's Nite Club
Mark Bar (Mark Hotel)
Martell's
Marty O'Briens
Match (Uptown)
Merchants
Mogos (formerly Beacon Hill Ale House)
Mo's Caribbean Bar & Grille
Moscow
Mug Shot Saloon
Murphy's Law
Mustang
Neary's
Oak Room, The (@ The Plaza)
O'Flanagan's
O'Flanagan's Old Ale House
Okie Dokie (a.k.a. Elsie's)
Opal
Ozone Bar & Lounge
Papa Joe's Original (formerly Nimrod)
Penang
Pig 'n' Whistle
Pour House, The
Quiet Man, The
Raccoon Lodge
Rain
Rathbones
Ref's Corner
Richter's Bar
Ruby's Tap House
Ryan's Daughter
Sam Beckett's
Session 73 (formerly Yorkville Brewery & Tavern)
Ship of Fools
Subway Inn
Sushi Generation
T.G. Whitney's
Tammany Hall
Tapas Lounge
Taperia Madrid
Tar Bar
Tool Box
Trilogy
Venus Room, The
Victory Café
Who's NYC
Wicked Wolf Restaurant
Willy's Bar & Grill
Works, The

**UPPER WEST SIDE**

420
All State Café
Alligator Alley
Amsterdam Billiard Club
Blondies
Boat Basin Café
Bourbon Street
Brother Jimmy's Bait Shack
Café Des Artistes
Calle Ocho
Candle Bar
Citrus Bar & Grill
City Grill, The
Cream
Dead Poet
Dive 75
Dive Bar
Drip
Dublin House
Eight of Clubs
Ernie's
Evelyn Lounge, The
Fez North
Firehouse
Fujiyama Mama
Gin Mill, The
Indigo Bar
Iridium Jazz Club
Ivy
Jake's Dilema

Jean Georges
Journey's Lounge
La Cocina
Latin Quarter
Malachy's
McAleer's Pub
Merlot
Miss Elle's Homesick Bar
Moonlighting (a.k.a. 511)
North West Restaurant & Lounge
P & G Café
P.D. O'Hurley's Bar & Grill
Parlour, The
Penang
Peter's
Planet Sushi
Potion Lounge
Prohibition
Raccoon Lodge
Rain
Rosa Mexicano
Ruby Foo's Dim Sum
Sushi Palace
Sabor
Saints
Saloon, The
Shark Bar
Tavern on the Green
Time Out (fomerly Boomers)
Triad
Venue and the Lava Lounge
Vermouth
Westside Brewing Co.
Wilson's
Xando Café & Bar (Uptown)
Yogi's

**WALL STREET**

Beekman, The
Bergin's
Cabana
Commuter Café
Dakota Roadhouse
Delmonico's
Divine Bar (Downtown)
Donald Sacks
Downtown
GB Shaw's Bar & Grill
Grace
Greatest Bar on Earth
Harry's at Hanover Sq
Il Porto
Jeremy's Ale House
Jim Brady's
John St. Bar & Grill
Johnny's Fish Grill
Le Marais
Let's Make a Daiquiri
Moran's (Edward Moran's)
Nassau Bar
North Star Pub
Paris Café
Ryan's Sports Bar
Seaport Café
Sequoia's
Square Rigger Pub
Suspenders
Swan's Bar & Grill
Tall Ship Bar & Grill
Wall St. Kitchen & Bar

**WASHINGTON HEIGHTS**

Blatino Bronx Factory

**WEST VILLAGE**

101
2i's
55 Bar
Absolutely 4th (formerly Karma)
Alegrias
Apple Restaurant & Bar
Arlo
Art Bar
Arthur's Tavern
Automatic Slims
Back Fence, The
Baggot Inn
Baktun
Bar 6
Bar d'O
Barrow Street Ale House
Bleecker Street Bar
Blind Tiger Ale House
Blue Note
Boots & Saddle
Bottom Line
Boughalem
Bowlmor Lanes
Braque
C3 Lounge
Caffé Torino
Caliente Cab Co.
Chi Chiz
Chicago B.L.U.E.S.
Chow
Chumley's
Clementine
Cody's
Comedy Cellar
Cooler, The
Cornelia Street Café
Corner Bistro
Cowgirl Hall of Fame
Crazy Nanny's
Cubby Hole, The
Culture Club
Daddy-O's
Demarchelier Lounge
Denizen
Dew Drop Inn
Do Hwa
Down the Hatch
Drover's Tap Room
Dugout, The
Duplex, The
Dylan
Eighty Eights
Fiddlesticks
Finally Fred's
Flannery's Bar
Fressen
Garage, The
Gaslight
Girl from Ipanema, The
Gonzales y Gonzales
Grange Hall, The
Halo
Hangar, The
Hell
Henrietta Hudson
Hog Pit
Hogs & Heifers
'ino
Isla
Ja
Jekyll & Hyde
Johnny's Bar
Julius
Junno's
Kava
L'Angolo
Lion's Den
Lips
Lotus
L-Ray
Lure, The
MacDougal St Ale House
Madame X

**WILLIAMSBURG**



## LISTINGS BY CATEGORY

### POOL TABLES

O'Flaherty's Ale House
Paddy Maguire's Ale
Park Ave. Country Club
Parkside Lounge
Pegasus
Phebe's
Pieces
Plug Uglies
Pourhouse
Rawhide
Red Rock West Saloon
Reservoir
Richter's Bar
Ryan's Daughter
Sam Beckett's
Ship of Fools
Ship's Mast
Sidewalk Café
Solas
Sophie's
Sporting Club
Starlight Bar & Lounge
Stinger Club
Stone Wall
Stoned Crow
Sweetwater Tavern
Swine on Nine
Tar Bar
Timboo's
Time Out
Toad Hall
Tool Box
Trilogy
Turkey's Nest
Two Potato
Village Idiot
Web, The
Welcome To The Johnsons
Whiskey Ward
Who's NYC
Works, The
Yabby's

**LIVE MUSIC**

101
147
169 Bar
2i's
55 Bar
5757 (@ The Four Seasons Hotel)
Acme Underground
Alegrias
Angel (formerly Dharma)
Angel's Share
Anyway Café
Arlene Grocery
Arthur's Tavern
B.B. King's Blues Club & Grill
B3
Babalu
Baby Jupiter
Back Fence, The
Baggot Inn
Bar 81( aka Verchovyna Tavern)
Bar 9
Bar d'O
Barracuda
Bellevue Bar
Bemelmans Bar (@ The Carlyle Hotel)
Bill's Gay Nineties
Birdland
Bishops Lounge & Grill
Bitter End
Black Betty
Black Sheep
Black Star
Blarney Star
Blue Note
Blue Water Grill
BMW
Botanica
Bottom Line
Bowery Ballroom
Brandy's Piano Bar
Broadway Lounge (Marriott Marquis)
Brownies
Bubble Lounge
Bull & Bear (@ The Waldorf Astoria)
C3 Lounge
Cabana
Café Nicole Bar
Café Remy
Café Wha?
Carnegie Club, The
CBGB's & OMFUG
CBGB's Gallery
Charleston, The
Chez Josephine
Chicago B.L.U.E.S.
Cibar
Ciel Rouge
C-Note
Cock, The
Continental
Cooler, The
Coopers Cars & Cigars
Copacabana
Copper Lounge (formerly Sweet Melissa's)
Cornelia Street Café
Crazy Nanny's
Cutting Room
Danny's Skylight Room
Deanna's
Delta Grill
Dempsey's Pub
Detour
Divine Bar
Don Hill's
Don't Tell Mama
Downtime
Duplex, The
Ear Inn
El Flamingo
Elbow Room
Enid's
Evelyn Lounge, The
Feinstein's
Fez
Finally Fred's
Flor de Sol
Galapagos
Garage, The
Gonzales y Gonzales
Greatest Bar on Earth
Groove, The
Halcyon
Helena's
Henrietta Hudson
Hogs & Heifers
Indigo Bar
Iridium Jazz Club
Izzy Bar
Jack Rose / Jack's Joint
Jake's Dilema
Japas St. Mark's
Jazz Standard
JB
Joe's Pub
Journey's Lounge
Judy's
Jule's Bistro
Kate Kearney's
Kavehaz
Kenny's Castaways
Knitting Factory
Lakeside Lounge
Latin Quarter
Le Regence Bar
Le Singe Vert
Leopard Lounge (Sin Sin)

**FOOD**

Boat Basin Cafe
Boca Chica
Bond St. Lounge
Bongo
Bottino
Bottom Line
Boughalem
Bowlmor Lanes
Braque
Brassierie 8 1/2
Brassierie Bit
Brassierie Centrale
Bread Bar at Tabla
Brew's
Brewsky's
British Open
Broadway Lounge
Brother Jimmy's Bait Shack
Bryant Park Grill
Bubble Lounge
Bull & Bear (@ The Waldorf Astoria)
Bull Moose Saloon
C.J.'s Knockouts Sports Bar
C3 Lounge
Cabana
Café Carlyle (@ The Carlyle Hotel)
Café Des Artistes
Café Gitane
Café Noir
Café Pierre
Cafeteria
Caffé Torino
Caliban
Calico Jacks Cantina
Caliente Cab Co.
Calle Ocho
Candela's
Canteen
Captain Café
Carnegie Club, The
Carnegie Hill Brewing Co.
Caroline's Comedy Club
Casa La Femme
Casa Mexicana
Casimir
Catwalk
Centro-Fly
Chaeria
Charleston, The
Chelsea Bistro & Bar
Chelsea Brewing Company
Chelsea Commons
Chez Es Saada
Chez Josephine
Chi Chiz
Chibi's Sake Bar
Chicama
Chow
Chumley's
Church Lounge (@ The Tribeca Grand Hotel)
Cibar
Cinema Classics
Circa Tabac
Citron 47
Citrus Bar & Grill
City Grill, The
City Hall
Clementine
Cloister Café
Club Macanudo
Cocktail Room
Coco Pazzo Café
Coffee Shop
Comedy Cellar
Commonwealth Brewery
Commune
Coopers Cars & Cigars
Copacabana
Copper Lounge
Cornelia Street Café
Corner Bistro
Coup
Cowboy Bar
Cowgirl Hall of Fame
Cub Room
Cutting Room
D.J. Reynold's
Daddy-O's
Danny's Skylight Room
Deanna's
Decade
Decibel
Delta Grill
Demarchelier Lounge
Delmonico's
Denial
Dennison
Dew Drop Inn
Dewey's Flatiron
Diner
Diva
Divine Bar (Downtown)
Divine Bar
Do Hwa
Doc Holidays
Dock's Oyster Bar
Donald Sacks
Dorrian's Red Hand
Down the Hatch
Downtown
Drip
Drover's Tap Room
Druids
DT/UT
Duke's
Dylan
Ear Inn
East of 8th
Eight Mile Creek
El Quijote
El Rio Grande
El Teddy's
Elaine's
Eleven Madison Park
Emerald Pub
Ernie's
Esperanto
ESPN Zone
Eugene
Eureka Joe's
Evelyn Lounge, The
Faces & Names
Failte
Fanelli's
Feinstein's
Fez
Fez North
Fiddlesticks
Film Center Café
Finnegan's Wake
Firehouse
First
Fitzgerald's
Five Points
Flamingo East
Flight 151
Flight 1668
Flor de Sol
Fressen
Fujiyama Mama
Gaf, The
Galaxy
Gamut Bistro Lounge, The
Garage, The
GB Shaw's Bar & Grill
Gemini Lounge
Gin Mill, The
Ginger
Ginger Man, The
Globe, The

Gonzales y Gonzales
Good Times Bar & Grill
Good World Bar & Grill
Googies
Gotham Bar & Grill
Gotham Comedy Club
Grace
Gramercy Tavern
Grand Bar
Grange Hall, The
Great Jones Café, The
Greatest Bar on Earth
Greenwich Café
Groove, The
Guastavino's
Guernica
H2K
Halcyon
Half King, The
Hallo Berlin
Halo
Hanratty's
Hard Rock Café
Harley Davidson Café
Harry Cipriani
Harry's at Hanover Sq
Heartland Brewery
Helena's
Hi-Life
Hog Pit
Hooters
Houston's
Howard Johnsons
H2K
Hudson B&B
Hunter's American Bar & Grill
Hush
i Restaurant & Lounge
I Trulli
Ideya
Iggy's
Iguana
Il Bagatto
Il Covo dell' Este
Il Porto
Il Violino Rosso
Independent, The
ino
Iridium Jazz Club
Isla
J. G. Melon
Jack Rose / Jack's Joint
Jameson's
Jazz Standard
JB
Jean Georges
Jekyll & Hyde
Jeremy's Ale House
Jim Brady's
Joe's Pub
John St. Bar & Grill
Johnny Fox's
Johnny's Fish Grill
Joshua Tree
Judge Crater's
JUdson Grill
Judy's
Jule's Bistro
Julius
Juniper Café
Junno's
Justin's
Kana Tapas Bar & Restaurant
Karavas Tavern
Kate Kearney's
Kava
Kavehaz
K-Dee's
Kennedy's
Ken's Broome St. Bar
Kevin St. James
King's Carriage House
Kinsale Tavern
Knickerbocker Bar & Grill
Kori
La Cocina
La Jumelle
La Maison De Sade
Lansky Lounge
La Nouvelle Justine
Lafayette Grill & Bar
Lakeside Lounge
L'Angolo
Lava Lounge
Layla
Le Bateau Ivre
Le Colonial
Le Figaro Café
Le Marais
Le Regence Bar
Le Singe Vert
Lemon, The
Library (@ The Regency)
Life Café
Lightship Frying Pan
Lips
Live Bait
Lola
L'Orange Bleu
Lot 61
Lotus
Lotus Club
L-Ray
Luahn
Luca Lounge
Lucien
Lucky Cheng's
Lucky Strike
Luke's Bar & Grill
Luna Park
Luvbuzz
M&R Bar
Mad River Bar & Grille
Malachy's
Marion's Continental
Markt
Mars 2112
Martell's
Marylou's
Match
Match (Uptown)
McAleer's Pub
McCarthy's
McCormack's
McDooley's
McFadden's
McGee's
McSorely's
Mekka
Mercer Bar
Merchants
Mercury Bar
Merlot
Mesopotania
Metronome
Mexican Radio
Mica Bar & Lounge
Michael Jordon's Steak House
Mickey Mantle's
Milady's
Milo's
Miracle Grill
Miri
Miss Elle's Homesick Bar
Mitch's Place
Molly's
Monkey Bar
Montague Street Saloon
Moomba
Morrell Wine Bar & Café
Mo's Carribean
Moscow

Motown Café
Mr. Bigg's Bar & Grill
Mudville 9
Mug Shot Saloon
Mug's Ale House
Mumbles
Murphy's Law
Mustang
Mustang Harry's
Mustang Sally's
n
Nathan Hale's Bar &-Grill
Negril
Nell's
Neva
Nevada Smith's
New Tokyo 18 Bar
Niagara
Nice Guy Eddie's
North West Restaurant & Lounge
North Star Pub
Novecento
Obeca Li
Oak Room
Odeon, The
Odessa Bar
Off the Wagon
O'Flaherty's Ale House
O'Flanagan's
O'Flanagan's Old Ale House
Old Stand, The
Old Town Bar
Oliva
Olive Garden
One & One
One 51
One if By Land, Two if by Sea
O'Nieal's Grand Street
Opal
Opaline
Oscar's
Oyster Bar & Restaurant
Ozone Bar & Lounge
P & G Café
P.D. O'Hurley's Bar & Grill
P.J. Clarke's
Paddy Maguires
Pageant
Palio
Panache
Pangea
Papa Joe's Original (formerly Nimrod)
Paris Café
Park Avalon
Park Ave. Country Club
Park Bar
Park Slope Brewing Company
Pastis
Patria
Patrick Kavanagh's
Pearl Oyster Bar
Peasant
Peculiar Pub
Penang
PenTop Bar Terrace, The
Peter McManus Café
Peter's
Pete's Tavern
Phebe's
Pierrot
Pig 'n' Whistle
Planet Sushi
Planet Thailand
Pop
Porter's (formerly Community Bar & Grill)
Potion Lounge
Pourhouse
Pravda
Prohibition
Puffy's Tavern
Push Café
Radio Perfecto
Rain
Raoul's
Redeye Grill
Regents
Relish
Reservoir
Revolution
Rhone
Rice
Right Bank Café
Rink Bar, The
Rio Mar
Rising Café
Rocking Horse Café Mexicano
Rodeo Bar
Rosa Mexicano
Round Bar, The (The Vodka Bar)
Ruby Foo's
Rubyfruit Bar & Grill
Ruby's Tap House
Rudy's Bar & Grill
Rue B
Russian Vodka Room
Ryan's Irish Pub
Ryan's Sports Bar
S.J. South & Sons
S.O.B.'s (Sounds Of Brazil)
Sabór
Sala
Saloon, The
Savoy
Scharmann's
Screening Room, The
Seaport Café
Sequoia's
Serena
Session 73
Shade
Shades of Green
Shark Bar
Ship of Fools
Ship's Mast
Sidewalk Café
Simone
Sin Sin
Slaughtered Lamb
Slipper Room
Sliver
SMF
Smiths
SOHO Kitchen & Bar
Spaghetti Western
Splitzzz
Sporting Club
Spy
Square Rigger Pub
St. Andrew's
St. Dymphna's
St. Mark's Ale House
Street car Cafe
Standard Notions
Stingy LuLu's
Sushi Generation
Suspenders
Sutton Grill
Sutton Place Rest & Bar
Swan's Bar & Grill
Sweetwater Tavern
Swift Hibernian Lounge
T.G. Whitney's
Tall Ship Bar & Grill
Tammany Hall
Tapas Lounge
Taperia Madrid
Tapika

Tavern on Jane
Tavern on the Green
Teddy's Bar & Grill
Telephone Bar & Grill
Temple Bar
Tennesse Mountain
Three of Cups Lounge
Time Out
Tivoli
Tonic Bar & Rest
Torch
Tortilla Flats
Tracy J's Watering Hole
Tribeca Grill
Trilogy
Turtle Bay
Twist Lounge
Typhoon Restaurant
Union Bar
Vandam
Velvet Lounge
Vera
Vera Cruz
Veritas
Vermouth
Veruka
Vice Versa
Viceroy
Victory Café
Village Lantern
Virage
Vong
Walker's
Wall St. Kitchen & Bar
Waterfront Ale House
Waterloo
Welcome To The Johnsons
Westside Brewing Co.
White Horse Tavern
Wicked Wolf Restaurant
Willy's Bar & Grill
Wilson's
Windfall
Xando Café & Bar
Xth Ave Lounge
Yabby's
Zanzibar
Zarela
Zum Schneider

**FRAT**

151
Alligator Alley
American Spirits
American Trash
Bank Café, The
Bar East (formerly Australia, The Bar)
Bar None
Barrow Street Ale House
Bear Bar
Bleecker Street Bar
Bourbon Street
Brother Jimmy's Bait-Shack
Bull McCabe's
Bull's Head Tavern
Carnegie Hill Brewing Co.
Cowboy Bar
Doc Watson's
Dorrian's Red Hand
Down the Hatch
Fat Black Pussy Cat
Firehouse
Fitzpatrick's
Gin Mill, The
Hogs & Heifers
Jake's Dilema
Jekyll & Hyde
Jeremy's Ale House
Joshua Tree
Kinsale Tavern
Lion's Den
Looking Glass
Mad River Bar & Grille
Martell's
Mo's Caribbean Bar & Grille
Mug Shot Saloon
Nevada Smith's
Off the Wagon
Park Slope Brewing Company
Polly Esther's
Quiet Man, The
Red Lion
Richter's Bar
Shades of Green
Ship of Fools
Slaughtered Lamb
Sporting Club
Spring Lounge
St. Mark's Ale House
Sutton Place Rest & Bar
Tammany Hall
Third & Long
Time Out (fomerly Boomers)
Village Vanguard
Who's NYC
Wreck Room

**DANCING/CLUB**

13
357
205 Club
2i's
Acme Underground
Alphabet Lounge
Aria
Asylum
Au Bar
Baktun
Bistro Latino
Blatino Bronx Factory
bOb
Bowery Ballroom
Café Remy
Café Wha?
Centro Fly
Chaeira
Chaos
Cheetah
China Club
Club New York
Cooler, The
Copacabana
Cream
Culture Club
Decade
Don Hill's
Downtime
Drinkland
El Flamingo
Escuelita
Etoile
Eugene
Exit
Flamingo East
Float
Fun
Greatest Bar on Earth
Guernica
Halo
Hell
Hush
Iguana
Ivy
Izzy Bar
Jack Rose / Jack's Joint
Jet Lounge
Joy
King
Latin Quarter

Lightship Frying Pan
Limelight, The
Lotus
Ludlow Bar
Madison's Nite Club
Mercury Lounge
Metronome
Monster, The
Moonlighting (a.k.a. 511)
Moscow
Naked Lunch
Nell's
Neva
Niva
NV/289 Bar Lounge
Obeca Li
Ohm
One 51
Parlour, The
Plant
Polly Esther's
Pyramid Club
Rebar
Red Rock West Saloon
Roxy, The
S.O.B.'s (Sounds Of Brazil)
Sapphire Lounge
Shine
Spa
Splash
True
Tunnel
Twilo
Twirl
Wakamba
Web, The
Webster Hall
Who's NYC
XVI (16)

**SPORTS BARS**

Abbey Tavern
Alligator Alley
Amsterdam Billiard Club
Back Page (formerly Entourage)
Bank Café, The
Bar None
Barfly
Bear Bar
Bishops Lounge & Grill
Blondies
British Open
Brother Jimmy's Bait Shack
Bull McCabe's
Bull Moose Saloon
C.J.'s Knockouts Sports Bar
Carnegie Hill Brewing Co.
Dempsey's Pub
Doc Watson's
Dublin House
Dugout, The
Duke's
ESPN Zone
Flight 1668
Gin Mill, The
Googies
Headlines
Jeremy's Ale House
Jimmy Walker's
John St. Bar & Grill
Joshua Tree
Kinsale Tavern
Mad River Bar & Grille
McDooley's
Mickey Mantle's
Mitch's Place
Mug Shot Saloon
Mug's Ale House
Mulligan's
Nevada Smith's
Off the Wagon
O'Flanagan's
O'Flanagan's Old Ale House
Old Stand, The
Paddy Maguire's Ale
Park Ave. Country Club
Peter's
Rathbones
Ref's Corner
Reservoir
Richter's Bar
Ryan's Sports Bar
Sam Beckett's
Ship of Fools
Splitzzz
Sporting Club
St. Mark's Ale House
Sutton Grill
Sutton Place Rest & Bar
Swan's Bar & Grill
T.G. Whitney's
Tammany Hall
Third & Long
Time Out (fomerly Boomers)
Triple Crown

**DATE/ROMANTIC**

147
212
205 Club
55 Bar
5757 (@ The Four Seasons Hotel)
Absolutely 4th (formerly Karma)
Angel (formerly Dharma)
Angel's Share
Aquavit
Asia De Cuba
Astor
Au Bar
Aubette
Auction House
AZ
B Bar (a.k.a. Bowery Bar)
B3
Babalu
Balthazar
Bar 9
Bar Demi
Bar Veloce
Baraza
Belmont Lounge
Bemelmans Bar (@ The Carlyle Hotel)
Big Sur
Bistro Latino
Black Betty
Blu Lounge
Bond St. Lounge
Bottino
Brassierie 8 1/2
Bread Bar @ Tabla
Bubble Lounge
C3 Lounge
Cachette
Café Carlyle (@ The Carlyle Hotel)
Café Des Artistes
Café Pierre
Caffé Torino
Caliban
Candela's
Canteen
Casa La Femme
Casimir
Chaeira
Chase
Chez Es Saada

**OUTDOOR SPACE**

Doc Watson's
Druids
DT/UT
Duplex, The
Ear Inn
East of 8th
Eight of Clubs
El Rio Grande
El Teddy's
Evelyn Lounge, The
Excelsior
Finally Fred's
Finnegan's Wake
Firehouse
Five Points
Flamingo East
Flight 1668
Garage, The
Gate, The
Gin Mill, The
Good World Bar & Grill
Great Hall Balcony (MET)
Half King, The
Hallo Berlin
Harley Davidson Café
Heartland Brewery
Henrietta Hudson
Il Violino Rosso
Independent, The
International Bar
Iona
Jean Georges
Jeremy's Ale House
Johnny Fox's
Jule's Bistro
Kana Tapas Bar & Restaurant
La Cocina
Last Exit
Layla
Le Bateau Ivre
Le Figaro Café
Let's Make a Daiquiri
Life Café
Liquor Store Bar
L'Orange Bleu
Luca Lounge
Luke's Bar & Grill
Luna Park
Luvbuzz
M&R Bar
Madame X
Martell's
Match (Uptown)
McAleer's Pub
Merchants
Mica Bar & Lounge
Miracle Grill
Miss Elle's Homesick Bar
Mitch's Place
Montague Street Saloon
Moran's (Edward Moran's)
Morrell Wine Bar & Café
Musical Box
Mustang
Nancy Whiskey Pub
No Malice Palace (formerly Delia's)
North West Restaurant & Lounge
Novecento
Odeon, The
O'Flaherty's Ale House
Park Slope Brewing Company
Pastis
PenTop Bar Terrace, The
Pete's Tavern
Pierrot
Planet Sushi
Potion Lounge
Prohibition
Radio Perfecto
Raoul's
Recess
Red Lion
Redeye Grill
Ref's Corner
Relish
Revival
Right Bank Café
Rink Bar, The
Rising Café
Riviera Café & Sports Bar
Rudy's Bar & Grill
Ryan's Irish Pub
S & T Bar (Stock & Tankard)
Saloon, The
Scharmann's
Seaport Café
Sequoia's
St. Dymphna's
Standard Notions
Sushi Generation
Sweet & Vicious
Tavern on the Green
Teddy's Bar & Grill
Telephone Bar & Grill
Time Out (fomerly Boomers)
Tortilla Flats
Townhouse, The
Velvet Lounge
Vera Cruz
Vermouth
Viceroy
Village Lantern
Westside Brewing Co.
White Horse Tavern
Willy's Bar & Grill
Xando Café & Bar (Downtown)
Xando Café & Bar (Uptown)
Yabby's

**CIGAR FRIENDLY**

147
212
169 Bar
205 Club
2A
53rd St. Cigar Bar
55 Bar
5757 (@ The Four Seasons Hotel)
7B (Vazac's)
9C
Angelo & Maxie's
Aubette
Auction House
B Bar (a.k.a. Bowery Bar)
Bahi
Bar 54
Bar Veloce
Beekman Bar & Books
Beer Bar @ Café Centro
Big Sur
Bill's Gay Nineties
Bishops Lounge & Grill
Blarney Stone
bOb
Botanica
Bourbon Street
Boxcar Lounge
Brady's Bar
Brandy's Piano Bar
Brassierie Bit
Brewsky's
British Open
Brooklyn Ale House

Brother Jimmy's Bait Shack
Bubble Lounge
Bull & Bear (@ The Waldorf Astoria)
Bull McCabe's
Bull Moose Saloon
Café Noir
Café Pierre
Caffé Torino
Caliban
Candela's
Captain Café
Carnegie Club, The
Casa Mexicana
Catwalk
Chaos
Charleston, The
Chi Chiz
Church Lounge (@ The Tribeca Grand Hotel)
Cibar
Cinema Classics
Circa Tabac
City Hall
Club Macanudo
Cocktail Room, The
Commuter Café
Copper Lounge
Cowboy Bar
Cream
Cub Room
D Lounge
Dakota Roadhouse
Dead Poet
Decade
Denizen
Dewey's Flatiron
Doc Watson's
Down the Hatch
Downtime
Downtown
Dublin House
Dylan
Eleventh St. Bar
Emerald Pub
Etoile
Fat Black Pussy Cat
Feinstein's
Finally Fred's
Fitzpatrick's
Five Points
Flannery's Bar
Flight 1668
Float
Flute
Fressen
Fubar
Gaf, The
Gaslight
GB Shaw's Bar & Grill
Gin Mill, The
Girl from Ipanema, The
Good Times Bar & Grill
Grand Bar
H2K
Harry Cipriani
Harry's at Hanover Sq
Headlines
Hog Pit
Holland Bar
Houston's
Hudson B&B
Ideya
Iggy's
Indigo Bar
Iona
Ivy
Izzy Bar
Ja
Jameson's
Jim Brady's
Jimmy's Corner
Joe's Bar
John St. Bar & Grill
Joshua Tree
Journey's Lounge
JUdson Grill
Jule's Bistro
Justin's
Kate Kearney's
Kavehaz
Kettle Of Fish
Knickerbocker Bar & Grill
Korova Milk Bar
Lafayette Grill & Bar
Lakeside Lounge
Lansky Lounge
Last Exit
Latin Quarter
Le Bateau Ivre
Le Regence Bar
Lemon, The
Library (@ The Regency)
Lightship Frying Pan
Limelight, The
Liquor Store Bar
Local 138
Looking Glass
L'Orange Bleu
Lotus Club
L-Ray
Luahn
Luna Lounge
Lure, The
MacDougal St. Ale House
Mad River Bar & Grille
Madame X
Madison's Nite Club
Manitoba's
Marcel Lounge
Marty O'Briens
Marylou's
Match (Uptown)
Max Fish
McAleer's Pub
McDooley's
McSorely's Old Ale House
McSwiggan's
Milano's
Milk and Honey
Milo's
Mitch's Place
Mona's
Morrell Wine Bar & Café
Motor City Bar
Mr. Bigg's Bar & Grill
Mug's Ale House
Mustang
Nell's
Niagara
No Moore
North West Restaurant & Lounge
NV/289 Bar Lounge
NW3
Oasis Lounge
Ohm
Old Stand, The
O'Nieal's Grand Street
Opal
Oscar's
P.J. Clarke's
Pageant
Park Ave. Country Club
Parlay Lounge
Patrick Kavanagh's
Peculiar Pub
PenTop Bar Terrace, The
Pete's Candy Shop
Pig 'n' Whistle
Polly Esther's
Pour House, The
Puck Fair
Raoul's

Red Lion
Red Rock West Saloon
Relish
Reservoir
Revolution
Right Bank Café
Rink Bar, The
Room, The
Rose Mary's
Greenpoint Tavern
Rudy's Bar & Grill
Rue B
Ryan's Daughter
Ryan's Sports Bar
S & T Bar (Stock & Tankard)
Sala
Scharmann's
Scratcher, The
Session 73 (formerly Yorkville Brewery & Tavern)
Shade
Shades of Green
Ship of Fools
Slipper Room
Smalls
Solas
Sophie's
Spike, The
Sporting Club
Spy
Square Rigger Pub
St. Mark's Ale House
Stingy LuLu's
Stoned Crow
Subway Inn
Suspenders
Sutton Grill
Sweet & Vicious
Swift Hibernian Lounge
Swine on Nine
T.G. Whitney's
Tall Ship Bar & Grill
Tammany Hall
Tar Bar
Tavern on the Green
Telephone Bar & Grill
Tenth Street Lounge
Terra Blues
Third & Long
Thirsty Scholar
Tivoli
Toad Hall
Tonic Bar & Rest
Triad
Turkey's Nest
Twilo
Velvet Lounge
Venue and the Lava Lounge
Vera Cruz
Vice Versa
Vig Bar, The
Village Idiot
Virage
Walker's
Wall St. Kitchen & Bar
WCOU (formerly Tile Bar)
Whiskey Ward
Wilson's
Windfall
Wonder Bar
Wreck Room
Xth Ave Lounge
XVI (16)
Yabby's
Zanzibar

## GOOD BEER & WINE LIST

147
212
5757 (@ The Four Seasons Hotel)
Alva
Angelo & Maxie's
Angel's Share
Apple Restaurant & Bar
Aquavit
Asia De Cuba
Astor
Asylum
Au Bar
Aubette
AZ
B3
Balthazar
Bar 54
Bar 6
Bar 81 (a.k.a. Verchovyna Tavern)
Bar 89
Bar Demi
Bar Veloce
Barfly
Barrow Street Ale House
Beekman Bar & Books
Belgo Nieuw York
Belmont Lounge
Bishops Lounge & Grill
Black & White
Black Betty
Blarney Star
Blind Tiger Ale House
Bond St. Lounge
Bongo
Bottino
Boughalem
Bourbon Street
Boxcar Lounge
Braque
Brassierie 8 1/2
Bread Bar @ Tabla
Brewsky's
Bubble Lounge
Bull & Bear (@ The Waldorf Astoria)
Burp Castle
C3 Lounge
Café Carlyle (@ The Carlyle Hotel)
Café Noir
Caffé Torino
Calle Ocho
Candela's
Carnegie Club, The
Carnegie Hill Brewing Co.
Chelsea Bistro & Bar
Chelsea Brewing Company
Chez Josephine
Chibi's Sake Bar
Church Lounge (@ The Tribeca Grand Hotel)
City Hall
Cloister Café
Club Macanudo
Collins Bar
Cub Room
d.b.a.
Dewey's Flatiron Diner
Divine Bar
El Quijote
El Teddy's
Eleven Madison Park
ESPN Zone
Etoile
Failte
Fanelli's
Feinstein's
Fez North
Fiddlesticks
Five Points
Flor de Sol
Gamut Bistro Lounge,

The
Garage, The
Ginger Man, The
Globe, The
Good World Bar & Grill
Gotham Bar & Grill
Guernica
H2K
Hallo Berlin
Harry Cipriani
Hudson B&B
I Trulli
Il Covo dell'EST
Il Violino Rosso
'ino
Iona
Iridium Jazz Club
JUdson Grill
King Cole Bar (@ The St. Regis)
Le Colonial
Le Marais
Library (@ The Regency)
L'Ivre
L-Ray
Luahn
Lucien
Lush
Markt
Mercer Bar
Metronome
Mica Bar & Lounge
Miri
Morrell Wine Bar & Café
Novecento
Oak Room, The (@ The Plaza)
One if By Land, Two if by Sea
Opaline
Other Room,The
Palio
Pangea
Parlour, The
Peculier Pub
Poolbeg St.Pub
Porter's
Potion Lounge
Raoul's
Redeye Grill
Room, The
Ruby's Tap House
Rue B
Russian Vodka Room
Savoy
SMF
SOHO Kitchen & Bar
St. Andrew's
Swift Hibernian Lounge
Tavern on the Green
Twist Lounge
Vandam
Vera
Veritas
Von
Wall St. Kitchen & Bar
Whiskey Bar, The
Whiskey Ward
Zum Schneider

**ANNOYING DOOR POLICY**

357
g
2i's
Aria
Asia De Cuba
Au Bar
B Bar (a.k.a. Bowery Bar)
Balthazar
Centro Fly
Chaos
Chez Es Saada
China Club
Church Lounge (@ The Tribeca Grand Hotel)
Club New York
Cream
Downtime
Drinkland
El Flamingo
Etoile
Exit (formerly Carbon)
Float
Gemini Lounge
Gonzales y Gonzales
Idelewild
Joy
Justin's
Lansky Lounge
Lava Lounge
Lotus
Lounge at 203 Spring, The (formerly Lily's)
Madison's Nite Club
Milk & Honey
Monster, The
Moomba
Moonlighting (a.k.a. 511)
Morgans Bar
Naked Lunch
NV/289 Bar Lounge
Ohm
Parlay Lounge
Peasant
S.O.B.'s (Sounds of Brazil)
Serena
Spa
Spy
Sway
Tenth Street Lounge
True
Tunnel
Twilo
Twirl
Veruka

**SHECKY'S PICKS**

13
44
288 Bar (Tom & Jerry's)
5757 (@ The Four Seasons Hotel)
147
Absolutely 4th (formerly Karma)
Alphabet Lounge
Angel
Angel's Share
Anotheroom
Aria
Arizona 206
Arlene Grocery
Art Bar
Astor
Aubette
Auction House
AZ
Baby Jupiter
Bahi
Baktun
Balthazar
Bar 6
Bar Code
Bar Demi
Bar d'O
Bar Veloce
Baraza
Barracuda
Barramundi
Bellevue Bar
Bitter End
Black and White
Blind Tiger Ale House
Blue Note
Blue Water Grill

bOb
Bond Street
Bongo
Boston Comedy Club
Bottino
Boughalem
Bowery Ballroom
Bowlmor Lanes
Brassierie 8 1/2
Bread Bar @ Tabla
Cachette
Café Des Artistes
Café Noir
Cafeteria
Caliban
Candela
Canteen
Carolines Comedy Club
Casa La Femme
Casimir
CBGB's & OMFUG
Centro Fly
Chase
Chelsea Commons
Chez Es Saada
Chibi's Sake Bar
Chicama
Chumley's
Church Lounge (@ The Tribeca Grand Hotel)
Cibar
Ciel Rouge
Circa Tabac
Citrus
City Hall
Clementine
Club Macanudo
C-Note
Coffee Shop
Comedy Cellar
Cooler, The
Corner Bistro
Coup
Crazy Nanny's
Cub Room
d.b.a.
Denial
Divine Bar
Don Hills
Don't Tell Mama
Double Happiness
Drinkland
Druids
DT/UT
Duplex, The
Dylan
Ear Inn
Eau
Eight Mile Creek
El Teddy's
Escuelita
Esperanto
Eugene
Evelyn Lounge, The
Failte
Fanelli's
Firehouse
First
Flute
Fressen
Fun
g
Galapegos
Gamut Bistro Lounge,
Good World Bar & Grill
Grace
Gramercy Tavern
Grand Bar
Great Hall Balcony (MET)
Guastavino's
Guernica
H2K
Half King, The
Hell
Hush
i
'ino
I Trulli
Ice Bar
Joe's Pub
JUdson Grill
Junnos
Justins
King Cole Bar
Kori
Lansky Lounge
Le Colonial
Lei Bar
Leopard Lounge (Sin Sin)
Liquids
Liquor Store Bar
Local 38
Lot 61
Lotus
L-Ray
Luca Lounge
Lucky Strike
Ludlow Bar
Lush
Mercer Bar
Mexican Radio
Milk and Honey
Molly's
Moomba
Musical Box
n
Nancy Whiskey Pub
New Tokyo 18
Niagra
No Moore
No Malice Palace
North West Restaurant & Lounge
NW3
Obeca Li
Odeon, The
Old Town Bar
Oliva
One 51
O'Nieal's Grand Street
Opaline
Opium Den
Orchard Bar
Otheroom
Passerby
Pastis
Patria
Peasant
Peculier Pub
Peters
Phoenix, The
Puck Fair
Push Café
Raoul's
Red Bench
Red Rock West Saloon
Reservoir
Rhone
Rivertown Lounge
Rocking Horse Café
Mexicano
Room, The
Rue B
Russian Vodka Room
Sala
Screening Room, The
Ship of Fools
Siberia
Simone
Sin Sin
Solas
Spa
Standard
Sweet & Vicious
Temple Bar
Torch
Tortilla Flats
Tunnel
Typhoon Restaurant

Village Underground
Walker's
Wall St. Kitchen & Bar
Waterloo
Webster Hall
Zum Schneider

**DOG FRIENDLY**

13
19th Hole
288 Bar (Tom & Jerry's)
9C
Ace Bar
American Trash
Astor
Back Fence, The
Bar 81 (a.k.a. Verchovyna Tavern)
Bar Odeon
Bellevue Bar
Blarney Rock
Blarney Stone
BMW
Boxcar Lounge
Brewsky's
Brooklyn Ale House
Cinema Classics
Dead Poet (formerly The Snug)
Dempsey's Pub
Ear Inn
Edge, The
Eleventh St. Bar
Emerald Pub
Enid's
Failte
Finally Fred's
Fish Bar
Gaf, The
Gate, The
Gin Mill, The
Ginger (formerly Carry Nation)
Holiday Lounge
Iggy's
Jake's Dilema
Joe's Bar
Kavehaz
KGB
Lakeside Lounge
Library, The
Lightship Frying Pan
Liquor Store Bar
Local 138
Looking Glass
Lotus Club
Lucy's
McDooley's
McSorely's Old Ale House
Mona's
Odeon, The
Parkside Lounge
Puffy's Tavern
Rawhide
Right Bank Café
Route 85A
Sam Beckett's
Siberia
Sidewalk Café
Sweetwater Tavern
Swift Hibernian Lounge
Swine on Nine
Tapas Lounge
Tavern on Jane
Timboo's
Toad Hall
Victory Café
Village Idiot
Virage
Von
WCOU
White Horse Tavern
WXOU Radio

**AFTER WORK SPOTS**

420
288 Bar (Tom & Jerry's)
53rd St. Cigar Bar
55 Bar
5757 (@ The Four Seasons Hotel)
7A
7B (Vazac's)
Abbey, The
Absolutely 4th (formerly Karma)
All State Café
Alligator Alley
America
American Trash
Angel's Share
Annie Moore's
Anotheroom
Antartica
Aquavit
Arizona 206
Asia De Cuba
AZ
B Bar (a.k.a. Bowery Bar)
Back Page (formerly Entourage)
Bandito
Bank Café, The
Bar 54
Bar 6
Bar 89
Bar 9
Bar None
Bar Odeon
Bar on A
Barclay's Bar & Grill
Barfly
Barrymore's
Beauty Bar
Beer Bar @ Café Centro
Belmont Lounge
Bemelmans Bar (@ The Carlyle Hotel)
Birdland
Bishops Lounge & Grill
Black & White
Black Sheep
Black Star
Blarney Rock
Blarney Star
Blarney Stone
Blind Tiger Ale House
Bliss Bar & Lounge
Blu
Blue Water Grill
Boiler Room
Bond Street
Bongo
Boots & Saddle
Botanica
Bottino
Boughalem
Bourbon Street
Bowlmor Lanes
Boxcar Lounge
Braque
Brassierie 8 1/2
Brassierie Bit
Brassierie Centrale
Bread Bar @ Tabla
Brew's
Brewsky's
Bridge Bar, The
Brooklyn Ale House
Brother Jimmy's Bait Shack
Bryant Park Grill
Bubble Lounge
Bull & Bear (Waldorf Astoria)
Bull McCabe's
Bull Moose Saloon
Bull's Head Tavern

Café Noir
Café Remy
Caliban
Candle Bar
Carnegie Club, The
Carnegie Hill Brewing Co.
Casa Mexicana
Catwalk
Chase
Chelsea Commons
Chi Chiz
Church Lounge (@ The Tribeca Grand Hotel)
Cibar
Citron 47
Citrus Bar & Grill
City Hall
Clementine
Cloister Café
Club Macanudo
Coco Pazzo Café
Coffee Shop
Collins Bar
Commune
Commuter Café
Coopers Cars & Cigars
Copacabana
Corner Bistro
Crazy Nanny's
Cub Room
Cutting Room
D Lounge
d.b.a.
Dakota Roadhouse
Danny's Skylight Room
Deanna's
Delmonico's
Dewey's Flatiron
Divine Bar
Dock's Oyster Bar
Donald Sacks
Down the Hatch
Downtown
Druids
Due South
Dugout, The
Ear Inn
Eight of Clubs
El Rio Grande
El Teddy's
Eleven Madison Park
Emerald Pub
ESPN Zone
Eugene
Evelyn Lounge, The
Failte
Fanelli's
Fez North
Fiddlesticks
Film Center Café
Firehouse
First
Fitzpatrick's
Flannery's Bar
Flight 151
Flight 1668
Flute
Fubar
Galaxy
Garage, The
GB Shaw's Bar & Grill
Gin Mill, The
Ginger Man, The
Globe, The
Good World Bar & Grill
Grace
Grange Hall, The
Great Jones Café, The
Greatest Bar on Earth
Guastavino's
Guernica
H2K
Halo
Harry's at Hanover Square
Heartland Brewery
Houston's
Iggy's
Iguana
International Bar
Irish Pub
Irish Treasury
Ivy
Izzy Bar
Jake's Dilema
Jameson's
JB
Jekyll & Hyde
Jeremy's Ale House
John St. Bar & Grill
Johnny Fox's
Johnny's Bar
Johnny's Fish Grill
Joshua Tree
JUdson Grill
Judy's
Julius
Kate Kearney's
Kava
Kennedy's
Ken's Broome St. Bar
Kevin St. James
King Cole Bar (@The St. Regis)
King's Carriage House
Knickerbocker Bar & Grill
Le Colonial
Le Regence Bar
Lemon, The
Library, The
Liquor Store Bar
Live Bait
Lola
Looking Glass
Lotus Club
L-Ray
Luca Lounge
Luke's Bar & Grill
Luna Park
MacDougal St. Ale House
Mad River Bar & Grille
Marie's Crisis Café
Marion's Continental
Max Fish
McAleer's Pub
McSorely's Old Ale House
Mekka
Merc Bar
Mercer Bar
Merchants
Mercury Bar
Merlot
Mexican Radio
Mica Bar & Lounge
Michael Jordon's Steak House
Mickey Mantle's
Milo's
Miri
Mitch's Place
Mogos (formerly Beacon Hill Ale House)
Molly's
Mona's
Monkey Bar
Monster, The
Moran's (Edward Moran's)
Morgans Bar
Morrell Wine Bar & Café
Mr. Bigg's Bar & Grill
Mudville 9
Muldoon's Irish Pub
Mulligan's
Murphy's Law
Mustang

n
Nancy Whiskey Pub
Nassau Bar
Nathan Hales
No Moore
North River Bar
North Star Pub
O'Flaherty's Ale House
O'Flanagan's
O'Flanagan's Old Ale House
Old Stand, The
Old Town Bar
One & One
O'Nieal's Grand Street
Opal
Oscar Wilde
Oscar's
Other Room,The
Otis
Oyster Bar & Restaurant
P.J. Clarke's
Paddy Maguire's Ale
Paddy Reilly's
Palio
Pangea
Park Avalon
Park Ave. Country Club
Park Bar
Pastis
Patrick Kavanagh's
Peculier Pub
Pegasus
PenTop Bar Terrace, The
Peter's
Pete's Tavern
Phebe's
Pieces
Pierrot
Pig 'n' Whistle
Pop
Pourhouse
Pravda
Puffy's Tavern
Raccoon Lodge
Recess
Red Rock West Saloon
Redeye Grill
Ref's Corner
Relish
Revolution
Rhone
Rivertown Lounge
Rodeo Bar
Room, The
Round Bar, The (The Vodka Bar)
Ruby's Tap House
Ryan's Daughter
Ryan's Irish Pub
Ryan's Sports Bar
S.J. South & Sons
Saints
Saloon, The
Scandal
Scratcher, The
Session 73 (formerly Yorkville Brewery & Tavern)
Shades of Green
Siberia
SOHO Kitchen & Bar
Sophie's
Spaghetti Western
Splitzzz
Sporting Club
Spring Lounge
Square Rigger Pub
St. Mark's Ale House
Stinger Club
Stoned Crow
Street Car Café
Subway Inn
Suspenders
Sutton Grill
Sutton Place Rest & Bar
Swan's Bar & Grill
T.G. Whitney's
Tall Ship Bar & Grill
Tammany Hall
Tar Bar
Tavern on Jane
Teddy's Bar & Grill
Third & Long
Thirsty Scholar
Tivoli
Toad Hall
Tonic Bar & Rest
Tortilla Flats
Triad
Tribeca Grill
Trilogy
Triple Crown
Turkey's Nest
Turtle Bay
Twist Lounge
Typhoon Restaurant
Ty's
Union Bar
Venue and the Lava Lounge
Vera
Vig Bar, The
Von
Walker's
Wall St. Kitchen & Bar
Whiskey Bar, The
Whiskey Blue
Whiskey Park
Whiskey Ward
White Horse Tavern
Wicked Wolf Restaurant
Willy's Bar & Grill
Windfall
Works, The
WXOU Radio
Yabby's
Zanzibar

**HOTEL BARS**

44 (@ The Royalton)
53rd St Cigar Bar
5757 (@ The Four Seasons Hotel)
Asia De Cuba
Bar 54
Bemelmans Bar (@ The Carlyle Hotel)
Broadway Lounge (Marriott Marquis)
Bull & Bear (@ The Waldorf Astoria)
C3 Lounge
Café Carlyle (At The Carlyle Hotel)
Café Nicole Bar
Café Pierre
Church Lounge (@ The Tribeca Grand Hotel)
Cibar
D Lounge
Feinstein's
Gramercy Park Hotel
Grand Bar
Halcyon
Harry Cipriani
Jean Georges
Journey's Lounge
King Cole Bar (@The St. Regis)
Le Bateau Ivre
Le Regence Bar
Library @ The Regency
Marcel Lounge
Mark Bar (@ The Mark Hotel)
Mercer Bar

Merlot
Monkey Bar
Morgans Bar
Oak Room, The (@ The Plaza)
Oscar's
PenTop Bar Terrace, The
Tall Ship Bar & Grill
Twist Lounge
Wet Bar
Whiskey Bar, The
Whiskey Blue
Wilson's

**NEIGHBORHOOD SPOTS**

288 Bar (Tom & Jerry's)
7A
Abbey, The
Ace Bar
Alchymy
All State Café
Annie Moore's
Anotheroom
Antartica
Anyway Café
Apple Restaurant & Bar
Arlo
Automatic Slims
Back Fence, The
Baggot Inn
Bahi
Bank Café, The
Bar 54
Bar East
Bar None
Bar on A
Barmacy
Barramundi
Barrow Street Ale House
Barrymore's
Beauty Bar
Bellevue Bar
Bergin's
Big Bar
Bishops Lounge & Grill
Bitter End
Black Sheep
Black Star
Blarney Cove
Blarney Rock
Blarney Star
Blarney Stone
Bleecker Street Bar
Blind Tiger Ale House
Blue and Gold
BMW
Boca Chica
Boiler Room
Bouche Bar
Bourbon Street
Brady's Bar
Brassierie
BitBrassierie Centrale
Brew's
Brewsky's
British Open
Brooklyn Ale House
Bull McCabe's
Bull Moose Saloon
Bull's Head Tavern
Café Gitane
Calico Jacks Cantina
Caliente Cab Co.
Chelsea Commons
Cherry Tavern
Chumley's
Citrus Bar & Grill
Club Car, The
C-Note
Cody's
Commonwealth Brewery
Copper Lounge (formerly Sweet Melissa's)
Cornelia Street Café
Corner Bistro
d.b.a.
Daddy-O's
Dempsey's Pub
Dew Drop Inn
Dewey's Flatiron
Dick's Bar
Dive 75
Doc Holidays
Dorrian's Red Hand
Downtown
Drip
Drover's Tap Room
DT/UT
Dublin House
Dusk
Ear Inn
Edge, The
Eleventh St. Bar
Ellen O'Dees
Emerald Pub
Enid's
Ernie's
Esperanto
Eureka Joe's
Failte
Finally Fred's
Finnegan's Wake
Fish Bar
Fitzgerald's
Fitzpatrick's
Flannery's Bar
Flight 151
Flight 1668
Gaf, The
Gaslight
Gate, The
GB Shaw's Bar & Grill
Ginger Man, The
Girl from Ipanema, The
Great Jones Café, The
Great Lakes
Greenwich Café
Half King Bar
Hallo Berlin
Headlines
Heartland Brewery
Hi-Life
Hogs & Heifers
Hunter's American Bar & Grill
Iggy's
Iggy's Kick Ass Bar
Il Bagatto
Il Covo dell'EST
Indigo Bar
International Bar
Iona
Irish Pub
J. G. Melon
Jack Rose / Jack's Joint
Jameson's
Jeremy's Ale House
Jimmy Walker's
Johnny Fox's
Johnny's Bar
Judge Crater's
Judge Roy Bean
Kana Tapas Bar & Restaurant
Kate Kearney's
Kava
Kennedy's
Kevin St. James
Kinsale Tavern
Leshko's
Library, The
Living Room
Lucky Strike
Luke's Bar & Grill
Luna Park

M&R Bar
MacDougal St. Ale House
Manitoba's
Martell's
Max Fish
McCarthy's
McCormack's
McGee's
McSwiggan's
Milady's
Miracle Grill
Moran's (Edward Moran's)
Mo's Caribbean Bar & Grille
Muldoon's Irish Pub
Mulligan's
Musical Box
Mustang
Mustang Harry's
Mustang Sally's
Nancy Whiskey Pub
Nevada Smith's
Nice Guy Eddie's
No Idea
North River Bar
Odeon, The
Old Homestead Inn, The
Old Town Bar
One & One
P&G Café
P.J. Clarke's
Paddy Maguire's Ale
Paddy Reilly's
Panache (formerly L'Attitude)
Parlour, The
Peter McManus Café
Peter's
Pete's Candy Shop
Pete's Tavern
Phoenix, The
Pig 'n' Whistle
Plug Uglies
Poolbeg St.Pub (formerley Glocca Mora)
Pour House, The
Pourhouse
Puck Fair
Push Café
Quiet Man, The
Radio Perfecto
Rathbones
Raven, The
Red Lion
Ref's Corner
Reservoir
Rice
Rivertown Lounge
Riviera Café & Sports Bar
Rocking Horse Café Mexicano
Room, The
Rose Mary's Greenpoint Tavern
Route 85A
Rubyfruit Bar & Grill
Ruby's Tap House
Rudy's Bar & Grill
Ryan's Daughter
Ryan's Irish Pub
S.J. South & Sons
Sam Beckett's
Scratcher, The
Shades of Green
Shark Bar
Sidewalk Café
Solas
Spaghetti Western
Splitzzz
Spring Lounge
St. Dymphna's
Standard Notions
Suspenders
Sutton Grill
Swim
Tammany Hall
Taperia Madrid
Tapika
Tavern on Jane
Third & Long
Toad Hall
Triple Crown
Turtle Bay
Victory Café
Walker's
Wall St. Kitchen & Bar
Waterfront Ale House
Welcome To The Johnsons
White Horse Tavern
WXOU Radio
Xando Café & Bar (Uptown)
Xunta
Yogi's
Zum Schneider

**DIVE BARS**

119 Bar
7B (Vazac's)
Abbey, The
Ace Bar
Alligator Alley
American Spirits
American Trash
Androgyny
Another Bar NYC
Arlene Grocery
Baby Doll Lounge
Bandito
Bar 81( a.k.a. Verchovyna Tavern)
Bar East
Bear Bar
Beauty Bar
Billy's Stopless
Blarney Cove
Blarney Rock
Blarney Stone
Bleecker Street Bar
Blue and Gold
BMW
Boots & Saddle
Botanica
Bourbon Street
CBGB's & OMFUG
Cleo's 9th Ave. Saloon
Cock, The
Continental
Coyote Ugly
Dead Poet
Dive Bar
Doc Holidays
Edge, The
Eight of Clubs
Fat Black Pussy Cat
Flannery's Bar
Gin Mill, The
Good Times Bar & Grill
Grassroots Tavern
Hog Pit
Holiday Lounge
Holland Bar
Iggy's Kick Ass Bar
Jake's Dilema
Jeremy's
Jimmy's Corner
Joe's Bar
Johnny's Bar
Lakeside Lounge
Lion's Den
Living Room
Looking Glass
Lucy's
Lure, The
MacDougal St. Ale House

Malachy's
Mars Bar
McAleer's Pub
McDooley's
McSwiggan's
Milady's
Milano's
Mogos (formerly Beacon Hill Ale House)
Mona's
Motor City Bar
Mudville 9
Mug Shot Saloon
Muldoon's Irish Pub
Nancy Whiskey Pub
North River Bar
O'Connor's Bar
Okie Dokie (a.k.a. Elsie's)
Old Homestead Inn, The
Olympic Lounge
P.J. Clarke's
Parkside Lounge
Polly Esther's
Pour House, The
Pourhouse
Raccoon Lodge
Rawhide
Refs Corner
Red Rock West Saloon
Rocky Sullivans
Rodeo Bar
Rose Mary's
Greenpoint Tavern
Rudy's Bar & Grill
Savoy Lounge
Ship's Mast
Siberia
Smiths
Sneakers
Sophie's
Stella's
Stoned Crow
Subway Inn
Sweetwater Tavern
Swine on Nine
Timboo's
Turkey's Nest
Village Idiot
Wakamba

**SWANKY BARS**

147
212
357
44 (@ The Royalton)
5757 (@ The Four Seasons Hotel)
Alphabet Lounge
Angel
Angels Share
Aria
Astor Bar
Asylum
Aquagrill
Asia De Cuba
Au Bar
Aubette
Auction House
Aura (formerly Fred's Beauty)
Avenue A Sushi
AZ
B-Bar
Babalu
Balthazar
Bar 6
Bar 89
Bar Demi
Bar d'O
Bar Veloce
Baraza
Barclay's Bar & Grill
Barracuda
Beekman Bar & Books
Belmont Lounge
Bemelmans Bar
Big Sur
Black & White
Bliss
Blu
Blue Water Grill
Bond Street
Bongo
Bottino
Boxcar Lounge
Brasserie 8 1/2
Bread Bar at Tabla
Bubble Lounge
Bull & Bear (Waldorf Astoria)
Cachette
Cafe Carlyle
Cafe Des Artists
Cafe Ocho
Café Pierre
Caliban
Candela
Canteen
Casa La Femme
Catwalk
Centro-Fly
Chaos
Chase
Chez Es Saada
Chibi's Sake Bar
Chicama
China Club
Church Lounge (@ The Tribeca Grand Hotel)
Cibar
Circa Tabac
Citrus
City Hall
Clementine
Club Macanudo
Cocktail Room
Coopers Cigar Bar
Commune
C-3
D Lounge
Decade
Decibel
Delmonico's
Denial
Denizen
Diva
Divine Bar
Double Happiness
Drinkland
Eau
Eight Mile Creek
Eleven Madison Park
Esperanto
Etoile
Eugene
Evelyn Lounge
Feinstein's
Fez
Fez North
53rd St. Cigar Bar
Firebird Cafe
Five Points
Flamingo East
Flute
Fressen
g
Globe, The
Gotham Bar & Grill
Grace
Gramercy Tavern
Grand Bar (@ The SoHo Grand)
Guastavino's
Guernica
Halo
Harry Cipriani
Hell
Hudson B&B
H2K

i Restaurant & Lounge
Ice Bar
Ideya
Idlewild
Independent, The
'ino
Iridium Jazz Club
Isla
Ja
Jean Georges
Jet Lounge
Joe's Pub
Journey's Lounge
Joy
Judson Grill
King Cole Bar (@ The St. Regis)
Kush
La Linea
Lansky Lounge
Lava Lounge
Le Colonial
Lemon, The
Leopard Lounge (Sin Sin)
Level X
Library (@ The Regency)
Limelight, The
Liquids
L'Ivre
Loki Lounge
Lola
L'Orange Bleu
Lot 61
Lotus
Lounge @ 203 Spring
L-Ray
Luahn
Luca Lounge
Lush
Luvbuzz
Madame X
Mark Bar (@ The Mark Hotel)
Markt
Match (Uptown)
Merc Bar
Mercer Bar
Merchants
Metronome
Mica Bar & Lounge
Michael Jordon's Steak House
Milk & Honey
Milo's
Monkey Bar
Moomba
Morgans Bar
Musical Box
n
Nell's
No Malice Palace (formerly Delia's)
North West Restaurant & Lounge
Nowbar
Obeca Li
Ohm
Oliva
One 51
One if By Land, Two if by Sea
O'Nieal's Grand Street
Opal
Opaline
Opium Den
Orchard Bar
Oriont
Oyster Bar
Ozone Bar & Lounge
Pageant
Palio
Pangea
Parlay Lounge
Pastis
Pentop Bar & Terrace
Pierrot
Pop
Porter's (formerly Community Bar & Grill)
Potion Lounge
Pravda
Prohibition
Raoul's
Red Bench
Regent
Relish
Rhone
Round Bar(@ The Royalton)
Rue B
Russian Vodka Room
Sabor
Savoy
Screening Room, The
Serena
Shade
Shampu
Shine
Simone
Sin Sin
Slipper Room
Solas
Spy Bar
Sway
Swim
Tapas Bar
Temple Bar
Tenth Street Lounge
Tonic
Torch
Townhouse
Tribe
True (formerly Vanity)
Tunnel
Twist Lounge
Union Bar
Vandam
Velvet Lounge
Veritas
Vermouth
Veruka
Vig
Vice Versa
Village Lantern
Void
Waterloo
Wet Bar
Whiskey Bar, The
Whiskey Blue
Whiskey Park
XR Bar
Zanzibar
Zinc Bar

**NEW HOT/HIP BARS**

169 Bar
205 Club
2i's
357
Absolutely 4th (formerly Karma)
Androgyny
Angel (formerly Dharma)
Angelo & Maxie's
Anyway Café
Aria
Art Bar
Asia De Cuba
Asylum
Au Bar
AZ
B3
Babalu
Baktun
Balthazar
Bar Code
Bar Demi
Bar Odeon

Baraza
Bellevue Bar
Black & White
Bliss Bar & Lounge
Blu
Blu Lounge
Bond Street
Bongo
Bottino
Brassierie 8 1/2
Bubble Lounge
Cabana
Cachette
Calle Ocho
Captain Café
Casa Mexicana
Catwalk
Centro Fly
Chaeira
Chaos
Chase
Chez Es Saada
Chicama
China Club
Church Lounge (@ The Tribeca Grand Hotel)
City Hall
Clementine
Cocktail Room, The (formerly Reminiscence)
Commune
Cooler, The
Cutting Room
Dave's Tavern
Diner
Do Hwa
Dusk
Dylan
Eau
Eight Mile Creek
Esperanto
ESPN Zone
Eugene
Exit (formerly Carbon)
Fat Black Pussy Cat
Fish Bar
Float
Fressen
Fun
Galapagos
Ginger (formerly Carry Nation)
Good World Bar & Grill
Grace
Guernica
H2K
Half King Bar
Halo
Hell
Idelewild
Il Covo dell'EST
'ino
Iona
Isla
Jean Georges
Joe's Pub
Joy
Juniper Café
Justin's
Le Marais
Leopard Lounge (Sin Sin)
Level X
Loki Lounge
Lot 61
Lotus
Lounge at 203 Spring, The (formerly Lily's)
Luahn
Lush
Luvbuzz
MacDougal St. Ale House
Marcel Lounge
Marty O'Briens
McFadden's
Mercer Bar
Milk & Honey
Milo's
Miri
Moomba
Morgans Bar
Morrell Wine Bar & Café
n
Niva
No Malice Palace (formerly Delia's)
Obeca Li
Oliva
One 51
Opal
Orchard Bar
Park Bar
Parlay Lounge
Passerby
Pastis
Peasant
Pete's Candy Shop
Planet Sushi
Plant (formerly Latin In Manhattan)
Porter's (formerly Community Bar & Grill)
Pourhouse
Puck Fair
Rebar
Recess
Relish
Rhone
Route 85A
Rue B
Sabor
Sala
Scandal
Shampu
Slipper Room
SMF
Spa
Splash
Stinger Club
Stingy LuLu's
Sway
Teddy's Bar & Grill
Thirsty Scholar
Tivoli
Tribe
True (formerly Vanity)
Twist Lounge
Vera
Veritas
Village Underground
Waterloo
Whiskey Blue
Whiskey Park
Whiskey Ward
Zanzibar
Zum Schneider

## PICK UP SPOTS

13
147
288 Bar (Tom & Jerry's)
5757 (@ The Four Seasons Hotel)
7B (Vazac's)
Absolutely 4th (formerly Karma)
Apple Restaurant & Bar
Arizona 206
Art Bar
Astor
Asylum
Au Bar
Aubette
Auction House
Aura (formerly Fred's Beauty)
Automatic Slims

Back Fence, The
Bahi
Baktun
Bar 6
Bar 9
Bar Demi
Bar d'O
Bar None
Bar, The
Baraza
Barmacy
Belmont Lounge
Black & White
Black Star
Bliss Bar & Lounge
Blu
Blu Lounge
bOb
Bond Street
Boots & Saddle
Bourbon Street
Bryant Park Grill
BS New York Video (formerly The Comfort Zone)
Bubble Lounge
Café Noir
Canteen
Catwalk
Chase
Chelsea Commons
Chez Es Saada
Chez Josephine
Chicama
China Club
Church Lounge (@ The Tribeca Grand Hotel)
Citron 47
Clementine
Cleo's 9th Ave. Saloon
Cock, The
Cocktail Room, The (formerly Reminiscence)
Coffee Shop
Collins Bar
Commonwealth Brewery
Commune
Copacabana
Copper Lounge (formerly Sweet Melissa's)
d.b.a.
Dive 75
Dive Bar
Divine Bar (Downtown)
Divine Bar
Dorrian's Red Hand
Drinkland
Dugout, The
Duke's
Duplex, The
Eau
Eight of Clubs
El Quijote
El Rio Grande
El Teddy's
Etoile
Eugene
Fat Black Pussy Cat
Fiddlesticks
First
Flamingo East
Fubar
Fun
Galapagos
Gemini Lounge
Ginger Man, The
Good World Bar & Grill
Googies
Grace
Guernica
Hell
Henrietta Hudson
Ice Bar
Jet Lounge
Le Colonial
Level X
Lotus
Luna Park
Lush
Luvbuzz
Mercer Bar
Monkey Bar
Moomba
Morgans Bar
Mustang
Naked Lunch
Ohm
One 51
Opium Den
Pageant
Peter's
Phoenix, The
Rebar
Shampu
Shark Bar
Standard, The
Tammany Hall
Tunnel
Vice Versa
Wakamba
Wall St. Kitchen & Bar
Webster Hall
Xando Café & Bar

### COMEDY CLUBS

Boston Comedy Club
Caroline's Comedy Club
Comedy Cellar
Dangerfield's
Gotham Comedy Club
New York Comedy Club

### GAY/LESBIAN

Androgyny
Bar d'O
Bar, The
Barracuda
Blatino Bronx Factory
Blu
Boiler Room
Boots & Saddle
Brandy's Piano Bar
Bridge Bar, The
BS New York Video (formerly The Comfort Zone)
Caffé Torino
Candle Bar
Chase
Chi Chiz
Cleo's 9th Ave. Saloon
Cock, The
Crazy Nanny's
Cubby Hole, The
Dugout, The
Duplex, The
Eight of Clubs
Escuelita
Excelsior
Garage, The
Ginger (formerly Carry Nation)
Hangar, The
Hell
Henrietta Hudson
Judy's
Julie's
Julius
King
Lips
Lure, The
Marie's Crisis Café
Meow Mix
Monster, The
Nowbar
Olympic Lounge
Oscar Wilde
Pegasus

Phoenix, The
Pieces
Pyramid Club
Rawhide
Rising Café
Rose's Turn
Rosie Too!
Rubyfruit Bar & Grill
Scandal
Sneakers
Spike, The
Splash
Starlight Bar & Lounge
Stella's
Stone Wall
Tool Box
Townhouse, The
Twilo
Twirl
Two Potato
Ty's
Viceroy
Web, The
Wonder Bar
Works, The

**THE OLDER SCENE**

5757 (@ The Four Seasons Hotel)
Abbey Tavern
Barrymore's
Beekman Bar & Books
Bemelmans Bar (@ The Carlyle Hotel)
Blue Note
Boiler Room
Boots & Saddle
Bottom Line
Boughalem
British Open
Café Carlyle (@ The Carlyle Hotel)
Café Des Artistes
Café Nicole Bar
Café Pierre
Coopers Cars & Cigars
Copacabana
D Lounge
Decade
Delmonico's
Dock's Oyster Bar
Don't Tell Mama
Fanelli's
Feinstein's
FireBird Café, The
Flor de Sol
Gotham Bar & Grill
Gotham Comedy Club
Gramercy Park Hotel
Gramercy Tavern
Great Hall Balcony (MET)
Great Jones Café, The
Harry Cipriani
Harry's at Hanover Square
Hudson B&B
Hunter's American Bar & Grill
I Trulli
Iridium Jazz Club
J. G. Melon
Jack Rose / Jack's Joint
Jazz Standard
Judge Roy Bean
JUdson Grill
Julie's
Kennedy's
Kettle Of Fish
King Cole Bar (@ The St. Regis)
Knickerbocker Bar & Grill
Le Colonial
Le Regence Bar
Marie's Crisis Café
Mark Bar (@ The Mark Hotel)
Marylou's
Mercer Bar
Merlot
Miss Elle's Homesick Bar
Monkey Bar
Mumbles
Nancy Whiskey Pub
Oak Room, The (@ The Plaza)
Odeon, The
Old Homestead Inn, The
One if By Land, Two if by Sea
Oyster Bar & Restaurant
P.J. Clarke's
Panache (formerly L'Attitude)
Peter McManus Café
Porter's (formerly Community Bar & Grill)
Rathbones
Rose's Turn
Rosie Too!
Russian Vodka Room
Saloon, The
Savoy Lounge
Smiths
Tall Ship Bar & Grill
Tavern on the Green
Townhouse, The
Wall St. Kitchen & Bar
Whiskey Park
White Horse Tavern
Wilson's
Xunta